OXFORD STUDIES IN ROMAN SOCIETY AND LAW

General Editors

Paul du Plessis Thomas A. J. McGinn

OXFORD STUDIES IN ROMAN SOCIETY AND LAW

The aim of this monograph series is to create an interdisciplinary forum devoted to the interaction between legal history and ancient history, in the context of the study of Roman Law. Focusing on the relationship of law to society, the volumes will cover the most significant periods of Roman Law (up to the death of Justinian in 565) so as to provide a balanced view of growth, decline, and resurgence. Most importantly, the series will provoke general debate over the extant to which legal rules should be examined in light of the society which produced them in order to understand their purpose and efficacy.

Compiling the *Collatio Legum Mosaicarum et Romanarum* in Late Antiquity

ROBERT M. FRAKES

OXFORD
UNIVERSITY PRESS

OXFORD
UNIVERSITY PRESS

Great Clarendon Street, Oxford OX2 6DP

Oxford University Press is a department of the University of Oxford.
It furthers the University's objective of excellence in research, scholarship,
and education by publishing worldwide in

Oxford New York

Auckland Cape Town Dar es Salaam Hong Kong Karachi
Kuala Lumpur Madrid Melbourne Mexico City Nairobi
New Delhi Shanghai Taipei Toronto

With offices in

Argentina Austria Brazil Chile Czech Republic France Greece
Guatemala Hungary Italy Japan Poland Portugal Singapore
South Korea Switzerland Thailand Turkey Ukraine Vietnam

Oxford is a registered trade mark of Oxford University Press
in the UK and in certain other countries

Published in the United States
by Oxford University Press Inc., New York

First published 2011

British Library Cataloguing in Publication Data
Data available

Library of Congress Cataloging in Publication Data
Data available

Typeset by RefineCatch Limited, Bungay, Suffolk
Printed in Great Britain
on acid-free paper by
MPG Books Group, Bodmin and King's Lynn

ISBN 978–0–19–958940–1

3 5 7 9 10 8 6 4 2

For Hannah and Lilith

Preface

In the summer of 2000, during a stroll through the Englischer Garten after I had just finished the draft of my first monograph, Professor Dieter Nörr asked me if I had any ideas for my next book. I replied that I found the *Collatio Legum Mosaicarum et Romanarum* (also known by some scholars as the *Lex Dei*) a fascinating topic and wanted to delve into that further. He replied '*Die Collatio? Dass ist spannend!*' The topic did indeed turn out to be suspenseful, even seductive. The work's curious blend of biblical and Roman legal texts has proved a siren's song for me, as it had to many previous scholars, which is why I am writing this preface over nine years later.

I must thank several sources for aiding me in trying to unravel the mysteries of the work. The Alexander von Humboldt-Stiftung provided me with fellowship support at the Leopold Wenger Institute for Legal History and Papyrus Research at the University of Munich at various stages that proved to be critical for my research. I am especially grateful to Dieter Nörr and Alfons Bürge for their encouragement of this project. The community of scholars at the Leopold Wenger Institute provided hospitality and useful insights into ancient law while Hubert Kauhold even gave me instruction in Syriac. Many colleagues in the USA and UK also provided advice at various steps in the formulation of this book. H. A. Drake read through the five chapters of the historical study in draft form and David Banta combed through the English translation. I accepted most of their helpful suggestions (and any remaining errors are due to my own obstreperousness). Many other scholars were kind enough to respond to my email queries from Western Pennsylvania.

Preliminary attempts at some of the aspects of this study were published in the *Harvard Theological Review*, *Index: Quaderni camerti di studi romanistici*, *Quaderni Urbinati di Cultura Classica*, *Zeitschrift der Savigny-Stiftung für Rechtsgeschichte (Romanistische Abteilung)*, and *Religious Identity in Late Antiquity* (Toronto, 2006). I thank the editors for their kind permission to publish revised versions of my work as part of a larger argument. I presented other aspects of my research at conferences in Philadelphia, Chicago, and Oxford where I benefited from responses offered by various audiences. Archives and libraries across Europe provided not only copies of manuscripts and early printed editions, but also direct access to the texts themselves. Ginger McGiffin of the Carlson Library Interlibrary Loan Department of Clarion University did outstanding work in securing loans (and multiple renewals of loans) of various scholarly works for me. A sabbatical leave from Clarion University in 2007 gave me the opportunity to draft this research into book form that I revised through the course of 2008 and 2009. I am especially grateful to Judith Evans Grubbs, Paul Du Plessis, Thomas McGinn, and OUP's anonymous external readers for their constructive criticism as well as Hilary O'Shea's counsel at the Press. At any place where my work fails to persuade, the fault lies with me and not them. At times, I feared the product would end up like Professor Grady Tripp's fourth book in Michael Chabon's 1995 novel *Wonder Boys* and literally never end. The chiding of my daughters helped my book avoid that fate.

Copyright Acknowledgements

Contents

Abbreviations xiii

Introduction 1

Part I The Collator

1 Approaching the Collator's World 11

A. Diocletian's Inheritance 12

B. Religion, Law, and Politics under the House of Constantine 17

C. Church and State in the Mid Fourth Century 24

D. Law, Religion, and the Age of Theodosius I 26

E. Conclusion: Roman Law after the Fall of the West 32

2 Dating the Work 35

A. Medieval and Early Modern Encounters with the *Collatio* 36

B. Internal Evidence 51

C. Closing the Window 59

D. Conclusion: A Single Collator 64

3 The Collator's Sources 66

A. Jurists and Laws 66

B. The Collator's Bible 82

C. Conclusion: The Collator's Library 97

4 The Collator's Method 99

A. Structure 99

B. Using Texts 111

C. Conclusion: The Collator at Work 121

5 The Collator's Identity and Purpose 124

A. Questions of Identity 125

B. The Religious Angle 129

C. The Collator's Audience and Purpose 140
D. Conclusion: The Christian Collator 149

Part II The Work (*Collatio Legum Mosaicarum et Romanarum*)

Sigla 155

Latin Text 157

English Translation 202

Commentary 242

Tables 311

Works Cited 323

Indexes 355

Abbreviations

AARC	*Atti dell'accademia romanistica costantiniana*
AE	*L'Année épigraphique*
AJP	*American Journal of Philology*
ANRW	H. Temporini et al. (eds.), *Aufstieg und Niedergang der römischen Welt: Geschichte und Kultur Roms im Spiegel der neueren Forschung*
Ant. Tard.	*Antiquité Tardive*
BHAC	*Bonner Historia-Augusta Colloquium*
BIDR	*Bullettino dell'Istituto di Diritto Romano*
CG	*Codex Gregiorianus*
CH	*Codex Hermogenianus*
CIL	*Corpus Inscriptionum Latinarum*
CJ	*Codex Iustinianus*, P. Krüger, ed. (Berlin, 1877)
Coll.	*Collatio Legum Mosaicarum et Romanarum*
Const. Omn.	*Constitution Omnem* (second preface to Justinian's Digest)
CP	*Classical Philology*
CR	*Classical Review*
CQ	*Classical Quarterly*
CSEL	*Corpus Scriptorum Ecclesiasticorum Latinorum*
CTh	T. Mommsen and P. M. Meyer (eds.), *Theodosiani libri XVI cum Constitutionibus Sirmondianis*, 2 vols. (Berlin, 1905, publ. 1904)
Dig.	*Digesta Iustiniani Augusti*
FIRA	S. Riccobono et al. (eds.), *Fontes Iuris Romani Antejustiniani*, 2nd edn, 3 vols. (Florence, 1940–3)
GRBS	*Greek, Roman, and Byzantine Studies*
HLL4	R. Herzog and P. L. Schmidt (eds.), *Handbuch der Lateinischen Literatur der Antike* (Munich, 1997), VIII(4)
HLL5	Herzog, R. and Schmidt, P. L. (eds.), *Handbuch der LateinischenLiteratur der Antike* (Munich, 1989) VIII(5)
HTR	*Harvard Theological Review*
ILS	H. Dessau, *Inscriptiones Latinae Selectae*, 3 vols. (Berlin, 1892–1916)

JECS	*Journal of Early Christian Studies*
JEH	*Journal of Ecclesiastical History*
JRS	*Journal of Roman Studies*
JTS	*Journal of Theological Studies*
LE	*Laws of Eshnunna*
LH	*Code of Hammurabi*
LRV	*Lex Romana Visigothorum*
MGH	*Monumenta Germaniae Historica*
NPNF	*Nicene and Post-Nicene Fathers of the Church*
NRSV	*New Revised Standard Version Bible*
PBSR	*Papers of the British School at Rome*
PLRE	A. H. M. Jones, J. Morris, and J. Martindale (eds.), *Prosopography of the Later Roman Empire*, vol. I.
PS	*Pauli Sententiae*
QUCC	*Quaderni Urbinati di Cultura Classica*
RAC	*Reallexikon für Antike und Christentum*
RE	*Real-Encyclopedie der klassischen Altertumswissenschaft*, Pauly-Wissowa (-Kroll)
REAug	*Revue des études augustiniennes*
REL	*Revue des études latines*
RHE	*Revue d'histoire ecclésiastique*
RIDA	*Revue internationale des droits de l'antiquité*
SDHI	*Studia et Documenta Historiae et Iuris*
TAPA	*Transactions and Proceedings of the American Philological Association*
TR	*Tijdschrift voor Rechtsgeschiedenis*
ZRG (R.A.)	*Zeitschrift der Savigny-Stiftung für Rechtsgeschichte (Romanistische Abteilung)*

Introduction

'The great mystery of the *Collatio legum Mosaicarum et Romanarum* can be regarded as solved.'[1]

So wrote David Daube, one of the greatest twentieth-century scholars of ancient law, in 1943. By that time, this enigmatic work had already puzzled scholars for over a century. Some of its many mysteries included the identity of the author of the work, when he wrote it, and why he chose to compile together strictures from the Hebrew Bible with statements from the Roman jurists and some Roman legal texts. Indeed, the original title of the work itself is unknown. While the manuscripts themselves have forms of *Lex Dei quam praecipit Dominus ad Moysen* ('The Law of God which the Lord gave to Moses'), early modern scholars labeled it the *Collatio Legum Mosaicarum et Romarum* ('Collation of the Laws of Moses and of the Romans').[2] In my own work I have wrestled with which name to use for the compilation. Ultimately, since the title of *Collatio* (and the accompanying abbreviation of 'Coll.' for passages in the work) has been the scholarly convention for over a century, I have decided to adopt it throughout this study. The *Collatio* proves to be especially fascinating because it stands at the intersection of legal, religious, and political history during a pivotal period in late antiquity.

Daube could feel confident that the mystery had been solved for several reasons. Scholars from the sixteenth through nineteenth centuries had discovered medieval manuscripts of the work and had made preliminary editions.[3] Theodor Mommsen used these

[1] D. Daube, '*Collatio* 2. 6. 5,' in I. Epstein *et al.* (eds.), *Essays in Honor of the Very Reverend Dr. J. H. Hertz* (London, 1943), 111–29 (republished in David Daube, *Collected Studies in Roman Law* (Frankfurt, 1991), I, 107–22).

[2] See P. Jörs, 'Collatio legum Mosaicarum et Romanarum', *RE* (Stuttgart, 1900), IV, cols. 367–70 at 367 on early modern scholars in late 1500s.

[3] The first edition of the *Collatio* can be found in P. Pithou (ed.), *Fragmenta Quaedam Papiniani, Pauli, Ulpiani, Gaii, Modestini, aliorumque veterum Iuris auctorum ex integris ipsorum libris ante Iustiniani Imp. tempora collecta, et cum Moysis legibus collata* (Paris, 1573), 1–54 for text and 66–112 for commentary (I would like to thank the staff of the Lesesaal Altes Büch of the University of Munich library for access to this important early edition). Nineteenth-century editions include F. Bluhme (ed.), *Lex Dei sive Mosaicarum et Romanarum legum collatio* (Bonn, 1833)

manuscripts in conjunction with earlier editions of the work for the basis of a modern text that he edited in 1890 (although he confessed in the preface he did not quite understand how the manuscripts interrelated).[4] Mommsen's text has been used as the basis for every subsequent modern edition and translation, including the 1913 English translation by the eminent rabbi Moses Hyamson.[5] But Daube was especially impressed by the work of the Italian legal scholar Edoardo Volterra, who proposed in 1930 a new religious identity, date, and purpose for the author of the work that to Daube resolved all of these nettlesome issues (on Volterra's conclusions, see discussions in chapters 2 and 5 below).[6]

However, over sixty years of scholarship since Daube's confident statement has shown that the enigma of the Collator is not so easily revealed. A major advance, unavailable to Mommsen, Volterra, or even Daube at the time he wrote, was the textual work of Fritz Schulz who finally established the correct relationship of the manuscripts in 1946.[7] Also, the last sixty years have seen a large amount of research in the history of Roman law, including study of the surviving texts of the Roman jurists, close examination of the technicalities of law-making in the Roman Empire, and analysis of the editorial process involved

(subsequently included in E. Böcking, A. von Bethmann-Hollweg, and E. Pugge (eds.), *Corpus Iuris Anteiustiniani* (Bonn, 1841), I, 308–86)); P. Huschke, 'Lex Dei sive Mosaicarum et Romanarum Legum Collatio' in Huschke (ed.), *Iurisprudentia Anteiustiniana* (Leipzig, 1860; 6th edn, 1927), II(2), 325–94.

[4] T. Mommsen (ed.), *Mosaicarum et Romanarum Legum Collatio* in Paul Krüger, T. Mommsen, and Wilhelm Studemund (eds.), *Collectio Librorum Iuris Anteiustiniani* (Berlin, 1890), III, 107–98 at 123–4.

[5] M. Hyamson, *Mosaicarum et Romanarum Legum Collatio* (Oxford, 1913). For Hyamson's fascinating life, see his obituary in *American Jewish Year Book* 51 (1951), 541. On Hyamson's study of the *Collatio*, see the reviews by A. F. Murison in *CR* 27 (1913), 274–7 and J. S. Blake Reed, *JRS* 3 (1913), 150–1. For other texts depending on Mommsen, see N. Smits, *Mosaicarum et Romanarum legum Collatio* (Haarlem, 1934); P. Girard (ed.), 'Mosaicarum et Romanarum Legum Collatio' in P. Girard, and F. Senn (eds.), *Textes de Droit Romain*, 7th edn (Paris, 1967), I, 547–90; J. Baviera (ed.), 'Mosaicarum et Romanarum Legum Collatio' in S. Riccobono *et al.* (eds.), *FIRA*, II, 541–89; J. E. Spruit and K. E. M. Bongenaar (eds.), 'Mosaicarum et Romanarum Legum Collatio' in Spruit and Bongenaar (eds.), *Fragmenta Vaticana, Collatio, Consultatio, Scholia Sinaitica, Probus* (Zutphen, 1987), 129–89; as well as, most recently, Martha Elena Montemayor Aceves (ed.), *Mosaicarum et Romanarum Collatio (Comparacion de Leyes Mosaicas y Romanas)* (Mexico City, 1994).

[6] E. Volterra, *Collatio Legum Mosaicarum et Romanarum* (Rome, 1930).

[7] F. Schulz, 'The manuscripts of the "Collatio Legum Mosaicarum et Romanarum"' in M. David, B. A. van Gröningen, and E. M. Meijers (eds.), *Symbolae van Oven* (Leiden, 1946), 313–32 (reprinted in *BIDR* 55 (1951), 50–69).

in the creation of the great fifth and sixth-century law codes (the *Theodosian Code* and the *Code of Justinian*).[8] Likewise, scholars of biblical texts have made substantial advances that can also shed light on the Collator and his work. Lastly, the study of late antiquity, the period when the Collator wrote, has become a field in its own right.[9]

Part of the intriguing tension in late antiquity derives from the interaction between different religious traditions (Christians, Jews, and the stew of traditional rites and beliefs usually summed up by the title 'Graeco-Roman religion'). While Christians and Jews are, on the surface at least, easy enough to comprehend as labels, the others are more difficult to label by means of a single term. The last century has seen scholars moving back and forth from 'pagan' to 'polytheist' to identify such folk.[10] The believers in traditional gods had no word for their own religion, nor did those who melded such belief with an idea of a greater god force.[11] 'Pagan' as a label for non-Christians is

[8] Such works include, but are not limited to, those of F. Wieacker, *Textstufen Klassischer Juristen* (Göttingen, 1960); T. Honoré, *Gaius* (Oxford, 1962); D. Liebs, *Hermogenians Iuris Epitomae* (Göttingen, 1964); T. Honoré, *Tribonian* (London, 1978); D. Liebs, *Die Jurisprudenz im spätantiken Italien (260–640 n. Chr.)* (Berlin, 1987); J. Harries and I. Wood (eds.), *The Theodosian Code: Studies in the imperial law of late antiquity* (London, 1993); T. Honoré, *Emperors and Lawyers*, 2nd edn (Oxford, 1994); J. Harries, *Law and Empire in Late Antiquity* (Cambridge, 1999); T. Honoré, *Law in the Crisis of Empire, 379–455 AD* (Oxford, 1998); J. F. Matthews, *Laying Down the Law: A study of the Theodosian Code* (New Haven, 2000); D. Liebs, *Römische Jurisprudenz in Gallien* (Berlin, 2002); T. Honoré, *Ulpian: Pioneer of human rights*, 2nd edn (Oxford, 2002); D. Liebs, *Römische Jurisprudenz in Africa*, 2nd edn (Berlin, 2005); A. J. B. Sirks, *The Theodosian Code: A study* (Friedrichsdorf, 2007); J. Harries, *Law and Crime in the Roman World* (Cambridge, 2007); and C. Humfress, *Orthodoxy and the Courts* (Oxford, 2007). A. Watson (ed. and tr.), *The Digest of Justinian*, 4 vols. (Philadelphia, 1985) and M. Crawford (ed.), *Roman Statutes*, 2 vols. (London, 1996) have brought Roman law from its beginnings to the sixth century CE to a wider audience. A team of scholars led by Bruce Frier is currently revising an English translation of the *Code of Justinian* and T. D. Barnes has informed me he is currently working on a study and new translation of the *Theodosian Code*.

[9] For a recent overview of the development of the modern study of late antiquity, see R. M. Frakes and E. D. Digeser (eds.), *Religious Identity in Late Antiquity* (Toronto, 2007), 3–9.

[10] T. D. Barnes, 'Monotheists all?', *Phoenix* 55 (2001), 142–62 at 142.

[11] For 'pagan monotheism' see G. Fowden, *Empire to Commonwealth: Consequences of monotheism in late antiquity* (Princeton, 1993), 5–6 and 37–60; P. Athanassiadi and M. Frede (eds.), *Pagan Monotheism in Late Antiquity* (Oxford, 1997), 1–20; M. L. West, 'Towards monotheism' in Athanassiadi and Frede, 21–40; and M. Frede, 'Monotheism and pagan philosophy in later antiquity' in Athanassiadi and Frede, 41–67. For another view, see M. Edwards, 'Pagan and Christian in the age of monotheism' in S. Swain and M. Edwards (eds.), *Approaching Late Antiquity: The transformation from early to late empire* (Oxford, 2004), 211–34.

problematic because it originated as a pejorative term meaning a rural, unsophisticated person and began to be so used by Christians in the early fifth century. While that might make 'polytheism' more attractive as a label, such a term does not clearly reveal those who did accept an overarching god force (and polytheism, too, was used in a hostile way by Christians).[12] Ultimately, unless we want to be saddled with a cumbersome lengthy phrase, we must choose some kind of label. This book will use 'pagan' with the understanding that it will be used as a broad umbrella term to include both those worshipping traditional 'polytheistic' gods as well as late antique non-Christian (and non-Jewish) monotheists and monists who believed in a powerful overarching divinity.

The Collator seems to have had a straightforward schema for the *Collatio*. He divided his work into sixteen titles, or sections (although scholars have differed over why he chose the ones he did). These titles included homicide; severe injury; cruelty toward slaves; adultery; *stuprum* (the term which the Collator used for male homosexuality); incest; theft; perjury; not admitting the testimony of family members; deposit; cattle rustling; arson; moving boundary markers; kidnapping; a combined title treating astrology, sorcery, and Manichaeism; and, lastly, inheritance.[13] While scholars both before and after Daube were unimpressed with the Collator as an author and described him as 'a scholarly non-entity', 'to some degree an imbecile', and 'a person of mediocre talents', because of the 'odd', 'superficial', and 'uniquely flawed' nature of such a compendium, such judgements can make him all the more revealing of his age for us.[14]

[12] Barnes, 'Monotheists all?', 142 citing his earlier *From Eusebius to Augustine* (Aldershot, 1994), x–xi.

[13] Coll. 1. *De Sicariis et Homicidis*; Coll. 2. *De Atroci Iniuria*; Coll. 3. *De Iure et Saevitia Dominorum*; Coll. 4. *De Adulteriis*; Coll. 5. *De Stupratoribus*; Coll. 6. *De Incestis Nuptis*; Coll. 7. *De Furibus et de Poena eorum*; Coll. 8. *De Falso Testimonio*; Coll. 9. *De Familiaris Testimonio non admittendo*; Coll. 10. *De Deposito*; Coll. 11. *De Abactoribus*; Coll. 12. *De Incendiariis*; Coll. 13. *De Termino Amoto*; Coll. 14. *De Plagiariis*; Coll. 15. *De Mathematicis, Maleficis, et Manichaeis*; and Coll. 16. *De Legitima Successione.*

[14] See S. Solazzi, 'Per la Data della "Collatio Mosaicarum et Romanarum Legum"' in his *Scritti di Diritto Romano* (Naples, 1960), III, 481–502 at 484 (originally published in *Atti della R. Acc. di Scienze morali e politiche di Napoli* 57 (1935), 263–91) for 'nullita scientifica' and 'discretamente imbecille'. For 'mediocre talents', see J. Harries, 'How to make a law code' in M. Austin, J. Harries, and C. Smith (eds.), *Modus Operandi: Essays in honor of Geoffrey Rickman* (London, 1998), 63–78 at 68. For 'odd' ('*merkwürdige*'), see L. Wenger, *Die Quellen des römischen Rechts* (Vienna,

While nineteenth-century historians, following the lead of Leopold von Ranke, believed that they could describe history 'as it actually happened' (or *wie es eigentlich gewesen*) by studying the actions of the elites who dominated political events, this positivistic view has been challenged by scholars influenced by the Frankfurt and *Annales* Schools who have aimed at a more total history.[15] In this vein, the study of the Collator, his background, and his work can show us how a non-elite writer viewed the world in which he lived. While it certainly is important to understand the broader political context, examining the Collator within his age can provide a corrective to a view of late antiquity that examines only emperors and bishops of large cities.

To approach this analysis, I have taken Mommsen's text of the *Collatio* as a first step, but then compared it against the surviving manuscripts of the work together with the Apograph (an early handwritten copy) made by Joseph Scaliger.[16] I then examined alternate readings in other editions of the *Collatio*, from the sixteenth century onward. This analysis, together with the use of Schulz's stemma, led to my making approximately a hundred small changes to Mommsen's text (which still leaves the majority of his text as sound). One of Mommsen's great strengths was that he had already produced the modern edition of the *Digest* (the famous sixth-century compendium of the Roman jurists compiled by Tribonian and his staff at the behest of the Emperor Justinian).[17] With such a deep knowledge of the jurists' prose and texts, at times Mommsen naturally emended the text of the *Collatio* to fit the corresponding passages in the *Digest*. However, the texts from which the compilers of the *Digest* were

1953), 545; for 'superficial', see F. Schulz, *History of Roman Legal Science* (Oxford, 1946), 313; for 'uniquely flawed' ('*een werk met zulke eigenaardige fouten*'), see Smits, *Collatio*, 178.

[15] For von Ranke's famous quotation, see his 'Vorrede zur ersten Ausgabe', *Geschichten der romanischen und germanischen Völker von 1494 bis 1514*, 3rd edn (Leipzig, 1885), vii. In general, on changing trends in historiography, see P. Novick, *That Noble Dream: The 'objectivity question' and the American historical profession* (Cambridge, 1988).

[16] The Apograph of Joseph Scaliger (Scal. 61 at ff. 107–26) is housed in the Scaliger Institute of the library of the University of Leiden. I would like to thank the staff of the University of Leiden library for allowing me access to the manuscript in the summer of 2007.

[17] T. Mommsen and P. Krüger (eds.), *Digesta Iustiniani Augusti* (Berlin, 1870); reprinted as *Corpus Iuris Civilis I: Institutiones et Digesta*, 21st edn (Zurich, 1970).

working had already altered over the centuries from the original versions of the jurists and the *Digest* itself was the product of centuries of textual transmission.[18] At places where I have proposed a change to Mommsen's Latin text of the *Collatio*, I have given a footnote showing what reading he had and the grounds for my suggested change so any interested readers can weigh the arguments for different reconstructions. I then used that revised text as the basis for my new English translation (the first one in nearly a hundred years). While legalistic prose is seldom elegant (either in antiquity or in the present), one of my goals is to provide a clear rendering of this fascinating though difficult work for readers who do not have Latin. Although at times it was tempting to leave some legal expressions in Latin, I have attempted to a large degree to avoid that and whenever there are Latin expressions, I give explanations. The revised text and new English translation are followed by a brief commentary that provides more historical and legal information on the different texts compiled in the *Collatio*. All three of these tools (Latin text, English translation, and Commentary) serve as the basis for my new historical study of the Collator that can, I hope, provide a non-elite view of the last years of the fourth century.

This study will attempt to view the Collator and his work as a window on his age. To approach that goal, an introductory chapter (especially useful for non-specialist readers) will sketch the continuity of interest in Roman law in the broader changing political and religious landscape of the Roman Empire, with special attention to developments in the fourth century CE. The second chapter will attempt to unravel the knotty question of dating the work and place the Collator within that age. A subsequent chapter will examine his sources for his statements from the Roman jurists, Roman law, and the Hebrew Bible. The next chapter will closely examine his methodology in using those sources. A last chapter will suggest what the Collator's purpose may have been in constructing his work and how that might shed new light on his time.

It is my intention that the resulting work will be useful not only to historians of the Roman Empire, but also to medievalists, scholars of religion, and legal historians (and, as such, fits the mission of this

[18] See, among others, O. Gradenwitz, *Interpolationen in den Pandekten: kritische Studien* (Berlin, 1887) and W. Kalb, *Die Jagd nach Interpolationen in den Digesten: sprachliche Beiträge zur Digestenkritik* (Nürnberg, 1897). See the lucid overview of early scholarship in Wieacker, *Textstufen Klassischer Juristen*, 9–24.

series in trying to create interdisciplinary dialogue between scholars who have interests in Roman society and law). At times I will thus provide some broad historical context while at other times I will focus on particular problems. Reaching such a diverse audience can be a challenging task and I hope that this work will be comprehensible to readers with a general knowledge while still being of interest to specialists. While the research and writing of this book has at times led me to critique work of earlier scholars, I am grateful for their insight and, following the twelfth-century Bernard of Chartres, if I can see further, it is only because I stand on the shoulders of giants. Ultimately, I hope this work will become a useful resource for future examinations of the *Collatio* for readers from a variety of backgrounds.

Part I

The Collator

1

Approaching the Collator's World

Coll. 7. 1. 1: Just as the Twelve Tables order a thief in the night to be killed in any case[, or a thief in the daytime] if he dares to defend himself with a weapon, know oh Jurists, that Moses ordained this earlier, just as a close reading shows.

[Coll. 7. 1. 1: *Quod si duodecim tabularum nocturnum furem [quoquo modo, diurnum] autem si se audeat telo defendere, interfici iubent, scitote, iuris consulti, quia Moyses prius hoc statuit, sicut lectio manifestat.*]

In passages such as this one, the anonymous Collator of the late antique *Collatio* shows how he intends to compare quotations from Roman and biblical law for his audience of 'jurists'. What is especially fascinating is that he reaches as far back as the famous *Lex duodecim tabularum* (or 'Law of the Twelve Tables') of the early Roman Republic for one of his allusions to Roman law.[1] To approach the Collator and his world, with its devotion to traditional law and its tumult of religious and political change, this chapter will sketch out a survey of significant historical developments that helped shape the late antique world of the Collator (with special attention given to law and religion in the fourth century). This approach to the Collator's world will help non-specialist readers understand the dynamic context in which he wrote his work.

There is a tension in modern scholarship on the later Roman Empire between the traditional view, most clearly laid out by the eighteenth-century Edward Gibbon, of violent political and religious change and the more recent model championed by Peter Brown and others of the importance of continuities between the classical world

[1] The Twelve Tables traditionally date to 451 BCE. See Crawford, *Roman Statutes*, II, 555–721.

and that of the late antique periods of the fourth and fifth centuries CE.[2] Of course, there were often wars and changes of regime in the history of the Roman state—and to some degree it is delusional to argue that these did not at times affect its citizens. On the other hand, there certainly must have been many times when the shift of the reins of centralized power made little difference to the man in the Roman street (or to people on the periphery of political centres).

One approach to examining the tension between the traditional model of event-oriented history and the school of continuity can be to look at it through the lens of Roman law. While Roman society was not a monolithic unchanging block, its culture tended to be conservative, especially in the province of law. Lawyers in late antiquity were still trained, at some level, in the legislation of the republic (although they did not have the actual texts of those laws themselves, but rather knew them through quotations and commentaries in the works of the jurists).[3] Indeed, the fact that much of our evidence for earlier Roman law comes from the *Theodosian Code* (or *Codex Theodosianus*) of 429–38 CE and the *Corpus Iuris Civilis* (including the *Code of Justinian* and especially the *Digest*) compiled from 529–34 CE shows how much continuity there was in that aspect of late Roman society.

A. DIOCLETIAN'S INHERITANCE

The Roman Empire that emerged from the chaos of the mid third century presents a model of change and continuity. While the early emperors of the Principate had mostly utilized a republican façade (fashioned by Octavian) as the basis of the legitimacy of power, the early-to-mid third century saw an increasing amount of instability and violence due to a rising number of usurpers and civil wars. This situation was exacerbated by external threats such as Germanic folk movements in the west and a revived Persian Empire in the east. Such chaos seems to have accelerated an increased religiosity in both the

[2] For Gibbon, see his *Decline and Fall of the Roman Empire* (New York: Modern Library edition, n.d.). For Brown, see, among other works, *The World of Late Antiquity* (London, 1971).

[3] See comments of Harries, *Law and Empire in Late Antiquity*, 6–18.

population of the Roman Empire and in the discourse of power.[4] This increase led to more interest in all types of religions (including increasing conversions to Christianity). It also led to a renewed interest in earlier models of kingship that looked to religion as the basis of legitimacy.[5] The dynamic Emperor Diocletian (r. 284–305) reconsolidated the Roman state by creating a new model of empire in the late third century that built upon this increasing religiosity as well as on traditional aspects of Roman law.[6]

Diocletian achieved this goal through several means. He defeated Rome's external enemies for the time being and embarked on a wide-ranging plan to reorganize the Roman state. After some experimentation, he created an imperial college that eventually had two senior emperors (known as augusti) and two junior emperors (or caesars). These tetrarchs were based strategically throughout the empire near problem zones. He massively increased the size of the civil service, partly due to the new fourfold nature of administration but also due to new urban legislation that created more officials for every community that had the status of city in the Roman Empire.[7] Because he appealed to the traditional Roman gods as the basis of his legitimacy by fostering worship of divine comrades of the tetrarchs

[4] Although dated in many respects, E. R. Dodds, *Pagan and Christian in an Age of Anxiety: Some aspects of religious experience from Marcus Aurelius to Constantine* (Cambridge, 1965) is still central to this view. See more recently, P. Brown, *The Making of Late Antiquity* (Cambridge, MA, 1978); C. Haas, 'Imperial religious policy and Valerian's persecution of the Church', *Church History* 52 (1983), 133–44; and D. Potter, *Prophecy and History in the Crisis of the Roman Empire* (Oxford, 1990).

[5] See esp. J. Rives, 'The Decree of Decius and the religion of empire', *JRS* 89 (1999), 135–54. E. R. Goodenough, 'The political philosophy of Hellenistic kingship', *Yale Classical Studies* 1 (1928), 55–102, is still useful for its discussion of Hellenistic texts. For more recent studies of political philosophy in this period, see D. J. O'Meara, *Platonopolis: Platonic political philosophy in late antiquity* (Oxford, 2003) and E. D. Digeser, 'Religion, law and the Roman polity: The era of the Great Persecution' in C. Ando and J. Rüpke (eds.), *Religion and Law in Classical and Christian Rome* (Stuttgart, 2006), 68–84.

[6] See T. D. Barnes, *The New Empire of Diocletian and Constantine* (Cambridge, MA, 1981); S. Williams, *Diocletian and the Roman Recovery* (London, 1985); F. Kolb, *Diocletian und die erste Tetrarchie: Improvisation oder Experiment in der Organisation monarchischer Herrschaft?* (Berlin, 1987); S. Corcoran, *The Empire of the Tetrarchs: Imperial pronouncements and government* AD *284–324*, 2nd edn (Oxford, 2000); A. Demandt *et al.* (eds.), *Diokletian und die Tetrarchie* (Berlin, 2004); and S. Corcoran, 'Before Constantine' in N. Lenski (ed.), *The Cambridge Companion to the Age of Constantine* (Cambridge, 2006), 35–58.

[7] On the increase in bureaucracy, see recently, C. Kelly, *Ruling the Later Roman Empire* (Cambridge, MA, 2004), 107–13.

(which thus provided a religious sanction for his reign),[8] he launched an empire-wide policy of persecution of the increasing number of Christians by an edict of 303.[9] In addition to Christianity, other forms of perceived religious deviance, such as Manichaeism and magic also were subjects of increasing government interest.[10]

However, there were also aspects of continuity in the appreciation of the empire's legal heritage under Diocletian and his successors. For instance, the Twelve Tables (long a standard part of Roman legal education) had been the subject of juristic commentaries in the Roman Empire.[11] Subsequently, these commentaries (and their references to the Twelve Tables) continued to be studied through Diocletian's reign and into the Collator's day in late antiquity, as the quotation at the beginning of this chapter shows. Likewise, later republican statutes (such as the *Lex Aquilia* regarding damage to another's property and the various *leges Corneliae* of the Dictator Lucius Cornelius Sulla on murder and injury) also were topics for juristic commentaries that, in turn, continued to be the bases of legal study and practice in the fourth century and via such sources appear in the *Collatio*.[12] Moreover, the edict of the urban praetor (while not a statute) became critical for legal procedure and the Emperor Hadrian even ordered the jurist Salvius Iulianus to make a standard

[8] A. D. Nock, 'The emperor's divine *comes*', *JRS* 37 (1947), 102–16.

[9] See recently, E. D. Digeser, 'Christian or Hellene? The Great Persecution and the problem of identity' in Frakes and Digeser, *Religious Identity in Late Antiquity*, 36–57. On the earlier persecution of Decius (r. 249–51), see Rives, 'Decree of Decius', 135–54 and O. F. Robinson, *Penal Practice and Penal Policy in Ancient Rome* (London, 2007), 116–48.

[10] See Coll. 15. On Manichaeism, see P. Brown, 'The diffusion of Manichaeism in the Roman Empire', *JRS* 59 (1969), 92 –103; S. Lieu, *Manichaeism in the Later Roman Empire and Medieval China*, 2nd edn (Tübingen, 1992); S. Lieu, *Manichaeism in Mesopotamia and the Roman East*, 2nd edn (Leiden, 1999); S. Lieu, *Manichaean Texts from the Roman Empire* (Cambridge, 2004). On the changes in view of magic, see J. Rives, 'Magic in Roman law: The reconstruction of a crime', *Classical Antiquity* 22 (2003), 313–39 and his 'Magic, religion, and law' in C. Ando and J. Rüpke (eds.), *Religion and Law in Classical and Christian Rome* (Stuttgart, 2006), 47–67. The fundamental work of C. Pharr, 'The interdiction of magic in Roman law', *TAPA* 63 (1932), 269–95 is still useful.

[11] Cicero, *De Legibus* 2. 23. 59 on learning the Twelve Tables in boyhood. See also his comments in *De Oratore*, 1. 44. 195. Recently on the Twelve Tables, see J. Harries, *Cicero and the Jurists: From citizens' law to the lawful state* (London, 2006), 171–5.

[12] On the formulaic knowledge of republican statutes by the jurists, see Harries, *Law and Empire*, 13–14. See also Wenger, *Die Quellen*, 488–530.

edition of it (that is partly preserved in later quotations).[13] Imperial legislation (whether it took the form of *edicta*, *decreta*, or *rescripta*; all of which fall under the broad umbrella of *constitutio*) had joined that of the republic in both legal study and practice and I have at times used the generic 'law' to translate both *lex* and *constitutio* unless it makes a difference in our understanding.[14] Such earlier legislation of the republic and empire continued to be valid, and studied, under Diocletian and Constantine and later into the Collator's day and was often central to passages quoted in the *Collatio*.

Other aspects of continuity in the legal sphere in the late empire can be seen in the respect given to the work of the earlier Roman jurists. The first two centuries of the empire saw the evolution of what legal historians call the 'Classical Period' of the Roman jurists.[15] While 'jurists' can include working lawyers, legal experts, and teachers of law, modern scholars tend to use the term to describe Roman lawyers who studied the earlier, and still valid, laws of the Roman state and interpreted them for students, judges, and, later, even emperors.[16] The jurists worked closely with the imperial staff in

[13] On the origins of the edict, see A. Watson, *Law Making in the Later Roman Republic* (Oxford, 1974), 45–58. On its influence, see Harries, *Law and Empire*, 14–15. For a thorough study of the growth of the praetor's power, see T. C. Brennan, *The Praetorship in the Roman Republic*, 2 vols. (Oxford, 2000), esp. I, 130–2 on the edict. On Salvius Julianus, see W. Kunkel, *Die Römischen Juristen: Herkunft und soziale Stellung*, 2nd edn (Cologne, 1967), 157–66 and D. Nörr, 'Drei Miszellen zur Lebensgeschichte des Juristen Salvius Julianus,' in A. Watson (ed.), *Daube Noster* (Edinburgh, 1974), 233–52. Already in the first century BCE, there is evidence of a large body of legal commentaries such as that of Servius Sulpicius Rufus on the Edict of the Urban Praetor. See further, Schulz, *Roman Legal Science*, 40–9; Watson, *Law Making*, 159–68; Kunkel, *Die Römischen Juristen*, 25, 39–40.

[14] For a standard overview, see H. F. Jolowicz and B Nicholas, *Historical Introduction to the Study of Roman Law*, 3rd edn (Cambridge, 1972), 368–70. On the 'legal heritage' of late antiquity, see Harries, *Law and Empire*, 1–30. For a sweeping study that argues that such *rescripta* show how the empire worked, see F. Millar, *The Emperor in the Roman World* (London, 1977), esp. 240–52.

[15] On the dating of the Classical Period, see Schulz, *Roman Legal Science*, 99–140; F. Schulz, *Classical Roman Law* (Oxford, 1951), 2–3; and Jolowicz and Nicholas, *Roman Law*, 6 and 405–20. See also B. Frier, *The Rise of the Roman Jurists: Studies in Cicero's Pro Caecina* (Princeton, 1985).

[16] Schulz, *Roman Legal Science*, 2, argued jurists could include any lawyer dedicated to jurisprudence (or 'every vocational activity in the sphere of law'), but more often scholars refer to those engaged in theoretical studies and working with the imperial administration rather than more typical working lawyers. See Jolowicz and Nicholas, *Roman Law*, 374–94; A. Carcaterra, *Le definizioni dei giuristi romani: Metodo mezzi e fini* (Naples, 1966); L. Ceci, *Le etimologie dei giureconsulti romani* (Rome, 1966); and R. Martini, *Le definizioni dei giuristi romani* (Milan, 1966). This

the first and second centuries and continued to do so under Diocletian, Constantine, and their successors.[17] While it is true that we see fewer original theoretic works of jurisprudence after 235, more recent scholars have argued for greater continuity in Roman legal thinking than the traditional view holds (and analysis of the *Collatio* can support such an argument).[18]

Another important legal development that the fourth century inherited is the so-called 'Antonine Constitution' of 212 that spread Roman citizenship to all free people in the empire and had the added benefit of raising taxes.[19] Thereafter, the distinction of *honestiores* (literally 'more honest ones,' meaning the distinguished citizens) and *humiliores* (humbler or common citizens) became progressively more important in Roman law (and appears in passages of the jurists cited by the Collator).[20]

type of juristic activity, such as the work of Marcus Antistius Labeo under Augustus, seems to be the norm for the next several centuries, and was even categorized into two schools. See further, Pomponius, *Enchiridion* (in *Digest* 1. 2. 2). See also, Schulz, *Roman Legal Science*, 102–20; Kunkel, *Römischen Juristen*, 32–4, 114; Jolowicz and Nicholas, *Roman Law*, 378–80; and D. Liebs, 'Rechtsschulen und Rechtsunterricht im Prinzipat' in H. Temporini (ed.), *ANRW* (Berlin and New York, 1976), II(15), 197–286.

[17] D. Liebs, 'Juristen als Sekretäre den römischen Kaiser', *ZRG (R.A.)* 100 (1983), 485–509. On lawyers in the government under Diocletian, see Schulz, *Roman Legal Science*, 262–4, A. H. M. Jones, *The Later Roman Empire, 284–602: A social, economic, and administrative survey* (London, 1964; reprint Baltimore, 1986), 42–52, esp. 49. On Hermogenianus as a case study, see D. Liebs, *Hermogenians Iuris Epitomae* and his 'Hermogenians Prätorianerpräfektur inschriftlich bezeugt', *ZRG (R.A.)* 107 (1990), 385–6.

[18] See J. Harries, 'Violence, victims, and legal tradition in late antiquity' in H. A. Drake (ed.), *Violence in Late Antiquity: Perceptions and practices* (Aldershot and Burlington, VT, 2006), 85–102, esp. 85–7. On the importance of historical context for Roman legal historians, see the cautionary words of E. A. Meyer, *Legitimacy and Law in the Roman World: Tabulae in Roman belief and practice* (Cambridge, 2004), 2–5.

[19] See L. De Giovanni, 'Effecti della Constitutio Antoniniana: un' ulteriore prospettiva d'indagine' in *Fraterna Munera: Studi in onore di L. Amirante* (Salerno, 1998), 145–59; P. Romanelli, '*Constitutio Antoniniana*', *Romanitas* 4 (1962), 29–41; Z. Rubin, 'Further to the dating of the *Constitutio Antoniniana*', *Latomus* 34 (1975), 430–6; C. Sasse, *Die Constitutio Antoniniana* (Wiesbaden, 1958); and A. N. Sherwin-White, *The Roman Citizenship*, 2nd edn (Oxford, 1973), 380–94.

[20] See P. Garnsey, *Social Status and Legal Privilege in the Roman Empire* (Oxford, 1970), 221–76; R. Rilinger, *Humiliores-Honestiores: zu einer sozialen Dichotomie in Strafrecht der römischen Kaiserzeit* (Munich, 1988); and R. Bauman, *Crime and Punishment in Ancient Rome* (London, 1996), 124–36.

B. RELIGION, LAW, AND POLITICS UNDER THE HOUSE OF CONSTANTINE

With the persecution of Christians well under way, and with what appeared to be a smoothly functioning system of imperial succession and provincial and urban administration, Diocletian retired in 305. Internal struggle quickly broke out again with Constantine, the son of one of Diocletian's caesars, emerging as a powerful figure within the Roman state after the Battle of the Milvian Bridge in 312. Constantine adopted and adapted Diocletian's reforms and continued to expand the civil service and, like his predecessors, to use lawyers in his administration.[21] He kept the system of a college of emperors, but relied on family connections for his caesars (especially after the deposition of Licinius in 324).[22] He reached out to Christianity as a basis for legitimacy in several ways. Although Galerius had already issued an edict of toleration in 311, Constantine and Licinius reiterated and clarified the end of Diocletian's persecution in 313 in a decree known traditionally as the 'Edict of Milan'.[23] Since this document plays such an important role in the history of the fourth century and in constructing the religious landscape of late antiquity in the Collator's life, it is important to look at it closely (as it is related by Lactantius):

When I, Constantine Augustus, and I, Licinius Augustus, happily met at Milan and had under consideration all matters which concerned the public advantage and safety, we thought that, among all the other things that we saw would benefit the majority of men, the arrangements which above all needed to be made were those which ensured reverence for the Divinity, so that we might grant both to Christians and to all men freedom to follow

[21] Jones, *Later Roman Empire*, 100–4; Jolowicz and Nicholas, *Roman Law*, 427; C. Kelly, 'Bureaucracy and government' in Lenski, *Age of Constantine*, 183–204; and C. Humfress, 'Civil law and social life' in Lenski, *Age of Constantine*, 205–25.

[22] See R. M. Frakes, 'The dynasty of Constantine down to 363' in Lenski, *Age of Constantine*, 91–107 at 91–5.

[23] See Lactantius, *De Mortibus Persecutorum*, 33–5 (on Galerius); 48. 2–12 (on the edict of Milan); Eusebius, *HE* 10. 5. 2–14. On the misleading title, see O. Seeck, 'Das sogenannte Edikt von Mailand', *Zeitschrift für Kirchengeschichte* 12 (1891), 381–6. For recent discussion, see H. A. Drake, *Constantine and the Bishops* (Baltimore, 2000), 162–5, 193–8; E. D. Digeser, *The Making of a Christian Empire: Lactantius and Rome* (Ithaca and London, 2000), 122–3. For discussion of the Edict of Galerius, see Drake, *Constantine and the Bishops*, 142–53; Digeser, 'Religion, law and the Roman polity', 69–70.

whatever religion each one wished, in order that whatever divinity there is in the seat of heaven may be appeased and made propitious towards us and towards all who have been set under our power.[24]

It is important to note that this decree, even though related by the Christian scholar Lactantius (tutor to Constantine's son Crispus), granted toleration for all religions in the state. Moreover, the explicit grant of freedom to both Christians and all others, no matter what their religion, suggests that Constantine was constructing a religiously tolerant discourse for his empire. The additional phrase *quicquid divinatis* ('whatever divinity') acknowledges a central God force that might be perceived in different manifestations by Christians and pagans.

Constantine went on to support Christianity further. For instance, he extended legal authority to decisions of bishops as arbiters (the *episcopalis audientia*).[25] While he allowed Jewish leaders some secular privileges, in the religious sphere the emperor ordered the punishment of Jews who attacked converts to Christianity and banned the circumcision of slaves by Jews.[26] Ultimately, Constantine's use of Church councils to ensure domestic stability demonstrates his vision of the use of the Church structure in his empire.[27]

[24] Lactantius, *De Mortibus Persecutorum*, 48. 2:

Cum feliciter tam ego [quam] Constantinus Augustus quam etiam ego Licinius Augustus apud Mediolanum convenissemus atque universa quae ad commoda et securitatem publicam pertinerent, in tractatu haberemus, haec inter cetera quae videbamus pluribus hominibus profutura, vel in primis ordinanda esse credidimus quibus divinitatis reverentia continebatur, ut daremus et Christianis et omnibus liberam potestatem sequendi religionem quam quisque voluisset, quo quicquid <est> divinitatis in sede caelesti, nobis atque omnibus qui sub potestate nostra sunt constituti, placatum ac propitium posit existere.

Latin text and English translation from J. L. Creed (ed.), *Lactantius: De Mortibus Persecutorum* (Oxford, 1984). See also the Greek translation in Eusebius, *HE*, 10. 5. 1–14 which does not preserve the more inclusive religious language.

[25] On the *episcopalis audientia*, see Harries, *Law and Empire*, 191–211; Drake, *Constantine and the Bishops*, 322–5; Frakes, *Contra Potentium Iniurias: The Defensor Civitatis and late Roman justice* (Munich, 2001), 195–229; and N. Lenski, 'Evidence for the *Audientia Episcopalis* in the new letters of Augustine' in R. Mathisen, *Law, Society, and Authority in Late Antiquity* (Oxford, 2001), 83–97. See most recently, Humfress, *Orthodoxy and the Courts*, 157–62 on late Roman laws as evidence for the 'bishop's court'.

[26] *CTh* 16. 8. 2–4 gave some Jewish religious leaders exemptions from compulsory public service; *CTh* 16. 8. 1 punished any Jews who stoned Christian converts with death by burning and *CTh* 16. 8. 5 punished Jews who disturbed converts to Christianity; and *Con. Sirm.* 4 forbade the circumcision of slaves by Jews.

[27] See Drake, *Constantine and the Bishops*, 238–68.

While Christianity was now a legal religion in that it was no longer outlawed by the edict of persecution,[28] and gained increasing government support under Constantine, it is important to remember that traditional pagan religion was still tolerated and, moreover, still followed by the majority of the population of the Roman Empire during Constantine's reign.[29] Indeed, he probably built traditional pagan temples as well as churches in his new capital city of Constantinople.[30] Scholars remain divided over the extent to which traditional rites were suppressed during Constantine's reign, but he may have restricted large-scale public sacrifices by officials on the order of the tetrarchs.[31] He certainly issued laws guarding against some forms of private divination and 'black magic' (i.e. magic used to hurt others).[32] So, in legislation he specified that

[28] On Roman policy toward Christianity in the mid to late third century, see P. Keresztes, 'The imperial Roman government and the Christian Church II: From Gallienus to the Great Persecution' in W. Haase (ed.), *ANRW* (Berlin and New York, 1979), II(23.1), 375–86.

[29] While Gibbon, *Decline and Fall*, I, 436 (Ch. 15) felt sure that Christians were only 5 percent of the empire in 312, more recent scholars have seen them as a larger minority by Constantine's reign. For the growth of Christianity, see R. Stark, *The Rise of Christianity* (Princeton, 1996), 4–13 (esp. 7 for Table 1.1); R. von Haehling, *Die Religionszugehörigkeit der hohen Amtsträger des römischen Reiches seit Constantins I. Alleinherrschaft bis zum Ende der Theodosianischen Dynastie (324–450 bzw. 455 n. Chr.)* (Bonn, 1978); R. Bagnall, *Egypt in Late Antiquity* (Princeton, 1993), 278–89; M. R. Salzman, *The Making of a Christian Aristocracy* (Cambridge, MA, 2002); Mark Edwards, 'The beginnings of Christianity' in Lenski, *Age of Constantine*, 137–58; A. D. Lee, 'Traditional religions' in Lenski, *Age of Constantine*, 159–79.

[30] Zosimus, *Historia Nova*, 2. 31–2 (on Constantine and pagan temples). On pagan priests playing a role in the inauguration of the city, see G. Dagron, *Naissance d'une capitale* (Paris, 1974), 37–41.

[31] Doubted as early as Gibbon, *Decline and Fall*, I, 722–3 (Ch. 21), who felt the law would surely have been included in the *Theodosian Code* if it had existed. For modern debate, see S. L. Greenslade, *Church and State from Constantine to Theodosius* (London, 1954), 22–3; T. D. Barnes, *Constantine and Eusebius* (Cambridge, MA, 1981), 210–12; H. A. Drake, Review of Barnes, 'Constantine and Eusebius' in *AJP* 103 (1982), 462–6; T. D. Barnes, 'Constantine's prohibition of pagan sacrifice', *AJP* 105 (1984), 69–72; R. Malcolm Errington, 'Constantine and the pagans', *GRBS* 29 (1988), 309–18; S. Bradbury, 'Constantine and the problem of anti-pagan legislation in the fourth century,' *CP* 89 (1994), 120–39; Averil Cameron and S. Hall (tr.), *Eusebius: Life of Constantine* (Oxford, 1999), 242–8. The testimony of Julian, no fan of Constantine, states that Constantine only despised the temples, while his sons demolished them (*Or.* 7. 228b–c).

[32] *CTh* 9. 40. 1; *CTh* 9. 16. 2 = *CJ* 9. 18. 3; *CTh* 9. 16. 1 = *CJ* 9. 18. 3. Such concerns date at least back to the *Lex Cornelia de sicariis et veneficiis*. See further, M. Dickie, *Magic and Magicians in the Greco-Roman World* (London, 2001), 142–272; Rives, 'Magic in Roman law', 313–39 and his 'Magic, religion, and law: The case of the *Lex Cornela de sicariis et veneficiis*' in C. Ando and J. Rüpke (eds.), *Religion and Law in*

haruspices (soothsayers who consulted the entrails of sacrificed animals) who conduct private divinations should be punished,[33] but allowed that such activity at public shrines for the good of the empire should be permitted.[34] In other legislation Constantine warned magicians who cast spells to hurt others, but allowed that magic used for good would not be punished.[35]

With the construction of such an apparently religiously tolerant atmosphere and on the eve of a major military expedition against Persia in 337, Constantine fell gravely ill, asked for Christian baptism, and died.[36] Constantine's sons (Constantine II, Constantius II, and Constans), who succeeded him as augusti after his death in 337, continued his policies, especially that of support for the Church and use of Church councils as well as further legislation restricting sacrifices and private divination.[37] They also seem to allow some toleration for traditional pagan worship in temples for a while. For instance, in 342, an edict of Constantius II and Constans (*CTh* 16. 10. 3) explicitly protected traditional pagan temples from harm due to their connection with Roman traditions.

The middle road between favouring Christianity and tolerating aspects of paganism continued for a few years. In November of 353,

Classical and Christian Rome (Stuttgart, 2006), 47–67. Pharr, 'Interdiction of Magic,' 272–5, prefers the Native American label of 'Bad Medicine' as a translation because the root of the word Latin word *venenum* denotes both medicine and potion.

[33] For further on the position of *haruspex*, which grew out of Etruscan religion, see K. Thulin, 'Haruspices', *RE* (Stuttgart, 1912), VII(2), cols. 2341–468; F. Lucrezi, 'Constantino e gli aurispici', *Atti dell' academia di scienze morali e politiche* 97 (1987), 171–98; G. Luck, *Arcana Mundi: Magic and the occult in the Greek and Roman worlds*, 2nd edn (Baltimore, 2006), 309–11; Dickie, *Magic and Magicians*, 155–6, 284–7.

[34] *CTh* 9. 16. 1 = *CJ* 9. 18. 3. On emperors' concern that private divination was associated with the desire for regime change, see Dickie, *Magic and Magicians*, 251–2; A. Lotz, *Der Magiekonflikt in der Spätantike* (Bonn, 2005), 99–103.

[35] *CTh* 9. 16. 3 = *CJ* 9. 18. 4. Barnes, *New Empire*, 74 adopts Seeck's dating of 318. On the consulships of the emperors, see further, R. Bagnall *et al.*, *Consuls of the Later Roman Empire* (Atlanta, 1987), 170–3. For the argument that 'magic' should be perceived as a fluid heuristic category in the Roman Empire until *c.*300 CE when it becomes seen as a religious offence, see Rives, 'Magic in Roman law', 334–5. Constantine's legislation may have been the grounds for the execution of Sopater when he was accused of casting a spell to stop the grain ships from entering the harbour at Constantinople, probably after 329 (Zosimus, *Historia Nova*, 2. 40; Eunapius *VS*, 6. 2–3).

[36] Eusebius, *VC*, 4. 62–4.

[37] See *CTh* 16. 10. 2 and see Barnes, *Constantine and Eusebius*, 377 n. 15; T. D. Barnes, *Athanasius and Constantius* (Cambridge, MA, 1993), 102, where he attributes the law to Constans; and Bradbury, 'Legislation', 126–9.

Constantius issued a constitution (part of which survives as *CTh* 16. 10. 5) stipulating that the secret nocturnal sacrifices which the usurper Flavius Magnus Magnentius (r. 350–August 353) had allowed were now abolished. This law seems to have followed in the tradition of the legislation of Constantine against domestic, and thus secret, sacrifices (as well as in the tradition of Constantine's supporters accusing Maxentius of black magic).[38] However, Constantius was still impressed by many of the temples in Rome when he visited in April of 357.[39] Moreover, in the east, traditional pagan temples were still open and crowded (at least until 354).[40]

The practice of religious toleration toward open pagan practices was restricted in a series of laws in the mid 350s. In a constitution of February 20 of 356 (surviving as *CTh* 16. 10. 6), Constantius (now with Julian as his caesar) ordered that anyone proven 'to devote their attention to sacrifices or to worship images' should be executed.[41] In another law (preserved as *CTh* 16. 10. 4 = *CJ* 1. 11. 1) that has been dated to December of 356, the emperors order that the pagan temples should be closed and that everyone should abstain from sacrificing, under threat of execution.[42] This law may be linked to a decision of Constantius II to remove the Altar of Victory from the Senate house the next year (a bone of contention for traditional pagans for the next several decades up to the time when the Collator compiled the *Collatio*) and appears on the surface at least to be a serious attempt at a general ban on sacrifice.[43] Shortly afterward,

[38] Lactantius, *DMP*, 44; Eusebius, *HE*, 8. 14. 5; *VC*, 1. 36. See Libanius, *Or.* 1. 98–9 relating how a bisexual boy prostitute, in league with Libanius' rivals, made the accusation that Libanius cast spells against Constantius II and Gallus with the aid of the severed heads of two girls. For comments on anti-divination legislation in this period, see Dickie, *Magic and Magicians*, 255–6.

[39] Ammianus, 16. 10. 4.

[40] See Lib. *Or.* 1. 102.

[41] C. Pharr (ed. and tr.), *The Theodosian Code* (Philadelphia, 1952), 472–3.

[42] The dating is problematic because of the editorial handling of the versions of the law preserved in the *Theodosian Code* and the *Code of Justinian*, and in the conflict between the dating information in the address and subscription. In both cases, the law is addressed to Taurus, as Praetorian Prefect, an office he held from 355–61 (*PLRE*, I, 879–80). The subscription in *CTh* 16. 10. 4 yields 346, but *CJ* 1. 11. 1 gives instead 354. O. Seeck, *Regesten für Kaiser und Päpste* (Stuttgart, 1919), 41–2, 203 suggested a dating to the first of December of 356 for this law, which *PLRE*, I, 879–80, follows.

[43] Libanius, *Or.* 1. 118–19, states Julian restored blood sacrifices at public temples. See also, Julian, *Misopogon*, 360d–361b.

Constantius issued a constitution in January of 357 (partly surviving as *CTh* 9. 16. 4 = *CJ* 9. 18. 5) forbidding anyone to consult *haruspices*, *mathematici* ('astrologers'), or *harioli* ('diviners'). This, in turn, was followed by a law (preserved by *CTh* 9. 16. 6 of July 357) that included a clause stipulating that suspected diviners should be interrogated by means of torture, even if of high rank and in the emperor's court. The fear of secret divination appears to be a continuation of Constantine's policy but seems to have expanded.

The watershed event in the expansion on the ban against sacrifices under Constantius seems to be the usurpation of Magnentius.[44] A capable and experienced general of Germanic origins, he rose against Constans and reached out to both Christians and pagans for support (although a Christian himself).[45] Even allowing for standard vitriolic against usurpers, Constantius II, who was raised as a Christian, may have considered the repercussions of Magnentius' policy and decided not only to repeal the usurper's allowance of secret sacrifices, but to go further and expand his father's restriction of sacrifices.[46]

Ironically, Constantius continued to use the traditional title of *pontifex maximus* (literally 'greatest bridge builder' = chief priest of the traditional Roman pagan religions). Symmachus later recounted how Constantius continued to fill empty slots among the pagan priests and maintained the privileges of the Vestal Virgins and guarded the traditional rituals.[47] Indeed, a Roman official's calendar from this time lists both Christian and traditional pagan holy days.[48] Moreover, testimony from Ammianus Marcellinus suggests that even Constantius' law against sacrifices was not enforced.[49] Ammianus also relates that Constantius ordered that an obelisk which had a dedication to the Sun god be erected in honour of the gods of

[44] Lotz, *Magiekonflikt*, 105–8.

[45] See J. Ziegler, *Die religiösen Haltung der Gegenkaiser im 4. Jr. n. Chr.* (Opladen, 1970), 53–69; Barnes, *Athansius and Constantius*, 102.

[46] See Ammianus, 14. 5 on Constantius purging Magnentius' followers.

[47] Symmachus, *Rel.* 3. 7.

[48] See M. R. Salzman, *On Roman Time: The Codex Calendar of 354 and the rhythms of urban life in late antiquity* (Berkeley, 1990).

[49] See Ammianus, 19. 10. 1–4 where he relates how Tertullus, the urban prefect, sacrificed at a temple in Ostia to calm the seas to allow food supplies to be delivered to Rome (probably in 359). See Greenslade, *Church and State*, 27, who suggests that such constitutions represent desires rather than enforceable laws.

Rome in 357.[50] The evidence, then, on Constantius' policy after 353 is complex. His laws may have banned divination sacrifices and then all sacrifices, but he does not seem to have enforced them seriously. Constantius had to contend with multiple military and political threats during his reign (such as Magnentius, Persians, Germanic tribes, and fear of his own caesars) and perhaps did not have time to follow through on his new policy.[51]

It is plausible that the number and percentage of Christians in the population of the Roman Empire continued to rise under the reigns of the sons of Constantine (337–61). Thus, it is dramatic that Constantine's half-nephew Julian actively sought to restore the empire to paganism when he claimed the title of augustus in 360. After Constantius died en route to confront Julian,[52] the usurper was accepted as the legitimate augustus and endeavoured to support paganism (but perhaps of a more syncretistic sort than Diocletian) through several means including banning Christians from teaching positions, eliminating Constantine's tax exemptions for clergy, creating a parallel pagan episcopal system, and rebuilding the Temple in Jerusalem.[53] Some adroit careerists may have followed his lead and apostacized to paganism for political advancement but, if so, their ambitions were frustrated as Julian fell mortally wounded during his invasion of Persia in June of 363.[54]

[50] Ammianus, 17. 4. On the obelisk, see also Salzman, *On Roman Time*, 220–1, and G. Kelly, *Ammianus Marcellinus: The allusive historian* (Cambridge, 2008), 225–30.

[51] For an overview, see Frakes, 'The dynasty of Constantine down to 363' in Lenski, *Age of Constantine*, 91–107; R. Malcolm Errington, *Roman Imperial Policy from Julian to Theodosius* (Chapel Hill, 2006), 14–17.

[52] Ammianus, 21. 15. 3, relates Constantius' death and his desire that Julian succeed him.

[53] See R. Browning, *The Emperor Julian* (Berkeley, 1976); G. Bowersock, *Julian the Apostate* (Cambridge, MA, 1978); R. Braun and J. Richer (eds.), *L'Empereur Julien: De l'histoire à la légende* (Paris, 1978); P. Athanassiadi-Fowden, *Julian and Hellenism* (Oxford, 1981); J. Bouffartigue, *L' Empereur Julien et la culture de son temps* (Paris, 1992); R. Smith, *Julian's Gods* (London and New York, 1995); and S. Tougher, *Julian the Apostate* (Edinburgh, 2007).

[54] Ammianus, 25. 3. 6–23, on the death of Julian. For a suggestion that Ammianus might have shifted from Christianity to paganism under Julian, see T. D. Barnes, *Ammianus Marcellinus and the Representation of Historical Reality* (Ithaca, 1998), 79–94.

C. CHURCH AND STATE IN THE MID FOURTH CENTURY

A middle ground policy that allowed both Christianity and some aspects of paganism continued for a short time. Jovian's brief reign from June of 363 to February of 364 followed Julian's death. Infamous for ceding several eastern provinces to Persia in a disastrous peace treaty,[55] Jovian seems to have followed a religiously tolerant course. Although a Christian, he started his reign by having the *haruspices* interpret the entrails of sacrificed animals.[56] Pagans, naturally, praised his policy of toleration.[57]

This tactic seems to have been followed in the main by his immediate successors. After Jovian's early death, Valentinian was elected by a group of military and administrative leaders and started a new dynasty in February of 364.[58] To ensure against future succession crises, within a month Valentinian made his brother Valens his co-augustus (skipping the junior emperor position of caesar perhaps to guard against possible usurpation conspiracies). After a serious illness, Valentinian also made his eight-year-old son Gratian another co-augustus in 367. Valentinian and Valens were Christians, but did not actively persecute pagans. Instead, they focused, like Constantine, on magic and, in Valens' case, attacked heresy.[59] Indeed, while Christian leaders, such as Irenaeus of Lyons, had wrestled with heresy as early as the second century, such concern accelerated after Constantine ended the great persecution, and even more

[55] See R. C. Blockley, *East Roman Foreign Policy* (Leeds, 1992), 26–30.

[56] Ammianus, 25. 6. 1.

[57] See Themistius, *Or.* 5. 70 b. For further on Jovian and toleration, see J. Vanderspoel, *Themistius and the Imperial Court* (Ann Arbor, 1995), 148–53.

[58] N. Lenski, *Failure of Empire: Valens and the Roman state in the fourth century* AD (Berkeley, 2002), 14–67. See Errington, *Roman Imperial Policy*, 293 n. 10, on debate over whether Jovian or Valentinian and Valens should be credited with reversal of some Julian's pagan legislation.

[59] Regarding their fear of magic, see the vivid descriptions in Ammianus, 28. 1; 29. 1; 30. 5. 11 and Libanius *Or.* 1. 171. See also, J. Matthews, *The Roman Empire of Ammianus* (London, 1989), 209–26. On treatment of heresy, see Lenski, *Failure of Empire*, 234–63; Errington, *Roman Imperial Policy*, 175–88. On allowing sacrifice, see Ammianus, 19. 12. 12.

after the death of Julian.[60] For example, we find in the *Panarion* ('medicine chest') of Epiphanius from 374–6 a laundry list of targeted heresies.[61]

Although they probably did most of the work in reversing Julian's anti-Christian legislation, Valentinian and Valens can still be seen as following in Constantine's model regarding religious toleration. Evidence exists that pagan shrines continued to be used.[62] They banned nocturnal sacrifices (again) in the constitutions surviving as *CTh* 9. 16. 7–8, but apparently allowed the burning of incense before pagan images.[63] The Pannonian emperors even continued to use the traditional title of *pontifex maximus* for the chief priest of Rome.[64] They may have pursued this course to maintain stability and ensure their newly won legitimacy. This situation changed in the next generation when Gratian rejected the robe associated with that traditional title and removed the Altar of Victory in 382.[65] After Valentinian's death, allegedly after suffering a stroke during a fit of rage,[66] Valens and Gratian were joined as augusti by Valentinian II (Valentinian's son by his second wife Justina). Since he was only four years old at the time of his accession, his reign was probably influenced by Gratian for some time.[67]

These Pannonian emperors faced a serious challenge that continued beyond their reign into the early fifth century. In 376 the

[60] See R. M. Grant, *Irenaeus of Lyons* (London, 1997); D. Gwynn, *The Eusebians: The polemic of Athanasius of Alexandria and the construction of the 'Arian controversy'* (Oxford, 2007).

[61] For a recent translation, see F. Williams, *The Panarion of Epiphanius of Salamis*, 2 vols. (Leiden, 1987–90). See also recently, Y. Kim, 'Epiphanius of Cyprus and the geography of heresy' in Drake, *Violence in Late Antiquity*, 235–51.

[62] Lib. *Or.* 1. 143 on a shrine of Asclepius (probably dated to 367). See also his epp. 137, 706–8, 1300 for earlier attempts at healings (probably in 363 and 364).

[63] Libanius, *Or.* 30. 7.

[64] Lenski, *Failure of Empire*, 214–18.

[65] Zosimus, *Historia Nova*, 4. 36. See further, O. Seeck, 'Gratianus (3)' in *RE* (Stuttgart, 1912), VII(2), cols. 1831–40 at 1838; Greenslade, *Church and State*, 72–4; Alan Cameron, 'Gratian's repudiation of the pontifical robe', *JRS* 58 (1968), 96–102; Drake, *Constantine and the Bishops*, 403; and Lenski, *Failure of Empire*, 215. See also the revisionist argument of R. Lizzi Testa, 'Christian emperor, Vestal Virgins and priestly colleges: Reconsidering the end of Roman paganism', *Ant. Tard.* 15 (2007), 251–62.

[66] Ammianus, 30. 6.

[67] Ammianus, 30. 10. See further, N. McLynn, *Ambrose of Milan* (Berkeley, 1994), 84–5; Lenski, *Failure of Empire*, 357. On Justina's possible connection to the house of Constantine, see Frakes, 'Dynasty', 96–7; D. Woods, 'The Constantinian origin of Justina (Themistius, *Or.* 3.43b)', *CQ* 54 (2004), 325–7.

Visigoths, who had been allowed to settle on the Danube frontier by Valens following their defeat by the Huns, rose in rebellion.[68] Valens hastened to stop them, but was soundly defeated at the disastrous Battle of Adrianople in 378 where he, like a large part of the eastern Roman army, perished.[69] Since Valentinian II was still only seven years old at this point, Gratian needed an imperial presence in the east to deal with the Visigoths as well as the ever-dangerous Persian frontier. Gratian chose the young officer Theodosius as *magister militum* and quickly promoted him to augustus in January of 379.[70]

D. LAW, RELIGION, AND THE AGE OF THEODOSIUS I

Political and religious developments intersected dramatically under this new emperor. Theodosius dealt with the Visigothic threat by settling a peace treaty with them and hiring many of them as the replacements for the lost eastern Roman army (the *foederati*).[71] His western co-augustus Gratian was subsequently overthrown and murdered by the forces of Magnus Maximus in 383.[72] Theodosius stalled for a time, perhaps to protect the eastern frontier against the Persian emperors Ardashir II (379–83) and Shapur III (383–8), and elevated his older son Arcadius to the status of augustus in 383. When Magnus Maximus invaded Italy in 387 and pushed out the young Valentinian II, Theodosius invaded from the east and quickly defeated Maximus in 388.[73] Although Valentinian II was technically

[68] Ammianus, 31. 1–6.

[69] Ammianus, 31. 13. On the defeat, see A. Ferrill, *The Fall of Rome: The military explanation* (London, 1986), 56–67; Lenski, *Failure of Empire*, 320–367.

[70] J. Matthews, *Western Aristocracies and Imperial Court,* AD *364–425*, 2nd edn (Oxford, 1990), 91–2; S. Williams and G. Friell, *Theodosius: The empire at bay* (New Haven, 1994), 20–6; Honoré, *Law in the Crisis of Empire*, 1; Errington, *Roman Imperial Policy*, 28–9.

[71] Although chastised by some modern historians for this decision, it did stabilize the eastern frontier for the rest of his reign. See comments of Ferrill, *Fall of Rome*, 68–70; Williams and Friell, *Theodosius*, 29–35; Honoré, *Crisis of Empire*, 2.

[72] See Matthews, *Western Aristocracies*, 173; Williams and Friell, *Theodosius*, 36–42; and Errington, *Roman Imperial Policy*, 31–2.

[73] Zosimus, *Historia Nova*, 4. 45–7. See also comments of Matthews, *Western Aristocracies*, 224–5; Ferrill, *Fall of Rome*, 70–1; Williams and Friell, *Theodosius*, 62–3; McLynn, *Ambrose*, 292–4; and Errington, *Roman Imperial Policy*, 33–7.

in power in the west, Theodosius remained there three years before returning to the east in the summer of 391.[74]

It was during this period that Theodosius had dramatic confrontations with Ambrose, the Bishop of Milan. Like earlier Christian emperors since Constantine, Theodosius was probably raised in a Christian environment. So, already in February of 380 he issued a constitution (surviving as *CTh* 16. 1. 2) stipulating that Catholic Christianity was the only valid form of the faith, although he still tolerated traditional pagan belief.[75] Up to this time, Christian emperors had, like Constantine, held off on baptism until near their death (a practice not confined to the upper class).[76] Due to a serious illness, Theodosius had thought he was dying in 380 and begged for baptism.[77] He recovered and after that time became naturally more susceptible to pressure from Church leaders because of his fear of accumulating sin and risking his chance for salvation.

When Theodosius was in the west after the campaign against Magnus Maximus, the influence of Western Church leaders, such as Ambrose, grew. When Theodosius heard that a Christian mob had burned a synagogue in the eastern town of Callinicum in 388, the emperor ordered the local bishop to ensure the Jewish place of worship was rebuilt. Around this time, the emperor also heard that a mob of monks in Syria had beaten some Gnostic heretics and Theodosius apparently ordered that the monks who had beaten the heretics also be punished.[78] However, Ambrose reproached the emperor for his lenient treatment of non-Catholics in both cases and Theodosius reversed himself on his decision regarding the

[74] See Ferrill, *Fall of Rome*, 71; Matthews, *Western Aristocracies*, 225–38; Williams and Friell, *Theodosius*, 64; and McLynn, *Ambrose*, 294–8. On the impact of Theodosius' entry into Rome in 389, see Matthews, *Roman Empire of Ammianus*, 9–12.

[75] See Zosimus, *Historia Nova*, 4. 29. 2, on the continuation of worship in pagan temples in the beginning of Theodosius' reign. See also discussion by Williams and Friell, *Theodosius*, 52–4, and R. Malcolm Errington, 'Christian accounts of the religious legislation of Theodosius I', *Klio* 79 (1997), 398–443.

[76] See Augustine, *Confessions*, 4. 4. 8, on how a boyhood friend changed after he was baptized when he thought he was dying (probably in the 370s or early 380s).

[77] Zosimus, *Historia Nova*, 4. 34. 4, implies Theodosius' disease might have struck in winter 381–2. Sozomen, 7. 4, states instead winter 380–1, which most scholars accept.

[78] For clarification of these being two separate events, see McLynn, *Ambrose*, 301–2.

Bishop of Callinicum.[79] In 388–9, Theodosius still worked well with the traditional pagan elite of Rome by appointing pagans to high office. For instance, Symmachus was appointed consul for 391 and Virius Nicomachus Flavianus was made first quaestor, perhaps from October of 388 to June of 390, and then praetorian prefect of Italy, Africa, and Illyricum in early 390.[80]

This even-handed treatment changed as a result of the most famous episode with Ambrose, which, ironically, is also the murkiest.[81] The episode revolves around an event that occurred in Thessalonica sometime before the summer of 390 and is colourfully related by Sozomen.[82] A crowd of the town's inhabitants, fearing a favourite charioteer would not be released in time for an upcoming race, rioted and killed a local military commander. When the emperor heard the news, he apparently punished the town's population by ordering the massacre of thousands of them.[83]

In response, Ambrose again upbraided Theodosius—this time by refusing him communion until he performed penance for his

[79] Ambrose, *ep.* 74. See also, McLynn, *Ambrose*, 298–309; Errington, *Roman Imperial Policy*, 239–41.

[80] See T. Honoré (ed.), *Virius Nicomachus Flavianus* (Konstanz, 1989), 10–14; Honoré, *Crisis of Empire*, 59–70; McLynn, *Ambrose*, 310–12; Errington, *Roman Imperial Policy*, 241–3. For date of his prefecture, see *PLRE*, I, 347–9. For a fascinating study of his life, see also C. W. Hedrick, *History and Silence: The purge and rehabilitation of memory in late antiquity* (Austin, 2000).

[81] I am grateful for comments on a preliminary analysis of this event that I presented in the summer of 2007 at the North American Patristics Society. On this dramatic event, see McLynn, *Ambrose*, 315–30; C. W. R. Larsen, 'Theodosius and the Thessalonian Massacre revisited—Yet again', *Studia Patristica* 10 (1970), 297–301; F. Kolb, 'Der Bussakt von Mailand: Zum Verhaltnis von Staat und Kirche in der Spätantike' in H. Boockman, K. Jürgensen, and G. Stottenberg (eds.), *Geschichte und Gegenwart: Festschrift für K. D. Erdmann* (Neumünster, 1980), 41–74. W. Ensslin, *Die Religionspolitik des Kaisers Theodosius d. Gr.* (Munich, 1953) is still of interest and Williams and Friell, *Theodosius*, 67, provides a general overview.

[82] Sozomen, *HE*, 7. 25. 1–9. On this event, see C. Hohenlohe, *Ursprung und Zweck der Collatio Legum Mosaicarum et Romanarum* (Vienna, 1935), 11–12; Ensslin, *Religionspolitik*, 67; and N. Q. King, *The Emperor Theodosius and the Establishment of Christianity* (Philadelphia, 1960), 68–70. R. Malcolm Errington, 'The praetorian prefectures of Virius Nicomachus Flavianus', *Historia* 41 (1992), 439–461 at 454, suggests sometime in 390 as a possible date for the arrest.

[83] Sozomen, *HE*, 7. 25. 4–7. See Ambrose, *ep.* 51; Theodoret, 5. 18. See also Williams and Friell, *Theodosius*, 67–8 and J. Curran, 'From Jovian to Theodosius' in Averil Cameron and P. Garnsey (eds.), *The Cambridge Ancient History*, XIII: *The Late Empire*, AD *337–425* (Cambridge, 1998), 78–110.

actions.[84] In an action that must have sent both Constantine and Julian spinning in their graves, Theodosius publicly repented for his actions, possibly on Christmas day of 390. While this action may have been a public relations coup for both Theodosius and Ambrose,[85] in hindsight it established a precedent for the domination of Church over state that would evolve further in the medieval west (reaching its zenith in the Investiture Contest at Canossa in 1077 when Pope Gregory VII forced Emperor Henry IV to do penance to regain political power after his excommunication).[86] Finally, in February of 391, Theodosius, in conjunction with Valentinian II and Arcadius, issued a constitution which ordered: 'No person shall pollute himself with sacrificial animals; no person shall slaughter an innocent victim; no person shall approach the shrines, shall wander through the temples, or revere the images formed by mortal labour, lest he become guilty by divine and human laws.'[87] The law went on to specify that any governor who commits these crimes must pay a fine as well as their staff members who did not report such crimes. The traditional view of this law is that it effectively made Christianity the official religion of the Roman Empire by outlawing pagan worship.[88] However, this law also, like perhaps those of Constantius II, might not have been meant to have a wide-ranging impact.[89] While this

[84] Sozomen, 7. 25. 1–2 (see colourful English translation by C. D. Hartranft (tr.), *The Ecclesiastical History of Sozomen*, NPNF (New York, 1890), II, 393–4).

[85] See the intriguing analysis by McLynn, *Ambrose*, 323–330. For a traditional view, see Ensslin, *Religionspolitik*, 67–9.

[86] Pope Gelasius had argued for a separation of powers in 494, but the papal reform movement developed new ideas based on the study of canon law in the eleventh century. See further, U.-R. Blumenthal, *The Investiture Controversy: Church and monarchy from the ninth to the twelfth century* (Philadelphia, 1988); C. Morris, *The Papal Monarchy: The Western Church from 1050 to 1250* (Oxford, 1989); and I. Robinson, *The Papacy, 1073–1198: Continuity and innovation* (Cambridge, 1990).

[87] English translation from Pharr, *The Theodosian Code*, 473. *CTh* 16. 10. 10: *IDEM AAA AD ALBINUM PRAEFECTUM PRAETORIO. nemo se hostiis polluat, nemo insontem victimam caedat, nemo delubra adeat, templa perlustret et mortali opere formata simulacra suspiciat, ne divinis adque humanis sanctionibus reus fiat.* (Latin text, T. Mommsen and P. M. Meyer (eds.), *Theodosiani Libri XVI* (Berlin, 1905), 899–900.)

[88] See the discussion by King, *Emperor Theodosius and the Establishment of Christianity*, 77–82 and Williams and Friell, *Theodosius*, 119–25.

[89] See Errington, 'Christian accounts of the religious legislation of Theodosius I', 398–443. It does appear, however, that we have fewer attested pagan priests after 391 (for instance, Coelia Concordia, cited in *CIL* VI, 2145, is the last attested Vestal Virgin).

constitution and subsequent ones banning worship at temples in Egypt (*CTh* 16. 10. 11 dated to June of 391) and an expansion to banning not just sacrifice of animals, but also burning incense or pouring out an offering of wine (*CTh* 16. 10. 12 dated to November of 392), might not have been directly influenced by Ambrose, it is plausible they were part of a growing Christian programme that Theodosius was developing as he returned to the east.[90] Contemporary pagan reactions centre more on complaints that public funding for sacrifices has been stopped, implying that Theodosius' legislation had more impact on that issue than on any other area.[91]

The pagans would have one last champion. In less than a year, Valentinian II was found dead, possibly by his own hand, by his *magister militum* Arbogast at Vienne (in Gaul) in 392.[92] Arbogast then fostered the elevation of Eugenius, a teacher of rhetoric and *magister scrinii*, as augustus on August 22 of 392.[93] Theodosius rejected the offers of cooperation from Eugenius (and Arbogast) and instead elevated his younger son Honorius to the status of augustus in January of 393 in preparation for the coming military campaign against the western usurper.[94] When hope for a peaceful resolution seemed lost by spring of 393, Eugenius journeyed to Rome where he was recognized as augustus by elements of the traditional pagan elite. While it is now held that Eugenius was a Christian, he reached out to the traditional pagan elite of Italy and allowed Symmachus to return the Altar of Victory to the Senate House in Rome (earlier removed by Constantius II in 357, probably replaced by Julian, and

[90] See McLynn, *Ambrose*, 331–3, against traditional view of Ambrose standing behind this legislation.

[91] See Zosimus, *Historia Nova*, 4. 59. 2–3. On Theodosius allowing pagans to continue to hold high office, see Prudentius, *Contra Symmachum*, 615–30. For a request in the summer of 392 by both pagan and Christian senators in Rome for Valentinian to restore pagan privileges, see Ambrose, *De Obitu Valentiniani*, 19–20.

[92] The primary sources are in conflict over whether Arbogast murdered Valentinian II or if he committed suicide. See Zosimus, *Historia Nova*, 4. 54. 3; Sozomen, 7. 22; and Rufinus, *HE*, 11. 31. See further, Matthews, *Western Aristocracies*, 238–9; B. Croke, 'Arbogast and the death of Valentinian II', *Historia* 25 (1976), 235–44; Williams and Friell, *Theodosius*, 127–8; and McLynn, *Ambrose*, 335–7.

[93] J. Straub, 'Eugenius', *RAC* 6 (1966), cols. 860–77; Matthews, *Western Aristocracies*, 238–9; J. Szidat, 'Die Usurpation des Eugenius', *Historia* 28 (1979), 487–508; and Williams and Friell, *Theodosius*, 129–30.

[94] Matthews, *Western Aristocracies*, 239; Errington, *Roman Imperial Policy*, 39–41.

then removed again by Gratian in 382).[95] The 'pagan outreach' campaign of Eugenius was fostered by Nicomachus Flavianus, the prefect of Italy who also revived several traditional pagan festivals.[96] After claiming that an oracle had prophesied that Christianity would perish 365 years after its foundation (which he believed would be in 394, since he dated the crucifixion to 29 CE), Nicomachus Flavianus promised that after the pagan victory he would turn cathedrals into stables and conscript priests into the Roman armies.[97] Unfortunately for the pagan-friendly camp, Theodosius' forces were able to defeat the army of Eugenius in a two-day battle in September of 394 on the banks of the Frigidus river (in modern Slovenia) with the help of a strong wind, which later Christian writers interpreted as divinely sent.[98] Nicomachus Flavianus and Arbogast committed suicide afterward.

With the death of Eugenius and Arbogast, the tide had turned against the pagans. Theodosius ruled in concert with his two sons for the weeks remaining until his death in January of 395. His sons then took the natural path of taking different halves of the empire (with Arcadius in the east and Honorius in the west). Although this was standard practice from the period of the tetrarchy onward, and even had earlier precedents, in retrospect the death of Theodosius in 395 seems to mark a milestone after which the empire was never successfully unified. Arcadius and Honorius were dominated by their

[95] See, obliquely, Ambrose, *ep.* 57. On the attempts to restore the Altar of Victory, see J. Wytzes, *Der Streit um den Altar der Viktoria* (Leiden, 1936) and Errington, *Roman Imperial Policy*, 126–7. On Eugenius'actions, see Matthews, *Western Aristocracies*, 239–41. For Symmachus' career, see recently C. Sogno, *Symmachus: A political biography* (Ann Arbor, 2006), esp. 45–50 on his third *Relatio*.

[96] See comments in the anonymous *Carmen contra Paganos*, 103–15. See further, B. Croke and J. Harries, *Religious Conflict in Fourth-Century Rome* (Sydney, 1982), 52–72; Matthews, *Western Aristocracies*, 241–2; Honoré, *Flavianus*, 9; and Errington, *Roman Imperial Policy*, 140–1. While earlier scholars held for a 'Circle of Symmachus' and their role in a 'pagan revival', see comments of Alan Cameron, 'The date and identity of Macrobius', *JRS* 55 (1965), 25–38.

[97] Paulinus, *V. Ambr.* 31. See further, Matthews, *Western Aristocracies*, 245–6, who conjectures that this might be the source for the anonymous false prophecy recounted in Augustine, *City of God*, 18. 54. See also, Honoré, *Flavianus*, 9.

[98] O. Seeck and G. Veith, 'Die Schlacht am Frigidus', *Klio* 13 (1913), 451–67. See, more recently, Ferrill, *Fall of Rome*, 71–5; Williams and Friell, *Theodosius*, 134–5; M. Springer, 'Die Schlacht am Frigidus als quellenkundliches und literaturgeschichtliches Problem' and M. Kovac, 'Bora or summer storm: Meterological aspect of the Battle of Frigidus' in R. Bratoz (ed.), *Westillyricum und Nordostitalien in der Spätrömischen Zeit* (Ljubljana, 1996), 45–93 and 109–19, respectively.

advisors (Arcadius by Rufinus, Eutropius, and, arguably, Eudoxia and Honorius by Stilicho).[99] They had to deal with increased folk movements of Germanic tribes and, most especially, the powerful Alaric, leader of the Visigoths who eventually sacked Rome in 410.[100] While Honorius ruled until 423, his western zone saw continual incursions of Germanic tribes. Ultimately, he was be succeeded by his nephew Valentinian III during whose reign the transformation of the west accelerated. After his murder in 455, the west saw a series of emperors of uneven quality culminating in the short reign of Romulus Augustulus, traditionally seen as the last western emperor when he was deposed by the Germanic chief Odoacer in 476.[101]

E. CONCLUSION: ROMAN LAW AFTER THE FALL OF THE WEST

Interest in the laws of the Roman state would outlast the Western Roman Empire and the continuing influence of Roman jurisprudence helped preserve both the *Collatio* and variant versions of its sources. As various Germanic tribal groups set up their kingdoms in the remains of the western state (with Anglo-Saxons in Britain, Visigoths in Spain, Ostrogoths in Italy, and Franks in what would become France), some knowledge of aspects of Roman imperial law continued in both secular and Church archives and even in practice.[102] The Visigoths under Alaric II composed their own redaction of late Roman laws (and some jurisprudence) in the *Lex*

[99] Ferrill, *Fall of Rome*, 86–116. In general, see also Alan Cameron, *Claudian: Poetry and propaganda at the court of Honorius* (Oxford, 1970) and Alan Cameron and J. Long, *Barbarians and Politics at the Court of Arcadius* (Berkely, 1993).

[100] On the Germanic tribes and their effects, see most recently, P. Heather, *The Fall of the Roman Empire: A new history of Rome and the Barbarians* (Oxford, 2006). On the tradition that Pope Innocent allowed pagan sacrifices to aid in repelling Alaric, see Zosimus, *Historia Nova*, 5. 41.

[101] Gibbon, *Decline and Fall*, II, 339–42 (ch. 36); Ferrill, *Fall of Rome*, 159–61. On the historiography on this event, see the comprehensive study by B. Croke, 'AD 476: The manufacture of a turning point', *Chiron* 13 (1983), 81–119.

[102] See, among others, P. Barnwell, 'Emperors, jurists and kings: Law and custom in the late-Roman and early-medieval West', *Past and Present* 168 (2000), 6–29.

Romana Visigothorum or *Breviarium*.[103] Other Germanic tribes adopted some aspects of Roman law while Church leaders also explored models of that great legal system.[104] While the Visigothic kingdom fell to the Moslems in 711, the Franks resisted that threat under the leadership of Charles Martel. His son established a dynasty that reached its zenith in the next generation under Charlemagne who tried to recapture aspects of Roman learning, including Roman law.

The Eastern Roman Empire lasted much longer (and Roman law logically continued to play a central role in that state). After the death of Arcadius in 408, his son Theodosius II came to the throne where he ordered what was probably the first effective imperial codification of Roman imperial law—the *Theodosian Code* in 438.[105] His eventual successor Justinian undertook an even more arduous compilation of Roman imperial laws in the sixth century—the *Corpus Iuris Civilis* which included the *Code of Justinian* (containing some material that the compilers of the *Theodosian Code* might not have had), the *Novels* (or new laws issued by Justinian), the *Institutes* (a textbook clearly based on the earlier work of the jurist Gaius), and, importantly for comparative purposes with the *Collatio*, the *Digest* (the long handbook of extracts from the works of the great Roman jurists).[106] While his successors had to deal with the Persian threat in the east, and later the Slavs in the north, and still later the Moslems in the

[103] See recently, J.-D. Rodriguez-Martin, 'A handbook for Alaric's Codification', *RIDA* 3, Série 46 (1999), 451–63; J. Matthews, 'Roman law and Barbarian identity in the late Roman West' in S. Mitchell (ed.), *Ethnicity and Culture in Late Antiquity* (London, 2000), 31–44; J. Matthews, 'Interpreting the *Interpretationes* of the *Breviarium*' in Mathisen, *Law, Society, and Authority in Late Antiquity*, 11–32; and D. Liebs, 'Zur Überlieferung und Entstehung des Breviarium Alaricianum', *AARC* 14 (2003), 653–71.

[104] A. Arjava, 'The survival of Roman family law after the Barbarian settlements' in Mathisen, *Law, Society, and Authority in Late Antiquity*, 33–51.

[105] Although the *Codex Hermogenianus* and *Codex Gregorianus* may have been officially authorized, the *Theodosian Code* was clearly a tool of government policy. See further, W. Turpin, 'The purpose of the Roman law codes', *ZRG (R.A.)* 104 (1987), 620–30. On Theodosius II and his code, see Harries and Wood, *The Theodosian Code*, Matthews, *Laying Down the Law*; F. Millar, *A Greek Roman Empire: Power and belief under Theodosius II (408–450)* (Berkeley, 2006); and, most recently, Sirks, *Theodosian Code*.

[106] For a recent overview of scholarship on Justinian's legal work, see C. Humfress, 'Law and legal practice in the age of Justinian' in M. Maas (ed.), *Cambridge Companion to the Age of Justinian* (Cambridge, 2005), 161–84. See also A. Biscardi, 'Nuovi Spunti sulle Fonti del Diritto nell' età del Tardo Impero', *AARC* 10 (1995), 327–34.

south, they continued to study and use aspects of Roman law and jurisprudence for centuries (as demonstrated by the tenth-century codification, the *Basilika*) before their ultimate defeat by the Moslem Turks in 1453.[107]

The Collator lived and wrote during the complex world of late antiquity (although, as we shall see, scholars have had different answers to the question of exactly when he wrote). For centuries the Roman state saw military crises, religious change, as well as the study and editing of Roman law and Roman jurisprudence. The Collator was the product of traditional Roman juristic education in the late empire. At the same time, he and his world were affected by the broad political and religious developments in the Roman Empire. To track exactly the effects of that influence, the next chapter will place the Collator within the proper historical context in this changing Roman state.

[107] On the *Basilika*, see G. Heimbach (ed.), *Basilicorum libri* LX, 3 vols. (Leipzig, 1833–43); F. Pringsheim, *Zum Plan einer neuen Ausgabe der Basiliken: Begründung ihrer Notwendigkeit und Gesichtspunkte für ihre Herstellung* (Berlin, 1956); and H. Scheltema (ed.), *Basilicorum libri LX*, 17 vols. (Groningen, 1953–88).

2

Dating the Work

Hincmar, *Responsio* 12: He who sleeps with a man in the manner of a woman, both have sinned, let them die. From whence also the Roman laws point out in the chapter 'Concerning Those Who Commit *Stupra*', as all, reading, will find. And if it is thus determined concerning male with male, what would the laws say if they encountered the male (and a brother) with a sister in the manner of sodomite male practice?

[Hincmar, Responsio 12: *Qui dormierit cum masculo coitu femineo, uterque operatus est nefas, morte moriantur. Unde et leges Romanae decernunt in capitulis de stupratoribus, quo legens quisque inveniet. Et si de masculo cum masculo ita decernitur, quam adinventionem leges invenient de masculo et fratre cum sorore ex concubito masculi sodomitano?*][1]

So wrote Bishop Hincmar of Reims in 860 in his attempt to exonerate the Frankish Queen Theutberga from accusations made by her husband Lothar II (a great-grandson of Charlemagne) of incestuous anal sex with her brother prior to their marriage, leading somehow to impregnation and abortion.[2] In Hincmar's text we encounter the first explicit external reference to the *Collatio* by allusion to the chapter *De Stupratoribus* (or 'Concerning Those Who Commit *Stupra*', i.e. illicit intercourse). Analysis of such references as that by Hincmar can help us understand the manuscript tradition of

[1] *Responsio* 12, in L. Böhringer (ed.), *De Divortio Lotharii Regis et Theutbergae Reginae* (Hannover, 1992), 178.

[2] For a recent study of the political aspects of this conflict, see S. Airlie, 'Private bodies and the body politic in the divorce case of Lothar II', *Past and Present* 161 (1998), 3–38. Part of this chapter appeared in an earlier form as R. M. Frakes, 'The manuscript tradition of the *Lex Dei*', *ZRG (R.A.)* 124 (2007), 290–304, but has been revised on the basis of further consultation with early editions as well as discussions with various scholars and now recast as part of a broader argument. See also recently L. Loschiavo, 'La legge che dio trasmise a Mosè. Fortuna medioevale di un' operetta volgare', *Rechtsgeschichte* 2 (2003), 72–86.

the *Collatio* and its use in the Middle Ages. Examining the early modern encounter with the work can further clarify the manuscript tradition. Finally, such analysis can provide the first step in the search for the date when the anonymous Collator wrote his work in late antiquity.

Setting the *Collatio* in historical context is critical for analysing the thought world of the Collator and his purpose in constructing his work. The Collator gives no single explicit description of when he was writing. However, a few clues from external and internal evidence (that is, what others said about the *Collatio* and what the Collator himself states within the work) can aid in dating the work. Scholars have disputed the interpretation of these clues and have suggested a range of dates spanning from the late third to the sixth century.[3] To define the date for the work, it is critical to establish the date before which it must have been written (or *terminus ante quem* in traditional scholarly parlance) and the date after which the work must have been written (or *terminus post quem*). To accomplish this, we shall have to enter into study of the manuscript tradition, external testimony, and certain important passages within the work. Re-examination of both external and internal evidence provides a clearer understanding of the date for the composition of the *Collatio* and confirms a date in the last decade of the fourth century.

A. MEDIEVAL AND EARLY MODERN ENCOUNTERS WITH THE *COLLATIO*

The first step is to establish the manuscript tradition of the work. There are three surviving manuscripts of the *Collatio*: the ninth-century B (*Codex Berolinensis* Lat. Fol. 269), the tenth/eleventh century V (*Codex Vercellensis* n. 122), and W (*Codex Vindobonensis* n. 2160) which traditionally was also dated to the tenth or eleventh

[3] Indeed, while A. Jacobs, '"Papinian commands one thing, our Paul another": Roman Christians and Jewish law in the *Collatio Legum Mosaicarum et Romanarum*' in C. Ando and J. Rüpke (eds.), *Religion and Law in Classical and Christian Rome* (Stuttgart, 2006), 85–99 at 88–9 relates the range of dates provided by scholars, he does not commit himself to anything beyond the fourth century after 315.

century, but seems more likely to have come from the late ninth century.[4] While nineteenth- and early twentieth-century scholars were unsure of the exact connection between these three manuscripts, in 1946 Fritz Schulz produced a convincing stemma that subsequent scholars of the *Collatio* have accepted:[5]

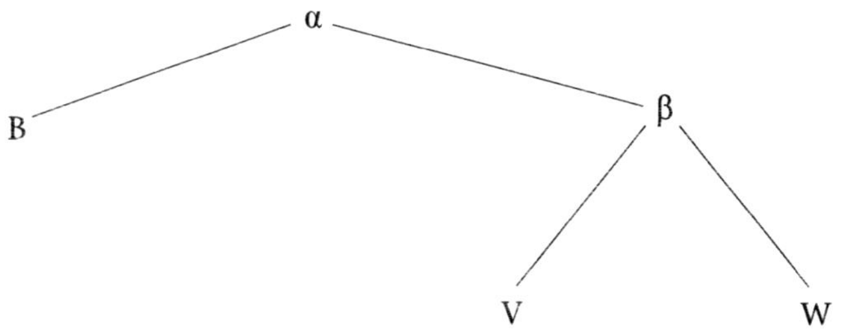

While Schulz's stemma successfully explained the relationships of the three surviving manuscripts, it did not deal with two fragments surviving in other works, with allusions by the canons of Merovingian Church councils, statements by Hincmar, or with observations by several early modern scholars. While Schulz's stemma of the surviving manuscripts is certainly correct, analysis of possible further stages of the manuscript tradition can flesh out this skeletal diagram (and I will provide a fuller new version at the end of this section). Such an approach can help us better understand the interest in and use of the *Collatio* in late antiquity and the Middle Ages and can thus provide the first steps toward the dating of the work.

To make progress in gaining a fuller view of the transmission process of the *Collatio* from the original author's hand to the

[4] For the dating and standard labels of the manuscripts, see Mommsen, *Collatio*, 109–110; Schulz, 'Manuscripts of the Collatio Legum Mosaicarum et Romanarum', 314–15. Most recently, see W. Kaiser, *Die Epitome Iuliani* (Frankfurt, 2004), 123–4, who suggests a dating to the first half of the eleventh century is possible for V and, 153–4, the third quarter of the ninth century is possible for W, following the work of B. Bischoff, *Die südostdeutschen Schreibschulen und Bibliotheken in der Karolingerzeit* (Wiesbaden, 1980), II, 168. I would like to thank the Staatsbibliothek zu Berlin Handschriftenabteilung for allowing me access to the manuscript and for later providing a copy of Lat. Fol. 269, the Österreichische Nationalbibliothek for sending me a microfilm copy of W, and the Biblioteca Capitolare di Vercelli for providing a microfilm copy of V.

[5] From Schulz, 'Manuscripts', 315. See also the comments of H. L. W. Nelson and U. Manthe, *Gai Institutiones III. 1–87: Intestaterbfolge und sonstige Arten von Gesamtnachfolge* (Berlin, 1992), 8–15 who use a variant of Schulz's stemma.

versions that survive we need to look closely at intervening steps with appropriate labels. Following traditional rules of paleography, we can label the lost autograph (the original manuscript written by the Collator) of the *Collatio* as χ.[6] Can we trace the use of χ in late antiquity and the early Middle Ages before Hincmar? If so, this could help set when the work itself could have been written. It appears that the *Collatio* was probably used in Merovingian Church councils, dating at least as early as the third Council of Orleans in 538, based on study of the canons stemming from those synods.[7] It may well have been used again in 567 at the Council of Tours and then at the Council of Mâcon in 585.[8] There is some distance between those cities (and especially between Tours and Mâcon). Moreover, while Tours and Orleans were at times in the same Frankish state (later called Neustria), Mâcon was in Burgundy. Because all three councils reflect interest in the work, and are spread over space and time during a fairly unstable period,[9] it seems likely that already by the mid 500s there must have been several copies of χ in circulation (a layer of the manuscript tradition that I have termed sub-χ) that were used by Church leaders in the Frankish kingdoms and in Burgundy long before Hincmar.

Examination of another legal text can help in charting the interest in the *Collatio* in the sixth and seventh centuries. Analysis of the manuscript tradition of the handbook of Byzantine law called the *Epitome* of Julian affirms that the *Collatio* was in some demand in the early Middle Ages and was recopied probably more than once. The Byzantine law teacher Julian composed his *Epitome* as a didactic introduction to the *Novels* of the Emperor Justinian in 554 in Constantinople. His work made its way to Italy, much of which Justinian had re-conquered from the Ostrogoths from 535–52 and

[6] For a standard work on such an approach, see M. L. West, *Textual Criticism and Editorial Technique* (Stuttgart, 1973).

[7] See P. Mikat, *Die Inzestverbote des Dritten Konzils von Orléans (538): Ein Beitrag zur Geschichte des Fränkischen Eherects* (Opladen, 1993), 38–40 and P. Mikat, *Die Inzestgesetzgebung der merowingisch-fränkischen Konzilien (511–626/27)* (Padeborn, 1994), esp. at 57–8. For the development of the interest of Merovingian Church councils on incest, see *ibid.*, 39–40.

[8] See comments of Mikat, *Inzestgesetzgebung der merowingisch-fränkischen Konzilien*, 125–6 on the Council of Tours of 567 and 130–1 on the Council of Mâcon.

[9] See Gregory of Tours, *HF*, Books 3–5. For a standard scholarly work on the foundations of Frankish society in this period, see R. van Dam, *Leadership and Community in Late Antique Gaul* (Berkeley, 1985), esp. 177–277.

where the Byzantines maintained a foothold for centuries. The *Collatio* was bound together with the *Epitome* of Julian at some point early in the textual tradition after 560 when the *Epitome* was received in the west.[10] While it is impossible to date this stage of the manuscript tradition exactly, the fact that the *Collatio* was considered of high enough interest in the second half of the sixth century (as confirmed by its use in the Merovingian Church councils) suggests that there were probably several copies of sub-χ in circulation, copies of which might have been bound with the *Epitome* of Julian after 560 (a hypothetical stage of the manuscript tradition that I have labelled sub-χ2).[11]

Another late Merovingian legal text can provide further insight into the popularity of the *Collatio* in the eighth century. When the Merovingian throne was vacant under the domination of the *Major Domus* Charles Martel, Odilo (the Duke of Bavaria and Charles Martel's son-in-law) ordered the compilation of the *Lex Baiuvariorum* (or 'Laws of the Bavarians') *c*.740.[12] While earlier scholars believed that this work was based on traditional Germanic oral laws, the standard scholarly view now holds that the work is more likely the product of a synthesis of Germanic and Roman law in the Merovingian period.[13] Although the sources of the compiler of the *Lex Baiuvariorum* have been debated by scholars, it appears that the *Collatio* was one of them.[14] It is plausible, then, that the scribe of the *Lex Baiuvariorum* had access to a manuscript of the sub-χ2 stage of the manuscript tradition of the *Collatio*.

[10] For compilation with Julian's *Epitome*, see Kaiser, *Epitome Iuliani*, 122–71.

[11] Frakes, 'Manuscript tradition', 304. See Nelson and Manthe, *Gai Institutiones III. 1–87*, 14–15 on the difficulty of knowing the exact date of the compilation of the *Epitome Iuliani*.

[12] For early editions of the work, see K. Beyerle, *Lex Baiuvariorum* (Munich, 1926); E. von Schwind (ed.), *Lex Baiwariorum*, MGH, *Leges nationum Germanicarum*, 5, 2 (Hannover, 1926; reprinted 1997) and K. A. Eckhardt, *Germanenrechte, Texte und Übersetzungen*, II(2): *Alamannen und Bayern* (Weimar, 1934). For an English translation, see T. Rivers, *Laws of the Alamans and Bavarians* (Philadelphia, 1977). See also W. Brown, Review of E. von Schwind (ed.), *Lex Baiwariorum* in *The Medieval Review* (online), 00.05.02.

[13] See H. Siems, 'Lex Baiuvariorum' in *Handwörterbuch zur deutschen Rechtsgeschichte* 2 (Berlin, 1978), 1887–901. See also, more recently, Brown's review of von Schwind as well as H. Siems, 'Lex Baiuvariorum' in *Reallexikon der Germanischen Altertumskunde*, 18 (Berlin, 2001), 304–15. I am grateful to Professor Siems for his comments to me on this important source in the autumn of 2007.

[14] A. von Daniels, *De Saxononici speculi origine ex juris communis* (Berlin, 1852); C. R. Sachsse, Review of von Daniels in *Kritische Zeitschrift für die gesammte*

When Pepin III (more famously known as Pepin 'the Short') reconsolidated the Frankish Kingdom in 751 and started the Carolingian dynasty with papal blessing, it is likely that many of the existing manuscripts of the *Collatio* would have been brought into one large state. When his son Charlemagne later supported the work of Alcuin and his assistants, many classical works were recopied during the Carolingian Renaissance and this movement also led to the recopying of the *Collatio.* For over a century, scholars have noticed that B was most likely from the ninth century and was copied from a lost forerunner that was already written in minuscule possibly in the eighth century.[15] In Schulz's examination of the manuscript tradition, he agreed with a ninth-century dating for B and confirmed that B was a copy of a lost forerunner that he labelled α.[16] Schulz went on to argue that α also was a copy of an even earlier forerunner written in minuscule (a stage of the tradition that I have labelled proto-α).[17] If it is correct to assume that sub-$\chi 2$ marks the binding of a copy of the *Collatio* with the *Epitome* of Julian in the late sixth or seventh century, the early eighth-century proto-α might then have been a copy of sub-$\chi 2$. To allow for proto-α to be copied to α, and then further copied to B by the early-to-mid ninth century, it would appear plausible that copies of the *Collatio* were generated from the mid eighth century onward. β, a sibling of B which was the lost hyparchetype (or forerunner) of V and W was probably also copied from α in the early or mid ninth century. This dating range is supported by the argument that W was already copied in the third quarter of the ninth century in northern Italy.[18] Therefore, when Hincmar felt pressed to defend Theutberga from at least some of the shocking charges made by her estranged husband, the bishop's

Rechtswissenschaft 1 (1853), 173–216; von Daniels, *Alter und Ursprung des Sachsenspiegels* (Berlin, 1853); von Daniels, *Handbuch der deutsche Reichs-und Staatenrechtsgeschichte* (Tübingen, 1859), I, 219–21. Most clearly, see Beyerle, *Lex Baiuvariorum*, lvi–lix (lix: '*wahrscheinlich ist, dass er weiterhin auch die Lex Dei vor sich hatte*').

15 Mommsen, *Collatio*, 109–10, 124.

16 Schulz, 'Manuscripts', 318–19.

17 See further Nelson and Manthe, *Gai*, 12–14. On the development of minuscule in the mid to late eighth century, see B. Bischoff, *Latin Palaeography: Antiquity and the Middle Ages*, tr. D. Ó. Crónín and D. Ganz (Cambridge, 1990), 100–9, 112–18. See also R. M. Frakes, 'The *Collatio* and the *Codex Gregorianus* (Observations on Coll. I. 10, VI. 4, VI. 6, XV. 3)', *Index* 33 (2005), 293–300 at 293.

18 See Kaiser, *Epitome Iuliani*, 153–4; Bischoff, *Die südostdeutschen Schreibschulen und Bibliotheken in der Karolingerzeit*, 168.

library must have profited from the work of Carolingian scribes who had copied B from α.[19]

We must return to the salacious quotation that started this chapter. Hincmar exonerated Theutberga from the accusation of abortion by arguing that anal intercourse, while sinful whether between two men or between a brother and a sister, cannot lead to the conception of a child.[20] What is central for this study is that the Bishop of Reims cites directly and explicitly from the work in this passage.[21] Because his testimony from the *Collatio* is so important in providing the first direct quotation from the Collator's work, as opposed to the Merovingian examples that show probable influence, we must look at it in detail. In the quotation from Hincmar's *De Divortio* cited at the beginning of this chapter, the bishop was describing both biblical and Roman prohibitions of unnatural sex. Indeed, it is important to note that the Bishop of Reims quoted from the Hebrew Bible (Leviticus 20: 13) immediately before our passage. By constructing the passage in this way, Hincmar follows the model of the *Collatio* by citing first biblical law and then, subsequently, a quotation derived from Roman law. Moreover, the *Collatio* does indeed have a title devoted to *De Stupratoribus* (Title 5) that starts with a citation from Leviticus 20: 13 and then follows with a Roman law against homosexual prostitution.[22] It would appear conclusive, then, that Hincmar thus had access to a manuscript of the *Collatio*.

It is noteworthy that Hincmar does not actually quote the Collator's Latin translation from Leviticus that is in the text of the *Collatio*, but uses the Vulgate translation of Jerome.[23] This

[19] On the copying of manuscripts under Hincmar, see F. M. Carey, 'The Scriptorium of Reims during the archbishopric of Hincmar (845–882 A. D.)' in L. Webber Jones (ed.), *Classical and Mediaeval Studies in Honor of Edward Kennard Rand* (New York, 1938), 41–60, esp. at 41–4. Indeed, Carey, 44, points out that Hincmar spent his youth at the monastery of St Denys and it is tempting to conjecture that he might have already encountered the *Collatio* there. See also Böhringer, 1, for Hincmar's youth at St. Denys.

[20] Böhringer, 178. I am grateful to Dr Böhringer for her comments on this passage in 2005.

[21] A third general allusion to the *Collatio* may also appear at *Responsio* 5 (Börhinger, 138), where Hincmar generally refers to the view of Roman law on adultery, but he does not cite the work directly.

[22] On this law, see further R. M. Frakes, '*Item Theodosianus*? (Observations on Coll. V. 3. 1)', *QUCC* n. s. 71(2) (2002), 163–8 and discussion later in this chapter.

[23] Leviticus 20: 13 (Stuttgart Vulgate), *Qui dormierit cum masculo coitu femineo uterque operatori sunt nefas, morte moriantur.*

substitution is probably because Hincmar would have been well schooled in this translation as a bishop and by the second half of the ninth century the translation of Jerome was the more common text of the Bible in use in the Frankish kingdoms as Alcuin encouraged its use and duplication during the Carolingian Renaissance.[24]

However, Hincmar does not call the *Collatio* by that title in this passage or by its alternate modern title of *Lex Dei*, but instead refers to it simply as *leges Romanae* ('Roman laws'). Because of the disparity between the title in the manuscripts and the description in the text of Hincmar, some scholars have played with possible reconstructed titles such as *Lex Dei quam praecipit Dominus ad Moysen et lex Romana quomodo convenient.*[25] However, Hincmar seems to be simply comparing Roman law to that of the Bible. Hincmar might well have not been implying that the title of the work originally had *lex* or *leges Romanae* in it, but instead the work was his source for some of his knowledge of Roman law. Moreover, the part of the *Collatio* to which Hincmar alluded was indeed a Roman law of the late empire (also surviving in abbreviated form in *CTh* 9. 7. 6). More revealing is the implication of Hincmar's phrase *quo legens quisque inveniet* ('as anyone reading it will find').[26] This clause implies that there might have been several copies of the *Collatio* available to clerics when he wrote in the second half of the ninth century. Obviously, if Hincmar had had the only copy of an obscure law book, he would not have implied that many people could find the passage to which he alludes (and the diction implies that work and not another of a handful of Roman law books that were extant in the mid ninth century).[27] Moreover, as we have seen, examination of the manuscript tradition makes this unlikely, since proto-α, α, B, and β (if not also sub-χ2) may well have been available in archives in the different Frankish kingdoms of Hincmar's day.

[24] B. Metzger, *The Early Versions of the New Testament: Their origin, transmission, and limitations* (Oxford, 1977), 341–4.

[25] If so, such a title may have been original or may have been inserted into the manuscript tradition by the scribe of B or an earlier lost forerunner. See further, Mommsen, *Collatio*, 128; Hyamson, *Mosaicarum et Romanarum Legum Collatio*, xxxi; Liebs, *Italien*, 162–3.

[26] Hyamson, xiii; Liebs, *Italien*, 174.

[27] On possible allusions to the *Theodosian Code* in the Middle Ages, see D. Walters, 'From Benedict to Gratian: The Code in medieval ecclesiastical authors' in Harries and Wood, *The Theodosian Code*, 200–16. See also, M. Conrat, *Geschichte der Quellen und Literatur des Römischen Rechts im früheren Mittelalter* (Leipzig, 1891), I.

This passage is not the only one in Hincmar's *De Divortio* that shows influence from the *Collatio*. Slightly later in his work, describing the punishment of adultery, the Bishop of Reims writes:

Sicut in primo libro legis Roman[a]e capitulo VI de stupratoribus et in capitulo VII de incestis et turpibus nuptiis praecipitur et in ceteris, quae Christiana iura depromunt, iusti iudices legere possunt.[28]

[Just as it is instructed in the first book of the Roman law in Chapter 6 concerning those who commit *stupra* and in Chapter 7 on incestuous and disgraceful marriages and in others, righteous judges can read what Christian laws promulgate.]

Hincmar had already alluded to the title *De Stupratoribus* of the *Collatio* in our earlier example. However, the surviving manuscripts of the *Collatio* list the title *De Stupratoribus* as number five, not six. Moreover, the next title in Mommsen's text is *De Incestis Nuptis* and is numbered six, not seven. Mommsen explained this problem with the astute observation that in the manuscript now known as B, a scribal error in the last sentence before the beginning of Title 5 reads *Expl(icit) Titulo Quinto* (or 'here ends Title 5'). So, if Hincmar were reading this section of the *Collatio*, he might take for granted that the title that follows (*De Stupratoribus*) must be Title 6 and the one thereafter (*De Incestis Nuptiis*) must be seven. Since V and W do not have this line, this scribal mistake in B supports the view that Hincmar used the manuscript later known as B.[29] The scribe of B may have made this comment either through an error, or by interpreting Coll. 1. 5–13 as a distinct title from Coll. 1. 1–4 (and thus subdivided Title 1 into two units).[30]

While Mommsen apparently solved that problem, we have one other minor discrepancy between the *Collatio* and Hincmar's text. The phrase *et turpibus* ('and disgraceful') used in this second passage of Hincmar's work does not appear in the three surviving manuscripts of the *Collatio*. Thus, either the phrase *et turpibus* was in a lost manuscript of the *Collatio* that Hincmar used (either instead of B or together with B), or he added it to the text for clarification, or Hincmar was doing here what he did with the phrase *leges Romanae*

[28] *Responsio* 12, Böhringer, 184–5.

[29] Mommsen, *Collatio*, 112. This is supported by Hyamson, xiii–xiv.

[30] Mommsen, *Collatio*, 128–9; Liebs, *Italien*, 162. See further, Hyamson, 58, who inserts *De Causalibus Homicidis* into his Latin text as a subheading at Coll. 1. 5.

in the previous citation and was merely speaking descriptively. Title 6 of the *Collatio* does indeed deal with defining incestuous marriages, but only in the biblical parts of the title is the disgraceful aspect of such stressed, and we can assume that Hincmar was persuaded by that. Thus, we can keep Mommsen's explanation of the faulty numbering of the titles as being due to Hincmar's accepting the mistake of the scribe of B and adding his own emphasis on disgraceful unions.

There is one last problem with this passage. Scholars from the time of Mommsen onward have noticed that the descriptive phrase *in primo libro* that Hincmar uses in alluding to the *leges Romanae* preserved in the *Collatio* is problematic. One surviving manuscript, W, does seem to preserve this identification at the very beginning of the *Collatio* immediately after the title of the work, but before the beginning of Title 1. However, we have a dilemma because Mommsen's explanation of the errors in enumerating Titles 5 and 6 works so well for identifying Hincmar's manuscript as B. Might Hincmar have used both B and β, the Carolingian forerunner of W, or perhaps an earlier manuscript that also kept the formula *primus liber*? Or, as some have suggested, did the phrase *primus liber* pertain to the placement of the *Collatio* in a larger collected codex of several works?[31] We can dispense this latter solution, because in all three of our surviving manuscripts, the *Collatio* is deep within a similar ordering of late Roman laws and translations of early Byzantine legal texts, and probably followed that order for some time in the manuscript tradition at least in α, if not already in proto-α or sub-$\chi 2$.[32]

Many scholars accept the reading as genuine and place the phrase *primus liber* at the beginning of their editions of the text with no brackets.[33] If this clause indeed existed in the archetype of the work, the phrase must have somehow been preserved in W, and not in B and V. Some have even speculated that there might originally have been two books or major parts of the *Collatio* and our surviving

[31] Hyamson, xiv n. 2 reflecting on Friedrich Carl von Savigny, *Geschichte des Römischen Rechts im Mittelalter* (Heidelberg, 1850), II, 280–3.

[32] Mommsen, *Collatio*, 114–16; Schulz, 'Manuscripts,' 324–9; Kaiser, *Epitome Iuliani*, 167–71.

[33] Mommsen, *Collatio*, 136; Hyamson, 56; Smits, *Collatio*, 72; Girard, 'Mosaicarum et Romanarum'; Aceves, *Mosaicarum et Romanarum Legum Collatio*, 1.

manuscripts contain only the first part dealing with criminal law and the hypothetical second, now lost, part treated private law.[34]

Hincmar's usage may present a simpler solution. Perhaps, like in the other two examples of his work, Hincmar meant the phrase *primus liber* to be descriptive to his audience, not an actual citation of part of the title of part one of the *Collatio*. Thus, it is possible that he used *primus liber* to describe the *Collatio* as the 'first' (or 'earliest') book of Roman law in a chronological sense. Examination of Hincmar's sources for Roman law shows that the *Collatio* is indeed chronologically the earliest.[35] While there were earlier collections of Roman law such as the Edict of the Urban Praetor or, even earlier, the Twelve Tables, such works did not survive into the Middle Ages (or even late antiquity) and were certainly already lost by 860. The *Codices* of Gregorianus and Hermogenianus of the 290s can arguably be called the first Roman law codes, and were available to the compilers of the *Theodosian Code* and the *Code of Justinian* as models. However, Justinian's sixth-century law code ended any official use for the earlier law codes of Diocletian's time and they seem to have dropped out of usage a generation or two after 534.[36] Therefore, the *Collatio* might well be described the 'first' or earliest book of Roman law available to Hincmar in 860.[37] This conclusion is satisfactory because it follows the style of Hincmar in describing the works he was citing. Also, such a view frees us from wrestling with a hypothetical lost second part of the *Collatio*, for which we have no evidence. Lastly, it also liberates us from the problem of how the phrase *liber primus* could have been seen by Hincmar in the B manuscript that clearly does not have it. As Schulz noted, the scribe of W made several emendations to the manuscript and it seems more

[34] Liebs, *Italien*, 172; H. L. W. Nelson, *Überlieferung, Aufbau und Stil von Gai Institutiones* (Leiden, 1981), 113–16; G. Pugliese, 'A suggestion on the Collatio', *Israel Law Review* 29 (1995), 161–75, at 163. Most importantly, see Mommsen, *Collatio*, 118, 128–9, and 198 where he ends his text with *reliqua desunt*.

[35] Confirmed by the source index in Böhringer, 275. See earlier view of H. E. Dirksen, 'Hincmar, Erzbischof von Rheims, als Kenner der Quellen des römischen Rechts' in F. D. Sanio (ed.), *H. E. Dirksen's Hinterlassene Schrift zur Kritik und Auslegung der Quellen römischer Rechtsgeschichte und Alterthumskunde* (Leipzig, 1871), II, 130–41.

[36] See Humfress, 'Law and legal procedure in the age of Justinian', 164–6.

[37] In general, on Hincmar's relative lack of interest in classical works, see Carey, 'Scriptorium of Reims', 43–4.

likely that the phrase *primus liber* in W is also a conjecture.[38] The similarity of *primus liber* in W and *in primo libro* in Hincmar's work was naturally too tempting for Mommsen (and scholars dependant upon him) to resist in conjuring up some kind of connection and thus to develop of theory of two separate parts of the *Collatio*.

The *Collatio* was copied at least twice more in the Middle Ages after Hincmar's day. The manuscript known as W (after Wien or Vienna), dated to the third quarter of the ninth century, was made known to the scholarly community by K. W. Lancizolle in 1822.[39] V (the *Codex Vercellensis*) was probably copied in the tenth or eleventh century and was discovered by Friederich Bluhme in the cathedral archive in Vercelli in northern Italy coincidently in the same year.[40] If the locations the manuscripts were found are an indication of where they might have been made (which is not always the case), it is at least plausible that their lost forerunner manuscript, β, might have already been in northern Italy by the late ninth century, since the state that later would be called the Holy Roman Empire included Austria and large parts of northern Italy.

Examination of two additional quotations from the *Collatio* further illustrate the work's relative popularity in the Middle Ages. A quotation from Coll. 1. 7 appears in a collection of canons written in the eleventh century in northern Italy.[41] Since it appears that V was copied around the same time as the *Codex Vallicelliano*, presumably also in northern Italy, scholars logically suggested that the fragment of the *Collatio* quoted in the *Codex Vallicelliano* might have been connected to the V manuscript. However, analysis of the textual variants suggests that the fragment is instead closer to B than to V

[38] In describing one of the emendations of W, Schulz, 'Manuscripts', 317, calls the scribe of W 'bold as ever'. Likewise, Schulz, 'Manuscripts', 324–9, pointed out that B and V, probably following their lost forerunners α and β, placed the *Collatio* in the middle of the *Dictatum de Consiliariis*. However, W, through conjecture, remedied this error by leaving that work in its entirety and placing the *Collatio* at the end of the codex. I would like to thank Wolfgang Kaiser for his comments on this issue.

[39] Mommsen, *Collatio*, 111–12; Hyamson, xxi; Schulz, 'Manuscripts', 315; Kaiser, *Epitome Iuliani*, 154. On Lancizolle's work and career, see G. Haenel, *Iuliani epitome latina Novellarum Iustiniani* (Leipzig, 1873), vii and H. Brandt, 'Lancizolle (de Leuze de L.), Karl Wilhelm v.' in *Neue Deutsche Biographie* (Berlin, 1892), XIII, 474–5.

[40] Bluhme, *Lex Dei*; Mommsen, *Collatio*, 110; Hyamson, xxii–xxiii; Schulz, 'Manuscripts', 314; Kaiser, *Epitome Iuliani*, 122.

[41] *Codices Vallicelliano* B. ii.; Vatican n. xiii. 39; and Monte Cassino, n. ii, 16. See further, Mommsen, *Collatio*, 113–14; Hyamson, xxvi, n. *; Loschiavo, 'La legge', 77.

and W.[42] While the fragment could have been independently copied from β, there are not enough consistent similarities to V and W to support this hypothesis. The scribe of this work, then, more likely had access to B.

Analysis of one last medieval fragment of the *Collatio*, specifically from the beginning of Title 10 (*De Deposito*) that survives in the *Codex Bellovacensis* of the ninth century (which also holds an important role for scholarship on the *Breviarium*) can clarify the expanded use of the work.[43] This ninth-century manuscript was found in Beauvais (in northern France) and is now in Paris (BN Lat. 9652).[44] Since it contains a quotation of part of the *Collatio*, it is attractive to suppose that it might have been related to B, β, or α. However, analysis of the text preserved in this fragment when compared with B shows some variants. Title 10, like almost every title of the *Collatio*, begins with a quotation from Hebrew law followed by a quotation from a Roman jurist. So, here we find in Coll. 10 quotations from Exodus 22: 7, 8, 11 followed by a passage from the jurist Modestinus. Mommsen noticed that in this quotation from Exodus, the scribe of the *Codex Bellovacensis* used the Vulgate Latin text rather than the biblical text quoted in the *Collatio*.[45] This usage of Jerome's Latin Bible is similar to that of Hincmar and probably reflects the widespread use of the Vulgate in the age after Alcuin. At other places in the same passage, however, the scribe of *Bellovacensis* differed from both B and the Vulgate.[46]

The passage has enough differences to B, and indeed to V and W, that the Bellovocensian scribe either must have had a different manuscript than either B or β in front of him (in addition to his

[42] See *apparatus criticus* at Mommsen, *Collatio*, 139, which shows that for *perierit*, V gives *ferierit*, and B, W, and Vallicell. all give *fuerit*. Likewise, for *ictus* in the part of this quotation from the *Sententiae* of Ps. Paulus (preserved at *Digest* 48. 8. 17), B and Vallicell., give *iocus*, W gives *botos*, and V gives *votus*. While V and Vallicell. both give *quoque ipsos*, B gives *quoque ipso* (very similar, and no doubt a minor error) while W gives *ipsos quoque*.

[43] Mommsen, *Collatio*, 114; Hyamson, xxvi, n. *.

[44] See further, G. Dolezalek, *Verzeichnis der Handschriften zum römischen Recht bis 1600* (Frankfurt, 1972), II: no pagination. See comments by Loschiavo, 'La legge', 77.

[45] Mommsen, *Collatio*, 169.

[46] For instance, the scribe of *Bellovacensis* has *Moyses respondit* instead of B's *Moyses dicit*. Also, *Bellovacensis* has *aurum* (gold) in addition to *argentum* (silver), adds *fuerit*, and has different forms for some of the verbs. See, again, the apparatus at Mommsen, *Collatio*, 168–9. The influence of the Vulgate can be seen in the Bellovacensian scribe adding *dominus domus* instead of simply *dominum*.

Vulgate Bible) or he was making multiple emendations or changes. Since he seems to make only one emendation based on the Vulgate, it is more likely that he was using a different manuscript of the *Collatio* that is now lost. Since there are differences from the readings in B and β, and since the *Codex Bellovacensis* dates from the ninth century, then its scribe most likely did not use α, but possibly a lost sister manuscript of B and β that I have tentatively labelled γ.[47]

Study of encounters between early modern scholars and the *Collatio* can further clarify the manuscript tradition and the earlier use of the work. In the first half of the sixteenth century, Joannes Tilius (or Jean du Tillet), the humanist scholar and Bishop of St Brieuc (and later of Meaux) found what he called a 'few fragments' (*fragmenta pauca*) of the *Collatio* when he visited northern French monasteries in 1544 during one of his searches for manuscripts.[48] Unfortunately, the location he gives is very imprecise. Beauvais does lie in northern France and it is tempting to connect Du Tillet's description to the source of the *Codex Bellovacensis*. The fragmentary nature of Du Tillet's discovery does not match the fuller versions of the manuscript that we see in B, V, or W and must reflect a partial version that has since been lost. It is tempting to connect Du Tillet's *pauca fragmenta* with the hypothetical γ that might have been the source for the quotation in the *Codex Bellovacensis*.

In 1570 Pierre Pithou discovered a codex of the *Collatio* in a library that he described as being in the area of the 'Sequani' or 'Mandubii'.[49] By using these names, Pithou was displaying his

[47] Frakes, 'Manuscript tradition', 301–2.

[48] Pithou, *Fragmenta*, 66: '*ac memini Jo. Tilium antiquae eruditionis hominem, cum de veterum iurisconsultorum reliquiis sermo esset, narrare solitum habuisse aliquando se eius operis fragmenta pauca* ... ' See further the comments of Mommsen, *Collatio*, 112–13. On the Du Tillet brothers (both named Jean) as scholars, see D. Kelly, 'Jean du Tillet, archivist and antiquary', *Journal of Modern History* 38 (1966), 337–54, and C. H. Turner, 'Jean du Tillet: A neglected scholar of the sixteenth century', appendix V in J. K. Fotheringham (ed.), *The Bodleian Manuscript of Jerome's Version of the Chronicle of Eusebius, reproduced in Collotype* (Oxford, 1905), 48–63. The younger Jean du Tillet discovered several works of Roman jurisprudence as well as a manuscript of the Hebrew Bible.

[49] Pithou, *Fragmenta*, 66: '*Illud affirmare liquet quae nunc damus ex antiquissima Sequanorum aut Mandubiorum potius bibliotheca* ... ' See also the comments of F. Blu[h]me, 'Über Pithou's Handschrift der Lex Dei, oder Legum Mosaicarum et Romanarum Collatio', *Zeitschrift für geschichtliche Rechtswissenschaft* 10 (1842), 298–308; Mommsen, *Collatio*, 109–10; Hyamson, xv; and Kaiser, *Epitome Iuliani*, 95–7.

knowledge of classical history (as a good late Renaissance scholar would) because these two tribes were ancient Celtic groups that Julius Caesar described in his *Commentaries on the Gallic Wars* in the first century BCE. Unfortunately, Pithou's location is unclear as the ancient Sequani dominated the Seine valley and the Mandubii controlled much of central Gaul in Caesar's day. This manuscript was the basis of Pithou's 1573 edition of the *Collatio* that he shared (together with the manuscript itself) with some of his friends, including the famous scholars Jacobus Cujacius (or Jacques Cujas) and Ludwig Charondas (or Loys Charondas Le Caron).[50]

The latter of these, Charondas, would quote from this manuscript of the *Collatio* in his edition of Justinian's *Digest* in 1575. Happily, Charondas is much more precise for the location of the home of Pithou's manuscript. Charondas stated that the manuscript was discovered in the library of the Abbey of St Denys.[51] Modern scholars have noted that Charondas' quotations from the *Collatio* match those of Pithou. Thus, Pithou's manuscript must have been found in St Denys that would indeed have been in the ancient territory of the Sequani. This is the manuscript that would later be housed in the State Library in Berlin, from which it is labelled B, and serves as the best manuscript of the work.[52]

Other early modern scholars have interacted with this manuscript. For example, Joseph Scaliger apparently had access to the manuscript of the *Collatio* from St Denys when he was staying in the house of Cujas.[53] Scaliger made a fine, clear copy of the manuscript by hand, the famous Apograph of Scaliger.[54] While earlier scholars were not sure if Scaliger's Apograph marked a separate manuscript than that of St Denys,[55] it now seems certain that it is a copy of B, which can

[50] Hyamson, xiv–xvi. For a brief overview of Cujas' life and career, see Sir John MacDonell and E. Manson (eds.), *Great Jurists of the World* (Boston, 1914), II, 89–94. For Charondas' life, see J. Buhlmann and D. Gilman (eds.), *Louis Le Caron, Dialogues* (Droz, 1986), 11–20.

[51] Mommsen, *Collatio*, 109; Hyamson, xiv–xv; and Kaiser, *Epitome Iuliani*, 98–100.

[52] Mommsen, *Collatio*, 110; Hyamson, xviii; and Schulz, 'Manuscripts', 314. Although see comments of Kaiser, *Epitome Iuliani*, 100–1.

[53] See discussion in A. Grafton, *Joseph Scaliger: A study in the history of classical scholarship*, I: *Textual Criticism and Exegesis* (Oxford, 1983), 122–3.

[54] Scal. 61 at ff. 107–26 housed in the Scaliger Institute of the University of Leiden. I thank the staff of the Institute for allowing me to view the Apograph in the summer of 2007.

[55] See the discussion in Hyamson, xvii–xviii. To some degree, the controversy was abetted by D'Orville's copy of Pithou's edition where he marked corrections based on

still be useful in readings in any parts of B that might have been damaged since the early 1570's when Scaliger made his copy.[56]

While Pithou, Bluhme, and Huschke all made important early editions of the *Collatio* based on the manuscripts that were available at the time they worked, Mommsen produced a more thorough modern edition in 1890. However, Mommsen himself allowed he was unclear as to the relationship between the manuscripts. He was aware that B was the oldest based on paleography, but he could not understand how sometimes W alone had what appeared to be the correct reading based on Latin style. Schulz was able to lead the connections between the manuscripts out of Mommsen's impasse by noting the scribe of W's penchant for clever emendations and thereby produced his accepted stemma of the surviving manuscripts reproduced at the beginning of this section.

Re-examination of the use of the *Collatio* in the Middle Ages suggests that there were several intermediary steps in the manuscript tradition. Such re-examination allows us to re-evaluate the place of external fragments in conjunction with V, W. and especially B, and even Scaliger's Apograph for places where B might have been damaged since the 1570s, for approaching the text.[57] Most significantly for this book, such re-examination of the manuscript tradition indicates that the work must date before the sixth century and was read, used, and copied fairly regularly by clerics and Church leaders from the early Merovingian period through to the eleventh century.[58]

Scaliger's Apograph, as well as his own emendations, not all of which are correct (e.g., in Coll. 1. 7 he changed *dimidia* to *demedia*; at Coll. 5. 3. 2 he changed *Minerua* to *Minerae*). I would like to thank the staff of the Bodleian Library for allowing me access to Ms. D'Orville 334 in Duke Humfrey's Library in the summer of 2007.

[56] On the Apograph and B, see Mommsen, *Collatio*, 109–10; Hyamson, xvii–xviii; and Schulz, 'Manuscripts', 51.

[57] See West, *Textual Criticism and Editorial Technique*, 86, for uses of apographia.

[58] For a scholarly debate over whether Alfred the Great of England was influenced by the *Collatio*, see P. Wormald, *The Making of English law: King Alfred to the twelfth century* (Oxford, 1999), 418–25, and B. Carella, 'The source of the Prologue to the laws of Alfred', *Peritia* 19 (2005), 91–118, which seems to prove it played no role. On the potential influence of the *Collatio* on the Irish author of an early eighth-century text, see P. Fournier, 'Le Liber ex lege Moysi et les tendances biblique du droit canonique irlandais,' *Revue Celtique* 30 (1909), 221–34. It is possible that the author of the *Liber ex lege Moysi* saw the *Collatio*, but used the Vulgate instead for his Biblical quotations. On the possible influence of the *Collatio* on the mysterious Pepo (the earliest professor of Roman law at Bologna *c.*1075), see Loschiavo, 'La legge,' 76.

We can then display the expanded stemma in historical context as follows:

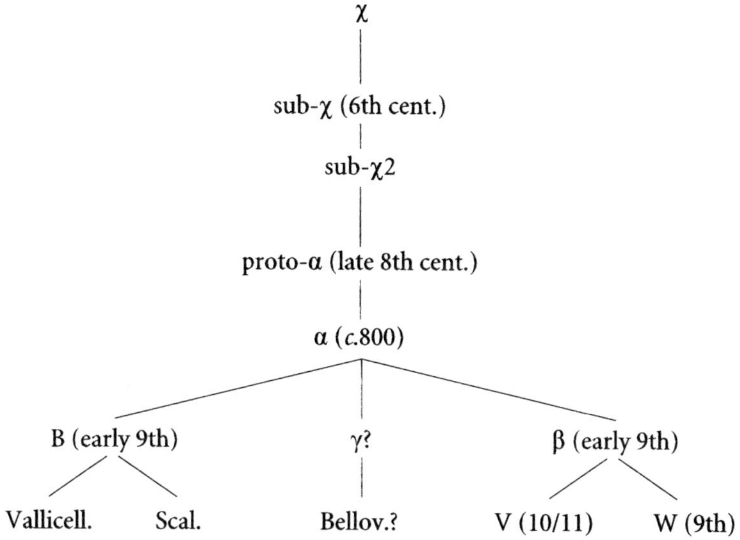

B. INTERNAL EVIDENCE

To focus in further on the date of the composition of the work we must turn to the *terminus post quem*—the date after which the Collator must have written the work. We can approach this goal by examining internal evidence from the *Collatio*. While scholars have pointed to various parts of the *Collatio* as evidence for differing hypothetical contexts, whether because of authors the Collator cites or because of influence of various laws and developments, a close examination of these earlier theories and the passages on which they were based reveals that the Collator wrote his work sometime shortly after 390.

It was long ago noticed by scholars that the Collator cited five Roman jurists by name as his sources of much of his knowledge of Roman jurisprudence. These five happen to be the same famous five jurists, dating from the second and third centuries, who were given authoritative status in legal arguments by the so-called 'Law of Citations' of the Emperors Theodosius II and Valentinian III that was issued in 426 and survives in the *Theodosian Code* (*CTh* 1. 4. 3).[59] Some scholars have taken this as proof that the Collator must have been writing after 426 and thus was following the Law of Citations by citing from those five jurists.[60] However, it is logical that the Law of Citations would not have been issued in 426 in these terms, if the five had not already had recognized superior status in the legal community.[61] We know that their works were actively used and recopied in the fourth century and thus we are not forced to accept a *terminus post quem* of 426, but could allow the Collator to be working earlier. Quotations from the five jurists could then serve as an example of the popularity of the five jurists that later led to their canonization in *CTh* 1. 4. 3. Further examination of internal evidence can reveal how much earlier than 426 the Collator might have written.

While the Collator quotes from the famous five jurists by name, more recent work on these works allegedly by them indicates that while some of the works quoted are authentic writings of the five jurists, others are later creations dating from the third and early

[59] *CTh* 1. 4. 3:

IMPP. THEOD(OSIUS) ET VALENTIN(IANUS) AA. AD SENATUM URBIS ROM(AE). POST ALIA. Papiniani, Pauli, Gai, Ulpiani atque Modestini scripta universa firmamus ita, ut Gaium quae Paulum, Ulpianum et cunctos ceteros comitetur auctoritas lectionesque ex omni eius corpore recitentur. Eorum quoque scientiam, quorum tractatus atque sententias praedicti omnes suis operibus miscuerunt, ratam esse censemus, ut Scaevolae, Sabini, Iuliani atque Marcelli omniumque, quos illi celebrarunt, si tamen eorum libri propter antiquitatis incertum codicum collatione firmentur. Ubi autem diversae sententiae proferuntur, potior numerus vincat auctorum, vel, si numerus aequalis sit, eius partis praecedat auctoritas, in qua excellentis ingenii vir Papinianus emineat, qui ut singulos vincit, ita cedit duobus. Notas etiam Pauli atque Ulpiani in Papiniani corpus factas, sicut dudum statutum est, praecipimus infirmari. Ubi autem eorum pares sententiae recitantur, quorum par censetur auctoritas, quos sequi debeat, eligat moderatio iudicantis. Pauli quoque sententias semper valere praecipimus. ET CETERA. DAT. VII ID. NOVEMB. RAVENNA DD. NN. THEOD(OSIO) XII ET VALENT(IANO) II AA. CONSS.

Latin text from Mommsen, *Theodosiani Libri XVI*, 34.

[60] See Pithou, *Fragmenta*, 66: '*videri eum Theodosii iunioris temporibus vixisse, et post consultatum quidem ipsius xv* [sic *xvi*] *quo demum codex editus legitur*'; G. Haenel (ed.), *Codex Theodosianus* (Bonn, 1842), col. 846, and G. E. Heimbach, Review of Haenel's *Codex Theodosianus* in *Neue Jenaische Allgemeine Literatur-Zeitung* 2, no. 175–7 (Leipzig, 1843), 709–20 at 719. See criticism by P. Huschke, 'Über Alter und Verfasser der Legum Mosaicarum et Romanarum Collatio', *Zeitschrift für geschichtliche Rechtswissenschaft* 13 (1846), 1–49 at 2–3. More recently, see Solazzi, 'Per la data', 500–1. Even more recently, a dating after the Law of Citations has been championed again. See E. Schrage, 'La date de la "Collatio Legum Mosaicarum et Romanarum", étudiée d'après les citations bibliques' in J. A. Ankum *et al.* (ed.), *Mélanges Felix Wubbe* (Fribourg, 1993), 401–17, at 416–17, and adopted by B. Shaw, 'Raising and killing children: Two Roman myths', *Mnemosyne* 54 (2001), 31–77 at 65 n. 88.

[61] See comments of H. E. Dirksen, 'Über die Collatio Legum Mosaicarum et Romanarum' in *Hinterlassene Schriften*, 2, 100–29 at 115–16, and Hyamson, xlvi.

fourth centuries. This research can aid us in clarifying a *terminus post quem* for the *Collatio*. The most famous example is the work disproving the authenticity of the *Sententiae* of Paulus. This handbook, the juristic work most cited by the Collator was, most scholars now believe, composed of passages lifted from the famous jurist's works, if not also from other jurists, by a late third- or early fourth-century compiler.[62] Likewise, the *Liber singularis et titulo de Iniuriis* is probably a late classical (*c.*300 CE) revision of that part of Paulus' *Commentary*.[63] This basic terminus is confirmed by the Collator's use of such earlier legal compendia as the *Codex Gregorianus* dating to 291 and the *Codex Hermogenianus* dating to 295. Thus, re-dating of some of the Collator's legal sources gives us an initial *terminus post quem* of the late third or early fourth century, a period when several scholars believe the Collator wrote.[64]

Examination of some passages within the *Collatio* can further close the window of time when the Collator composed his work from this initial *terminus post quem* of the late third or early fourth century and the *terminus ante quem* of the sixth-century Church councils. The most famous of these sections occurs in Title 5 of the *Collatio*, entitled *De Stupratoribus* (perhaps best translated as 'Concerning Those Who Engaged in Illicit Sexual Intercourse') to which Hincmar alluded in his defence of Theutberga. After quoting a biblical injunction (Leviticus 20: 13) against male homosexuality at Coll. 5. 1. 1 and then a statement from the *Sententiae* of Pseudo Paulus (Ps. Paulus) at Coll. 5. 2. 1 relating to homosexual rape of Roman citizens, at Coll.

[62] See D. Liebs, 'Die pseudopaulinischen Sentenzen I', *ZRG (R.A.)* 112 (1995), 151–71. See also the description in ch. 3.

[63] See D. Liebs in Herzog and Schmidt, *HLL4*, 156–7.

[64] See Volterra, *Collatio*, 95–100; E. Levy, Review of Volterra in *ZRG (R.A.)* 50 (1930), 698–705 at 703; G. Scherillo, Review of Volterra in *Archivo giuridico* 104 (1930), 255–65; Daube, '*Collatio* 2. 6. 5', 111–29; A. Masi, 'Contributi ad una Datazione della "Collatio Legum Mosaicarum et Romanarum"', *BIDR* 3 (1961), 285–321 at 321; more recently, G. Barone-Adesi, *L'eta della "Lex Dei"* (Naples, 1992), 144; Pugliese, 'Suggestion', 171; A. M. Rabello, 'La Datazione della Collatio Legum Mosaicarum et Romanarum e il Problema di una sua seconda redazione o del suo uso nel corso del quarto secolo' in *Humana Sapit: Etudes d'Antiquité tardive offerts à Lellia Cracco Ruggini* (Brepols, 2002), 411–22 at 414–21. See also Rabello's earlier 'Alcune note sulla "Collatio Legum Mosaicarum et Romanarum" e sul suo luogo d'origine' in *Scritti sull'Ebraismo in memoria di Guido Bedarida* (Florence, 1966), 177–86; 'Sull'ebraicita' dell'autore della "Collatio Legum Mosaicarum et Romanarum"', *La Rassegna mensile di Israel* 33 (1967), 339–49; and 'Sul Decalogo "Cristianizzato" e l'autore della "Collatio Legum Mosaicarum et Romanarum"', *La Rassegna mensile di Israel* 55 (1989), 133–5.

5. 3. 1 the Collator introduces a constitution of Theodosius I, posted in May in Rome in an unstated year, against homosexual prostitution with the preface (in Mommsen's Latin text): *Hoc quidem iuris est: mentem tamen legis Moysi imperatoris Theodosii constitutio ad plenum secuta cognoscitur. <Item Theodosianus>*. Hyamson translated this: 'This indeed is the law. But a constitution of the Emperor Theodosius followed to the full the spirit of the Mosaic Law. (Likewise the *Theodosian Code*).'[65]

This passage is not only important for revealing the personal view of the Collator toward homosexuality but is critical for clarifying the dating of his work, and so we must take a look at earlier scholarly arguments carefully.[66] The famous early modern legal scholar Jacques Godefroy suggested that the phrase *item Theodosianus* in this passage showed that the anonymous compiler had taken the constitution directly from the *Codex Theodosianus* (thus he wrote '*Theodosianus*') when he was compiling the *Collatio* which would then have to be after 438 when this law code was promulgated.[67] Since the surviving version of the same constitution in the *Codex Theodosianus* (*CTh* 9. 7. 6) which gives the year as 390 is much shorter than the version surviving in the *Collatio*, Godefroy argued that the more complete text of this constitution dropped out of the manuscript tradition of the *Theodosian Code* and was later reintroduced in an abbreviated version lifted from the *Breviary* of Alaric sometime later in the textual transmission of the work.[68]

Although ingenious, this solution is overly convoluted and Huschke proposed an alternate explanation in 1846 that has become the accepted view. Huschke argued that an early copyist of the *Collatio* who knew the corresponding version of the law in the *Theodosian Code* inserted the reference *item Theodosianus* (that is, 'in the same manner, the Theodosian') into the manuscript to signify

[65] Hyamson, 83.

[66] See Frakes, 'Item Theodosianus? (Observations on Coll. 5, 3, 1)', 163–8.

[67] On the promulgation of the *Theodosian Code*, see Harries, *Law and Empire in Late Antiquity*, 59–69; Harries, 'The background to the Code' in Harries and Wood, *The Theodosian Code*, 1–16; J. Matthews, 'The making of the text' in Harries and Wood, 19–44; A. J. B. Sirks, 'The sources of the Code' in Harries and Wood, 45–67; and, in general, J. Matthews, *Laying Down the Law*, 1–9; Sirks, *Theodosian Code*, 178–214.

[68] See J. Godefroy, *Codex Theodosianus* (Leipzig, 1738; revision of earlier edition of Lyons, 1665), 69: *Aperte enim ex Codice Theodos. eam allegat author seu Pariator ille. Item, inquit, Theodosianus: Imppp. Valentinianus, Theodosius, et Arcadius Augusti.*

the connection to that law code.[69] Mommsen, Jörs, and Hyamson all adopted this suggestion and thus dated the *Collatio* to a window of time from 390 to 438 (which has influenced much subsequent scholarship).[70] Hyamson strengthened that argument by going so far as to translate *item Theodosianus* with 'Likewise the Theodosian Code' when there is no *Codex* mentioned in the Latin text of the *Collatio* (strictly following the Latin would give instead 'Likewise [the] Theodosian').[71]

Most modern editors have accepted Huschke's thesis that the phrase *item Theodosianus* is an interpolation by placing it in parenthesis in their texts of the *Collatio*.[72] However, before Huschke's suggestion, Gustav Haenel hazarded that the phrase *item Theodosianus* was an incorrect emendation of *Item* (or *Idem*) *Theodosius* to *Item Theodosianus* by a copyist early in the manuscript tradition.[73] Analysis of the style throughout the *Collatio* and of its most important manuscript (B) indicates that Haenel's proposal is most likely correct.[74] In this phrase, *idem* is grammatically correct and *item* is not.[75] That is, the text probably would not read 'likewise the *Theodosian Code*' when the exact 'constitution of the Emperor Theodosius' was cited in the preceding sentence. Rather than adopting Huschke's explanation that *item Theodosianus* was the interpolation of a learned copyist making a connection to the *Codex Theodosianus*, it is easier to believe that the Collator was following his standard practice and here used *idem* to refer back to an author mentioned earlier in the same title—in this case the Emperor Theodosius in the sentence immediately preceding it.[76] Indeed, close examination of this passage in B (the Berlin manuscript) shows that the phrase occurs in thicker ink and larger letters at the beginning

69 Huschke, 'Alter und Verfasser', 2–6, esp. 5–6.

70 See, for instance, Wenger, *Die Quellen*, 546–8.

71 Mommsen, *Collatio*, 127 and 154; Jörs, 'Collatio,' 369; Hyamson, 83. For Hyamson's explicit acceptance of the interpolation theory, see xxxvi–xxxviii.

72 In addition to Mommsen and Hyamson, see *FIRA*, II, 557; Smits, *Collatio*, 90–2; and, most recently, Aceves, *Mosaicarum et Romanarum*, 16.

73 Haenel, *Codex Theodosianus*, cols. 845–6: *clarum est, antiquitus non scriptum fuisse Item Theodosianus*, sed *Item* (s. *Idem*) *Theodosius*, *v. Theodosius a librariis deinde mutatum esse in Theodosianus, cuius mutationis non desunt in libris manuscriptis exempla*.

74 See Frakes, '*Item Theodosianus*?', 163–8.

75 See Jörs, 'Collatio', 369.

76 See Frakes, '*Item Theodosianus*', 166–7.

of a new 'Capital', or chapter, as is often the case with a cited author throughout the work.[77]

Rather than reading *item Theodosianus* ('in the same way the Theodosian'), we should, following Haenel, adopt *idem Theodosius* ('the same Theodosius') as referring back to Theodosius mentioned in the *constitutio Theodosii* in the sentence before. A slip from *Theodosius* to *Theodosianus* would be a simple mistake to make in copying a manuscript. Moreover, it must be pointed out that the text of the *Collatio*, like most ancient works that had to go through 1,000 years of manuscript tradition until the Renaissance and finally the perfection of moveable type *c.*1450, has many errors of spelling and grammar where cases are changed, letters are left out of words, nouns are changed into adverbs, as well as many other mistakes. As B was derived from α, the change of the text from *idem Theodosius* to *item Theodosianus* may already have stood at least in α. Although there may have possibly been a few copies of the *Codex Theodosianus* in existence in Merovingian and Carolingian France,[78] the *Sirmondian Constitutions* which preserve some constitutions of Theodosius (*Con. Sirm.* 2 and 3) were also in circulation, as was as the *Breviary* of Alaric.[79] Therefore, it is by no means certain that an early medieval scribe would automatically take a reference to a law of Theodosius to mean something in the *Codex Theodosianus.* Since there are so many scribal errors, and the Collator had a pattern of using *idem* within the *Collatio*, and since there is doubt that a scribe would have had even encountered the *Theodosian Code*, it is a simpler solution not to postulate an anonymous legal scholar as a scribe in the seventh, eighth, or ninth century making such an interpolation and accept the reading as *idem Theodosius.*

This correction clarifies that there is no direct connection between the *Collatio* and the *Codex Theodosianus.* The Collator neither cites it like he does the Codes of Hermogenianus and Gregorianus nor does

[77] Again, I appreciate access to the manuscript granted me by the staff of the Staatsbibliothek zu Berlin Handschriftenabteilung. For a facsimile of Berlin manuscript, see Hyamson. Among other examples are: Coll. 2. 4, Coll. 2. 6, Coll. 3. 1. 1. See also my '*Item Theodosianus*', 165–6.

[78] See Wood, 'Code in Merovingian Gaul' in Harries and Wood, *The Theodosian Code*, 161–71 at 162–3.

[79] On the Sirmondian Constitutions, see most recently M. Vessey, 'The origins of the Collectio Sirmondiana' in Harries and Wood, *The Theodosian Code*, 178–99. On the Breviary of Alaric (or *Lex Romanarum Visigothicorum*), see Wood, 'The Code' 162–6.

he make use of laws such as *CTh* 3. 12. 4 of 415 on incest, which is the topic of Title 6 of the *Collatio* and thus might have fitted perfectly.[80] The version of the law against homosexual prostitution found at Coll. 5. 3. 1 that is preserved in the *Theodosian Code* (*CTh* 9. 7. 6) has the subscription *in foro Traiani VIII. Id. Aug. Valentiniano A. IV et Neotoerio Coss*) while that preserved in Coll. 5. 3 has *atrium Minervae* as the promulgation location. The reason for the difference probably results from the work of the compilers of the *Theodosian Code* (who often used the formula *in foro traiano*).[81] Since Valentinian and Neotoerius held the consulship together in 390, it would appear that we have a clear *terminus post quem* of May of 390 for the *Collatio*. Moreover, the phrase *atrium Minervae* implies that the Collator might have even seen the law in Rome.[82] The publication of the *Theodosian Code* likewise gives us an earlier *terminus ante quem* of 438 (and thus before Hincmar and the Merovingian Church councils). So, at face value, the Collator must have compiled his work sometime between 390 and 438.

One objection to such a dating range, first raised by Edoardo Volterra in 1930, is the chronological isolation of the citation of the constitution against homosexuality (at Coll. 5. 3. 1) from the other citations of imperial laws that derive from the *Codex Hermogenianus* and *Codex Gregorianus* (from the 290s) within the *Collatio*.[83] Volterra argued that the absence of laws from the intervening years suggested that the law of Theodosius must have been an interpolation drawn from the *Theodosian Code* into the *Collatio* at an early stage in its transmission. Here Volterra was influenced by the difficulty of the reading of *item Theodosianus* that was of such concern to Huschke.[84] But we have seen that Haenel's correction to *idem Theodosius* resolves the difficulty. And the Collator does seem to cite the law in a similar way to other passages if we accept that reading and more recent scholars have leaned toward accepting the law of Theodosius as part of the original work.[85] Indeed, it is important to remember

[80] Already noticed by Huschke, 'Alter und Verfasser', 8. See also, Hyamson, xlv–xlviii.

[81] See Liebs, *Italien*, 165–7.

[82] See further, *ibid.*, 166–70.

[83] See Volterra, *Collatio*, 95–100 (esp. 96–7).

[84] *Ibid.*, 98–100.

[85] See Smits, *Collatio*, 18–22; Liebs, *Italien*, 163–8; L. V. Rutgers, *The Jews in Late Ancient Rome: Evidence of cultural interaction in the Roman diaspora* (Leiden, 2000), 215–17; and Frakes, 'Religious identity', 131–5.

that if we accept Volterra's alleged interpolation of the constitution of Theodosius at Coll. 5. 3. 1, the original hypothetical Title 5 of the *Collatio* would have been remarkably brief and would have in fact been the shortest title of the entire work.[86] Since we would then have something so out of proportion to the rest of the work, we should not rush to cut something out of the text that stands in all three manuscripts and thus must have stood in the work very early.

Moreover, there could be other explanations for the seeming gap in legislation quoted by the Collator from the time of the *Codex Hermogenianus* and *Codex Gregorianus* and the law of Theodosius in 390 that seemed important for the argument from silence that Volterra used. The first possibility could simply be that the Collator had no other contemporary laws at his disposal (whether due to personal circumstances or to lack of access to an archive). There is scholarly debate over how imperial laws were collected and maintained at the regional level and it is important to remember that even the imperially authorized collections of law that resulted in the *Theodosian Code* and *Code of Justinian* did not succeed in finding all laws and we have no evidence that the Collator was at the highest levels of the imperial government to facilitate such access.[87] Another explanation for the seeming lack of imperial edicts, slightly more complex but perhaps more intriguing, is that the Collator may have been employed as a low-ranking rescripts official in one of the legal secretariats and naturally gravitated to the standard rescripts collection that was in general use, and that imperial edicts were, for the most part, outside his remit.[88] Lastly, the Collator seems to have had special interest in sexual deviance from biblical law and so the contemporary constitution of Theodosius may have struck his interest strongly when he was composing his work.[89]

[86] First raised by Smits, *Collatio*, 162. See also comments of Liebs, *Italien*, 163.

[87] For scholarly debate on the types of legal archives in late antiquity, see O. Seeck, 'Die Zeitfolge der Gesetze Constantins', *ZRG (R.A.)* 10 (1899), 1–44, 177–255; Sirks, 'The sources of the Code' in Harries and Wood, *The Theodosian Code*, 45–67; J. Matthews, 'The making of the text' in Harries and Wood; Matthews, *Laying Down the Law*, 280–93; and Sirks, *Theodosian Code*, 109–77.

[88] I would like to thank an anonymous external reader for Oxford University Press who suggested this possibility. On officials involved with rescripts, see Harries, *Law and Empire*, 26–31.

[89] See commentary at Coll. 5. 3 and Coll. 6. 7.

C. CLOSING THE WINDOW

Working from the material within the *Collatio* and not accepting a theory based on an argument of silence and supposed interpolation, gives us a window of 390 to 438 for the composition of the *Collatio* which, given the nature of the evidence, is the most plausible. We can close this probable window of time even further. While the constitution against homosexual prostitution was released when Valentinian II, Theodosius, and Arcadius were co-augusti, the additional phrase in the *Collatio* of *constitutio Theodosii* implies that Theodosius was the sole powerful legitimate ruler in the eyes of the Collator. We have seen that Theodosius had elevated his older son Arcadius to the rank of augustus in January of 383 in the face of the usurpation of Magnus Maximus.[90] By 390, Arcadius would still have been only twelve or thirteen years old, and logically would have been guided by his father. Valentinian II had been recently restored to power after the defeat of Magnus Maximus by Theodosius. Although Theodosius dominated him as well, Valentinian II was still perceived as an augustus. However, as we have seen, he would mysteriously die on May 15 of 392. It is safe to say that the Collator produced his work in a window of time between 390, the date of the issuance of the law against homosexual prostitution, and January of 395, the death of Theodosius. Within this five-year span, it is most plausible that the Collator wrote sometime in the short window between Valentinian's death in 392 and 395, as Honorius was still only a child when he was made augustus during the usurpation of Eugenius in 393.[91] A likely place where the Collator wrote would be Italy since he seems to have somehow seen the version of the law against homosexual prostitution that was posted in the atrium of the temple of Minerva at Rome.

[90] Matthews, *Western Aristocracies*, 223–52; Errington, *Roman Imperial Policy*, 212–59.

[91] See further, Frakes, 'Item Theodosianus', 163–8; Liebs, *Italien*, 170. Aceves, *Comparación*, xxi–xxvii, cautiously suggests a date sometime in the early fifth century before 438—a window similar to that advocated by Jörs, 'Collatio', 367–70, and Hyamson, xlviii, who both suggested some time from 390 to 438. I. Ostersetzer, 'La "Collatio legum Mosaicarum et Romanarum", Ses origins—son but', *Revue des Études Juives* 97 (1934), 65–96, argues for an author in the east c.398. See also the earlier comments of Mommsen, *Collatio*, 127–8, and Dirksen, 'Über die Collatio', 104–11.

A few other passages in the *Collatio* might presumably help confirm when the Collator wrote. The first of these occurs at Coll. 14. 3. 6 after a long passage from Ulpian on the *Lex Fabia*. Here the Collator, in one of the several short passages where we hear his voice, comments that kidnapping is treated more harshly in recent times than in Ulpian's day. The critical passage here reads '*Sciendum tamen est ex novellis constitutionibus*' ('Nevertheless, it is to be known from recent constitutions'). Scholars have noticed the importance of this allusion for the dating of the *Collatio*, but have differed in their interpretations.[92] Versions of laws pertaining to kidnapping closer to the Collator's day have survived in edited form as *CJ* 9. 20. 7 (dated to December of 287) and *CTh* 9. 18. 1 (August of 315).[93] Now, to be sure, we must be certain of what the Collator meant by the form of *novella* (or 'new') here. The year 315 was certainly much closer to the Collator's time of the 390s than the early third-century Ulpian, or indeed the original *Lex Fabia*, which dates from the second or first century BCE.[94]

Analysis of contemporary late fourth-century usage of a form of *novella* in the *Historia Augusta* can help us understand the nuance of the word in the late fourth century. Despite sincere efforts by recent scholars, the author of this work is unknown and all that can be safely said is that he wrote in the 390s or shortly after 400.[95] In the biography of the Emperor Tacitus, the still anonymous author of the *Historia Augusta* (Tac. 1) states that the institution of an interregnum was created after the death of Romulus when the power of the city

[92] See Levy, Review of Volterra, 702–3; Solazzi, 'Per la Data', 483; Masi, 'Contributi ad una Datazione', 317–321; G. Cervenca, 'Ancora sul Problema della datazione della "Collatio Legum Mosaicarum et Romanarum"', *SDHI* 29 (1963), 253–60; P. De Francisci, 'Ancora intorno alla "Collatio Legum Mosaicarum et Romanarum"', *BIDR* 5 (1963), 97–101 at 97–8; M. A. De Dominicis, 'Ancora sulla Collatio Legum Mosaicarum et Romanarum', *BIDR* 8 (1966), 337–42 at 337–8.

[93] Huschke, 'Alter und Verfasser,' 4; Hyamson, xxxvi–xxxvii.

[94] Berger, 'Lex Fabia', *Encyclopedic Dictionary of Roman Law*, 552.

[95] The ground-breaking work of H. Dessau, 'Über Zeit und Persönlichkeit der Scriptores Historiae Augustae', *Hermes* 24 (1889), 337–92, established that this work was not written by several authors in the early fourth century as earlier scholars had believed. For recent attempts to identify the author, see the highly introspective S. Ratti, 'Nicomaque Flavien Senior auteur de l'Histoire Auguste' in *Historiae Augustae Colloquium Bambergense* (Mai, 2005), ed. G. Bonamente and H. Brandt (Bari, 2007), 305–17 as well as his 'Nicomaque Flavien Senior et l'Histoire Auguste: la découverte de nouveaux liens', *REL* 85 (2007), 204–19. For an effective demolition of this hypothesis, see F. Paschoud, 'Chronique d'historiographie tardive', *Ant. Tard.* 15 (2007), 349–64 at 361–2.

of Rome was new (*novella*). Since, following Livy (1. 16) who is probably the ultimate source of the author of the *Historia Augusta* on this point, Rome was founded in 753 BCE and Romulus' rule ended in 716 BCE, something could be comparatively 'new' or 'recent' for at least thirty-seven years in late fourth-century Latin usage.

Analysis of another form of *novella* appearing elsewhere in the *Collatio* can further show the nuance of the word in fourth-century Latin. At Coll. 15. 3. 3, the Collator cites a law of Diocletian (possibly from 302) drawn from the *Codex Gregorianus* that complains about the religion of Manichaeism as one of several new (*novellas*) and dangerous sects. This religion had started with the teachings of Mani in *c.*245 CE and had been crossing the cultural frontier of the Eastern Roman Empire at least since 260 when Manichees reached Alexandria in Egypt (and the Manichee missionary Mar Adda allegedly cured Zenobia).[96] In this law of *c.*302 (and also in the reception of the usage in the Collator's time), we have a window of over forty years for something being considered 'new' or recent.[97] It could well be that our example regarding the 'newer' laws of 287 and 315 alluded to at Coll. 14. 3. 6 appeared more recent than Ulpian's treatment to the Collator. Thus, the Collator could still be writing sometime *c.*392–5 and feel that laws from 287 (under Diocletian) and 315 (from Constantine's early reign) were relatively recent in contrast to the age of Ulpian or he may have encountered other imperial legislation from the fourth century regarding kidnapping that has not survived. In either case, he does not seem to have had widespread access to any kind of large archive of recent imperial constitutions that he could have used to flesh out several of his titles.

In addition to the clear citation of the constitution at Coll. 5. 3. 1 and the explicit allusion to legislation at Coll. 14. 3. 6, there are several other passages that some scholars have felt may show influence from fourth-century constitutions and thus might be useful in clarifying the time when the Collator wrote. The first of these relates to a passage from the *Sententiae* of Ps. Paulus at Coll. 3. 2. 1. In this

[96] See I. M. F. Gardner and S. N. C. Lieu, 'From Narmouthis (Medinat Madi) to Kellis (Ismart El-Kharab): Manichaean documents from Roman Egypt', *JRS* 86 (1996), 146–69; Brown, 'The diffusion of Manichaeism in the Roman Empire', 92–103.

[97] Scholars date the constitution anywhere from 297 to 302. See further, Barnes, *New Empire of Diocletian and Constantine*, 55 n. 41; Corcoran, *Empire of the Tetrarchs*, 135–6.

passage, Ps. Paulus states that a master should not be charged with murder if he accidentally beats a slave to death. Two laws of Constantine (surviving as *CTh* 9. 12. 1 = *CJ* 9. 14. 1 of 319 and *CTh* 9. 12. 2 of either 326 or 329) also allow the beating of slaves and stipulate that masters cannot be charged with murder who accidentally beat slaves to death. There has been active scholarly dispute over whether this passage in the *Collatio* (or the text of the laws) may have suffered from an interpolation sometime in the fourth century after either 319 or 329, since earlier commentary on Roman law seems to suggest a master could not beat a slave to death with impunity (see Gaius, *Inst.* 1. 53).[98] However, this passage in Gaius, which alludes to a law of Antoninus Pius, states only that a master cannot kill his slave *sine causa* ('without cause').[99] Since the passage from Ps. Paulus in the *Collatio* does not preclude this, and even states such a beating cannot be done with evil intent, we are not forced to accept that this Constantinian legislation influenced this passage from Ps. Paulus or the Collator.

Another alleged example of influence of fourth-century legislation has been proposed for Coll. 4. 12. In this extract, Ps. Paulus describes how fathers and husbands may kill adulterers and are also able to torture slaves in cases of adultery (presumably for their testimony as witnesses which is mentioned at Coll. 4. 11). A scholarly debate has raged over whether this passage suffers from an interpolation (either in the text of the *Collatio* here, or in the Collator's version of Ps. Paulus, or the surviving constitution) due to influence from a law of 385 that survives as *CTh* 9. 7. 4.[100] This constitution of Gratian, Valentinian, and Theodosius stipulates that torture must be used on household slaves to investigate charges of adultery. The law of 385 emanated after a time when Valentinian had prosecuted a large number of trials for adultery among the senatorial elite of Rome from 368 through much of the 370s.[101] A fragment of Ulpian's *De*

[98] See Solazzi, 'Per la Data', 494–6; Masi, 'Contributi', 313–17; Cervenca, 'Ancora', 267–72; De Francisci, 'Ancora', 100–1; De Dominicis, 'Ancora', 340–1; F. Lucrezi, *L'Uccisione dello schiavo in diritto ebraico e romana* (Turin, 2001), 62–73, 125–6; Lucrezi, 'Sulla data di redazione della Collatio alla luce di due costituzioni costantiniane', *AARC* 14 (2003), 599–613 at 600–5.

[99] Gaius, *Inst.* 1. 53. See W. M. Gordon and O. F. Robinson (tr.), *The Institutes of Gaius* (London, 1988), 46–7.

[100] See Masi, 'Contributi', 294–300; Cervenca, 'Ancora', 263–7; De Dominicis, 'Ancora', 339–40.

[101] Ammianus, 28.1. See Matthews, *Roman Empire of Ammianus*, 209–17.

Adulteriis preserved in the sixth-century *Digest* (40. 9. 12) states that slaves were already prohibited from being freed to prevent them from being tortured to give evidence in a case of adultery. In fact, this had been Roman law long before the fourth century and the law of 385. Thus, this law did not necessarily influence the text, but the recent atmosphere of concern may have increased the Collator's interest in the topic.

Yet another example of posited influence occurs at Coll. 7. 2. 1. In this passage, the Collator quotes again from the *Sententiae* of Ps. Paulus that a thief who breaks into a house at night can be killed with impunity. While it has been argued that this passage might have been influenced by a law of 391 that survives as *CTh* 9. 14. 2 that allows self-defence against brigands who enter fields at night, the legal concept must be somewhat universal as it so closely parallels Hebrew law at Exodus 22: 2–3 (as the Collator noticed).[102]

There are some grounds to question these cases of alleged influence of fourth-century legislation. Beyond that, we have to remember that when we are working with the *Collatio* we are dealing with one late Roman compiler's selection of passages from the jurists. His own sources for these statements may themselves have been edited or even flawed. Moreover, we have only a scattering of other testimony, and that is often later from the *Digest* or from the fifth- or sixth-century law codes. It could even be that the officials who drafted some of the constitutions that survived in edited form in the *Codex Theodosianus* or *Codex Justinianus* may have read versions of the same texts that the Collator did. Postulating which influences which can quickly become an unanswerable 'chicken or the egg' question.[103] By far the safest empirical course is to examine the evidence that we have: the Collator wrote not only after the composition of the *Codex Gregorianus* in 291 and the *Codex Hermogenianus* in 295, but also after 390 and the issuance of the law against homosexual prostitution, and quite possibly after 392, but before 395 (the death of Theodosius) and before the promulgation of the *Theodosian Code* in 438.

[102] See Solazzi, 'Per la Data', 498; Masi, 'Contributi', 307–13; Cervenca, 'Ancora', 258–63; De Francisci, 'Ancora', 97–101; De Dominicis, 'Ancora', 338–9.

[103] For the drafting process of late Roman law, see T. Honoré, 'The making of the Theodosian Code', *ZRG (R.A.)* 103 (1986), 133–222, esp. 136–56; J. Harries, 'The Roman Imperial Quaestor from Constantine to Theodosius II', *JRS* 78 (1988), 148–72; and Matthews, *Laying Down the Law*, 171–80.

D. CONCLUSION: A SINGLE COLLATOR

There has been one last challenge to the window of 392–5 (or, indeed, for any date) for the composition of the *Collatio* that must be addressed before we can safely accept that time frame. Influenced by the scholarly movement of viewing a text as an archaeological construct composed of several layers, Fritz Schulz argued that what modern scholars perceive as the single organic work of the *Collatio* was actually a construct that had been created by a series of different compilers over the course of several decades in the fourth century.[104] The first one of these hypothetical collators, he argued, compiled a collection of passages from the jurists and some laws from the *Codex Gregorianus* and *Codex Hermongenianus* in the early fourth century. This bald collection would have been analogous to, though shorter than, the so-called *Fragmenta Vaticana*—a surviving collection of statements from the jurists and laws divided into different titles collated sometime shortly after *c.*318.[105] Decades later, Schulz suggested, a second hypothetical author added passages from the Bible to this 'bare bones' legal collection. Toward the end of the fourth century, Schulz postulated, an additional compiler then interpolated the law of Theodosius from the early 390s into the existing text (at Coll. 5. 3. 1) and this compiler, or perhaps yet another, added some personal reflections on various passages.[106] Ultimately, Schulz argued: 'the comparison is unconsidered and superficial, the biblical passages having been tacked on without the least reflection . . . no reasonable man could have made so considerable an array of juristic materials for the purpose of making so superficial a comparison of them with Mosaic law'.[107]

[104] Schulz, *History of Roman Legal Science*, 313–15. For Schulz's use of this methodological approach, see W. Flume, 'Fritz Schulz+', *ZRG (R.A.)* 75 (1958), 499–506. Further, see Liebs, *Italien*, 163–5, on *Schichtentheorie* and overview in Frakes, 'Religious identity', 133–4. See also observations in Barone-Adesi, *L'eta della "Lex Dei"*, 185–93.

[105] Schulz, *Roman Legal Science*, 310–11; see also, Berger, 'Fragmenta Vaticana', *Encyclopedic Dictionary*, 476, who dates it to the second half of the fourth century. For texts of the *Fragmenta Vaticana*, see T. Mommsen (ed.), *Fragmenta Vaticana* (in Krüger, Mommsen, and Studemond (eds.), *Collectio Librorum Iuris Anteiustiniani*, 3) and *FIRA*, II, 463–540.

[106] Schulz, *Roman Legal Science*, 313–14 on Coll. 6. 7. 1, 7. 1. 1.

[107] Schulz, *Roman Legal Science*, 313.

While delightfully stirring, and even fascinating as an intellectual exercise, there are several drawbacks to Schulz's thesis. First, we have no internal or external evidence that there was such a string of anonymous compilers at work on creating this document (and at a visceral level, it seems improbable). Indeed, the structure of the work and the style of the short prefatory statements seem fairly uniform throughout the *Collatio.*[108] Likewise, as we have seen, if the constitution of Theodosius at Coll. 5. 3. 1 was indeed a later interpolation, the original length of Title 5 would have been disproportionately short in comparison with the other titles with just the short quotation from Leviticus (20: 13) and one passage from the *Sententiae.*[109] Secondly, Schulz is projecting his modern, positivistic view of what makes an effective work when he felt that a 'reasonable man' would have made it more balanced in the types of sources he used. Thirdly, the end product would still have been what Schulz felt could not have been created, so we would still be left with an 'unreasonable' Collator (albeit, the last one in a series of hypothetical compilers).

It is not necessary to posit a complex theory of the work as an evolving composition over the course of a century and Schulz's radical argument regarding the composition of the work has thus not been accepted. Instead, we are left with the fairly certain window of 392–5 for the composition of the *Collatio.* Based on its use by Church councils, its multiple layers of copies, and its use by Hincmar, the *Collatio* must have entered into official Church libraries in the west fairly quickly, perhaps already in the fifth century. With the dating of the work assured to the window from 392–5, we can now turn to the sources of the Collator.

[108] As earlier noticed by Dirksen, 'Über die Collatio', 105.

[109] See comments of Smits, *Collatio*, 162; Liebs, *Italien*, 163; Frakes, 'Religious identity', 134–5.

3

The Collator's Sources

Coll. 14. 3. 6: Nevertheless, it is to be known from recent constitutions that kidnappers are to be punished for the atrocity of their deeds by the sentence of death: although Paulus related in the specific cases above that the punishment imposed for such things is crucifixion or the mines for guilty parties of this sort.

[Coll. 14. 3. 6: *Sciendum tamen est ex novellis constitutionibus capitali sententia plagiatores pro atrocitate factis puniendos: quamvis et Paulus relatis supra speciebus crucis et metalli poenam huiusmodi reis inrogaverit poenam.*]

Passages such as these from the *Collatio* reveal it to be a comparative compendium of passages from other works. Its titles contain statements from the jurists, direct quotations from Roman imperial laws, and biblical passages. As such, the *Collatio* presents important evidence for the transmission of the texts of Roman jurists independently of the *Digest* of Justinian as well as some important biblical texts in a Latin translation. An examination of the Collator's juristic sources, especially useful for ancient historians and theologians, shows how the classical Roman jurists continued to play a critical part in legal education in the late fourth century. A close analysis of his biblical texts can moreover show where the Collator stood in relation to the Bible (a subject of great debate). Lastly, examination of the sources the Collator had available to him can give insight into the library the Collator had at his disposal.

A. JURISTS AND LAWS

Scholars have, of course, noted the heavy use of juristic sources in the *Collatio* since the nineteenth century. The work of Franz Wieacker in the twentieth century has especially demonstrated the importance of the *Collatio* as an external control on the transmission of the texts from the jurists that appear in the *Digest*.[1] Wieacker has shown that the anonymous author of the *Collatio* often worked from different versions of the texts from those used by Tribonian and his staff in the sixth century and, moreover, the versions that the Collator was using in the late fourth century were probably already altered from those that the jurists themselves had earlier written.[2]

On the surface, the Collator cites several works of many important Roman jurists. In a brief overview of texts cited throughout his compilation (see fully Table I: The Collator's Alleged Sources), one encounters works attributed to Paulus, Ulpian, Modestinus, Papinian, and Gaius—the five major jurists whose works would later be codified in the famous Law of Citations in *CTh* 1. 4. 3 of 426 as having the greatest worth in legal disputations. The Collator's preference for them in the late fourth century indicates that their weight was already felt strongly in the legal community, and perhaps also in administrative circles. The Collator also cites laws from legal collections such as the *Codex Gregorianus* and *Codex Hermogenianus* as well as at least one contemporary constitution, while alluding to at least two others.

Since Hyamson last provided an overview of the Collator's juristic sources in 1913,[3] there has been much scholarly progress as to the authenticity of some of these works. In addition to the revised view of the *Sententiae* of Ps. Paulus (which will be discussed below), monographic works attributed to some of the jurists such as Paulus' *Liber singularis de adulteriis* and Papinian's work of the same title are now considered to be later derivations of longer works of the original jurists, possibly by followers of their school.[4] Likewise, the *Liber singularis regularum* attributed to Ulpian should instead be credited as a work of a student or follower of his school, even though it was already considered a work of Ulpian's by the fourth century.[5]

[1] Wieacker, *Textstufen*. On Tribonian and his work on the *Digest*, see, among others, Honoré, *Tribonian*; D. Pugsley, 'On Tribonian and his Latin style' in R. Ruedin (ed.), *Melanges en l'honneur de Carlo Augusto Cannata* (Basel, 1999), 171–7; and T. Honoré, 'How Tribonian Organized the Compilation of Justinian's Digest', *ZRG (R.A.)* 121 (2004), 1–43.

[2] Wieacker, *Textstufen*, 231–70.

[3] Hyamson, *Mosaicarum et Romanarum Legum Collatio*, 277–80.

[4] See Wieacker, *Textstufen*, 419–22.

[5] Honoré, *Ulpian*, 206–12.

Moreover, there has been substantial attention to earlier Roman jurists and their influence in Roman society.[6] The following section will first introduce the Collator's sources by following the attributed names (but will include warnings against probable spurious works) before turning to the Collator's biblical source.

(i) Paulus

Iulius Paulus is one of the most well-known Roman jurists of the classical period of Roman law. Although his exact origin is unknown, he may have been born *c.*160, perhaps in a province.[7] He studied in Rome under the jurist Quintus Cervidius Scaevola and became a lawyer. He worked under Papinian (see further below) when that jurist served as praetorian prefect. Paulus may have served as *magister memoriae* and was a member of the *consilium principis.*[8] The Emperor Elagabalus (r. 218–22) may even have married his daughter, before divorcing her to marry a Vestal Virgin.[9] The jurist was banished, but recalled by the Emperor Severus Alexander (r. 222–35). He also worked as a teacher of law and was a prolific author of law books ranging from legal educational works to monographs to commentaries.[10]

(a) Paulus, Liber responsorum *(or* Book of Responses*)*

Ironically, although the Collator cites six alleged works of the jurist, this is probably the only work of Paulus that the Collator cites that is

[6] See, for example, R. A. Bauman, *Lawyers in Roman Republican Politics: A study of the Roman jurists in their political setting, 316 BC – 82 BC* (Munich, 1983); *Lawyers in Roman Transitional Politics: A study of the Roman jurists in their political setting in the late Republic and Triumvirate* (Munich, 1985); and *Lawyers and Politics in the Early Roman Empire: A study of the Relations between the Roman jurists and the emperors from Augustus to Hadrian* (Munich, 1989).

[7] D. Liebs, in Herzog and Schmidt, *HLL4*, 150–2.

[8] For overviews of Paulus, see T. Honoré, *Emperors and Lawyers*, 2nd edn (Oxford, 1994), 21–4; C. Maschi, 'La conclusione della giurisprudenza classica all'età dei Severi. Iulius Paulus' in H. Temporini (ed.), *ANRW* (Berlin, 1976), II(15), 667–707. A. Berger, 'Iulius Paulus', *RE* (Stuttgart, 1917), X(1), cols. 690–752 is still useful. It is somewhat ironic that in a footnote at the beginning of Berger's 62–column article, Berger begs the reader's forgiveness that he was only able to put the overview together in a short amount of time.

[9] A. Birley, *Septimius Severus: The African emperor* (London, 1999), 190–3. The tradition on Elagabalus is admittedly quite hostile.

[10] Most recently, see Liebs, *HLL4*, 150–75 on Paulus' works.

actually authentic. This work, originally in twenty-three books, consisted of the jurist's responses to various legal problems.[11] It was probably finished during the reign of Severus Alexander, perhaps when the jurist returned from exile.[12] It could be that the jurist composed much of it during his period in exile. The work had an important role in legal education up to the period of Justinian's legal innovations.[13] The Collator cites this work once.[14]

(b) Ps. Paulus, Liber singularis de iniuriis *(or* Single Book concerning Injuries*)*

This reference may be to a work of Paulus or to a Pseudo-Paulus, or it may never have existed as such. The Collator cites the alleged work twice.[15] One of the cited passages in the *Collatio* (Coll. 2. 5) is very close to Justinian's *Institutes*, 4. 4, as scholars have noted (a passage which ultimately probably was derived from Paulus' *Commentary on the Edict*, Book 55). So, it could be that this *Liber singularis* is a late classical (*c.*300 CE) revision of that part of Paulus' *Commentary.*[16]

(c) Ps. Paulus, Liber singularis de poenis paganorum *(or* Single Book concerning the Punishments of Peasants*)*

This work is cited once, or perhaps twice, in the *Collatio* and also in four places in the *Digest.*[17] Although Berger accepted it as authentic, Liebs must be right in arguing that it was a late classical revision of an earlier work of Paulus.[18] The Collator, writing at the end of the fourth century no doubt believed it was truly a work of Paulus and so cited it.

[11] O. Lenel (ed.), *Palingenesia Iuris Civilis*, 2 vols. (Graz, 1960 reprint), I, cols. 1223–51. See further, Wieacker, *Textstufen*, 377–81.

[12] Liebs, *HLL4*, 173–4, although Berger, 'Iulius Paulus', cols. 730–1 suggests it may have been started under Elagabalus. Wieacker, *Textstufen*, 377, holds for a period from 233–5.

[13] Berger, 'Iulius Paulus', col. 731.

[14] Coll. 10. 9.

[15] Coll. 2. 5 and 2. 6.

[16] See Liebs, *HLL4*, 156–7.

[17] Lenel, *Paling.*, I, cols. 1178–9. Coll. 11. 6 and perhaps 12. 6.

[18] Berger, 'Iulius Paulus', col. 721; Liebs *HLL5*, 71 citing his earlier 'Römische Provinzialjurisprudenz' in H. Temporini (ed.), *ANRW* (Berlin, 1976), II(15), 288–362 at 316–19.

(d) Ps. Paulus, Liber singularis de poenis omnium legum *(or* Single Book concerning the Punishments of All Laws*)*

This work is cited twice in the *Digest* and once in the *Collatio.*[19] Again, the standard view a century ago was that it was a genuine work of Paulus.[20] However, this too, like the *Liber singularis de poenis paganorum* mentioned above, was composed later,[21] perhaps derived from Paulus' works. Since we see a tendency for these spurious works, which were probably not consciously conceived as deceitful but rather derivative, to be written in the late third and early fourth century, this one may also date from that time frame.

(e) Ps. Paulus, Liber singularis de adulteriis *(or* Single Book concerning Adultery*)*

Although one hundred years ago scholars considered this book an authentic work of Paulus,[22] it is now considered to be a later compilation derived from the jurists. Wieacker had already noticed that these passages were probably not the original work of Paulus, but rather a shortened edited version of Paulus' longer three-book commentary *De Adulteriis* that is cited in the *Digest.*[23] The Collator cited the work four times in quick succession.[24] Aside from these citations in the *Collatio*, we have only one citation of the work in the *Digest* at 48. 16. 16.[25]

(f) Ps. Paulus, Sententiae *(or* The Opinions*)*

Of all the works attributed to Paulus, the Collator cited from the so-called *Sententiae* of Paulus (often termed PS by scholars) the most—fully twenty-eight times.[26] Thus, it is the single most-used juristic source by the Collator. The work, which apparently was a teaching manual for lawyers, survives in fragments from the *Fragmenta Vaticana* of *c.*320, the *Collatio*, the fifth-century *Consultatio*, the *Lex Romana Visigothorum* of 506, and the *Digest.* At the beginning of the twentieth century, scholars felt this was an authentic work of the great jurist Paulus. However, Beseler already began to doubt it could have really come from his hand due to stylistic reasons

19 Lenel, *Paling.*, I, col. 1178. Coll. 8. 2.
20 Berger, 'Iulius Paulus', col. 721.
21 Liebs, *HLL4*, 174.
22 Berger, 'Iulius Paulus', col. 715.
23 Wieacker, *Textstufen*, 421–2. On this longer work, see Berger, 'Iulius Paulus', col. 716. See further, Liebs, *HLL4*, 160.
24 Coll. 4. 2, 3, 4, 6.
25 Lenel, *Paling.*, I, cols. 953–4.
26 See Table I.

and hypothesized that it may have been the work of an unknown editor *c.*300 who culled important passages from Paulus' work to form a teaching guide.[27] Constantine ordered that it be considered a pre-eminent source in a constitution of 327 (*CTh* 1. 4. 2). The compilers of the *Digest* apparently felt it was genuine as they used it and cited it as a work of Paulus. While Berger and Levy attempted different clarifications of Beseler's thesis, more recently Liebs has argued that the *Sententiae* of Paulus have as little to do with Paulus as the *Dicta Marci Catonis ad filium* from the third century CE have to do with Cato the elder of the second century BCE![28] Liebs argued that the anonymous compiler of the *Sententiae*, possibly a North African, took passages not only from Paulus' works, but also from works attributed to Papinian, Ulpian, Modestinus, the *Codex Gregorianus*, the *Codex Hermogenianus*, and possibly others.[29]

Some of the echoes of the other jurists that Liebs indicates are close to passages in the *Sententiae*, others are a bit more distant. Some may even be explained by the works of the other jurists interacting with the original works of Paulus. For instance, in the passage of the *Sententiae* preserved at Coll. 4. 4. 1, Papinian is cited, so a supposed similarity to a passage in the *Sententiae* being culled from Papinian might instead be explained by the original Paulus having read Papinian (which is chronologically possible), and then the compiler of the *Sententiae* reading Paulus.[30] It seems most likely that the compiler of the *Sententiae* drew from works written by several jurists, but nonetheless probably drew mostly from those of Paulus. So instead of Paulus himself as the original compiler, we should look instead to an anonymous legal editor of *c.*300 from somewhere in the Western Mediterranean (possibly Africa, Gaul, or Italy)—a time frame that fits so many other spurious works attributed to Paulus (which the compiler of the *Sententiae* and his contemporaries probably thought were genuine). The Collator's knowledge of this

[27] G. Beseler, *Beiträge zur Kritik der römischen Rechtsquellen* (Tübingen, 1910–20), 1: 99 and 4: 336.

[28] D. Liebs, *Römische Jurisprudenz in Africa*, 2nd edn (Berlin, 2005), 41–128 at 43. Earlier, see E. Levy, 'Paulus und der Sentenzenverfasser', *ZRG (R.A.)* 50 (1930), 272–94.

[29] Liebs, *Africa*, 58–111. See Liebs, 'Die pseudopaulinischen Sentenzen II', *ZRG (R.A.)* 113 (1996), 132–242 for a *palingensia* (a reconstruction of the surviving fragments) of the *Sententiae* to update that of P. Krüger, *Pauli Libri Quinque Sententiarum* in *Collectio Librorum Iuris Anteiustiniani, Tomus Alter* (Berlin, 1878).

[30] As opposed to Liebs, *Africa*, 58–9.

text, and apparent ready use of it, indicates that he was familiar with what had become the best-known handbook for Roman law by the mid fourth century.

(ii) Ulpian

Together with Paulus, Domitius Ulpianus (or Ulpian) is one of the most cited Roman jurists in later works such as the *Digest*. This pattern holds for the *Collatio* where works attributed to Ulpian are cited twenty-three times. Ulpian, like his younger contemporary Paulus, was active in Severan Rome. Originally from Tyre, Ulpian was a lawyer who followed an equestrian career path where he drafted rescripts under Septimius Severus and then was appointed, at least from 205, *magister libellorum* where he was in charge of imperial rescripts.[31] He may have been impressed by the spread of Roman citizenship under Caracalla in the Antonine Constitution of 212.[32] This law might have motivated him, a provincial himself, to write his large number of legal works to explain elements of Roman law to new citizens and to the new large number of resulting lawyers (although he might have composed some of his works before 212).[33] His official career would go on to include service as the praetorian prefect under Severus Alexander in 222, when he was killed by the praetorian guard either before June of 224 or in 228.[34] Ulpian wrote

[31] On Ulpian, see P. Jörs, 'Domitius Ulpianus', *RE* (Stuttgart, 1905), V(1), cols. 1435–509; G. Crifò, 'Ulpiano. Esperienze e responsabilità del giurista' in H. Temporini (ed.), *ANRW* (Berlin, 1976), II(15), 708–89. More recently, see Honoré, *Ulpian*. Honoré's methods and conclusions for not only Ulpian but also for his other works are stimulating and controversial (and stand at the centre of much current discourse on Roman law). See, among others, A. Rodger, 'Behind the scenes in Roman law', Review of Honoré's *Tribonian, Emperors and Lawyers*, and *Ulpian* in *Oxford Journal of Legal Studies* 3 (1983), 383–404; P. Birks, Review of Honoré's *Ulpian* in *The Irish Jurist* 18 (1983), 151–81; D. Liebs, Review of Honoré's *Ulpian* in *Gnomon* 56 (1984), 441–50; B. Frier, 'Law on the Installment Plan', Review of Honoré's *Ulpian* in *Michigan Law Review* 82 (1984), 856–68; Alan Watson, *Times Literary Supplement* (16 February, 1985), 164; and F. Millar, 'A new approach to the Roman jurists', *JRS* 76 (1986), 272–80.

[32] See the controversial argument of Honoré, *Ulpian*, 22–6; 76–86.

[33] See the interpretation of Honoré, *Ulpian*, 23–6; 88–94. For the view that Ulpian may have written some works earlier, see Frier, 'Law on the Installment Plan', 863.

[34] See Dio, 80.2.2. See also Honoré, *Ulpian*, 27–33, for the earlier dating. See R. Bauman, 'The death of Ulpian: The irresistible force and the immovable object', *ZRG (R.A.)* 112 (1995), 385–99 and Bauman, *Crime and Punishment*, 106, for date of 228. For a recent (and clever) return to 223, see S. Faro, 'Sull'anno della morte di Ulpiano', *Index* 30 (2002), 251–87.

many works ranging from commentaries to teaching manuals for law students. His reputation was praised by the author of the *Historia Augusta* in the late fourth century, showing that at the time when the Collator wrote Ulpian was still held in high esteem.[35] His works would go on to be used as a major part (anywhere from 1/3 to 2/5) of the *Digest*.[36]

(a) The Liber de officio proconsulis *(or* Book concerning the Office of the Proconsul*)*

The second most cited work by the Collator, after the *Sententiae*, is Ulpian's *Liber de officio proconsulis*. In this work, probably written *c.*213, Ulpian laid out rules for provincial administration.[37] Originally composed in ten books, the work treated the different judicial and legal duties of a provincial governor.[38] It is cited many times in the *Digest* as well as the *Collatio* and must have commanded great respect in the late empire.[39] The three books cited by the Collator (7, 8, and 9) seem to have treated the police and enforcement powers of the provincial governor.[40] The Collator cites this work thirteen times.[41]

(b) Ulpian's Institutionum Libri *(or* Books of the Institutes*)*

This work was a teaching manual chiefly dealing with civil law that Ulpian seems to have composed for law students.[42] Originally written in two books, he may have composed it sometime from 213 through

[35] See *HA*, *Vita Severi Alexandri* (Life of Severus Alexander), 15, 26, 31, 34. Honoré, *Ulpian*, 8; T. Honoré, 'Scriptor Historiae Augustae', *JRS* 77 (1987), 156–76.

[36] For 1/3, see Jörs, 'Ulpianus'; for 2/5, see Honoré, *Ulpian*, vii.

[37] See Bauman, *Crime and Punishment*, 194 n. 20. More fully, see Digeser, *Making of a Christian Empire*, 49–53, 60–2.

[38] See Jörs, 'Ulpianus', cols. 1452–3. For surviving fragments, see Lenel, *Paling.*, II, cols. 966–91.

[39] Wieacker, *Textstufen*, 391, calls it one of the most widely used handbooks of the classical jurists in antiquity. See also Schulz, *History of Roman Legal Science*, 243, on the purpose. See, most recently, A. Nogrady, *Römisches Strafrecht nach Ulpian: Buch 7 bis 9 De officio proconsulis* (Berlin, 2006).

[40] Jörs, 'Ulpianus', col. 1452. See also, Bauman, *Crime and Punishment*, 118, on the last four books of the work.

[41] Coll. 1. 3; 1. 6; 1. 11; 3. 3; 7. 4; 8. 7; 9. 2; 11. 7, 8; 12. 5; 13. 3; 14. 3; and 15. 2.

[42] Honoré, *Ulpian*, 192; Jörs, 'Ulpianus', cols. 1447–8. See also Berger, 'Institutiones', *Encyclopedic Dictionary*, 504.

214.[43] About fifteen fragments from this work survive in the *Digest*, and some other echoes survive elsewhere.[44] The Collator cites this work five times.[45]

(c) Ulpian, Libri ad edictum *(or* Books on the Edict*)*

The commentaries on the edict are very important juristic works. They treat the edict of the urban prefect, which, as we have earlier seen, generally included large parts of the edict of his predecessors and was put into a finalized form by Salvius Iulianus under the Emperor Hadrian.[46] The purpose of such commentaries was to give legal rules, and thus would obviously be of great use to practicing lawyers as well as to law students. Ulpian probably composed his massive 81-book commentary sometime from perhaps as early as 211 to possibly as late as 218.[47] In this major work, like his others, Ulpian seems to be committed to instructing lawyers, or potential lawyers, in the technicalities of Roman justice.[48] Many fragments of Ulpian's Commentary survive.[49] The Collator cites this work three times, but all three citations are from Book 18 (which seems to treat aspects of the *Lex Aquilia*).[50]

(d) Ps. Ulpian, Liber singularis regularum *(or* Single Book of Rules*)*

Although in Hyamson's day this work attributed to Ulpian was considered authentic, it is now thought to be spurious.[51] The work is

[43] Honoré, *Ulpian*, 193–6.

[44] Lenel, *Paling.*, II, cols. 926–30.

[45] Coll. 16. 5, 6, 7, 8, 9.

[46] See Lenel, *Edict Perpetuum*; U. von Lübtow, 'Die Aufgaben des römischen Praetors auf dem Gebiet der Zivilrechtspflege' in *Studi in onore di A. Biscardi* (Milan, 1983), IV, 349–412; and Brennan, *Praetorship in the Roman Republic*, I, 130–3, 462–5.

[47] See hypothetical argument of Honoré, *Ulpian*, 158–76, esp. conclusion on 176, for dating blocks of composition.

[48] See comments of Honoré, *Ulpian*, 92–3.

[49] Lenel, *Paling.*, II, cols. 421–884.

[50] Coll. 2. 4, 7. 3, 12. 7. See Lenel, *Paling.*, II, cols. 520–32.

[51] Honoré, *Ulpian*, 206–12. For dating, see F. Schulz, *Die Epitome Ulpiani der Cod. Vat. Reginae 1128* (Bonn, 1926), 8–9. For a radical new argument that this work actually dates to shortly after 180, and thus is not actually a revision of Ulpian's work, see M. Avenarius, *Der Pseudo-Ulpianische liber singularis regularum: Entstehung, Eigenart und Überlieferung einer hochklassischen Juristenschrift* (Göttingen, 2005) and the accompanying *Die Pseudo-Ulpianische Einzelschrift der Rechtsregeln (liber singularis regularum)* (Göttingen, 2005).

cited in the *Digest* once.[52] Honoré proposes that the anonymous author of the *Liber singularis regularum* tried to provide a 'nutshell type handbook' modelled on that of Gaius to serve as an approachable one-volume teaching manual on civil law.[53] The Collator, who probably thought it was by Ulpian as did others in late antiquity, cited it three times.[54]

(iii) Papinian

Aemilius Papinianus was considered to be the greatest of the classical jurists in late antiquity and even in the modern age.[55] He was very active in Severan Rome, and may have come to Rome from North Africa or Syria.[56] He was a lawyer, law teacher, and also served in a series of administrative positions. He may have served first as an assessor to the praetorian prefect, then composed rescripts in the office of the *magister libellorum* and then perhaps took over that position.[57] He became praetorian prefect himself, perhaps from 205–11, and tradition holds he was eventually put to death under the Emperor Caracalla in 212, following the emperor's murder of his brother and imperial colleague Geta (allegedly for refusing to make a speech to the senate defending Caracalla's action).[58] Papinian wrote several important legal treatises, seemingly influenced by his ethical beliefs.[59] The Law of Citations of 426 (*CTh.* 1. 4. 3) gave him the

[52] Lenel, *Paling.*, II, col. 1016 for references to *Digest* and *Tituli*, sometimes called the *Epitome Ulpiani.* See further, Schulz, *Die Epitome Ulpiani.* For more on the *Tituli*, see Honoré, *Ulpian*, 207–8.

[53] See further, Honoré, *Ulpian*, 207–12.

[54] Coll. 2. 2, 6. 2, 16. 4.

[55] For a recent reappraisal, see H. Ankum, 'Papinian, ein dunkler Jurist?', *Orbis Iuris Romani* 1 (1996), 5–32.

[56] P. Jörs, 'Aemilius Papinianus', *RE* (Stuttgart, 1893), I(1), cols. 572–5; E. Costa, *Papiniano, Studi di Storia interna del diritto romano* (Bologna, 1899), IV; W. Kunkel, *Herkunft und soziale Stellung der römischen Juristen* (Graz, Vienna, and Cologne, 1967), 224–6; V. Giuffrè, 'Papiniano: fra tradizione ed innovazione' in H. Temporini (ed.), *ANRW* (Berlin, 1976), II(15), 632–66. Papinian may have been related to Septimius Severus through the emperor's wife Julia Domna (see *HA*, *Vita Caracallae*, 8. 2: *ut aliqui loquuntur, ad finem etiam per secundam uxorem*).

[57] See Costa, *Papiniano*, 1–14; Jörs, 'Aemilius Papinianus', 572; A. Schiller, 'Provincial cases in Papinian', *Acta Juridica* 1 (1958), 221–42 at 224–5; and Ankum, 'Papinian', 5–6. See also the hypothesis of Honoré, *Emperors and Lawyers*, 76–81.

[58] See *HA*, *Vita Caracallae*, 3–4, 8 and *Vita Getae*, 6. 2–3; Aurelius Victor, 20. 33–4; Dio Cassius, 78.4; and Zosimus, *Historia Nova*, 1. 8.

[59] U. Manthe, 'Ethische Argumente im Werk Papinians', *Orbis Iuris Romani* 10 (2005), 143–66.

place of honour by giving his teachings the role of a tie-breaker, if the writings of the other four great jurists conflicted. Indeed, at some point in late antiquity before 533, third-year law students were known as 'Papinianists'.[60] His legend as an ethical martyr lived on in several early modern works.[61]

(a) Ps. Papinian, Liber singularis de adulteriis *(or* Single Book concerning Adultery*)*

We have testimony of two different works on adultery by Papinian: a version in two books and a version in one book (the *Liber singularis de adulteriis*).[62] The relationship between these two books is unclear, as is their dating.[63] The shorter version seems to be composed more of responses to legal problems.[64] It now seems likely that this shorter work is a late classical epitome of Papinian's earlier longer work.[65] The Collator cites this work six times, with five of the citations being in quick succession.[66] The nature of this work did jibe well with this title of the *Collatio* (on adultery).

[60] *Const. Omnem.* 4. See also, C. P. Sherman, 'The study of law in Roman law schools', *Yale Law Journal* 17 (1907–8), 499–512 at 505–6.

[61] The most famous is the tragedy *Grossmütiger Rechtsgelehrter oder Sterbender Aemilius Paulus Papinianus, Trauerspil* (Breslau, 1659) by Andreas Gryphius. On this work, see D. Nörr, 'Papinian and Gryphius. Zum Nachleben Papinians', *ZRG* 83 (1966), 308–33, and O. Behrends, 'Papinians Verweigerung oder die Moral eines Juristen', *Literatur und Rechts* 1 (1996), 243–91 (who also examines the jurist's ethical influence and death). Another dramatic version of the jurist's life and death is *Il Papiniano* included in the *Tragedie Cinque* (Naples, 1712) written by the great Italian jurist Giovanni Vincenzo Gravina (1664–1718). There is also an anonymous Tory work entitled *Letters of Papinian* (New York, 1779) addressed variously to John Jay and to the People of North America (presumably the author took the jurist's name as his *nom de plume* because of his ethical steadfastness). The 'Papinian' quoted in the epigraph of the second edition of the *Lyrical Ballads* (London, 1800) of Samuel T. Coleridge and William Wordsworth is probably not our jurist, but rather an allusion to the style of Papinus Statius (45/50–*c.*96). See further, D. Chandler, 'Who was Papinian?: The Meaning(s) of the Lyrical Ballad's epigraph', *English Language Notes* 39 (2002), 31–41.

[62] See Lenel, *Paling.*, I, cols. 803–7 for fragments of two-book versions; I, cols. 807–9 for fragments of one-book versions.

[63] Jörs, 'Aemilius Papinianus', col. 574.

[64] *Ibid.*; Ankum, 'Papinian', 8.

[65] Wieacker, *Textstufen*, 419–22; Giuffrè, 'Papiniano', 656–8; and Ankum, 'Papinian', 8.

[66] Coll. 4. 7, 8, 9, 10, 11; 6. 6.

(*b*) *Papinian*, Liber definitionum (*or* Book of Definitions)

This work was originally composed in two books. We have about 62 surviving fragments.[67] The style of the surviving fragments of the work suggests it had a simple style and elementary coverage treating a series of descriptions of legal concepts, probably addressing a twofold audience of law students and working lawyers.[68] The Collator cites the work once as it might not have dovetailed as well to his comparison of other texts.[69]

(*c*) *Papinian*, Liber responsorum (*or* Book of Responses)

This work originally existed in nineteen books. We have many surviving fragments in the *Digest*.[70] The fragments indicate that the work was a collection of responses to legal problems that might have been effective in teaching law students along the lines of the case method.[71] Papinian probably wrote it under the joint reigns of Septimius Severus and Caracalla (r. 198–211).[72] The Collator cites the work once.[73] It is possible that the casuistic nature of the work made it not as attractive to the Collator as the *liber singularis de adulteriis*.

(iv) Modestinus

Herennius Modestinus is sometimes considered the last of the great classical Roman jurists.[74] He seems to have come from the Greek-speaking Eastern Mediterranean and eventually made his way to Rome where he studied under Ulpian.[75] Probably of equestrian status, he, like Papinian Ulpian, and Paulus, entered into an administrative career. Honorè has suggested that he served in the office of

[67] Lenel, *Paling.*, I, cols. 809–13.

[68] Jörs, 'Aemilius Papinianus', col. 574. See also Ankum, 'Papinian', 9, on its didactic nature. See also Costa, *Papiniano*, 177–81.

[69] Coll. 2. 3.

[70] Lenel, *Paling.*, I, cols. 881–946. See comments of Costa, *Papiniano*, 127–76, 196–207.

[71] Berger, 'Papinianus', *Encyclopedic Dictionary*, 617; Ankum, 'Papinian', 9.

[72] Jörs, 'Aemilius Papinianus', col. 573; Ankum, 'Papinian', 9.

[73] Coll. 4. 5.

[74] S. Brassloff, 'Herennius Modestinus', *RE* (Stuttgart, 1912), VIII(1), cols. 668–75; Wenger, *Die Quellen*, 521–2; Kunkel, *Herkunft und soziale Stelle*, 259–61; and, more recently, T. Massiello, *I Libri excusationum di Erennio Modestino* (Naples, 1983).

[75] See Honoré, *Ulpian*, 17, 30, 35. See also Bauman, *Crime and Punishment*, 124, 156.

petitions and became *magister libellorum* under Severus Alexander, perhaps from late October of 223 to January of 226.[76] Later he certainly served as *praefectus vigilum.*[77] A teacher of law himself, he wrote several works, some in Latin and some in Greek (and thus might have been trying to reach a broad audience, possibly as a result of the Antonine Constitution of 212).[78] He wrote several works, fragments of which have survived. Arcadius Charisius praised his works at the end of the third century (*Dig.* 50. 4. 18. 26) showing the high esteem in which lawyers held him in late antiquity.[79] This high regard continued through the fourth and early fifth century to him being enshrined in the Law of Citations of 426 as one of the five great jurists.

(a) Modestinus, Liber differentiarum *(or* Book of Distinctions*)*

Modestinus wrote his *Liber differentiarum* originally in nine books, probably under the reign of Severus Alexander.[80] We have about forty-eight surviving fragments, mostly in the *Digest.*[81] From the surviving fragments, it looks as if the work treated controversial legal questions, which would have been of great use as a teaching manual.[82] The Collator quotes from this work two times.[83]

(v) Gaius

This is the last of the five classical jurists whom the Collator cites in the sense of where he falls in the *Collatio* (Title 16), but also the oldest. Gaius was born under the Emperor Hadrian (r. 117–38) at the latest.[84] A Roman citizen, Gaius' ultimate origins are disputed,[85]

[76] See controversial stylistic analysis of Honoré, *Emperors and Lawyers*, 101–7.

[77] Brassloff, 'Modestinus', 668–70.

[78] See Brassloff, 'Modestinus', 670.

[79] A typographical error in Brassloff, 'Modestinus', 675, gives citation as *Dig.* 50. 4. 8. 26. For an overview of the dating of Arcadius Charius to the late third century, see Frakes, *Contra Potentium Iniurias*, 32–3, esp. n. 64.

[80] Brassloff, 'Modestinus', 673.

[81] Lenel, *Paling.*, I, cols. 701–7.

[82] Berger, 'Modestinus', *Encyclopedic Dictionary*, 585.

[83] Coll. 1. 12 and Coll. 10. 2.

[84] B. Kübler, 'Gaius', *RE* (Stuttgart, 1910), VII(1), cols. 489–508 at 489; Honoré, *Gaius*, xi–xviii; G. Diosdi, 'Gaius, der Rechtsgelehrte (mit einer Bibliographie von R. Wittmann)' in H. Temporini (ed.), *ANRW* (Berlin, 1976), II(15), 605–31; and O. Stanojevic, *Gaius Noster, Plaidoyer pour Gaius* (Amsterdam, 1989). Although delightfully revisionist, R. Samter, 'War Gajus der männliche pseudonym einer Frau?', *Deutsche Juristenzeitung* 13 (1908), 1386–91, has not been accepted.

[85] Kübler, 'Gaius', 490.

as indeed is his whole name.[86] He probably studied in Rome,[87] but may have taught in the east (perhaps at the law school in Berytus). He lived until at least 178 and wrote several works of which the *Digest* preserves hundreds of passages.[88] His work would substantially influence later European law.[89]

(a) *Gaius,* Institutiones *(or* Institutes*)*

The *Institutiones* of Gaius was a teaching manual, probably derived from his lectures (*c.*160–1).[90] It is composed of four books for student use.[91] This work played a large role in the later composition of the *Institutes* of Justinian in the sixth century.[92] Luckily, B. G. Niebuhr rediscovered a palimpsest of this work in Verona in 1816.[93] The Collator cites once, but in an extremely long passage.[94]

(vi) The *Codex Gregorianus*

The *Codex Gregorianus* represents arguably the first late Roman law code, being assembled *c.*291 CE.[95] There is scholarly debate as to

[86] Honoré, *Gaius*, 12–17.

[87] For jurists influential in this period, see Bauman, *Lawyers and Politics in the Early Roman Empire.*

[88] Lenel, *Paling*, I, cols. 181–266.

[89] D. Kelly, 'Gaius Noster: Substructures of Western social thought', *American Historical Review* 84 (1979), 619–48.

[90] For recent text and commentary of Book III of Gaius' work, see the series of editions by H. L. W. Nelson and U. Manthe, *Gai Institutiones III. 1–87*; *Gai Institutiones III. 88–181: Die Kontraktsobligationen* (Berlin, 1999); *Gai Institutiones III. 182–225: Die Deliktsobligationen* (Berlin, 2007).

[91] Bauman, *Crime and Punishment*, 148–9.

[92] Berger, 'Gaius', *Encyclopedic Dictionary*, 481; Lenel, *Paling.*, I, col. 242; Wenger, *Die Quellen*, 602–8; and, more recently, see the essays collected in E. Metzger, *A Companion to Justinian's Institutes* (Ithaca, 1998), esp. G. MacCormack, 'Sources', 1–17.

[93] See description by Kelly, 'Gaius Noster', 619, esp. the recounting of Savigny's hopes ('*Das muss ein neues Leben unter unseren Juristen geben*!').

[94] Coll. 16. 2. 1–17.

[95] Liebs, *Italien*, 134. For further overview of the *Codex Gregorianus*, see Sirks, *Theodosian Code*, 4–8 and Corcoran, *Empire of the Tetrarchs*, 25–42, esp. at 37. P. Jörs, 'Codex Gregorianus', *RE* (Stuttgart, 1900), IV(1), cols. 161–4, is still useful as are G. Rotondi, 'Studi sulle fonti del codice giustinianeo' in *Scritti Giuridici* (Pavia, 1922), 110–283; G. Scherillo, 'Teodosiano, Gregoriano, Ermogeniano' in *Studi in memoria di U. Ratti* (Milan, 1934), 247–323; and Wenger, *Die Quellen*, 534–5. See also Hans-Julius Wolff, 'Vorgregorianische Reskriptensammlungen', *ZRG (R.A.)* 69 (1952), 128–53, on earlier law collections being restricted to defined topics. See Honoré, *Emperors and Lawyers*, 139–85, on the style of the texts that survive.

whether this work was originally made as a private collection or if it was ordered or abetted by the state.[96] It apparently became widely known, survived as a book into the fifth century when it was used as a source for the *Theodosian Code* in 438 (and was also used by the Visigoths).[97] Finally, it seems to have been used as a source by the compilers of the *Code of Justinian* in the early sixth century. The *Codex Gregorianus* itself was lost apparently after the compilation of the *Code of Justinian.* The *Codex Gregorianus* was also an important source for the Collator. This is fortunate for us because the *Collatio* provides an important vehicle for some fragments of this lost code.[98] The Collator cites this code seven times.[99]

(vii) *Codex Hermogenianus*

This second late Roman law code followed shortly after the *Codex Gregorianus* in Diocletian's reign.[100] It may have been released in Milan in 295.[101] The compiler Hermogenian was apparently *magister libellorum* and then later praetorian prefect, mirroring the path of some earlier jurists.[102] He also apparently wrote a work known as the *Iuris Epitomae.*[103] We have only a few fragments of the *Codex Hermogenianus* that apparently was short enough to be divided into titles, but not separate books.[104] The Collator quotes from this late

[96] See, among others, W. Turpin, 'The purpose of the Roman law codes', *ZRG (R.A.)* 104 (1987), 620–30; M. Sperandio, *Codex Gregorianus: origini e vicende* (Naples, 2005).

[97] See Jörs, 'Codex Gregorianus', 161. See further, *FIRA*, II, 633–65, 667–79.

[98] On the Collator's use of the Code, see further, Frakes, 'The Collatio and the Codex Gregorianus', For an overview of all the fragments, see P. Krüger, 'Codicis Gregoriani Fragmenta' in Mommsen, Krüger, and Studemond (eds.), *Collectio Librorum Iuris Anteiustiniani*, III, 236–42.

[99] Coll. 1. 8, 9, 10; 3. 4; 6. 4; 10. 8; and 15. 3.

[100] See P. Jörs, 'Codex Hermogenianus', *RE* (Stuttgart, 1900), VI(1), cols. 164–7 and Wenger, *Die Quellen*, 534–5. For more detail on the *Codex Hermogenianus*, see A. Cenderellli, *Ricerche sul 'Codex Hermogenianus'* (Milan, 1965); S. Corcoran, 'The publication of law in the era of the Tetrarchs: Diocletian, Galerius, Gregorius, Hermogenian' in Demandt *et al.*, *Diokletian und die Terarchie*, 56–73; and Sirks, *Theodosian Code*, 4–8.

[101] Liebs, *Italien*, 137; Corcoran, *Empire of the Tetrarchs*, 37.

[102] See Liebs, 'Hermogenians Prätorianerpräfektur inschriftlich bezeugt', 385–6; Honoré, *Emperors and Lawyers*, 163–81; and Corcoran, *Empire of the Tetrachs*, 76–7.

[103] See Liebs, *Hermogenians Iuris Epitomae.*

[104] P. Krüger, 'Codicis Hermogeniani Fragmenta' in Mommsen, Krüger, and Studemond, *Collectio Librorum Iuris Anteiustiniani*, III, 242–5.

Roman law code twice (but the second is an extended extract with several constitutions).[105]

(viii) Contemporary Laws

In addition to the juristic sources, and the *Codices* of Gregorianus and Hermogenianus, the Collator had some recent constitutions at his disposal at some level. While there has been debate among scholars as to how constitutions were released and collected in the later empire, the evolving view seems to be that some laws were held in provincial archives and then better and better central archives were kept after 380 in the east, and after 395 in the west.[106] Since the Collator made little use of such constitutions, it seems unlikely that he was actively working with such an archive in Rome or Milan where such laws may have been kept.

(a) Constitution of Valentinian, Theodosius, and Arcadius of 390 (Coll. 5. 3 = CTh *9. 7. 6)*

The clearest example of a contemporary constitution cited by the Collator occurs, as we have seen, at Coll. 5. 3 regarding homosexual prostitution. The statement at the end of the fuller version in the *Collatio* states that it was posted in the month of May in the *atrium Minervae* in Rome (while the version of the law surviving as *CTh* 9. 7. 6 provides the year as 390). Liebs argues that the atrium of Minerva may have been a legal archive as there was a large library associated with the temple here.[107]

(b) Novellae Constitutiones *(other 'Recent Constitutions')*

At Coll. 14. 3. 6, after a long passage from Ulpian on the *Lex Fabia*, the Collator, in a moment when we see his voice appearing as it occasionally does, comments that kidnapping is treated more harshly

[105] Coll. 6. 5; 10. 3, 10. 4, 10. 5, and 10. 6.

[106] See Seeck, 'Die Zeitfolge der Gesetze Constantins', 1–44, 177–251; Sirks, 'Sources of the Code' in Harries and Wood, *The Theodosian Code*, 45–67, esp. 46–53; Matthews, 'Making of the text' in Harries and Wood, 19–41; Matthews, *Laying Down the Law*, 168–99 ('Delivering the law') and 200–53 ('The editors at work'); and, most recently, Sirks, *Theodosian Code*, 109–38.

[107] Liebs, *Italien*, 166.

ex novellis constitutionibus ('from recent constitutions') than in Ulpian's day, although he allows that Paulus (actually referring to a quotation from the *Sententiae* of Pseudo-Paulus cited at Coll. 14. 2. 2) also suggested harsh penalties. While we saw in the last chapter how this passage is important for dating the work, the relevant thing here is that the Collator knew of at least some 'recent constitutions'. It is possible that these are the constitutions that later survived in edited form as *CJ* 9. 20. 7 dated to December of 287 and *CTh* 9. 19. 1 from August of 315. Or, he might be referring to constitutions that are now lost.

B. THE COLLATOR'S BIBLE

While the vast majority of the quotations compiled in the *Collatio* are from the Roman jurists, the Collator gave primacy to passages from the Bible with which he started each of the sixteen titles within the work. There has been a long scholarly dispute over the Collator's source for his Latin translations of quotations from the Hebrew Bible.[108] Theories suggest he either made his own translation from the Greek Septuagint, or worked directly from the Hebrew Scriptures themselves, or used the famous Latin translation of Jerome, or that he drew from an older Latin translation of the Bible (traditionally called the *Vetus Latina* or Old Latin Bible).[109] It has even been

[108] This section is a revision of aspects of my 'The *Lex Dei* and the Latin Bible', *HTR* 100 (4) (2007), 425–41. In the intervening years, I was able to expand aspects of the research through further close work with early Christian sources (both Greek and Syriac) and Hebrew Scripture. I then refashioned this research as part of a larger chapter on the Collator's sources. I would like to thank the Rev. Dr Robert Rigg for his comments regarding biblical scholarship and an array of biblical passages.

[109] Hyamson, xxxiii, suggests that the biblical quotations in the *Collatio* are either a 'free translation' from the Greek Septuagint or are from the 'Itala, properly styled the Vetus Latina'. However, at li, Hyamson also posits the Collator was hostile to Jerome because he chose not to use the Vulgate. See Volterra, *Collatio*, 53–86, for an argument that the Collator compared and contrasted the Septuagint with the Hebrew Scriptures in making his translations. On this theory, see further, B. Cohen, *Jewish and Roman Law* (New York, 1966), 5–6. Mommsen, *Collatio*, 130–4, believed the Collator used the *Vetus Latina*. F. Schulz, 'Die biblischen Texte in der Collatio Legum Mosaicarum et Romanarum', *SDHI* 2 (1936), 20–43, argued against Volterra's thesis of the Collator creating his own translations. Smits, *Collatio*, 31–43, suggests that the

suggested that the Collator did not use a Bible at all, but instead some sort of digested handbook of biblical quotations.[110] Examination of biblical passages from the *Collatio* in conjunction with other surviving Latin versions indicates that the Collator used some version of the Old Latin Bible. While analysis of the Collator's use of the Bible can also shed light on his methodology and purpose, and these will be examined in subsequent two chapters, knowing what kind of biblical source he had can complete our picture of the Collator's library.

Examination of the reception of the Hebrew Bible in the west and its translation into Latin can clarify the type of biblical sources available when the Collator composed his work in the early 390s. When working with the Hebrew Bible, it is important to recognize its constituent parts (and to avoid the Christian-centered term 'Old Testament'). The *Torah* (or 'Law') contains the first five books of the Hebrew Bible (Genesis, Exodus, Leviticus, Numbers, and Deuteronomy). These books were traditionally seen as being written by Moses after divine revelation.[111] These five books are also called the *Pentateuch* (or 'Five Books in a case'). The *Torah* or *Pentateuch* includes the 613 *Mitzvot* (or 'Commandments') by which Jews should live their lives. The *Torah* is a critical part of the *Tanakh* (an acronym for the three major parts of the Hebrew Bible: *Torah*, *Nevi'im* (or 'Prophets'), and *Ketuvim* (or 'Writings')).[112] *Mikra* (or 'Scriptures') is another term for the same three major portions (and thus is a synonym for *Tanakh*). *Halakhah* refers to the collective body of Jewish law including the 613 *Mitzvot* as well as later laws contained in the *Mishnah* (the *Talmud*, the *Midrashim*, and other Rabbinic texts).

Collator did not use the *Vetus Latina* as his source for the biblical quotations, but instead one of many Latin translations in circulation, believing that there was one distinct *Vetus Latina*, and not many.

[110] See H. Kaufhold, Review of G. Galbiati and S. Noja, *Precetti e Canoni giuridico-morali per arabi christiani*, I in *Oriens Christianus* 53 (1969), 266–70 at 267.

[111] The traditional view that Moses composed the Pentateuch was shaken by the documentary hypothesis of Julius Wellhausen, *Geschichte Israels*, 2 vols. (Berlin, 1878). See further, E. Nicholson, *The Pentateuch in the Twentieth Century: The legacy of Julius Wellhausen* (Oxford, 1998).

[112] The Masoretic Hebrew text of the Hebrew Bible itself was developed from an evolving tradition by Jewish scholars called Masoretes who systematized symbols for the inclusion of vowels and pronunciation for the Hebrew text in the sixth to the tenth centuries CE. For a modern scholarly text, see K. Elliger and W. Rudoph (eds.), *Biblia Hebraica Stuttgartensia* (New York, 1987).

Hebrew Scripture travelled to the Latin West together with the expansion of Christianity. As Christianity slowly spread in the first century CE, many early Christians used the Hebrew Bible through the translation of the Greek Septuagint.[113] Moreover, descriptions in the Gospels present Jesus quoting the words of Hebrew prophets as found in the Greek Septuagint translation. Of course, early Christian texts alluded to passages from the prophets in passages from the Septuagint as foreshadowing Christian truth. Moreover, the Christian liturgy included readings from the Hebrew Scriptures through the medium of the Septuagint.[114] By the end of the second century, Latin had grown in use among Christians in the west.[115] Already by 180, it appears likely that the martyrs of Scillium (in the Roman province of *Africa proconsularis*) may have had a Latin translation of at least some of Paul's letters.[116] While Paul's letters were the earliest Christian written texts, the Gospels were written *c.*65–95 and it would seem likely that if the Scillitan martyrs had a Latin translation of the Epistles of Paul, they also probably had Latin versions of the Gospels since they are such central texts for Christians.[117]

The North African theologian Tertullian appears to have used some kind of Latin version of the Hebrew Scriptures in the composition of his *Apologeticus* at the end of the second century.[118] While

[113] See, among others, M. Hengel, *The Septuagint as Christian Scripture: Its prehistory and the problem of its canon* (Edinburgh, 2002); A. Wasserstein and D. Wasserstein, *The Legend of the Septuagint: From classical antiquity to today* (Cambridge, 2007); and H. D. F. Sparks, 'The Latin Bible' in H. Wheeler Robinson (ed.), *The Bible in its Ancient and English Versions* (Oxford, 1940), 100–27 at 100. See the 24-volume *Septuaginta Vetus Testamentum Graecum*, ed. J. W. Wevers *et al.* (Göttingen, 1974–) for a modern scholarly text and A. Pietersma (tr.), *A New English Translation of the Septuagint* (Oxford, 2000).

[114] For example, see Justin, *Apol.* 1. 67.

[115] Jerome, *De Vir. Illust.* 34, 40, and 53. See further, Metzger, *Early Versions*, 287. For a standard study of Tertullian, see T. D. Barnes, *Tertullian* (Oxford, 1971).

[116] On this point, see Metzger, *Early Versions*, 288–9 and Arthur Vööbus, *Early Versions of the New Testament* (Stockholm, 1954), 37. See also Metzger's *The Canon of the New Testament: Its origins, development, and significance* (Oxford, 1997) for a lucid overview of the evolution of the New Testament canon.

[117] On the dating of the Gospels, see V. Taylor, *The Gospels: A short introduction*, 9th edn (London, 1960), 7–8; R. Brown, *An Introduction to the New Testament* (New York, 1997); and, in a recent accessible text, B. Ehrman, *The New Testament: A historical introduction to the early Christian writings*, 4th edn (New York and Oxford, 2008), 55–70. Regarding the Scillitan martyrs having Latin Gospels, see Metzger, *Early Versions*, 289, and Vööbus, *Early Versions of the New Testament*, 37.

[118] See J. Kenrick, 'The Versio Itala, its age, name and origin', *Theological Review* 11 (1874), 318–30 at 320, and Sparks, 'Latin Bible', 108.

Tertullian at times may have made his own translations from the Septuagint, he also used an already existing Latin translation.[119] Such a Latin version was also used by the mid third-century Cyprian of Carthage in his *Testimonia ad Quirinum*.[120] Cyprian's rival Novatian also apparently used the Latin translation of the Old Latin Bible.[121]

By the early third century, several Latin translations existed in the west.[122] Generally, scholars identified the African and the European versions of an Old Latin Bible. Some scholars argue that there may been a third, the *Itala* mentioned by St Augustine (354–430).[123]

Since Augustine's description of this version (*De Doctrina Christiana*, 2. 52–3 (2. 15. 21–2)) could greatly influence our view of what kind of Latin Bible that the Collator might have had, it is useful to reproduce it here. Discussing the significance of reading Scripture, Augustine stated:

> But inaccuracy must be excluded, for the attention of those who wish to know the divine scripture must first focus on the task of correcting the manuscripts, so that uncorrected ones give place to corrected ones, assuming that they belong to the same class of translation. Among actual

[119] H. A. A. Kennedy, 'Latin versions, The old' in J. Hastings (ed.), *A Dictionary of the Bible* (Edinburgh, 1900), III, 47–62 at 55. Regarding the influence of Tatian's *Diatesseron* on Latin translations of the Bible, see J. N. Birdsall, 'The New Testament text', in P. R. Ackroyd and C. F. Evans (eds.), *The Cambridge History of the Bible*, I: *From the Beginnings to Jerome* (Cambridge, 1970), 308–77 at 345. On the Syriac translation of the *Diatesseron*, see further A. Baumstark, 'Die Evangelienzitate Novatians', *Oriens Christianus*, 3rd series, 5 (1930), 1–14.

[120] See B. Metzger, *The Text of the New Testament: Its transmission, corruption, and restoration*, 3rd edn (Oxford, 1992), 73. Regarding the possibility of k (the scholarly label for the Bobbio manuscript of the Old Latin Bible) being composed outside of Africa, see Kennedy, 'Latin versions', 54, citing William Sanday, *Academy*, 11 May, 1889. On Cyprian, see further, among others, M. A. Fahey, *Cyprian and the Bible* (Tübingen, 1971) and, more recently, J. Patout Burns, *Cyprian the Bishop* (London and New York, 2002).

[121] See Kennedy, 'Latin versions', 55; J. N. Birdsall, 'The New Testament text' in Ackroyd and Evans, *Cambridge History of the Bible*, 308–77 at 371; Sparks, 'Latin Bible', 108. For further on Novatian, see A. d'Ales, *Novatien: Étude sur la théologie romaine au milieu du iiie siècle* (Paris, 1924); P. Mattei, 'L'anthropologie de Novatien: Affinités, perspectives, et limites', *REAug* 38 (1992), 232–59; and, most recently, J. Papandrea, *The Trinitarian Theology of Novatian of Rome: A study in third-century orthodoxy* (Lewiston, NY, 2008).

[122] L. Ziegler, *Die lateinischen Bibelübersetzungen vor Hieronymus und die Itala des Augustinus* (Munich, 1879), 131.

[123] See B. F. Westcott and F. J. A. Hort, *The New Testament in the Original Greek* (New York, 1882), II, 78–84; Sparks, 'Latin Bible', 107; Birdsall, 'New Testament text', 372.

translations the *Itala* should be preferred to all others, as it keeps more closely to the words without sacrificing clarity of expression.[124]

For well over a century, scholars have struggled with the concept of this mysterious *Itala* translation. Because it presents such a difficult issue, some have even tried to emend the text of this passage and thus solve the problem more easily.[125] One bold scholar argued that the text should read *Italia* instead of *Itala* (which might have meant the area between the Alps and the Po River in the late fourth and early fifth century).[126] Augustine might then have encountered this text when he was in northern Italy during the time leading up to his conversion. One other revisionist argument holds that the *Itala* was actually another name for Jerome's Vulgate translation of the Bible. However, there is no clear reason why this work would have been labelled as *Itala* and scholars have not accepted this hypothesis.[127] Therefore, any radical emendation of this passage creates even more problems than the existing text.[128]

The authority of Augustine had such an impact on succeeding generations that any known Latin Bible before that of St Jerome has been labelled *Itala* by many modern scholars.[129] However, there must

[124] Augustine, *De Doctrina Christiana*, 2. 52–3 (2. 15. 21–2): '*Nam codicibus emendandis primitus debet invigilare sollertia eorum qui Scripturas divinas nosse desiderant, ut emendates non emendati cedant, ex uno dumtaxat interpretationis genere venientes. In ipsis autem interpretationibus Itala ceteris praeferatur, nam est verborum tenacior cum perspicuitate sententiae.*' For Latin text and English translation, see R. P. H. Green (ed. and tr.), *Augustine: De Doctrina Christiana* (Oxford, 1995), 80–1. For discussion of the *De Doctrina Christiana*, see D. W. H. Arnold and P. Bright (eds.), *De Doctrina Christiana: A classic of Western culture* (Notre Dame, 1995).

[125] See Kenrick, 'Versio Itala', 321–2. For an overview of various suggested emendations, including one by Richard Bentley, to replace Itala, see Metzger, *Early Versions*, 291–3. On the fervour for emendation of Bentley, see Ulrich von Wilamowitz-Möllendorff, *Geschichte der Philologie* (Stuttgart, 1921; reprint, 1998), 35–7, and L. D. Reynolds and N. G. Wilson, *Scribes and Scholars*, 3rd edn (Oxford, 1991), 184–8.

[126] See Kenrick, 'Versio Itala', 322–8. On Augustine's conversion, see *Confessions*, Book 8 and Peter Brown, *Augustine of Hippo* (Berkeley, 1967), 106–14.

[127] F. C. Burkitt, *The Old Latin and the Itala* (Cambridge, 1896) and his 'Saint Augustine's Bible and the Itala', *JTS* 11 (1910), 258–68 and 447–58.

[128] See Constantine von Tischendorf, *Novum Testamentum Graece*, 7th edn (Leipzig, 1869), ccxli–ccxlii; Kenrick, 'Versio Itala', 328–9; Metzger, *Early Versions*, 291–3.

[129] See Kenrick, 'Versio Itala', 322–3; Hyamson's table on 153–8 (although earlier, at xxxiii, he allows *Vetus Latina* is a better label); Adolf Jülicher, *Itala: Das Neue Testament in altlateinischer Überlieferung* (Berlin, 1938).

have been several Latin translations in the west. Augustine's *Itala* was just one of many that we can call an 'Old Latin Bible' or *Vetus Latina* as a whole.[130] Moreover, Augustine himself describes how many versions of the Old Latin Bible were available slightly earlier in the same work cited above (*De Doctrina Christiana*, 2. 36 (2. 11. 16)):

> Translators of scripture from Hebrew into Greek can be easily counted, but not so translators into Latin, for in the early days of the faith any person who got hold of a Greek manuscript and fancied that he had some ability in the two languages went ahead and translated it.[131]

There is other evidence for Latin translations of the Bible from the beginning of the fourth century. During the Great Persecution of Diocletian, 34 Biblical manuscripts were seized in the town of Cirta in North Africa.[132] Since one provincial capital had so many copies that were found by the authorities, there might well have been thousands of copies of parts of the Bible in translation throughout the west.[133] Naturally, the text of many of these translations may have interacted with each other since the early third century.[134] While the style of the Old Latin Bible was fairly simple as a literal translation,[135] it was obviously used widely and became even more widespread after Constantine's reign.

[130] J. Schildenberger, 'Die Itala des hl. Augustinus' in B. Fischer and V. Fiala (eds.), *Colligere fragmenta: Festschrift Alban Dold* (Beuron, 1950), 84–102, who suggested that the *Itala* was one form. On collective term, see Kennedy, 'Latin versions', 47.

[131] Augustine, *De Doctrina Christiana*, 2. 36 (2. 11. 16): '*Qui enim Scripturas ex hebraea in graecam verterunt, numerari possunt, Latini autem interpretes nullo modo. Ut enim cuique primis fidei temporibus in manus venit codex graecus, et aliquantulum facultatis sibi utriusque linguae habere videbatur, ausus est interpretari*' (text and translation following Green, *Doctrina Christina*, 72–3).

[132] See *Gesta apud Zenophilum* in C. Ziwsa (ed.), *S. Optati Milevitani libri VII*, in *CSEL* 26 (Vienna, 1893), 187–8, following P. McGurk, 'The oldest manuscripts of the Latin Bible' in R. Gameson (ed.), *The Early Medieval Bible: Its production, decoration and use* (Cambridge, 1994), 1–23 at 1 n. 1. For recent studies of the scholarship regarding Diocletian's Persecution, see W. A. Löhr, 'Some observations on Karl-Heinz Schwartc's "Dioklctian's Christengesetz"', *Vigiliae Christianae* 56 (2002), 75–95, and Digeser, 'Christian or Hellene? The Great Persecution and the problem of identity', 36–57.

[133] For analysis of this example, see McGurk, 'Oldest manuscripts', 1.

[134] See Kennedy, 'Latin versions', 56.

[135] Regarding the Latinity of the Old Latin Bible, see Arnobius, *Adv. Gentes*, 1. 58. See further, H. Roensch, *Itala und Vulgata*, 2nd edn. (Marburg, 1875). The young, pre-Christian, Augustine was apparently not impressed by the Old Latin Bible (see further, *Confessions*, 3. 5; Sparks, 'Latin Bible', 110; and Brown, *Augustine of Hippo*, 42–4).

Perhaps because of the stylistic liabilities of the Old Latin Bible, Damasus, the Bishop of Rome, asked his secretary Jerome to start work on a new Latin translation in 382. Jerome quickly translated the Gospels by 383 and then turned to other parts of the New Testament.[136] He eventually settled in Bethlehem in 386 where he studied Origen's *Hexapla*, learned Hebrew, and began his Latin translation of the Hebrew Scriptures. Jerome probably completed his translation of the Books of Samuel and Kings sometime in 391.[137] Then he shifted to translating Proverbs, Job, Ecclesiastes, and Esdras from *c.*391 to 394. From 392 to 395 he also wrote his *De Viribus Illustribus* ('Concerning Famous Men') as well as several Biblical commentaries. Finally, Jerome finished his translation of the rest of the Hebrew Scriptures from *c.*398 to 405.[138] His Latin translation would eventually replace the Old Latin Bible over the course of centuries and was the commonly used text of the Bible in the west by the central Middle Ages.[139] Its place in the Roman Catholic Church would be later enshrined by the decision of the Council of Trent of the Counter Reformation in 1546 that assigned the title of 'Vulgate' to the Latin translation of Jerome.

When searching for the Collator's Latin Bible, we must first address the question of whether he might have used Jerome's Vulgate. The answer appears to be no, for two reasons. First, Jerome probably had not yet finished translating the books of Exodus, Numbers, Leviticus, and Deuteronomy at the time the Collator finished compiling his work between May of 392 and January of 395. Jerome had finished the books of Kings and Samuel in 391 and probably moved on to other parts of the Hebrew Scriptures sometime from 392 to 395. However, it seems likely that he did not complete his translation of the Pentateuch until sometime between 398 and 405. While it is impossible to extrapolate an exact rate of translation, the Pentateuch is lengthy and the Hebrew challenging

[136] See Sparks, 'Latin Bible', 111.

[137] See H. D. F. Sparks, 'Jerome as biblical scholar' in Ackroyd and Evans, *Cambridge History of the Bible*, 510–41 at 511–16. These books offer a history of Israel and Judah and in some traditions are called the 'Books of the Kingdoms.'

[138] See Sparks, 'Latin Bible', 112. For a recent chronology of Jerome's works, see M. Williams, *The Monk and the Book: Jerome and the making of Christian scholarship* (Chicago, 2006), 267–301.

[139] For the reception of Jerome's translation in late antiquity, see Rufinus, *Apol.* 2. 32–3.

and it is inconceivable that Jerome could have completely translated these books into Latin and that the Collator would have subsequently received them and then compiled his own work all by 395.[140]

Comparing and contrasting passages in the *Collatio* with parallel passages in the Old Latin Bible and the Vulgate provides another basis for arguing that the Collator used the Old Latin Bible and not Jerome's translation. Although no complete manuscript of the Old Latin Bible is extant, portions have survived and other fragments can be gleaned through the study of quotations in patristic authors and theologians.[141] Although there are partial surviving manuscripts of sections of the Old Latin Bible,[142] the largest single surviving portion of the Old Latin Bible is the Lyons manuscript (or *Codex Lugduniensis*) which contains about one-third of the Book of Genesis, one half of the Book of Exodus, three-quarters of the Books of Leviticus, and all of the Books of Numbers, Deuteronomy, Joshua, and almost all of the Book of Judges.[143] This collection of seven books (or Heptateuch) was successfully edited in two parts in the late nineteenth and beginning of the twentieth century.[144] The Lyons

[140] Hyamson, xxxiv, suggests that the Collator would not have used Jerome's translation because it was not yet formally adopted by the Church (although parts of Jerome's translation were certainly known in the fifth century). Hyamson's assertion, at li, that the Collator did not use Jerome's translation because there was hostility between the two of them would seem to contradict his other argument.

[141] The eighteenth-century Pierre Sabatier's work took the critical first steps in the reconstruction of the Old Latin Bible when he compiled all known extant fragments in his *Bibliorum sacrorum Latinae versiones antiquae seu Vetus Italica* (Reims, 1743). Sabatier, however, followed the relatively loose canons of scholarship of his time and did not always indicate what his sources were for his fragments of the Old Latin Bible. This problematic methodology is implied by Smits, *Collatio*, 57 and 63, and Schulz, 'biblischen Texte', 29 and 38, who must cite Sabatier himself as a source for passages from the *Vetus Latina*, because that scholar's marginal citations are unfortunately unclear.

[142] For instance, at Bobbio, Munich, Würzburg. See full list in Kennedy, 'Latin versions', 49–52 (manuscripts) and 52–3 (fragments in theological works).

[143] See Sparks, 'Latin Bible', 104.

[144] Ulysse Robert, *Pentateuchi Versio Latina Antiquissima e Codice Lugdunensi* (Paris, 1881) for Genesis, Exodus, Numbers and the first part of Deuteronomy from the famous Lyons manuscript discovered by Léopold Delisle; Ulysse Robert, *Heptateuchi parties posterioris versio Latina antiquissima e codice Lugdunensi* (Lyons, 1900) for Deuteronomy, Judges, and Joshua. Regarding the signficance of Robert's work, see N. McLean, 'The Lyons Old Latin Heptateuch', *JTS*, o. s. 2 (1901), 305–8; J. McIntosh, *A Study of Augustine's Versions of Genesis* (Chicago, 1912), 79–80; Max L. Margolis, 'Additions to Field from the Lyons Codex of the Old Latin', *Journal of the American Oriental Society* 33 (1913), 254–8.

manuscript dates to the sixth or seventh century, although it seems to be a copy of a Latin translation made sometime from the late third century to the late fourth century.[145]

Analysis of some passages from the Hebrew Bible in the *Collatio* confirms that the Collator did not make his own Latin translation from either the Septuagint or from the Hebrew text directly. Indeed, this analysis will also show that he did not use the Vulgate, but instead used a version of the Old Latin Bible as his source.[146] Analysis of a few passages serve to show his dependence upon this translation (and I will underline verbatim terms in Latin and provide English translations).

The first of these examples occurs at the beginning of the *Collatio*. Here, the text of Coll. 1. 1 (which quotes the law of Moses related at Numbers 35: 20–1) reads:

3. si autem per inimicitiam inpulerit eum vel inmiserit super eum aliquod vas ex insidiis et mortuus fuerit, 4. Vel per iram percusserit eum manu et mortuus fuerit, moriatur.

[3. And if, however, through hostility someone strikes him or throws an implement at him from an ambush and he dies, 4. or strikes him by hand through anger and he dies, let him die.][147]

For the corresponding passage (Numbers, 35. 20–1), the Old Latin Bible text of the Lyons manuscript reads:

20. Si autem per inimicitiam inpulerit eum, et inmiserit super eum omne vas ex insidia, et mortuus fuerit, 21. Vel per iram percusserit eum de manu, et mortuus fuerit, morti moriatur qui percusserit: homicida est: morti puniatur homicida.[148]

[145] On the dating, see Robert, *Pentateuchi*, cxli–cxlii; McClean, 'Lyons', 396.

[146] Hyamson, 153–8, presented the groundwork for such an analysis, but did not reach a firm conclusion. Moreover, he preferred the label 'Itala' that was in scholarly vogue in the early twentieth century as opposed to the more open-ended *Vetus Latina* or Old Latin Bible. Hyamson appears not to have seen the second volume of Robert's text of the Lyons manuscript that contained passages from the book of Deuteronomy also cited in the *Collatio*. Here I revise the diction of Smits, *Collatio*, 32, of using the phrase *Vetus Latina* to refer only to the single alleged *Itala* ('*Vetus Latina, meer bekend onder den naam van Itala*'), and use the broader label of 'Old Latin Bible' for Latin translations existing before Jerome's work.

[147] Unless noted otherwise, translations from the *Collatio* are my own.

[148] Robert, *Pentateuchi Versio Latina*, 308.

[20. If, moreover, someone through hostility strikes him, and throws any kind of implement at him from an ambush, and he dies, 21. or strikes someone through anger by hand, and he dies, let he who struck die: he is a murderer: murder is punished by death.][149]

The fact that so many common words appear in the passage in the *Collatio* and the Lyons manuscript of the Old Latin Bible suggests there might be a close relationship. Moreover, the only section that is not identical in the Lyons manuscript is the clarification that 'murder is punished by death' which might be an addition by a later scribe in the manuscript tradition. To show how close the similarity between the passage in the *Collatio* and the Lyons manuscript is, let us turn to the analogous passage in Jerome's Vulgate (Numbers 35. 20–1):

20. si per odium quis hominem impulerit vel iecerit quippiam in eum per insidias 21. aut cum esset inimicus manu percusserit et ille mortuus fuerit percussor homicidii reus erit.[150]

[20. If through hatred someone hits a human being or throws something at him through an ambush 21. or, since he was an enemy, he struck him by hand and that one died, the striker is guilty of murder.][151]

While the substance of Jerome's translation is similar, the stylistic difference in his text indicates that the Collator's Latin translation was much more similar to that seen in the Lyons manuscript.

The close relationship between the biblical text in the *Collatio* at Coll. 1. 1. 3–4 and that in the Lyons manuscript of the Old Latin Bible is not a unique case. At Coll. 1. 5. 1–4, for example, where the Collator quoted Numbers 35: 22–5, we read:

[149] My translation from the Lyons Codex of the Old Latin Bible.

[150] H. Quentin (ed.), *Biblia Sacra Iuxta Latinam Vulgatam Versionem ad Codicum Fidem. Libros Numerorum et Deuteronomii ex Interpretatione Sancti Hieronymi* (Rome, 1936), 280. The Stuttgart Vulgate text bears no major differences; see R. Weber *et al.*, *Biblia Sacra Iuxta Vulgatam Versionem* (Stuttgart, 1969).

[151] To render the comparison and contrast of the biblical passages for this chapter most clearly, I have also made the English translations from the Vulgate for this chapter. English translations include the Douay-Rheims version made by refugee English Catholic clerics at Douai and Reims from 1582–1609 during the English Reformation. Later revised by Bishop Richard Challoner in the eighteenth century with influence from the Protestant King James Version (KJV), this Catholic English translation would later be replaced by the Jerusalem Bible in 1966. For a readable survey of the creation of the KJV, see A. Nicolson, *God's Secretaries: The making of the King James Bible* (New York, 2003).

1. Si autem subito non per inimicitiam inmiserit super eum aliquod vas non ex insidiis 2. Vel lapidem, quo moriatur, non per dolum et ceciderit super eum et mortuus fuerit, si autem non inimicus eius fuerit neque quaesierit male facere ei, 3. Iudicabitis inter eum, qui percussit, et proximum mortui secundum iudicia haec, 4. Et liberabitis percussorem.

[1. If, however, someone neither through hostility nor from an ambush suddenly throws an implement or a stone at someone, 2. by which someone might die (not through intention), and it strikes someone and makes him dead, but he was not his enemy nor sought to do evil to him, 3. you shall judge between the person who struck and the relative of the dead man according to these judgments, 4. and you shall free the person who struck.]

In the Lyons manuscript of the Old Latin Bible, the analogous verse (Numbers 35: 22–5) reads:

22. Si autem subito, non per inimicitiam, inmiserit super omne vas non ex insidia, 23. Vel omnem lapidem quo moriatur non per dolum; et occiderit super eum, et mortuus fuerit, si autem non inimicus eius fuerit, neque quaesierit malefacere ei: 24. Et iudicabit synagoga inter eum qui percusserit et proximum sanguinis secundum iudicia haec. 25. Et liberavit synagoga percussorem a proximo sanguinis.[152]

[22. If, however, someone neither through hostility nor from an ambush suddenly throws any kind of implement or stone at someone, 2. by which someone might die (not through intention), and it strikes someone and makes him dead, but he was not his enemy nor sought to do evil to him: 24. And the Synagogue will judge between he who struck and the nearest of the blood relatives according to this justice. 25. And the Synagogue shall free he who struck from the nearest of the blood relatives. And let the Synagogue arrange that he be safe in the city, to which he had fled, and live there until the death of his high priest, who they anointed with holy oil.][153]

While the Collator condensed the text of the passage, other differences in the passages here are extremely minor and, in the case of *occiderit* as opposed to *ceciderit* might even be the product of scribal error.[154] Nonetheless, comparison of the text of the Biblical passage at Coll. 1. 5 with Numbers 35: 22–3 in the Lyons manuscript indicates that the Collator seems to be working from a text of the Old Latin Bible.[155]

[152] Robert, *Pentateuchi*, 308–9.

[153] My translation from the Lyons Codex of the Old Latin Bible.

[154] See Hyamson, 58.

[155] As opposed to the view of Ostersetzer, 'La Collatio', 75, who argues that the Collator here used the *Mishnah* (*Sanhedrin*, 1, 61) as his source for the Biblical quotation.

As before, we can contrast Numbers 35: 22–5 in the Vulgate:

22. quod si fortuito et absque odio 23. Et inimicitiis quicquam horum fecerit 24. et hoc audiente populo fuerit comprobatum atque inter percussorem et propinquum sanguinis quaestio ventilata 25. Liberabitur innocens de ultoris manu et reducetur per sententiam in urbem ad quam confugerat manebitque ibi donec sacerdos magnus qui oleo sancto unctus est moriatur.[156]

[22. Indeed, if by chance and without hatred 23. and hostility he do any of these things and this be proved in the hearing of the people and the case be aired between he who struck and the nearest of blood, 25. the innocent shall be freed from the hand of the avenger and shall be led back through sentence into the city in which he taken refuge and he will remain there until the high priest who was anointed with holy oil is dead.][157]

Although the meaning of the majority of this passage is similar to that in the Old Latin Bible and the *Collatio*, the Latin text is again markedly different. The key differences may stem from Jerome working more closely with the Hebrew than the translator of the Old Latin Bible.

Let us look at one last passage that will serve to demonstrate again the close relationship between the Collator's Bible and the Old Latin Version. At Coll 2. 1. 1–2 where the Collator draws from Exodus 21: 18–19:

1. Si autem contenderint duo viri et percusserit alter alterum lapide aut pugno et non fuerit mortuus, decubuerit autem in lectulo, 2. Et si surgens ambulaverit homo foris in baculo, sine crimine erit ille, qui eum percusserat praeter cessationis eius dabit ei et medico inpensas curationis.

[If two men fight and one strikes the other with a stone or with a fist and the man does not die, but lies in bed, 2. and if the man, rising, walks outside upon a staff, he who struck him will not be guilty of a crime, except he will compensate him for his disability and his doctor for the costs of treatment.]

We can again turn to the Lyons Codex of the Old Latin Bible for confirmation. The equivalent passage in the Lyons manuscript reads (Exodus 21: 18–19):

18. Si autem litigaverint duo viri, et percusserit quis proximum suum lapide aut ligno, et non fuerit mortuus, decubuerit autem in lecto, 19. Et si surgens ambulaverit homo foris cum baculo, innocens erit ille qui percusserit eum: verumtamen quo cessabit et medico curam illius dabit.[158]

[156] Quentin, *Biblia Sacra*, 281. The Stuttgart Vulgate again bears no major differences.

[157] My translation from the Vulgate.

[158] Robert, *Pentateuchi*, 175.

[18. If two men dispute and one strikes his neighbour with a stone or a piece of wood, and he does not die, but lays in bed, 19. And if the man, rising, walks from his door upon a staff, he who struck him will be innocent: Nevertheless, he shall give to him because of his disability and to his doctor for his care.][159]

The text in this passage from the *Collatio* demonstrates a close relationship with the corresponding portion of the Lyons manuscript of the Old Latin Bible. Furthermore, this passage in the Lyons manuscript might have been even closer to that in the *Collatio* earlier in the manuscript tradition. For example, the ablative form of 'fist' (*pugno*) in Coll. 2. 1. 1 must be correct as the Greek in the Septuagint reads πυγμῇ ('fist'). Mistakenly writing *ligno* for *pugno* would have been a simple transcription error for the copyist of the Lyons manuscript or a forerunner.[160] A further difference is the awkward construction at the end of the passage in the Lyons version. The Collator's use of a form of *cessatio* for the αργία in the Septuagint is much better. Scribal error might again account for this difference. Or it might be that an early translator of a forerunner manuscript in the transmission of the Old Latin Bible before the Lyons Codex could not think of a Latin word for αργία. Nevertheless, so many other parts of the passage in the *Collatio* and the Lyons Codex are again strikingly similar.

In contrast, Jerome's translation of this passage is again different. At Exodus 21: 18–19, the Vulgate reads:

18. Si rixati fuerint viri et percusserit alter proximum suum lapide vel pugno et ille mortuus non fuerit sed iacuerit in lectulo 19. si surrexit et ambulaverit foris super baculum suum innocens erit qui percussit ita tamen ut operas eius et impensas in medicos restituat.[161]

[If two men brawl and one strikes his neighbour with a stone or his fist and that one does not die, but lays in bed; 19. If he arises and walks from his door upon a staff, he who struck will be innocent, however he must repay him for his work and his medical expenses.][162]

[159] My translation from the Lyons Codex of the Old Latin Bible.

[160] See comments of Schulz, 'biblischen Texte', 26 and his 'Manuscripts', 324 on the passage suffering from corruption creeping in through glosses. Jerome correctly followed the Hebrew with *pugno* in the Vulgate.

[161] H. Quentin (ed.), *Biblia Sacra Iuxta Latinam Vulgatam Versionem ad Codicum Fidem. Libros Exodi et Levitici ex Interpretatione Sancti Hieronymi* (Rome, 1929), 186–7. The Stuttgart Vulgate text again bears no major differences.

[162] My translation from the Vulgate.

Although Jerome's meaning is naturally similar, the Latinity of the text of the Vulgate shows again it is more distant from that used by the Collator than that of the Lyons manuscript.

Other biblical passages quoted in the *Collatio* that have surviving counterparts in the Lyons manuscript version demonstrate similar connections.[163] While the Lyons manuscript does not present the entire text of the Old Latin Bible, other surviving parts of the *Vetus Latina* also seem to be more similar in their style to the quotations in the *Collatio* than the Vulgate.[164] These comparisons suggest that the Collator had a manuscript of the Old Latin Bible and did not rely on the translation of Jerome, or his own direct translation from either the Greek Septuagint or from the Hebrew Scriptures, or even a hypothetical collection of biblical sayings.[165] Furthermore, it seems very likely that his version must have been connected to that surviving in the Lyons manuscript. Biblical quotations from the *Collatio* that do not have matching sections in the Lyons version could serve as witnesses for the reconstruction of those parts not only of the Old Latin Bible, but of an ancestor to that version that survives in the Lyons codex.

It is tempting to ponder how large the Collator's Old Latin Bible might have been and what it contained. It certainly contained the books of Exodus, Leviticus, Numbers, and Deuteronomy. Pandects,

[163] For instance, Coll. 16. 1. 1–8 to Numbers 27: 2–11 in the Lyons manuscript. See further the comparative table in Smits, *Collatio*, 44–71.

[164] Compare, for example, Coll 6. 7. 9 to a quotation from Augustine's *Locutionum in Heptateuchum* 5 *(Deut.)* 59 from Deut. 27: 21; Coll. 7. 1. 2 to Augustine's *Quaestiones in Heptateuchum* 2 *(Exod.)* 84 on Exodus 22: 2. 3, Coll. 9. 1. 1 again to Augustine's *Quaestiones in Heptateuchum* 2 *(Exod.)* 71, Coll. 11. 1. 1 to Augustine's *Quaestiones in Heptateuchum* 4 *(Num.)* 10.

[165] Similarly, see Mommsen, *Collatio*, 134. Although Smits, *Collatio*, 38, hazarded that the Collator did not have the Bible in front of him, but was instead working from memory ('*misschien heeft de auteur van ons werk den tekst van het mozaisch recht niet voor zich gehad en uit het hoofd geciteerd*'), the close connection of the text of the *Collatio* and the Lyons manuscript suggests instead that the Collator did indeed have the Old Latin Bible before him and any minor changes can instead be explained by some slight editing on the Collator's part for stylistic reasons. Likewise, while Kaufhold's hypothesis of a collection of Biblical sayings is artful, again the close relationship between the Collator's quotations and the Lyons Codex show the Collator's close dependence. Although, most recently, Cohen, *Jewish and Roman Law*, 5–6 suggests that the study of the rabbinic *Halakhah* might be illuminating for the *Collatio*, again the close relationship between the *Collatio* and the Lyons Codex demonstrates that the Collator drew his knowledge of the Bible from the Old Latin Bible.

or complete one-volume Bibles, already existed in the Greek-speaking part of the Roman Empire in the fourth century, as can be seen in the *Codex Sinaiticus* and the *Codex Vaticanus*.[166] While some might suggest that there might have been Latin Pandects in the west in the fourth century by analogy, there is no firm evidence of such until the sixth century. The earliest surviving Latin Pandect is the *Codex Amiatinus* which was copied at the double monastery of Wearmouth-Jarrow in Northumbria sometime shortly before 716.[167] This Latin Bible was copied from another pandect, the now lost sixth-century *Codex Grandior* that was a product of the Vivarium monastery of Cassiodorus in the sixth century and which was purchased by the Northumbrian monks Ceolfrith and Benedict Biscop on their famous trip to Rome in 679–80.[168] There is also reference to a possible Pandect in Spain in the seventh century showing that the concept of pandects might have been spreading in this period in the west.[169] So, if our surviving evidence is any clue, most codices of the Old Latin Bible did not include both the 'Old' and 'New' Testament until the sixth century.[170] Old Latin translations of the Hebrew Scriptures might also have had only parts and not always a complete 'Old Testament.' Both the Pentateuch and the Heptateuch were common collections of books of the Hebrew Scriptures in late antiquity. While we can only work in shades of probability, since the

[166] See H. J. M. Milne and T. C. Skeat, *Scribes and Correctors of the Codex Sinaiticus* (London, 1938); T. C. Skeat, 'The Codex Vaticanus in the fifteenth century', *JTS*, n. s. 35 (1984), 454–65. For the fascinating account of the discovery of the *Codex Sinaiticus*, see Constantine von Tischendorf (tr.), *When Were Our Gospels Written?*, Religious Tract Society in London (New York, 1866). Parts of the *Codex Sinaiticus* survive in four locations: the British Library in London (where I was able to see it in the summer of 2007), the Russian National Library in St Petersburg, the Leipzig University Library, and St Catherine's monastery of Sinai in Egypt). There is a current project to digitize the text and make it available on the Internet.

[167] On this work, see H. J. White, 'The Codex Amiatinus and its birthplace', *Studia Biblica et Ecclesiastica* (Oxford, 1890), II, 273–309; R. L. S. Bruce-Mitford, 'The art of the Codex Amiatinus', *Journal of the British Archaeological Association*, 3rd series, 32 (1969), 1–25; M. B. Parkes, *The Scriptorium of Wearmouth-Jarrow* (Jarrow, 1982). For a recent study of the archaeological evidence for those monasteries, see Rosemary Cramp, *Wearmouth and Jarrow Monastic Sites* (Swindon, 2005).

[168] See P. Meyvaert, 'Bede, Cassiodorus, and the Codex Amiatinus', *Speculum* 71 (1996), 827–83, esp. 827–32. For a detailed view of Cassiodorus and the Vivarium, see J. J. O'Donnell, *Cassiodorus* (Berkeley, 1979), ch. 6. I am grateful for the inspiration of a lecture by the late Professor C. Warren Hollister in the fall of 1985 that originally sparked my interest in Benedict Biscop and his acquisitions.

[169] See McGurk, 'Oldest manuscripts', 2; Sparks, 'Latin Bible', 104.

[170] See Metzger, *Early Versions*, 293.

Pentateuch (or first five books of the 'Old Testament') is such a traditional grouping, and since the Collator certainly used four of the first five books, it is likely that the Collator most likely used an Old Latin translation of those five critical books of the Hebrew Scriptures in one codex.

C. CONCLUSION: THE COLLATOR'S LIBRARY

Close examination of internal references within the *Collatio* can thus provide us with a good view of the books at the Collator's disposal. Aside from a large part of the Old Latin Bible, his preference seems to have been for practical legal books and legal teaching manuals. These were probably the books he knew. By looking at the works he cites, we can gain an idea of the library available to the Collator. It is, of course, impossible to know if he owned these books himself or had access to a library that had them in its collections (although I lean toward the former). His usage suggests he had almost constant access to the *Sententiae* of Ps. Paulus and to at least parts of the works of Ulpian such as several books of the *Liber de officio proconsulis*, the *Libri ad edictum* (at least Book 18), and parts of the *Institutionum Libri*. His citations from Ulpian might have been either from separate volumes or perhaps he drew some passages from distinct volumes and some from one or more legal anthologies he might have had. It also looks like he had ready access to the *Codex Gregorianus* and the *Codex Hermogenianus*. He also quite probably had Gaius' *Institutes* at his disposal. Since this entire work has actually survived, analysis of Gaius' work shows that there is nothing else that could be directly used elsewhere in the *Collatio*, aside from the inheritance issues that the Collator cites in Title 16. So, it could well be that the Collator had all of Gaius' *Institutes* available to him, but he did not have the need to use it until Title 16 (where he certainly made up for it by using an extremely long quotation).

Many of these works of the Roman jurists would have been fairly lengthy and several were probably stand-alone codices.[171] If the

[171] On the preference for this form of book by the late fourth century, see C. H. Roberts and T. C. Skeat, *The Birth of the Codex* (London, 1983) and, more recently, J. A. Szirmai, *The Archaeology of Medieval Bookbinding* (Aldershot, 1999; reprint 2007), 1–31, who examines the binding structure of such *codices*.

surviving fragments of the *Sententiae* of Ps. Paulus are only a third of the entire work, the *Sententiae* could have run well over 300 modern pages if it had survived in its entirety,[172] so we can imagine him working with some long books. Other works that the Collator less frequently cites may have been in some kind of juristic handbooks. So, the infrequent citations to various *libri singulares* may reflect more cumbersome access due to some of these shorter legal monographs being bound together.

So, we can imagine the Collator either working in a library or using a good home collection of practical legal books that were popular in legal education by the mid to late fourth century. He might have had access to a few recent laws, but not many (as we saw in the last chapter).[173] Earnest in his research, the Collator was not a brilliant stylist in his own right, but rather a hard-working compiler. To understand how this diligent compiler came to set up his comparison the way he did, the next chapter will analyse the method of the Collator in using his sources.

[172] See further, Liebs, 'Die pseudopaulinischen Sentenzen II', 132–242, where the fragments alone run over a hundred pages.

[173] For instance, he did not use several laws that might have fit his plan such as *CTh* 3. 12. 1 and 2 (regarding incestuous marriages) from 342 and 355; *CTh* 9. 7. 1 and 2 (regarding adultery) from 326; *CTh* 9. 7. 3 (regarding homosexual marriage) from 342; and *CTh* 16. 5. 3 (regarding assemblies of Manichees) from 372 which suggests his access to contemporary legislation was imperfect.

4

The Collator's Method

Coll. 5. 3. 1: This is indeed law. However, a constitution of the emperor Theodosius is known to have followed to the full the meaning of the law of Moses.

[Coll. V. 3. 1: *Hoc quidem iuris est: mentem tamen legis Moysi imperatoris Theodosii constitutio ad plenum secuta cognoscitur.*]

While many scholars have felt the Collator had no method at all, but was instead working randomly or incompetently,[1] passages such as this one imply that the Collator did have a plan and a purpose in mind. This chapter will examine the structure of the work, how he used the texts he selected, and why he chose the passages he did. This approach indicates, as the passage above suggests, that the Collator not only sought to show the connections between biblical and Roman law, but did so more methodically than previously thought.[2] Close analysis of his methodology in making this comparison indicates that he was broadly following the second half of the Ten Commandments (Exodus 20: 2–17; repeated at Deuteronomy 5: 6–21). Furthermore, focused examination of how he quoted from his sources also suggests the manner in which he physically worked with his materials.

A. STRUCTURE

When the anonymous Collator of the *Collatio* compiled his work, he followed a fairly regular structure in which he began each of his

[1] See, for example, Solazzi, 'Per la Data', 484; Harries, 'How to make a law code', 68.

[2] See further, P. Garnsey and C. Humfress, *The Evolution of the Late Antique World* (Cambridge, 2001), 63.

sixteen titles with a citation from the Pentateuch (in a Latin translation).[3] Because the topic and order of the titles are the best clues to the Collator's structure, it is useful to list them here: Title 1 = Homicide; Title 2 = Severe Injury; Title 3 = Cruelty Toward Slaves; Title 4 = Adultery; Title 5 = *Stuprum* [Illicit Intercourse, by which the Collator means Male Homosexuality]; Title 6 = Incest; Title 7 = Theft; Title 8 = Perjury; Title 9 = Not Admitting the Testimony of Family Members; Title 10 = Deposit; Title 11 = Cattle Rustling; Title 12 = Arson; Title 13 = Moving Boundary Stones; Title 14 = Kidnapping; Title 15 = Astrologers, Sorcerers, and Manichees; and, lastly, Title 16 = Inheritance.

In these titles, the Collator followed the biblical passage with quotations from Roman jurists and Roman imperial constitutions with the implicit goal of comparing biblical and Roman law. While there has been dispute for nearly 150 years as to why he chose the sixteen titles that he did, after examining the titles and the scholarly debates, it seems most likely that the Collator modelled the structure of his work, and thus the selection of the titles, on the second half of the Ten Commandments. Not all scholars have accepted this theory, and even those who have do not always agree on which titles of the *Collatio* relate to which of the Ten Commandments.

In the nineteenth century, it had already occurred to some scholars that the content and, indeed, the order of some of these titles might have reflected the second half of the Ten Commandments or 'Decalogue' (a Greek term for 'Ten Words of the Law') that, following the biblical tradition, Moses received on Mt Sinai following the Exodus from Egypt on the way to Canaan *c.*1250 BCE.[4] However, reading the scholarly literature on this argument can be confusing because, while religious groups within the Judaeo-Christian tradition accept the same passages from Exodus and Deuteronomy as the revealed 'Ten Commandments', they divide and order the rules differently. So, the Jewish, Roman Catholic, Lutheran, and

[3] There are just a few exceptions when the Collator added extra biblical citations (e.g. Coll. 1. 5; 6. 7).

[4] On early scholarship, see von Daniels, *Handbuch der deutsche Reichs-und Staatenrechtsgeschichte*, I, 219–21. For scholarship on Moses and the Exodus, see recently Nahum M. Sarna and H. Shanks, 'Israel in Egypt: The Egyptian Sojourn and the Exodus' in H. Shanks (ed.), *Ancient Israel: From Abraham to the Roman destruction of the Temple*, 2nd edn (Washington, DC, 1999), 33–54.

non-Lutheran Protestant canonical lists of the Ten Commandments vary slightly.[5] While the particulars of the order of the first five commandments vary, the later half of the Ten Commandments dictate proper interactions within human society. For the purpose of comparing the *Collatio* with the Decalogue and for clarity of argument these can be listed as:[6]

6th Commandment:	You shall not murder
7th Commandment:	You shall not commit adultery
8th Commandment:	You shall not steal
9th Commandment:	You shall not bear false witness against your neighbour
10th Commandment:	You shall not covet your neighbour's house; you shall not covet your neighbour's wife, or male or female slave, or ox, or donkey, or anything that belongs to your neighbour

There are definite similarities between the order of some of the titles within the structure of the *Collatio* and the sixth to tenth commandments. For instance, Title 1 of the *Collatio* is against homicide, Title 6 is against adultery, Title 7 is against theft, and Title 8 is against false testimony, following not only the same prohibitions, but also the order of the sixth through ninth commandments. When scholars began to look at the other titles of the *Collatio* more closely, it seemed that many of them might also fit under the rubric of some of the Ten Commandments. For instance, the content of the passages from the Roman jurists in Titles 2 and 3 (severe injury and cruelty of masters) mostly deal with death, so they too could fall under the rubric of the sixth commandment. Likewise, Title 5 and 6 (concerning illicit intercourse and incest) might both conceivably fall under the rubric of the same seventh commandment as Title 4 (concerning Adultery). While Title 7 (Theft) could obviously be associated with the eighth

[5] For a modern Jewish English translation of the Hebrew Bible, see *Tanakh: A new translation of the Holy Scriptures* (Philadelphia, 1985: Jewish Publication Society of America), esp. 115 and 282 on the order of commandments. For the Lutheran order of the commandments, see J. Nelson and E. Drotning (eds.), *Luther's Small Catechism* (Minneapolis, 2001), 21–31. For the non-Lutheran Protestant order, see *The Book of Common Prayer* (Oxford, 1928), 578–9.

[6] Exodus 20: 13, Tr. *NRSV*.

commandment, Titles 8 (concerning False Testimony) and 9 (concerning not admitting the testimony of family members) could naturally fit under the ninth commandment (against bearing false witness).[7]

While the similarity between some of the commandments and the titles of the *Collatio* was already noticed in the mid nineteenth century, several scholars felt that the Collator followed them closely, not only for the obvious choices of Titles 1–9, but also for Titles 10–16, which seem at first glance to treat topics somewhat removed from the Ten Commandments. However, because of the topics of Titles 10–16, not all scholars were convinced.[8]

Mommsen accepted that Titles 1–15 of the *Collatio* were based on the Ten Commandments, but believed that Title 16 was the beginning of a second part of the *Collatio* that treated private law, the rest of which is now lost.[9] He held that view probably because the contents of the first fifteen titles dealt with aspects of criminal law. Moreover, we have already seen that W, one of the three surviving manuscripts of the *Collatio*, starts with the phrase *Liber primus* (the first book) implying that there might have been a *Liber secundus* (or second book) that treated private law and Title 16 might have been the first title of that second hypothetical, now lost, work. Scholars have continued to debate whether this title is, indeed, the last title of the *Collatio* or whether it is the first part of a second work (or second part) that dealt with private law.[10] However, since B and V, the other

[7] Von Daniels, *Handbuch*, 220–1; Conrat (Cohn), *Geschichte der Quellen und Literatur des Römischen Rechts*, 88–9 n. 2. See also, F. Triebs, *Studien zur Lex Dei* (Freiburg, 1905), I; *Studien zur Lex Dei*, II: *Das Römische Recht der Lex Dei über das Sechste Gebot des Dekalogs* (Freiburg, 1907); *Die Lex Iulia de adulteriis coercendis auf Grundlage der sog. Lex Dei (Collatio Legum Mosaicarum et Romanarum)* (Breslau, 1910), who feels the Collator certainly followed the commandments as far as Title 6. See Treibs, *Studien*, II, 1, where he states that 'der Redaktor der Lex Dei in den vorangegangen drei Titeln [i.e. Titles 1–3] das römische Recht über das fünfte Gebot des Dekalogs [in Catholic order, sixth in Protestant order] behandelt hat, geht er nunmehr in den folgenden drei Titeln (IV–VI) dazu über, das römische Recht über das sechste Gebot des mosaischen Gesetzbuches vorzulegen'.

[8] See, for instance, Dirksen, 'Über die Collatio Legum Mosaicarum et Romanarum', 112–15.

[9] Mommsen, *Collatio*, 128–9, 198. See recent echo that the *Collatio* is not complete in Jacobs, 'Roman Christians and Jewish law', 88.

[10] Mommsen, *Collatio*, 198, ends the text of the *Collatio* with '(*reliqua desunt*)' (i.e. 'the rest is lost') while Huschke in his edition felt it was complete. See also Liebs, *Jurisprudenz*, 172.

two surviving manuscripts, do not have this reading, and it is now accepted that B is the oldest (and best) of the three manuscripts, the phrase *Liber primus* was most likely a scribal addition by the copyist of W.

Most scholars of the *Collatio* after Mommsen have accepted his argument about Book 16 being the beginning of a second part of the work.[11] Some others have more creatively interpreted how the Collator used the Ten Commandments. For instance, Smits felt the Collator should have re-ordered some of the titles to have 11, 13, and 14 follow 8, since he believed that all these titles dealt with aspects of theft (and thus the sixth commandment).[12] More importantly, Smits noticed that Title 15 was problematic and suggested that it was part of criminal law since Manichaeism was against state law in the later Roman Empire. However, this observation forced him to acknowledge that this title was not directly linked to the Ten Commandments.[13] For the ensuing decades, Titles 15 and 16 would continue to be the thorniest problems for scholars in accepting the model of the Ten Commandments for the *Collatio*.[14]

[11] Hyamson, *Mosaicarum et Romanarum Legum Collatio*, xxx–xxxi, although accepting the Collator followed the Ten Commandments for Titles 1–15, is unsure about Title 16 (but left the clause *liber primus* at the beginning of his text). Girard, 'Mosaicarum', 590, accepts Mommsen's theory by ending his text with *La suite manque* ('the rest is missing').

[12] Smits, *Collatio*, 148. Smits also postulated that Title 12 (on Arson) must have come from biblical passages after the Decalogue that the Collator drew from to address criminal law from the Hebrew Bible.

[13] Smits, *Collatio*, 148. He also felt, 159–60, that Title 16 on succession marked a transition to civil law and wrestled with the concept of a first and second book, before ultimately concluding that the Collator wanted to write such a second book, but stopped after Title 16.

[14] For instance, Beyerle, *Lex Baiuvariorum*, lviii–lxi, firmly believed that both the Collator of the *Collatio* and the compiler of the *Lex Baiuvariorum* followed the model of the Decalogue throughout, although he allowed that sometimes both were using broad ideas drawn from it, and left undeveloped the problems of Titles 15 and 16. We have already seen that Schulz, *History of Roman Legal Science*, 313–14, argued the *Collatio* was not one single work (and thus implied there was no model). H. L. W. Nelson, *Überlieferung, Aufbau und Stil von Gai Institutiones* (Leiden, 1981), 113–16, argued that the Collator intended to write a two-volume work, but did not finish as he planned. Nelson argued that while Titles 1–9 might seem to follow some of the Ten Commandments, Titles 10–16 do not. He proposed that the Collator was actually basing his work on the *Sententiae* attributed to Ps. Paulus, a brave argument that no one since has adopted. While Liebs, *Italien*, 170–2, felt it was clear that the Collator based Titles 1–14 on the Ten Commandments, he avoids delving into Title 15 and played with Mommsen's theory regarding 16. Most recently, Jacobs, 'Roman Christians and Jewish law', 92–3, felt that Titles 1–14 followed the commandments, but 15 and 16 did not (and argues that the *Collatio* as it stands is not complete).

While following the theory that the Collator modelled his work on the Ten Commandments, Martha Montemayor Aceves has recently suggested that the Collator moved back and forth in his use of the commandments and, unlike earlier arguments, that he also based some of his titles on some of the first five of the commandments. So, although she follows most scholars in arguing that Titles 1–3 follow the sixth commandment, she suggests that Titles 4, 5, and 6 follow the seventh, Title 7 the eighth, and Titles 8 and 9 the ninth, and she makes some novel attributions for other titles. For instance, she argues that Titles 10–14 refer to the tenth commandment against coveting, Title 15 ('Concerning Astrologers, Sorcerers, and Manichees'), she felt refers to the first commandment ('You shall have no other gods before me'), and Title 16 ('Concerning Succession') she suggests should be placed under the rubric of the commandment 'Honour your father and mother' (the fourth commandment in the Catholic order, the fifth in the standard Protestant version).[15]

Scholars have continued to wrestle with Titles 15 and 16. For instance, Jill Harries argued that the Collator originally planned to follow the last five of the Ten Commandments, but tacked on Title 15 and 16 'at random' because he began to wander from his plan and could not resist moving on to new topics.[16] Luigi Loschiavo has most recently suggested that the Collator based Titles 1–15 on the Ten Commandments and that Title 16 marks something different (following Mommsen), but does not explain how Title 15 fits with the tenth commandment.[17]

Most recent scholars, then, understood that the Collator was at some level working within the conceptual framework of the Ten Commandments. So, they could place Title 10 (Deposit), 11 (Rustling), 12 (Arson), 13 (Moving Boundary Markers), and 14 (Kidnapping) under the umbrella of the tenth commandment ('You shall not covet') because the contents of those titles deal with personal gain at the expense of others. That is, confiscating some-

[15] Montemayor Aceves, *Mosaicarum,* xvi–xviii with table on xvii.

[16] Harries, 'How to make a law code', 68–9. She allowed that some scholars believed that there might have been a lost second part of the *Collatio,* but realized there is not evidence for it.

[17] Loschiavo, 'La legge', 79 n. 47. He felt Title 16 would have been of use to bishops who might use the *Collatio* as a handbook for mediating disputes.

one's deposit, stealing their animals, burning fields or farms for gain, taking another's land by moving a boundary marker, or taking another person through kidnapping. While we must deal with these titles more conceptually than Titles 1–9 to accept a link to the tenth commandment, this approach was probably the Collator's plan. Otherwise, the *Collatio* would have looked more like the eighth-century Irish *Liber ex Lege Moysi* and the Collator would have just directly cited the Ten Commandments themselves.[18] The same broad conceptual thinking used to include 10–14 under the rubric of the tenth commandment (against coveting) might be expanded to Titles 15 and 16 as well.

Such an approach works fairly well for Title 16.[19] Mommsen's concern that Title 16 followed private law as opposed to criminal law (and thus that this title marked a new section of the *Collatio*) is a distinction in Roman law important to modern European law, and to modern 'Romanists', as European specialists in Roman law call themselves. However, there is a problem with the argument that Title 16 marks a shift to private law because aspects of private law do show up earlier in the *Collatio*. Indeed, aspects of the *Lex Aquilia* in Title 12 could be considered to verge into private law, but the *Lex Aquilia* is complicated because it includes aspects of both private and criminal law.[20] Moreover, Title 10 of the *Collatio* concerning Deposit (*De Deposito*) deals with private law issues such as how one can sue for compensation of deposits.[21] The contents of Title 16 with their attention to the problem of who inherits when someone dies with or without a testament, in what order of succession, and in what situation could guard against coveting. That is, either one would

[18] Fournier, 'Le Liber ex Lege Moysi', 221–34; Carella, 'The source of the Prologue', 91–118.

[19] Certainly inheritance was an important aspect of Roman society. Plutarch's biography of Cato the Elder, 96, relates the apocryphal story that one of Cato's three regrets in life was that he lived one day without a testament (the other two being that he once travelled by boat when he could have travelled by land and that he once trusted his wife with a secret!).

[20] On the *Lex Aquilia* in the *Collatio*, see Coll. 2. 4, 7. 3, and 12. 7. For further on the *Lex Aquilia*, see R. Zimmerman, *The Law of Obligation: Roman foundations of the civilian tradition* (Cape Town, 1990), 953–1094 and sections of the commentary on the appropriate passages in the *Collatio*.

[21] For the classic description of the separation between public and private law in Roman law, see *Digest* 1. 1. 2 (Ulpian, *Institutes*, 1). For the Roman law of deposit, see Zimmerman, *Law of Obligation*, 205–20.

inherit according to law or one would not. If the legal technicalities were clear beforehand, some of the grounds for coveting (at least in the realm of fantasizing) would be removed. Moreover, we have seen that the phrase *Liber primus* which was a main prop for Mommsen's theory only shows up in the W manuscript, and not in B or V, and thus was most likely not in the autograph and serves only as a red herring.

Title 16 could conceptually fit under the rubric of the tenth commandment. Some might object that any law of property could do so and so the choice of succession is meaningless. We have seen aspects of concerns with property in the Collator's treatment of topics including cattle rustling (Title 11) and moving boundary stones (Title 13). Succession would be a natural further topic to fit under this rubric since Roman jurists loved to discuss it because succession was such a traditional theme of Roman jurisprudence.[22] Thus, we can accept Titles 10–14 and 16 as all possibly fitting under the stricture against coveting.

While Title 16 might plausibly fit under the rubric of the commandment against coveting, Title 15 presents a conceptual stumbling block, one that earlier scholars naturally tried to skirt, to the theory that the Collator was modelling his work on the Ten Commandments.[23] Although there have been noble efforts to link it to kidnapping or to the commandment to honour one's father and mother, there is no clear connection to either commandment and the Collator does not elsewhere refer back to the first five commandments.[24] While it is possible that Harries is right that this is a random addition,[25] the fact that the Collator apparently attempted to link his other titles to the Ten Commandments raises the possibility of searching for an alternate explanation. To conjecture what the Collator might have been doing here, we must look more closely at the Collator's methods and sources.

The title heading of Coll. 15 reads *De Mathematicis, Maleficis, et Manichaeis* ('Concerning Astrologers, Sorcerers, and Manichees').

[22] For instance, see discussion of the *Oratio* of 426 (which is the source for the Law of Citations and tacks on material on succession to apparently unrelated matters) in Harries, *Law and Empire in Late Antiquity*, 36–7, 50; Humfress, *Orthodoxy and the Courts in Late Antiquity*, 76–7.

[23] On recent scholars not developing Title 15, see Bianchini, Review of Barone-Adesi, 146.

[24] von Daniels, *Handbuch*, 221 and Montemayor Aceves, xvii, respectively.

[25] Harries, 'How to make a law code', 68–9.

While there were no biblical prohibitions against Manichaeism since it did not exist until the middle third century CE, there were certainly biblical injunctions against astrology and sorcery in Deuteronomy 18: 10–14 (that the Collator cites at the beginning of Title 15).[26] However, these biblical strictures against astrology and sorcery are not in the Ten Commandments themselves. If Titles 10–14 and Title 16 all relate to the tenth commandment against coveting, it might be possible that the Collator was casting about for more examples to include under that broad rubric when he finished Title 14. It is possible that he found them, and indeed the title name for what would become Title 15, in some of his favourite sources: the *De officio proconsulis* of Ulpian and the *Codex Gregorianus* (works that were probably constantly at hand along with the *Sententiae* of Ps. Paulus) which led him to move to this strange assortment of material in Title 15.

Examining the Collator's usage of his sources can aid us in approaching the problem of Title 15 and in hypothesizing a method to his madness here. The Collator last used Ulpian's *De officio proconsulis* at the end of Title 14 (Coll. 14. 3). He then may have leafed through it looking for an additional passage that pertained to coveting and found it at *De officio proconsulis* 7 under the Title *De Mathematicis et Vaticinatoribus* (or 'Concerning Astrologers and Soothsayers') which he quoted from at Coll. 15. 2. If he then looked through the *Codex Gregorianus*, one of his other favourite sources, the Collator would have found a similar title. And, indeed, at Coll. 15. 3, the Collator quotes from the Title '*De Maleficis et Manichaeis*' ('Concerning Sorcerers and Manichees') from the *Codex Gregorianus*.

Now the later *Theodosian Code* and the *Code of Justinian*, both modelled on the *Codex Gregorianus*, have similar titles (*CTh* 9. 16: '*De Mathematicis et Maleficis*' and the *Code of Justinian CJ* 9. 18: '*De Mathematicis et Maleficis*'). Because of the appearance of this title in both those later law codes, the phrase '*De Mathematicis*' may well have also originally stood as part of the title in the *Codex Gregorianus*, since it was the model for those later codes. Therefore,

[26] On Manichaeism, see Brown, 'Diffusion of Manichaeism', 92–103; Lieu, *Manichaeism in the Later Roman Empire and Medieval China*; Lieu, *Manichaeism in Mesopotamia and the Roman East*; and Lieu, *Manichaean Texts from the Roman Empire*. On Manichaeism and Coll. 15. 3, see Barone-Adesi, *L'età della Lex Dei*, 52–7.

if we put the surviving pieces of this title together, the phrase might have originally appeared as '*De Mathematicis, Maleficis, et Manichaeis*' in both the *Codex Gregorianus* and the *Collatio*. The citation of that part of the *Codex Gregorianus*, at Coll. 15. 3, could have become corrupt in the *Collatio* during the manuscript transmission already in α (if not earlier). Since Coll. 15. 3 is our only source for this part of the *Codex Gregorianus*, attempts to rebuild the text of that earlier lost law code were thus affected by the corrupted text.[27]

While this conclusion about the wording of the title might be valid, we still have to wrestle with the problem of why the Collator would have conceptually connected these topics with coveting. The astrology examples in the title may be dealt with fairly readily. The explanation for this part of the contents of Title 15 may lie in why people consulted astrologers, fortune-tellers, and magicians in the ancient world. While we have many horoscopes that survive on papyri and provide some information regarding what customers desired when they requested them, literary sources provide even more evidence.[28] From classical Greece we have famous examples such as Herodotus' description of Croesus asking if he would succeed in conquering Persia and Peisistratus asking to know the fortune of his sons.[29] From earlier Roman history, Livy describes Brutus consulting the oracle of Apollo at Delphi over who would have the most power in Rome.[30] So, at the aristocratic level of society, we see examples of the supplicant to the oracle seeking power and wealth.

Such views were naturally not isolated to the upper class. In the high Roman Empire, Plutarch described the normal functions of the oracle at Delphi in his dialogue on the subject.[31] He related that in his own day (*c.*100 CE) most questions to the oracle tended to deal with whether the questioner should make a journey, marry, lend

[27] Rives, 'Magic in Roman law', 334 n. 65, recently suspected that the title in the *Theodosian Code* might be compressed from an originally longer title in the *Codex Gregorianus*.

[28] See overview of inquiries to oracles in R. Lane Fox, *Pagans and Christians in the Mediterranean World from the Second Century* AD *to the Conversion of Constantine* (New York, 1988), 215–41.

[29] Herodotus, 1. 25–59.

[30] Livy, 1. 56. 9–13.

[31] For an English translation, see Plutarch, 'The Oracles at Delphi' in *Plutarch's Moralia*, vol. 5, tr. F. C. Babbitt (Cambridge, MA: Loeb Classical Library, 1936).

money, or about crops and herds.[32] Later in that century, *c.*180 CE, we have revealing information on the desires of those seeking advice from Lucian's satire on the career of the charlatan Alexander of Abonoteichus. Describing Alexander's youth, Lucian tells the reader how he became the assistant to 'one of those who advertise enchantments, miraculous incantations, charms for your love-affairs, "sendings" for your enemies, disclosures of buried treasure, and successions to estates'.[33]

Closer to the Collator's day, we can also see what people at a more typical level desired. In a standard set of questions to an oracle that survive on papyrus from the late third or early fourth century, we see standard questions such as whether someone would receive a present, a benefit, money, or profit.[34] Literary evidence from the 330s suggests most people probably consulted astrologers and sorcerers in the hopes of gaining money, property, or someone's love (as well as the old standby of learning how long one would live).[35] These topics fit well under the conceptual framework of the Tenth Commandment (do not covet your neighbour's wife, house, goods, animals) and this could have led the Collator to the citation in Ulpian.

The ultimate problem that must be dealt with when exploring the possible connection between Title 15 and the Ten Commandments, then, is the law against Manichaeism cited at Coll. 15. 3. Here I will take the lead of Harries and suggest that the Collator drifted to a topic that did not really connect because of the similarity of the titles within his sources. If we accept that the title '*De Mathematicis, Maleficis, et Manichaeis*' already existed in the *Codex Gregorianus*, then the compiler of that earlier law book had earlier linked Manichaeism to sorcery. In the text of the constitution of Diocletian preserved there, the powerful pagan emperor clearly perceived Manichaeism as an evil superstition. Indeed, Clyde Pharr suggested that the use of forms of the words *venenum* and *maleficium* in the text of this constitution showed a link to sorcery (and 'bad

[32] Plutarch, *De Pyth. Or.* 408c.

[33] Lucian, *Alexander the False Prophet*, 5, in *The Works of Lucian*, 4 vols., tr. A. M. Harmon (Cambridge, MA: Loeb Classical Library, 1925), 180–3.

[34] P. Oxy. XII 1477.

[35] See Firmicus Maternus, *Mathesis*, 2. 25. For an English translation, see J. R. Bram, *Ancient Astrology—Theory and Practice: Mathesis Libri VII by Firmicus Maternus* (Park Ridge, NJ, 1975).

medicine').[36] Now, Diocletian perceived any threat to acknowledging the divine legitimacy of his power as a danger, and Manichees certainly saw a higher force than his divine comrade Jupiter. Moreover, many fourth-century Christians saw the Manichees as evil as well. Augustine, a close contemporary of the Collator, indicates in the 380s that he had found Manichaeism a facile religion to follow since it solved the problem of theodicy (i.e. the existence of evil in a universe created by an all powerful good God) and it had the added bonus of allowing him to avoid confronting his own sins in his days as a student (*c.*370–5) and during his teaching career (*c.*375–86).[37] Indeed, Augustine continued to live with fellow Manichees when he moved to Rome in 383.[38]

The Collator of the *Collatio* may well have felt uncomfortable about the tennets of the Manichaean faith and obviously knew their religion was outlawed and might have been struck by the uses of technical terms for sorcery in the constitution of Diocletian. While we have seen that some scholars have argued that the Collator's inclusion of the quotations in Title 15 followed no plan at all,[39] it is plausible that he drew the citations at Coll. 15. 1 and 2 to connect directly to coveting and he added the constitution against Manichaeism at Coll. 15. 3 because of (1) it standing under a related title in the *Codex Gregorianus*, (2) it being an outlawed religion officially described as a superstition, similar to divination in that regard (and moreover was associated with *venenum* and *maleficium*), and (3) his own dislike of the heresy. His alleged transition to inheritance laws in Title 16 was then actually a reinforcement of the commandment against coveting which he had already been following since Title 10.

If this broad conceptual understanding of the titles in the *Collatio* is correct (with a small detour at Coll. 15. 3), then the Collator loosely followed the outline of the second half of the Ten Commandments throughout his work. This would help to explain why his work eventually was included in Church libraries in the early Middle Ages and why it was used in sixth-century Merovingian Church councils and, in the ninth century, by Hincmar. Lastly, the *Collatio* may well have been a model for at least one early medieval German

[36] Pharr, 'Interdiction of magic', 290–1.
[37] Brown, *Augustine of Hippo*, 46–60.
[38] See Augustine, *Confessions*, 5. 10.
[39] Harries, 'How to make a law code', 68–9.

law code (the *Lex Baiuvarioum*). At times, to give Harries her due, the Collator did stray a bit in Title 15, being pulled along by the texts he had at hand. However, he remained committed enough to the model of the Ten Commandments to return to the concept of coveting in inheritance in Title 16. The Collator of the *Collatio* then followed the following structure:

Commandment:	Title in *Collatio*:
6. You shall not murder =	1, 2, 3
7. You shall not commit adultery =	4, 5, 6
8. You shall not steal =	7
9. You shall not bear false witness =	8, 9
10. You shall not covet =	10–16

B. USING TEXTS

Tables 1 and 3 at the end of the book show that, although the Collator cited five jurists for comparative purposes, he tended to use some sources more than others. So, while Paulus and Ulpian (or at least works already attributed to them) receive many citations, Papinian (or works attributed to him) is only cited eight times (Coll. 2. 3; 4. 5; 4. 7; 4. 8; 4. 9; 4. 10; 4. 11; and 6. 6), Modestinus is only cited twice (Coll. 1. 12; 10. 2), and Gaius only once (Coll. 16. 2). There could be different explanations for the Collator's usage of these jurists. He may have simply preferred Paulus (and Ps. Paulus) and Ulpian as jurists for the purpose of his project in contrast to the works of Papinian and Modestinus, or knew them better, or just had them regularly at hand.

Let us look more closely at the Collator's tendency in citations from the jurists in Table 1. This table lists the authors as the Collator knew them (including what we now know as spurious works). We see that the Collator often cites several passages in succession from the same work and that he often moved back and forth from one work to another (whether he had independent volumes for all of his sources or a combination of some separate volumes and one or more legal anthologies). These tendencies in using his texts are only natural in that (a) the jurists tend to have related passages gathered together in titles and (b) human nature being what it is, it was easier for the Collator to use what was open and at hand.

Table 3 shows a simultaneous view of how the Collator used his sources. In Title 1 of the *Collatio*, the Collator moved back and forth between Book 5 of the *Sententiae* of Ps. Paulus and the Book 7 of Ulpian's *Liber de officio proconsulis*,[40] with an occasional detour into Book 4 of the *Codex Gregorianus*, and one lonely reference to Modestinus.[41] Even allowing for a few of the shorter works possibly standing in an anthology, the multitude of his citations to the *Sententiae* and to Ulpian's *de officio proconsulis* would suggest that they were separate works. Thus, for composing this part of the *Collatio*, the Collator had Book 5 of the *Sententiae* and Book 7 of Ulpian's *Liber de officio proconsulis* open and at hand. Indeed, they may well have been continually open since he returns to *Sententiae* 5 at Coll. 1. 13 after using Ulpian, Modestinus, and the *Codex Gregorianus* since his last citation from the Book 5 of the *Sententiae* at Coll. 1. 7.

Let us now look at how the Collator used these patterns of citation throughout his compilation by looking further at Table 3. After he explicitly used different works of Paulus (the alleged *de iniuriis* at Coll. 2. 5 and 6), the Collator returned to the fifth book of the *Sententiae* at Coll. 2. 7 and Coll. 3. 2. Here the steady usage from Title 2 to Title 3 of the *Collatio* reinforces the dependence of the Collator on the *Sententiae.*

Likewise, we see 'runs' of usage elsewhere. The Collator quotes from Papinian's *Liber singularis de adulteriis* five times in succession at Coll. 4. 7–11, and then returns to the second book of the *Sententiae* which he cites at Coll. 4. 12, 5. 2, and 6. 3. Then he jumped ahead to the fifth book of the *Sententiae* at Coll. 7. 2 before returning to the second book at Coll. 7. 5. Once again, the Collator had a run of material from the fifth book of the *Sententiae* at Coll. 8. 3, 4, 5, 6. He then used Ulpian's *De officio proconsulis* Book 8 at Coll. 8. 7 and 9. 2, in succession, implying that this work also may have been almost continually at hand. Indeed, in Titles 11 and 12 we see a long run of almost continuous usage of the *Sententiae* and Ulpian's *De officio proconsulis*, with only an occasional citation from Modestinus, the *Codex Hermogenianus*, and the *Codex Gregorianus* (and it is difficult to imagine that Modestinus' work would have been bound with the two codes).

40 PS Book 5 = Coll. 1. 2; 1. 4; 1.7; 1.13 and Ulpian, *De Officio Proconsulis* Book 7 = Coll. 1. 3, 6, 11.

41 CG 44 = Coll. 1. 8; 1. 9; 1. 10 and Modestinus, *Liber diff.* Book 6 = Coll. 1. 12.

The Collator clearly depended upon some works as sources, such as the *Sententiae* and Ulpian's *De officio proconsulis*, more than others. Indeed, the passage at Coll. 14. 3. 6 where the Collator reflects on how recent constitutions have returned to stern measures, as opposed to Ulpian's description, ends with a comparative reference to the *Sententiae*. That again would suggest he had both books open and at hand simultaneously. Such tendencies are noticeable throughout the work, with strings of citations, using apparent favourite works before finally ending with a long string of citations from Ulpian's *Institutes* (Coll. 16. 5–9). When he used the various shorter *libri singulares* (such as the *Liber singularis de adulteriis* of Ps. Paulus or the *Liber de singularis de adulteriis* of Ps. Papinian), the Collator would often just use them for a run of citations (and these shorter works might have stood together in one or more anthologies).[42]

Can we surmise anything further about the Collator's methodology by analysing his use of the Old Latin Bible? We have already seen in Chapter 3 that the Collator would at times condense the biblical passages to make the parallels with Roman law more evident (and this will be seen more fully in the appropriate parts of the commentary). A broader look at his use of the Bible can give even more information on his method. Table 2 lists his successive quotations from the Scriptures. The information in this table demonstrates that the Collator preferred when possible to use a run of quotations from a given text (as was also true in his use of Roman legal sources). So, as we have already seen, at Coll. 1. 1 and 5 he used Numbers 35: 16–17, 20–1 and Numbers 35: 22–5, respectively. It seems likely, then, that he might have kept his copy of the Old Latin Bible open to this section of Numbers when he was citing passages from Roman jurists in the interim at Coll. 1. 2–4. Likewise, at Coll. 4. 1, 5. 1, and 6. 1 the Collator successively went through Leviticus 20: 10, 13, and 11–12. Again, it seems probable that he kept his codex of the Old Latin Bible open to this section of Leviticus when he was working from Roman legal sources in the intervening other sections of those titles. The Collator's longest sequence of biblical quotations is to parts of Exodus (20 and 22) at Coll. 9. 1, 10. 1, 11. 1, and 12. 1. While he

[42] Ps. Paulus, *Liber singularis de adulteriis* at Coll. 4. 2; 4. 3; 4. 4; 4. 6 and Ps. Papinian, *Liber singularis de adulteriis* at Coll. 4. 7; 4. 8; 4. 9; 4. 10; and 4. 11.

had worked at Exodus 21 earlier, at Coll. 2. 1 and 3. 1 and later at Coll. 14. 1, this does not automatically imply that he had a separate volume for the translation of the Book of Exodus. It may instead be that he inserted some sort of book marks in his volume of the Old Latin Bible during the research phase of his project that enabled him to move quickly to sections that he thought were significant for his comparison of biblical and Roman law.

The way in which he used a series of quotations from given sections of texts gives insight into his methodology. While composing the *Collatio*, the Collator probably kept the Pentateuch of the Old Latin Bible and a wide number of Roman legal sources at hand (either at his home or in a library). He may have even had several of them open at any moment while he worked back and forth between his different texts teasing out connections between biblical and Roman law.

The Collator follows a standard approach starting each title with a short quotation from the Old Latin translation of the Hebrew Bible followed by statements from the Roman jurists and, occasionally, from some Roman imperial laws.[43] In all sixteen titles, the statements from the Roman jurists he selects almost always show similarities to the biblical strictures he quotes. Two examples will serve to illustrate his approach. At the beginning of Title 12 (*De Incendiariis* or 'Concerning Arsonists'), the Collator quotes from Exodus 22: 6: 'If a fire breaks out and it comes upon brush and engulfs threshing floors or grain or fields, he who set the fire must restore the estimated value.' His Latin translation here shows no significant variation from the corresponding Greek text of the Septuagint (which in turn follows the standard Hebrew text closely).[44] Following this biblical stricture, the Collator presents several passages from the *Sententiae* of Ps. Paulus,[45] a passage from Ulpian's *De officio proconsulis*,[46] and a long passage from Ulpian's *Liber ad edictum*.[47] In every case, the passages from the jurists treat arsonists and their punishment.

[43] The two titles where he added additional Biblical quotations, Title 1 (at 1. 5) and Title 6 (at 6. 7), can be explained. The first of these probably clarifies the difference between premeditated and accidental homicide (important for the similarity to Roman law). The second is more complex and seems to appear because these sexual crimes were particularly repulsive to the Collator (esp. bestiality which he moved to the end of the passage, possibly for emphasis).

[44] Although this portion of the Lyons Codex is missing, the Collator's translation is here similar to the Vulgate.

[45] Coll. 12. 2; 12. 3; 12. 4; and 12. 6. [46] Coll. 12. 5. [47] Coll. 12. 7.

We can see the pattern again at the beginning of Title 6 (*De Incestis Nuptiis* or 'Concerning Incestuous Marriages'). Here the Collator quotes from Leviticus 20: 11–12: 'Whoever lies with a woman who is the wife of his own father uncovers the private parts of his own father, let them both die: they are guilty.' Here and at Coll. 6. 7 his text is again similar to that relayed by other surviving Latin translations (but avoids the blood guilt conveyed by the Greek Septuagint and the Hebrew text).[48] The Collator then followed this commandment with quotations from Ps.-Ulpian's *Liber regularum singularis* (Coll. 6. 2), the *Sententiae* of Ps. Paulus (Coll. 6. 3), two imperial rescripts drawn from the *Codex Gregorianus* (at Coll. 6. 4) and *Codex Hermogenianus* (at Coll. 6. 5), and a passage from Ps. Papinian's *Liber singularis de adulteriis* (Coll. 6. 6). All of these passages relate to prohibitions of incestuous marriages and thus show something of his methodology.

Although the Collator does have a general pattern of quoting biblical passages and then quoting Roman jurists who treat similar concerns, at many places in his work he edits the biblical quotations (and, as we shall see, also the juristic ones). By examining the passages from the Bible in the *Collatio* and then comparing and contrasting them with those in the Lyons Codex of the Old Latin Bible, the Vulgate of Jerome, the Hebrew text, and the Septuagint, we can see that many times the Collator either trimmed out parts of the biblical text by skipping over sentences or subtly dropped words or even combined different passages from different books of the Bible. By examining some of these editorial changes, we can gain even better insight into the Collator's methodology and purpose.[49]

The Collator excised parts of the biblical quotations several times. For instance, at the beginning of Title 1 (*De Sicariis et Homicidis* or 'Concerning Assassins and Murderers'), the Collator quotes from Numbers 35: 16–17 and 20–1: '1. If someone strikes a person with an iron weapon and kills him, let him die. 2. Moreover, if someone strikes a person by hand with a stone by which he might die and he

[48] For instance, see Augustine, *Quaestionum in Heptateuchum*, 5 (*Locutiones De Iesu Nave*), 59: *Maledictus omnis, qui dormierit cum omni pecore* compared to Coll. 6. 7. 9: *maledictus, qui cum omni pecore*.

[49] I delivered a preliminary study of this aspect of the Collator as 'Patterns and puzzles in the *Lex Dei*' at the International Conference on Patristic Studies at the University of Oxford in the summer of 2007. I am grateful to the audience for their stimulating response.

dies, he is a murderer: let him die. 3. And if through hostility someone strikes him or throws an implement at him from an ambush and he dies, 4. or strikes him by hand through anger and he dies, let him die.' What is revealing here is that the Collator left out the verses at Numbers 35: 18 and 19 which read (in the *NRSV*) at 18 'Or anyone who strikes another with a weapon of wood in hand that could cause death, and death ensues, is a murderer; the murderer should be put to death' and at 19 'The avenger of blood is the one who shall put the murderer to death; when they meet, the avenger of blood shall execute the sentence.' These verses stand in both the Septuagint and the Lyons Codex of the Old Latin Bible and so were doubtless in the Latin Bible that the Collator consulted. While he may have excised verse 18 because of the redundancy of the 'weapon of wood' example, the 'avenger of the blood' mentioned in verse 19 refers to an aspect of ancient Hebrew law that did not have a counterpart in classical Roman law.[50] The fact that the Collator purposely left it out is confirmed by his also trimming off the end of verse 21 which repeats (in the *NRSV*) 'The avenger of blood shall put the murderer to death, when they meet.' In this case, then, it appears that the Collator was editing the biblical passage to exaggerate the similarity between biblical law and Roman law.

While this was a fairly large change of the text, several times the Collator made more subtle changes. At the beginning of Title 13 (*De Termino Amoto* or 'Concerning a Moved Boundary Marker'), the Collator quotes from Deuteronomy 19: 14: 'You shall not move the boundary markers of your neighbours that your fathers set up for your property.' We can plainly see his slight editing when we look at the Septuagint, the original Hebrew text, and the Old Latin Bible which stresses that the land was given by the Lord God. This stricture, the same as that stressed in the Shechem Dodecalogue at Deuteronomy 27: 17, discussed a form of theft that was condemned by both Hebrew and Roman law.[51] However, it is immediately apparent that the Collator excised the reference to the 'Lord God' which is apparent in the Greek phrase *κύριος ὁ θεός* in the Septuagint, the Tetragrammaton (the four-letter abbreviation used as a shorthand

[50] See Berger, 'Homicidium', in Berger, *Encyclopedic Dictionary*, 487–8 at 487: 'After a period of self-vengeance, homicide in historical times became a *crimen publicum*.'

[51] See G. von Rad, *Deuteronomy: A commentary*, tr. Dorotea Barton (Philadelphia, 1966), 129.

symbol for God) in the Hebrew text, and in the Latin *dominus deus* in the Lyons Codex of the Old Latin Bible. By trimming off this clause (and the reference to a Judaeo-Christian God), the Collator again underlined his agenda of showing the similarity between Hebrew and Roman law.

In his use of other biblical passages, the Collator does similar editing. Usually he left out references to abstruse points of ancient Hebrew law that had no parallels in Roman law. For instance, at Coll. 1. 5. 1–4 the Collator condensed the text of the passage.[52] Here, specifically, the Collator excised the parts of the biblical passage regarding the synagogue and cities of refuge from the blood avenger of the family. Sometimes, he combines biblical passages to make the similarity to Roman law clearer.[53] In other places the Collator makes some small editorial changes in the text of the biblical passages to make the similarity to Roman law stronger. For example, at the beginning of Title 10 (*De Deposito* or 'Concerning Deposit'), the Collator cuts out the description of the deposit of various kinds of animals mentioned in Exodus 22: 7–11 (oxen, donkeys, or sheep) and instead just leaves the items deposited as 'silver or a vase' which parallels the examples mentioned by the Roman jurists in that title.[54]

The Collator may have avoided using certain passages from the Bible that would have fit with the topics of his titles because they did not mesh well with Roman law. For instance, although Title 3 of the *Collatio* is entitled *De Iure et Saevitia Dominorum* ('Concerning the Law and the Cruelty of Masters'), the Collator did not include a stricture from the Hebrew Bible that guaranteed the manumission of male slaves after six year described at Exodus 21: 2. This omission is revealing as the Collator used nearby parts of the book of Exodus. Roman law had no similar regulation, and so the Collator did not include it. Likewise, he may have used Leviticus 20: 13 against homosexuality as opposed to Leviticus 18: 22 because it was more similar to the Roman law he would quote at Coll. 5. 3.[55]

[52] Noticed already by Hyamson, 58.

[53] For instance, Coll. 6. 1 combines Leviticus 20: 10 and Exodus 22: 16–17 (possibly because the Collator noticed that so many of his Roman juristic texts used in Title 4 treat the role of daughters).

[54] For instance, a law from the *Codex Hermogenianus* cited at Coll. 10. 4. 1 mentions an amount of silver and a passage from the *Sententiae* of Ps. Paulus quoted at Coll. 10. 10. 7 alludes to silver.

[55] As opposed to the view of Ostersetzer, 'La Collatio', 86 who suggests the Collator made this decision to make Jewish law appear more like Christian law.

Since the Collator does seem to be actively involved in some editorial polishing of the biblical texts, it is useful to see if he does the same thing in his use of Roman juristic texts. This is a more difficult task than working with the biblical quotations as most of the surviving variant texts for the Collator's passages from the jurists appear in the sixth-century *Digest* and may have suffered scribal errors in the nearly two hundred years since the Collator's day and also may have been the subject of editorial handling by Tribonian and his staff as they assembled the *Digest.*

Nonetheless, comparison of selected passages shows that the Collator also made minor editorial changes to his quotations from the jurists. Most of these consist of dropping sentences or clauses that did not directly pertain to his topics as stated in his title headings. For instance, at Coll. 1. 11, the Collator quotes from the seventh book of Ulpian's *De officio proconsulis* and we have a longer version of the same passage at *Digest* 48. 8. 4. The Collator does not quote the sentence surviving as *Dig.* 48. 8. 4 pr. which specifies that magistrates who illegally caused someone's death will be prosecuted. However, he keeps the sentence surviving as *Dig.* 48. 8. 4. 1, but then does not quote the sentence surviving as *Dig.* 48. 8. 4. 2 that those who create eunuchs are to be found guilty of breaking the *Lex Cornelia* and their goods should be transferred to the imperial fisc. On the other hand, the Collator keeps the detailed description about someone dying due to being tossed in a military cloak at a party that was not used by the compilers of the *Digest.* Presumably the Collator kept it because it was such a perfect example of accidental death (one of his themes in Title 1) whereas the Byzantine compilers of the *Digest* wanted to get to the heart of the matter. So, it would appear that the Collator selected from the jurists' works what he thought would fit best with the biblical stricture at the beginning of the title and with the theme of the title itself. Similarly at Coll. 1. 13, where the Collator quotes from the *Sententiae* of Ps. Paulus, he does not use the preceding sentence of the quotation that survives in the equivalent passage in the *Digest* (48. 6. 11) because it states that leaders of armed mobs who loot homes will receive capital punishment and Title 1 of the *Collatio* treats homicide, not looting or theft, as a crime.

The Collator followed this pattern elsewhere in his work. At Coll. 2. 4, the Collator quotes from Ulpian's *Liber ad edictum* and we have a longer version surviving as *Digest* 9. 2. 27. Analysing this passage in the *Digest* shows that the Collator took a section from the middle of the citation from Ulpian (at *Dig.* 9. 2. 27. 17) which fitted well with the theme of his second title on outrageous physical injuries. The sentences before this section in the *Digest* version treated examples of the *Lex Aquilia* (such as arson). Examples after the Collator's selected passage deal with other situations that would pertain to the *Lex Aquilia* such as torn clothing and overloaded mules. The Collator would later use a section of that passage that treated arson at Coll. 12. 7. Since the biblical stricture at Coll. 2. 1 dealt with fighting and physical injuries, the Collator used the part of Ulpian's quotation that fitted best. We see a similar case at Coll. 7. 3 where the Collator quoted again from Ulpian's *Liber ad edictum* (and a version of the passage survives as *Dig.* 9. 2. 5). Here again the Collator cut out details, such as the results of falling tiles or angry shoemakers which pertained to the *Lex Aquilia* (the theme of that part of the *Digest*) but did not fit the topic of theft (the theme of Title 7 and of the biblical stricture at Coll. 7. 1). Likewise, the compilers of the *Digest* cut out the section at the beginning of the Collator's passage (Coll. 7. 3. 1 which qualifies that killing a slave who is a thief is not an example of *iniuria*) because it was not critical for the Byzantine compilers.

At Coll. 12. 5, the Collator quotes from Ulpian's *De officio proconsulis* and we have a slightly longer version of this passage surviving at *Dig.* 47. 9. 12. Here the Collator cut out the first sentence of what survives in the version in the *Digest* (47. 9. 12. pr.) that describes an imperial rescript that allowed compensation of wrecked property. Since this sentence did not explicitly mention arson (the theme of Title 12), the Collator probably excised it.

These examples seem to show a pattern where the Collator selected from the passages from the jurists what he thought was most useful for his comparison between Roman and biblical law. With that in mind, we can turn to one last example of a surviving parallel passage in the *Digest* and in Title 10 (*De Deposito*) in the *Collatio* that has been the subject of some scholarly debate. At Coll. 10. 7, the Collator quotes from the *Sententiae* of Ps. Paulus and a shorter variant of that passage survives at *Dig.* 16. 3. 29. The Collator's quotation has several additional sentences defining the concept of deposit preceding where the *Digest* compilers began their quotation. Then the two works share a sentence (Coll. 10. 7. 9 = *Dig.* 16. 3. 29. pr.) from the *Sententiae* stating that a legal action is possible against someone who handles a deposit against the will of the person who had deposited it. The Collator follows this with a series of different deposit scenarios in which either the depositor or he with whom the object is deposited would have legal recourse. The *Digest* version then moves on to a sentence which the Collator does not have that states 'If deposited money is used with my permission by him with whom it has been deposited, as in the other good faith actions, he is compelled to pay me interest on that amount.'[56] Some scholars have felt that this sentence must have been an interpolation by Tribonian's staff since it is not in the passage from the *Collatio*.[57] Keeping in mind the Collator's pattern, he may well have excised this sentence, which originally might have come after that part of the passage from Ulpian preserved as Coll. 10. 7. 1–4, because it did not deal with defining deposit and guarding against the theft of deposited goods stated in the biblical stricture at Coll. 10. 1. 1. Using such methodology in his use of both biblical and juristic passages enables the Collator to make his comparison seem more vivid to his readers.

In addition to subtle editing of passages from the Roman jurists, the Collator also may have avoided using some recent Roman constitutions that did not mesh well with passages from the Bible. For instance, the Collator did not include a law of Constantius II from 355 (surviving as *CTh* 3. 12. 2) which prohibited marriage between a man and his sister-in-law, even after the death or divorce of his first wife, although he did have a title on incest (Title 6). Biblical law (Deut. 25: 5–10) allowed marriage to a dead wife's sister, but Roman law did not. Perhaps the Collator did not include it because it did not fit the comparison he was shaping that showed the similarities

[56] Dig. 16. 3. 29. 1: 'Si ex permissu meo deposita pecunia is penes quem deposita est utatur, ut in ceteris bonae fidei iudiciis usuras eius nomine praestare mihi cogitur'. Text and translation from A. Watson (ed. and tr.), *The Digest of Justinian*, 4 vols. (Philadelphia, 1985), 477–8.

[57] See C. Longo, 'Appunti sul Deposito Irregolare', *BIDR* 18 (1905), 121–56 at 125–7; G. Segre, 'Sul Deposito Irregolare in Diritto Romano', *BIDR* 19 (1907), 197–234 at 197–9; B. Kübler, 'Griechische Tatbestände in dem Werken der Kasuistischen Literatur', *ZRG (R.A.)* 29 (1908), 183–226 at 203; H. T. Klami, *'Mutua magis videtur quam deposita' Über die Geldverwahrung im Denken der Römischen Juristen* (Helsinki, 1969), 80–95 (with a review of the scholarly literature). F. Bonifacio, 'Richerche sul de Deposito Irregolare in Diritto Romano', *BIDR*, n. s. 8 (1947): 80–152 at 117–21 suggested that the clause at Coll. 10. 7. 9 pertained not to *depositum*, but to risk of damages (although it would appear the Ps. Paulus and the Collator both thought linked it to *depositum*).

between biblical and Roman law (although his access to recent laws does seem to be irregular).[58]

C. CONCLUSION: THE COLLATOR AT WORK

Examination of the Collator's use of his sources gives insight into how he worked in the last years of the fourth century. We have seen that he preferred, when possible, to use a series of passages from a source in succession. We have also seen that he would often return to a given section in a work after a break in use. Lastly, we have seen that he must have had the works in front of him as he picked and chose what parts of a passage he wanted to use to help his comparison along. All this insight is important when imagining how a writer composing such a text in late antiquity would actually work.

Recent scholarship on how ancient writers actually researched and wrote and what technology they had at their disposal can shed light on the Collator's methodology. We know that wax or wood tablets and related forms could be used for shorter compositions, but earlier writers in antiquity ultimately used papyrus rolls for their formal literary works. The codex book form increasingly grew in popularity throughout the first four centuries CE (and this was probably linked to the growth of Christianity which prized ready access to critical textual passages).[59] By the Collator's day in the 390s, it is quite likely that this was the most common form of book and his finished form would have probably been composed in a *codex*. Likewise, his Latin Bible (either a Pandect or at least the Pentateuch) and his juristic sources were probably also in codex form.

[58] A law prohibiting marriage to nieces earlier allowed by the emperor Claudius (*CTh* 3. 12. 1) of 342 might have fit better, but it could be that the Collator did not see it. The copy preserved in the *Theodosian Code* was given in Antioch while the law against marrying a sister-in-law surviving in *CTh* 3. 12. 2 was released at Rome and it is remotely possible that the Collator might have seen that one, just as he saw the constitution against homosexual prostitution he quoted at Coll. 5. 3. 1, but declined to use it.

[59] On the transition from the scroll to the *codex* as the most common form of book in late antiquity, see Roberts and Skeat, *The Birth of the Codex*; A. Grafton and M. Williams, *Christianity and the Transformation of the Book: Origen, Eusebius, and the Library of Caesarea* (Cambridge, MA, 2006), 8–15.

However, how did he physically use his sources and how did he write? Recent work has pointed out that, although tables had been used for centuries for banking and other purposes,[60] we have no evidence that ancient authors actually wrote on tables or desks in antiquity (as they did by the ninth century).[61] Instead, earlier ancient art depicts people writing on their laps, or dictating to literate slaves who did the same, in classical Greece and Roman society. In regard to reading texts, people may have sat or stood at a reading stand.[62] Artistic evidence does suggest readers used stands for books by the sixth century CE, as a famous image of Augustine from the Basilica of St John Lateran indicates. How would this have worked with the Collator? He must have had several books (probably *codices*) open while he worked, as Table 3 suggests.[63] While authors may have often dictated notes to scribes while conducting research in libraries, the similarities between the juristic passages in the *Collatio* to those in the *Digest* suggests that the Collator (or a scribe) was physically copying them while they were open.[64] He would have moved back and forth to them while copying down passages (making a few minor planned editorial changes as he did so). It is hard for a modern scholar to imagine how this would have been possible without working at some kind of table (at least as a staging area for the open *codices*). It is possible he had the books open on the floor around him

[60] The most famous reference from antiquity appears in the Gospels describing Jesus overturning the tables of the money changers during his cleansing of the Temple in Jerusalem (Mark 11: 15–19; Matt. 21: 12–17; John 2: 12–25).

[61] J. P. Small, *Wax Tablets of the Mind: Cognitive studies of memory and literacy in classical antiquity* (London and New York, 1997), 141–59. She is correct that the evidence is sparse. On the use of writing tables in the Middle Ages, see *ibid.*, 155. It is tempting to translate the *de scriniis* in Jerome *ep.* 57 (to Pammachius) as 'from the desk' (see further, W. H. Fremantle *et al.* (tr.), *Jerome: Letters and selected works*, NPNF, 2nd series, vol. 6 (New York, 1893)). See also, Jerome, *ep.* 49. 4 (to Pammachius)

[62] Small, *Wax Tablets*, 155–9. See further the comments of Grafton and Williams, *Transformation of the Book*, 214–21, while never quite getting down to the level of how the scribes actually wrote, postulated that Eusebius must have had a 'flock of secretaries and notaries' in his scriptorium to help produce his works.

[63] Although Small, *Wax Tablets*, 167–8, suggests we have no pictorial evidence for that until deep in the central Middle Ages (*c.*1200).

[64] On ancient research methods, see Small, *Wax Tablets*, 169–76. It is tempting to hypothesize that Origen may have had several Bible translations open while creating his *Hexapla*. In a similar way, Eusebius must have had access to several works at once while composing the *Canon* (or Table) for his *Chronicle*. On these works and their technical issues, see further, comments of Grafton and Williams, *Transformation of the Book*, 86–117 and 133–43.

and was writing on his lap or dictating to a scribe, but that would seem cumbersome (to us at least). Either the diligent Collator worked that way, or he did indeed write on some kind of table in the last years of the fourth century, as the transition to writing tables had to be made at some point, tables already existed and had been used in banking for centuries, and such a transition would be a logical effect of the transition to the codex and the Christian habit of checking references.

5

The Collator's Identity and Purpose

Matthew 19: 16. Then someone came to him and said, Teacher, what good deed must I do to have eternal life?' 17. And he said to him, 'Why do you ask me about what is good? There is only one who is good. If you wish to enter into life, keep the commandments.' 18. He said to him, 'Which ones?' And Jesus said, 'You shall not murder; You shall not commit adultery; You shall not steal; You shall not bear false witness; 19. Honor your father and mother; also, you shall love your neighbour as yourself.'[1]

Examination of the date, sources, and method of the Collator are of essential help in re-examining the purpose of the *Collatio.* As there is no stated purpose in the preface to the work, this has been the subject of great scholarly debate for over a century.[2] Closely intertwined with the problem of purpose are the questions of the identity and religious affiliation of the Collator. Positing different religious identities (especially Jewish or Christian) has led to an array of suggested purposes for this unique work. This chapter will examine clues both within the *Collatio* as well as within the context of the late fourth century which I have adopted for the work. Such an approach will suggest not only that the Collator was probably a Christian lawyer in the western part of the Roman Empire, but will also yield

[1] Tr. *NRSV.* Matthew 19: 16. '*Καὶ ἰδοὺ εἶς προσελθὼν αὐτῷ εἶπεν· διδάσκαλε, τί ἀγαθὸν ποιήσω ἵνα σχῶ ζωὴν αἰώνιον;* 17. *ὁ δὲ εἶπεν αὐτῷ· τί με ἐρωτᾷς περὶ τοῦ αγαθοῦ; εἷς ἔστιν ὁ ἀγαθός. εἰ δὲ θέλεις εἰς τὴν ζωὴν εἰσελθεῖν, τήρησον τὰς ἐντολάς.*18. *λέγει αὐτῷ· ποίας; ὁ δὲ Ἰησοῦς εἶπεν· τὸ οὐ φονεύσεις, οὐ μοιχεύσεις, οὐ κλέψεις, οὐ ψευδομαρτυρήσεις,* 19. *τίμα τὸν πατέρα καὶ τὴν μητέρα, καὶ, ἀγαπήσεις τὸν πλησίον σου ὡς σεαυτόν.*' Nestle-Aland, *Novum Testamentum Graece*, 27th edn (Stuttgart, 1993). This episode also appears in Mark 10: 17–19 and Luke 18: 18–20.

[2] Harries, 'How to make a law code', 68, and Wenger, *Die Quellen*, 546, suggest that an original preface where he laid out his purpose might have been lost in the manuscript tradition.

an understanding of his purpose that can give us a fuller view of how one Christian at the middle level of society in the last years of the fourth century understood Christianity and other religions and where he felt the right path for a Christian led (hinted at in the parable of the rich young man quoted above).

A. QUESTIONS OF IDENTITY

Early modern scholars postulated a variety of firm identities for the Collator. For instance, sixteenth-century scholars offered Licinius Rufinus, a Christian jurist writing in the early third century, as a possibility.[3] Huschke noticed this attribution did not work chronologically since there is evidence of fourth-century legislation in the work and offered the late fourth/early fifth-century Rufinus of Aquileia as the potential author and further suggested he wrote the work in the east when he was a priest in Jerusalem.[4] This identification also had difficulties.[5] Other scholars went so far as to suggest Ambrose (or one of his circle), Jerome, or Ambriosiaster as potential authors.[6]

[3] On the arguments of J. du Tillet, L. Charondas, and J. Cujas, see Hyamson, *Mosaicarum et Romanarum Legum Collatio*, xlix–li and xvi n. 2; Smits, *Collatio*, 8.

[4] See Huschke, 'Über Alter und Verfasser', 26–7. See further, Jörs, 'Collatio', col. 367; Hyamson, li–liii; Kaiser, *Epitome Iuliani*, 98–9. On the career of Rufinus of Aquileia, see F. X. Murphy, *Rufinus of Aquleia (345–411): His life and works* (Washington, DC, 1945); Philip R. Amidon, *The Church History of Rufinus of Aquileia, Books 10 and 11* (Oxford, 1997); and E. A. Clark, *The Origenist Controversy* (Princeton, 1992).

[5] See comments of Dirksen, 'Über die Collatio', 128–9.

[6] For the identification of Ambrose, see A. Rudorff, *Über den Ursprung und die Bestimmung der Lex Dei oder Mosaiacarum et Romanarum legum Collatio* (Berlin, 1868), 276–85. See further, the comments of Jörs, 'Collatio', col. 367; Hyamson, liii–lvi; and Ostersetzer, 'La Collatio', 69–70. Hohenlohe, *Ursprung*, 5–28, attempted to resurrect this identification by specifying the circle of Ambrose, unsuccessfully in the eyes of Bernhard Kübler in his review in *ZRG (R.A.)* 56 (1936), 361–2. However, Hohenlohe renewed his argument in 'Noch einmal Ursprung und Zweck der Collatio Mosaicarum et Romanarum Legum', *Archiv für Katholisches Kirchenrecht* 119 (1939), 352–64 and 'Um die Geheimnisse der "Collatio legum mosaicarum et romanarum"', *SDHI* 5 (1939), 486–90. Max Conrat (Cohn), 'Hieronymus und die Collatio', *Hermes* 35 (1899), 344–7, had earlier proposed St Jerome as the author instead. J. Wittig, *Der Ambrosiaster 'Hilarius'. Ein Beitrag zur Geschichte des Papstes Damasus* (Breslau, 1906), I, 53–7, was certain the author of the *Collatio* was Ambrosiaster, although the style of this late antique author seems not to match that of the Collator. More recently on Ambrosiaster, see Jacobs, 'Roman Christians and Jewish law', 95–7. In general, see Schrage, 'La date', 401–3.

In the last hundred years, most scholars have moved away from such firm identifications of exact individuals as possible authors of the work, noticing that there is no empirical evidence to support Ambrose's authorship and rightly observing that the style of the *Collatio* is much less elegant than that of the Bishop of Milan.[7]

Since there is not enough evidence to identify an exact person as the Collator, a better approach is to figure out what type of person he was. There are clues in the work to suggest what his education and occupation might have been. For instance, we have seen that the types of juristic sources the Collator used strongly suggest he was a lawyer. Not only does he use the celebrated five jurists (Paulus, Ulpian, Papinian, Modestinus, and Gaius), but he also had ready access to the *Codex Gregorianus*, the *Codex Hermogenianus*, and at least one fourth-century constitution.[8] He chose passages from the jurists that wrestled with such traditional Roman laws as the Twelve Tables, the *Lex Aquilia*, and the *leges Corneliae* (among others). In short, he seems to be a product of Roman legal education in the second half of the fourth century.[9] Looking at a few references to how he used such sources can confirm his occupation. Prefacing a quotation from Modestinus, he writes (at Coll. 1. 12) '*Modestinus . . . generaliter loquitur*' (or 'Modestinus . . . says generally') and describing a statement by Ulpian (Coll. 2. 4) he writes '*et cum diceret*' (or 'when he also says') implying that he had ready access to such legal works (and implying his audience may have had such access also). While not a brilliant original legal thinker, he seems to be a lawyer lifting passages from the great jurists of the Roman past (and from works that he thought were written by the great jurists) in order to show the similarities between biblical and Roman law.

Positing a career as a lawyer can be of further help in clarifying the Collator's probable education and even can suggest some ideas about his class background. Training for a career in law had traditionally grown out of the study of rhetoric in the Roman world. We can see

[7] See Hyamson, lvi. See the amusing comment of Solazzi, 'Per la data', 485, who rightly argues that the style is clearly not that of Ambrose ('*La buona fama di S. Ambrogio non è in pericolo*').

[8] On the Collator as lawyer, see Harries, 'How to make a law code', 70; Honoré, *Crisis of Empire*, 8.

[9] See Ammianus, 30. 16 on weak lawyers having forgotten the contents of their *codices* or law books ('*e quibus ita sunt rudes non nulli, ut numquam se codices habuisse meminerint*').

how such training worked in the autobiographical *Confessions* of St Augustine (who must have been a close contemporary of the Collator). Born in 354, his father had hopes that he would become a lawyer and perhaps enter the imperial administration. With that aim in sight, Augustine left his village school of Thagaste, went first for further schooling in Madoura, and then for advanced study in rhetoric at Carthage probably around 373.[10] However, like Martin Luther more than 1,000 years later, he frustrated his father's ambitions and did not pursue the study of law. In this decision Augustine bucked a trend as his contemporary Libanius, the great eastern professor of rhetoric, bemoaned that many students terminated their study of rhetoric early to concentrate on the jurists and law itself in centres of legal training at Berytus (Beirut) and Rome.[11] Augustine's friend Alypius did exactly this as he left the schools of rhetoric in North Africa for the law schools of Rome.[12]

The examples of Augustine, Alypius, and Libanius give us good insight into the background and training of lawyers in the latter half of the fourth century. It seems that most lawyers came from the middle level of Roman town or city society. Even Augustine's father Patricius, connected to the curial families of Thagaste, while periodically strapped for cash, saved enough for Augustine to have the opportunity of such training.[13] The goal, of course, was that this profession would be lucrative enough to ensure a good living as well as the opportunity to enter the ranks of the imperial civil service.[14] Some contemporaries, of course, found the motivations and actions

[10] Augustine, *Confessions*, Books 2 and 3.

[11] Libanius, *Or.* 2. 43–4; more generally at *Or.* 1. 154. For a recent study of Libanius and his students, see R. Cribiore, *The School of Libanius in Late Antique Antioch* (Princeton, 2007). For an examination of ancient Berytus including treatment of the law school, see L. Jones Hall, *Roman Berytus: Beirut in late antiquity* (London, 2004).

[12] Augustine, *Confessions*, 6. 7–10. For treatment of the theory that this section was written before the rest of the *Confessions*, see J. J. O'Donnell, *Augustine Confessions II: Commentary on Books 1–7* (Oxford, 1992), 360–2.

[13] On the expenses involved in higher education in the late empire, see R. Kaster, *Guardians of Language: The grammarian and society in late antiquity* (Berkeley, 1988), 21–5. For a description of law students in the sixth century, see Humfress, 'Law and legal practice in the Age of Justinian', 171–6. On the emphasis on the jurists in late antiquity, see Harries, *Cicero and the Jurists*, 49–50.

[14] On ambitions and rewards, see Kaster, *Guardians of Language*, 103–4. On law as a career, see Honoré, *Crisis of Empire*, 6–8; Jones, *Later Roman Empire*, 507–16 (esp. 510–13).

of some ambitious lawyers corrupt.[15] The Collator then might well have come from a similar background. His family (or family connections) probably had enough money to pay for his education, most likely first in rhetoric, then in law.[16]

To understand the Collator, it is helpful to look at him in the context of socio-economic status. It is tempting to label him as 'middle class' in that his position probably stood between the (often hereditary) upper class and the impoverished agricultural and manufacturing workers (both free and slave). Such a label however is misleading because the ancient world had nothing like the large middle class of modern western society.[17] In pre-industrial agricultural societies like the later Roman Empire, probably only about 10–15 per cent of the population (at the most) was not involved in food production.[18] That group would include an array of people descending in wealth and status from the wealthiest landowners and high-ranking administrative and military leaders to the civil servants and soldiers, from wealthy long-distance merchants to local salesmen and tradesmen. The Collator's education places him in the 10–15 per cent, but somewhere above a tradesman or legionary. However, the simple nature of his prose prefaces to quotations in his work suggests he was not from the highest level of the administration, but instead might have been either a working lawyer or a functionary in the judicial wing of the civil service. I have labelled him 'non-elite' as he seems to have rested below the level of the *clarissimi* (an honorific order of the late empire) and the leaders of Church or State, but was still a literate member of the population freed from food production.[19] He thus offers a glimpse of the worldview of the working non-elites who were the proto-middle class in the later Roman Empire. This sets him apart from such writers as Ambrose who came from a powerful elite background or Ammianus who certainly must

[15] See Ammianus, 30. 4. On this famous digression, see J. Matthews, 'Ammianus on Roman law and lawyers' in J. den Boeft *et al.*, *Cognitio Gestorum: The historiographic art of Ammianus Marcellinus* (Amsterdam, 1992), 47–57.

[16] On the expenses occurred in the study of Roman law in this period, see Cribiore, *School of Libanius*, 187–8.

[17] M. I. Finley, *The Ancient Economy*, 2nd edn (Berkeley, 1985), 48–51. See also the recent comparative analysis in B. G. Trigger, *Understanding Early Civilizations* (Cambridge, 2003), 142–66 ('Class Systems and Social Mobility').

[18] P. Crone, *Pre-Industrial Societies* (Oxford, 1989), 13–16.

[19] On such titles, see J. Lendon, *Empire of Honour: The art of government in the Roman world* (Oxford, 1997), 224–9 and J. Matthews, 'The Roman Empire and the proliferation of elites', *Arethusa* 33 (2000), 429–46.

have come from a wealthy family.[20] Augustine may have shared some attributes of background with the Collator, but his skills and ambition were such that he rose to high status first within the world of education and then within the Church. The Collator appears to have had not as much success, but as such can show us how a middling judicial functionary understood the process of conversion in the late fourth century.

There has also been dispute over where the Collator wrote his work, ranging from the eastern half of the Roman Empire, to Africa, to Italy.[21] While we cannot know exactly, the fact that he wrote in Latin, used a Latin translation of the Bible, and that his work was preserved in Western Church archives suggests he wrote in at least the western half of the Roman Empire. Since he quotes at least one constitution posted at Rome (at Coll. 5. 3. 1), it is likely that he might have at some point been in Italy and it is tempting to contemplate that he could have studied law at Rome. Indeed, the *Collatio* may have worked its way to Gaul in the early fifth century along with an exodus of lawyers after the Visigothic sack of Rome in 410.[22]

B. THE RELIGIOUS ANGLE

While the identification of the Collator as a Roman lawyer in the west seems probable, much more hotly argued is his religious affiliation. It is not likely that he was a pagan, since he had a Latin text of the Bible in front of him while he worked, was quite familiar with it, and perceived it as divinely inspired.[23] The debate focuses instead on whether the Collator was Christian or Jewish.[24] While the

[20] On Ambrose, see McLynn, *Ambrose of Milan*, 1–52. On Ammianus, see Matthews, *Roman Empire of Ammianus*, 67–80 and Barnes, *Ammianus Marcellinus and the Representation of Historical Reality*, 54–64.

[21] For the east, see Huschke, 'Alter und Verfasser', 26–7; for Africa, see Schrage, 'La date', 416; for Italy, see Liebs, *Italien*, 165–6.

[22] On the migration of lawyers from Italy to Gaul in this period, see Honoré, *Crisis of Empire*, 190; Liebs, *Italien*, 175–6.

[23] See Coll. 6. 1. 1 for *lex divina* and Coll. 16. 1. 1 for *scriptura divina*. See also Coll. 7. 1. 1 (*sicut lectio manifestat*) on reading the Bible. For a brief discussion of the possibility of a pagan Collator, see Smits, *Collatio*, 13–14.

[24] Part of this section is a revision of portions of my 'Religious identity and purpose', 126–47, based on comments of scholars and further research into Christian sources. I thank the late Professor Alan Samuel, editor-in-chief of Edgar Kent, Inc., for his support of this research.

standard scholarly view by the early twentieth century had been that the author was a Christian, this supposition was challenged in 1930 by an influential work of Edoardo Volterra.[25] This famous scholar of Roman law suggested that the *Collatio* might actually be the product of a Jewish Talmudic scholar in Italy writing an apologetic work explaining Judaism in the early fourth century to the Roman elite.[26] Following this argument, the organization of the *Collatio* would then make sense because such an anonymous Jewish Collator was attempting to show the similarities between Judaism and traditional Roman culture by compiling examples from Hebrew and Roman legal culture.[27]

After comparing and contrasting the Latin text of the citations of Hebrew law in the *Collatio* with both the Greek version of the Septuagint and the Hebrew text, Volterra suggested that the Collator made his translations by checking the Septuagint against the Hebrew text and then produced his own Latin translations.[28] Since Volterra had adopted a dating to the early fourth century for the work (based upon his rejection of the constitution of 390 quoted at Coll. 5. 3. 1 as an interpolation), he argued the Collator wrote when the apparatus of the Roman Empire was still mostly pagan. Thus, this hypothetical Jewish Collator might have directed his work at an audience of important Romans who might then recognize the similarities between Roman and Jewish culture and respect the antiquity of the Jews. This is certainly a provocative thesis and it is important that it was raised. Indeed, the fact that the Collator never mentions 'Jesus' or 'Christ' throughout the entire text might even seem to support it further. Volterra further hypothesized that the *Collatio* was originally a much longer work than what we see in the surviving manuscripts, and probably included an introduction explaining the author's identity and plan, but theorized that the work was severely edited by Christians in the medieval period to Christianize it and remove its original Jewish apologetic message.[29]

[25] Volterra, *Collatio.*

[26] *Ibid.*, 122.

[27] Marquard Freher, 'Parergon', reprinted in E. Otto (ed.), *Thesaurus Iuris Romani*, 2nd edn (Utrecht, 1733), I, cols. 852–948 at 872–3, had toyed with the idea of Jewish authorship for the *Collatio* in the early seventeenth century. On this possibility, see the comments of Hyamson, xlix, Volterra, *Collatio*, 108–9 n. 1, and Ostersetzer, 'La Collatio', 68. Volterra's treatment, however, is so much more fully developed that it can be seen as the first definitive articulation of the thesis.

[28] Volterra, *Collatio*, 53–86.

[29] Volterra, *Collatio*, 112.

Many were quickly drawn to Volterra's thesis (including immediate reviews by Ernst Levy and Gaitano Scherillo).[30] For instance, Israel Ostersetzer adopted the view that the Collator was Jewish, but revised the dating to the late fourth century, following the internal evidence of the *Collatio* (and thus accepting the constitution at Coll. 5. 3. 1). Ostersetzer argued that the Jewish Collator might have been attached to the staff of the Jewish patriarch and could have composed his work to try to convince the Roman government to continue to allow Jews some measure of internal arbitration.[31]

The thesis of a Jewish Collator is certainly stimulating. However, not all were unhesitatingly convinced by it. Nicolaas Smits argued that it would not be out of place for a Christian compiler to seek out passages from the Hebrew Scriptures if such an author was looking for laws to compare with Roman laws.[32] Smits went through the translated quotations from the Hebrew Bible in the *Collatio* and argued that the Collator did not definitely work from the original Hebrew, but instead might have used an older Latin translation of the Hebrew Bible (a western Old Latin Bible or *Vetus Latina* such as the *Itala*).[33] Smits also suggested that the Collator worked in the late fourth century or early fifth century, based on the constitution of Theodosius cited at Coll. 5. 3. 1 which Smits felt was not an interpolation, but rather originally part of the work.[34]

Smits' argument against Jewish authorship was supported by some work by Fritz Schulz. Schulz made a detailed analysis of the Biblical texts cited in the *Collatio* and argued that the text of the *Collatio* was imperfect and suggested several emendations to these passages.[35] These changes made the Latin translations of the biblical passages in the *Collatio* less like the Hebrew original and Greek Septuagint and more like existing versions of the Old Latin Bible. Schulz suggested that the Collator used such a Latin translation and that there were no grounds to suspect he was Jewish.

[30] See E. Levy, Review of Volterra, 698–703 (esp. 700–1 on identity), and G. Scherillo, Review of Volterra, 255–65.

[31] Ostersetzer, 'La Collatio', 65–96.

[32] Smits, *Collatio*, 15–17. See the comments of Liebs, *Italien*, 164.

[33] See further, Hyamson, xxxiii–xxxiv; Jörs, 'Collatio', col. 368; Mommsen, *Collatio*, 130–4; and Smits, *Collatio*, 31–43.

[34] Smits, *Collatio*, 15–23, 162–3, 183.

[35] Schulz, 'biblischen Texte', 20–43.

Even in the face of the criticism of Smits and Schulz, the hypothesis of a Jewish Collator, developed by Volterra and furthered by Ostersetzer, has received much support for several decades.[36] Although some researchers have laid out some reasons to doubt the Jewish identity of the Collator,[37] the Jewish Collator thesis has been supported forcefully by a larger group.[38] The most fully developed of these is that of Leonard Victor Rutgers. Because of the recent nature of his argument, his modifications to Volterra's thesis, and his thorough overview of earlier scholarship, I will give Rutgers' argument detailed attention.

Although Rutgers follows Volterra that the Collator was Jewish, he accepts that he used a Latin translation of the Septuagint other than that of Jerome for the source for his citations of Hebrew law.[39] He also accepts a late fourth-century dating based upon the constitution of Theodosius in the text at Coll. 5. 3 and follows the standard view that the Collator probably wrote in Italy.[40] Rutgers suggests that the structure of the *Collatio* being a series of quotations from Roman laws and jurists indicates that the Collator was not a jurist, nor even

[36] For instance, see Daube, 'Collatio 2. 6. 5'; Rabello, 'Alcune note sulla Collatio e sul luogo d'origine', 177–86; Rabello, 'Sull ebraicità dell autore della Collatio Legum Mosaicarum et Romanarum', 339–49; and Rabello, 'Sul Decalogo "Cristianizzato" e l'autore della "Collatio Legum Mosaicarum et Romanarum"', 133–5. For further scholarship on a Jewish identity of the Collator, see E. Levy's review of Volterra in *ZRG (R.A.)* 50 (1930), 698–705; P. De Francisci, 'Coll. 6. 7. 1 ss.', *IURA* 3 (1952), 222–4.

[37] Smits, *Collatio*, 161–79; Liebs, *Italien*, 162–74; Frakes, 'Religious identity and purpose', 131–43; Jacobs, 'Roman Christians and Jewish law', 85–99; and Frakes, 'Lex Dei and Latin Bible', 425–41.

[38] See J. Gaudemet, *La Formation du droit Seculier et du droit de l'eglise aux IV et V siecles* (Paris, 1957), 90–1; Rutgers, *The Jews in Late Ancient Rome*, 210–53; Barone-Adesi, *L'età della Lex Dei*; L. Cracco Ruggini, 'Ebrei e Romani a Confronti nell' Italia Tardoantica', *Italia Judica* (Rome, 1983), 38–65; Pugliese, 'A suggestion', 161–75. On Barone-Adesi's devotion to his mentor Volterra, see M. Bianchini's review of Barone-Adesi in *Iura* 43 (1992), 144–8. Rutgers republished his chapter as 'Jewish literary production in the Diaspora in late antiquity: The western evidence' in Rutgers, *The Hidden Heritage of Diaspora Judaism* (Leuven, 1998), 235–84. See further, Lucrezi, *L'uccisione dello schiavo*, 120–33; Lucrezi, 'Sulla Data di redazione', 611. See also K. L. Noethlichs, *Die Juden im christlichen Imperium Romanum [4.-6. Jahrhundert]* (Berlin, 2001), 200–2. See further, A. M. Rabello, 'La Datazione', 421. Although Lucrezi in his 'Lex Dei e comparazione Giruidico', *AARC* 15 (2005), 57–82, allows that there are two possibilities (Christian and Jewish) and both have problems, in his *La violenza sessuale*, 142, he opts again for a Jewish Collator.

[39] See Rutgers, *Jews in late ancient Rome*, 214.

[40] *Ibid.*, 216–18.

an original thinker (similar to the picture of Solazzi and Harries mentioned in the introduction to this book).[41] Rutgers felt that the Collator was not a Christian because he gave so much attention to Hebrew laws other than the Ten Commandments and suggested that Christian writers by this point saw such legalistic rules as irrelevant.[42] Rutgers argues that accepting an intended audience of pagan lawyers for the *Collatio* for a Christian compiler presupposes that the legal profession precluded conversion to Christianity. [43]

An important facet for the thesis of Jewish identity is that the Collator's purpose was to show the importance of Hebrew law to Christians who may have been playing a role in reducing the authority of Jewish law through legislation such as that surviving as *CTh* 2. 1. 10, dated to 3 February 398.[44] In this constitution, Arcadius and Honorius reduced the type of cases held before Jewish mediators to religious matters and to civil cases that both sides agreed could be held before such arbitrators.[45] But, it is important to recognize that the constitution surviving as *CJ* 1. 4. 7 (dated only a few months later from the same emperors to the same prefect) presents the same kind

[41] *Ibid.*, 215.

[42] See *Ibid.*, 222–32, where he cites Tertullian, *Adversus Iudaeos* and Ambrosiaster, *Quaestiones.* See also 233–6, where Rutgers compares the citations of Hebrew law in the *Collatio* with those of the Church Fathers in the series *Biblia Patristica*, ed. J. Allenbach (Paris, 1986: CNRS).

[43] For discussion of possibility of pagan intended audience, see Smits, *Collatio*, 177–8; Liebs, *Italien*, 170; and Frakes, 'Religious identity', 145–7.

[44] *CTh* 2. 1. 10:

IDEM AA. AD EUTYCHIANUM P(RAEFECTUM) P(RAETORI)O. Iudaei Romano et communi iure viventes in his causis, quae non tam ad superstitionem eorum quam ad forum et leges ac iura pertient, adeant solemni more iudicia omnesque Romanis legibus inferant et excipiant actiones: postremo sub legibus nostris sint. Sane si qui per conpromissum ad similitudinem arbitrorum apud Iudaeos vel patriarchas ex consensu partium in civili dumtaxat negotio putaverint litigandum, sortiri eorum iudicium iure publico non ventetur: eorum etiam sententias provinciarum iudices exequantur, tamquam ex sententia cognitoris arbitri fuerint adtributi. DAT. III NON. FEB. CONSTANT(INO)P(OLI) HONOR(IO) A. IIII ET EUTYCHIANO V. C. CONSS.

Latin text from Mommsen, *Theodosiani libri*, 75–6.

[45] Regarding *CTh* 2. 1. 10 of 398, see Rutgers, *Jews in Late Ancient Rome*, 239–50; Ostersetzer, 'La Collatio', 91. Rutgers, 248–50, attributes the creation of laws variously to 'lawgivers' and 'Roman authorities'. While this is generally correct, it should be stressed that the consistory and the *quaestor* would draft the law which the emperor(s) then had to approve. See further, Harries, 'Roman Imperial Quaestor', 148–72; Honoré, *Emperors and Lawyers*; and Harries, *Law and Empire in Late Antiquity*, 36–55.

of restrictions for cases held before bishops as Christian mediators.[46] The similar message of these constitutions when seen in the context of the Collator working between 392 and 395 (and thus only a few years earlier than these laws of 398) make the argument for a hypothetical Jewish Collator aiming his work at Christian administrators intent bent on reducing Jewish legal authority difficult to accept.

Other portions of the revised argument for Jewish authorship for the *Collatio* must likewise be examined carefully. The first point that must be addressed is the likelihood of a Jewish author using a Christian Latin translation of the Hebrew Bible as it appears the Collator did. A brief look at the development of the text of the Hebrew Bible indicates that the Hebrew *textus receptus* emerged after the first century CE with a proto-Masoretic text sometime in the second century, before it was systematized into the Masoretic text.[47] Some synagogues in fourth-century Italy probably still used the Hebrew Scriptures in Hebrew or Aramaic.[48] Since knowledge of Greek was certainly widely known in various parts of the dispersed Jewish community in the late empire, and shows up in a large number of Jewish inscriptions in Rome in this period, it could be that a

[46] *CJ* 1. 4. 7:

Idem AA. Eutychiano pp. Si qui ex consensu apud sacrae legis antistitem litigare voluerint, non vetabuntur, sed experientur illius (in civili dumtaxat negotio) arbitri more residentis sponte iudicium. Quod his obese non potuerit nec debebit, quos ad praedicti cognitioris examen conventos potius afuisse quam sponte venisse constiterit. D. VI K Aug. Mediolani Honorio A. IIII et Eutychiano conss.

Latin text from P. Krüger, *Codex Iustinianus* (Berlin, 1895). English translation adapted from S. P. Scott, *The Civil Law* (Cincinnati, 1932), XII and Justice Fred C. Blume, 'Annotated Justinian Code' (available at <http://uwacadweb.uwyo.edu/blume&justinian/>):

The Same Augusti to the Praetorian Prefect Eutychianus. If, by the consent of both parties, those who might wish to institute proceedings before a bishop of the Sacred Law, they shall not be forbidden to do so; but such proceedings shall only be instituted in civil matters before an arbiter who voluntarily presides. But the decision of the bishop cannot and should not prejudice those who have been summoned to the trial, instead of having voluntarily appeared. Given at Milan on the sixth of the Kalends of August, during the Consulate of the Emperor Honorius, Consul for the fourth time, and Eutychianus.

On this law, see further, Frakes, *Contra Potentium Iniurias*, 206–9.

[47] See S. Talmon, 'The Old Testament text' in Ackroyd and Evans, *The Cambridge History of the Bible*, I, 159–99; E. Würthwein, *Der Texte des Alten Testament* (Stuttgart, 1988), available in translation as *The Text of the Old Testament*, tr. E. F. Rhodes (Grand Rapids, 1995); and E. Tov, *Textual Criticism of the Hebrew Bible*, 2nd edn (Minneapolis, 2001).

[48] See A. Diez-Macho (ed.), *Neophyti 1. Targum Palestinense Ms de la Biblioteca Vaticana* (Madrid, 1968–1979), 19*–114*, for use of Aramaic Targumim of the Hebrew Scriptures in Italy.

Jewish author might have referred to the Greek text of the Septuagint for Hebrew laws if he did not have access to Hebrew or an Aramaic *Targum*.[49] While all those are likely vehicles for transmission of Hebrew law, it is unlikely that a Jewish Collator would have turned to a Christian Latin translation like the Old Latin Bible (derivative in its source of the Hebrew Bible from the Septuagint).

Would a Christian Collator in the late fourth century have used references to Hebrew laws or would such references be considered inappropriate by Christians in this period? Certainly, Christians in the first and second centuries continued to value the Ten Commandments (and some other laws of Moses). Indeed, while James the Just played an important role in producing the decree in Jerusalem that allowed Gentiles to be Christians if they avoided the flesh and licentiousness associated with blood sacrifice, he also seems to have felt that Christians should follow the Ten Commandments (James 2: 8–13; Acts 15: 4–29).[50] Moreover, the *Didache* (a manual for Christians from the second or even late first century) presents an overview of the importance of the sixth through tenth commandments (with a few additional crimes thrown in) that overlaps to a large degree with the topics of the Collator's titles.[51] The second-century

[49] On growth of the use of Greek language by Jews, see J. Finegan, *The Archeology of the New Testament* (Princeton, 1992), 325–6. On the use of the Greek Septuagint by the Jews, see L. Greenspoon, 'Mission to Alexandria: Truth and legend about the creation of the Septuagint, the first Bible translation', *Bible Review* 5 (1989), 34–41. See further Stark, *Rise of Christianity*, 57–8.

[50] On the importance of the Ten Commandments for James, see B. Witherington, *Jesus the Sage* (Minneapolis, 1994), 242–7; R. Bauckham, *James: Wisdom of James, Disciple of Jesus the Sage* (London, 1999), 142–51; H. Shanks and B. Witherington, *The Brother of Jesus* (New York, 2003), 127–41; See also R. Bauckham, 'James and the Gentiles (Acts 15. 13–21)' in B. Witherington (ed.), *History, Literature, and society in the Book of Acts* (Cambridge, 1996), 154–84.

[51] For a recent edition and translation of the *Didache*, see Bart D. Ehrman, *The Apostolic Fathers* (Cambridge, MA: Loeb Classical Library, 2003), I, 403–43 (esp. 418–20 for *Didache* 2. 1–3: 'And now the second commandment of the teaching. Do not murder, do not commit adultery, do not engage in pederasty, do not engage in sexual immorality. Do not steal, do not practice magic, do not use enchanted potions, do not abort a fetus or kill a child that is born. Do not desire what belongs to your neighbour, do not commit perjury, do not give false testimony, do not speak insults, do not bear grudges.'). The anonymous author of the *Didache* placed pederasty after adultery, like the Collator. For a recent argument that contemplates pushing the dating for the composition of the work before the Gospel of Matthew, see J. Draper, 'Torah and troublesome Apostles in the *Didache* community' in J. Draper (ed.), *The Didache in Modern Research* (Leiden, 1996), 340–63. For an approachable recent treatment of the *Didache*, see the comments of E. Pagels, *Beyond Belief: The secret Gospel of Thomas* (New York, 2003), 15–18.

Theophilus of Antioch also stressed the importance of keeping the Ten Commandments in his *Apologia* to the pagan Autolycus (seemingly as one of the bases for defending his faith).[52]

When Pliny the Younger served as governor of Bithynia (111–13 CE), he described in an epistle to the Emperor Trajan how Christians, although guilty of being Christians, did not commit fraud, theft, adultery, or break an agreement or refuse to return a deposit which seems to reflect a devotion to the Ten Commandments in the Christian community in second-century Bithynia (again strikingly close to the titles of the *Collatio*).[53] We have seen that the Collator himself followed the broad conceptual outline of the second half of the Ten Commandments (with occasional references to other passages outside the canonical Ten Commandments). While it is true that Christian theologians did cite Hebrew laws less frequently in the second to fourth centuries, Christians still naturally had respect for the Hebrew Bible. For example, Origen (*c*.185–*c*.254) stressed the connections of the Hebrew Scriptures with the New Testament in his *Hexapla* and other works.[54] Similarly, Tertullian saw the Pentateuch as inspired scripture—in direct contrast to the famous heretic Marcion of Sinope who attempted to exclude the legal books of the Hebrew Bible.[55] Indeed, Tertullian in his *Apologia* directly states that the laws of the Romans are derived from the divine law (*divina lege*)

[52] Theophilus, *To Autolycus*, 3. 9, on the divine law of Moses. On this author, see further R. M. Grant, 'Theophilus of Antioch to Autolycus', *HTR* 40 (1947), 227–56.

[53] Pliny, *ep*. 10. 96. 7: '*Affirmabant autem hanc fuisse summam vel culpae suae vel erroris, quod essent soliti stato die ante lucem convenire, carmenque Christo quasi deo dicere secum invicem seque sacramento non in scelus aliquod obstringere, sed ne furta ne latrocinia ne adulteria committerent, ne fidem fallerent, ne depositum appellati abnegarent.*'

[54] See F. Field (ed.), *Origenis Hexaplorum quae supersunt* (Hildesheim, 1964). See also Origen, *Hom. in. Num.*, 9. 4. See further, C. K. Barrett, 'The interpretation of the Old Testament in the New', in Ackroyd and Evans, *The Cambridge History of the Bible*, I, 377–411 at 410–11, and M. F. Wiles, 'Origen as biblical scholar' in Ackroyd and Evans, 454–89 at 483.

[55] See Tertullian, *De Pudic*. 6. 3. 4. See further, A. von Harnack, *Marcion: das Evangelium vom fremden Gott*, 2nd edn (Leipzig, 1924); R. P. C. Hanson, 'Biblical exegesis in the early Church' in Ackroyd and Evans, 423–4; R. M Grant, 'Marcion and the critical method' in P. Richardson and J. Hurd (eds.), *From Jesus to Paul: Studies in honour of Francis Wright Beare* (Waterloo, ON, 1984), 207–15; and P. Lampe, *From Paul to Valentinus: Christians at Rome in the first two centuries*, English tr. of *Die Christen in den ersten beiden Jahrhunderten* (London, 2003), 240–6.

of Moses.[56] The continuing influence of the account of Moses by the second century BCE Artapanus (perhaps part of his *Jewish History*), in the works of Clement of Alexandria (*c.*150–*c.*215 CE) and Eusebius (*c.*260–*c.*340 CE) confirms the importance of the Hebrew prophet to late antique Christians.[57]

Examination of the *Didascalia Apostolorum* can help confirm continued Christian interest in the image and laws of Moses. This work was purportedly composed by the Apostles, but actually comes from a Christian, possibly a convert from Judaism, in perhaps the second half of the third century.[58] The author made use of various works including the *Didache*. The *Didascalia* gives various instructions to Christians, including attention to the role of women in the Church and how Christians should interpret the laws of Moses. The anonymous author of this work argued that the Ten Commandments

[56] Tertullian, *Apologia* 45. 4: '*Dum tamen sciatis ipsas leges quoque vestras quae videntur ad innocentiam pergere de divina lege, ut antiquiore forma, mutuatas. Diximus iam de Moysi aetate*' ['Though at the same time you must recognize that your own laws, which seem to tend to innocence, drew from the divine law, which is the more ancient pattern. We have spoken already of the date of Moses']. Latin text and English translation from T. R. Glover (ed.), *Tertullian, Apology, De Spectaculis* (Cambridge, 1966), 196–7. See further the earlier comments of Jörs, 'Collatio', cols. 367–8, as well as the recent comments of Jacobs, 'Roman Christians and Jewish law', 8.

[57] See Clement of Alexandria, *Stromata* 1. 23. 154; Eusebius, *Prep. Evang.* 9. 18. 1; 9. 23. 1–4; and 9. 27. 1–37. On Artapanus, see E. Gruen, 'Fact and fiction: Jewish legends in a Hellenistic context' in P. Cartledge, P. Garnsey, and E. Gruen (eds.), *Hellenistic Constructs* (Berkeley, 1997), 72–88 at 84–7. See also, D. Tiede, 'Religious propaganda and Gospel literature' in W. Haase (ed.), *ANRW* (Berlin, 1984), XXV(2), 1705–29 at 1719. Lastly, see E. Schwartz, 'Artapanos', *RE* (Stuttgart, 1895), II(1), col. 1306.

[58] The work was probably originally composed in Greek, but also survives in Syriac and, partially, in Latin. For the Syriac text, see A. Vööbus (ed.), *The Didascalia Apostolorum in Syriac*, 2 vols. (Leuven, 1979). For the Latin text, see F. X. von Funk (ed.)., *Didascalia et Constitutiones Apostolorum* (Paderborn, 1905). For the Greek fragments, see J. V. Bartlet, 'Fragments of the *Didascalia Apostolorum*', *JTS* 18 (1916–1917), 301–9. For an English translation, see R. Hugh Connolly, *Didascalia Apostolorum* (Oxford, 1929). For the date, see P. Galtier, 'La Date de la Didascalia des Apotres', *RHE* 13 (1947), 315–51. See further, Funk, *Didascalia*, iv–v, who had earlier felt that a date to the first half of the third century was likely, but changed his mind in 1901. See also, M. Metzger, *Les Constitutions Apostoliques* (Paris, 1985), I, 16. For a provocative study examining the *Didascalia*'s role in between rabbinic Judaism and Christianity, see C. Fonrobert, 'The *Didascalia Apostolorum*: A mishna for the Disciples of Jesus', *JECS* 9 (2001), 485–509. The mid fourth-century *Constitutiones Apostolorum* were in part based on this work and can aid in its reconstruction. See further, F. X. von Funk, *Die apostolischen Konstitutionen, eine literarhistorische Untersuchung* (Rottenburg am Neckar, 1891) and D. A. Fiensy, *Prayers Alleged to be Jewish: An examination of the Constitutiones Apostolorum* (Chico, 1983).

at least, but not all the more recondite Jewish laws regarding diet and other rituals (the 'Second Legislation'), were central to Christianity. At *Didascalia* 6. 16. 1–2, he writes: 'The Law then consists of the Ten Words and the Judgments, which God spoke before that the People made the calf and served idols. For also that it is called the Law, (is) truly on account of the Judgments. This is the simple and light Law, wherein is no burden, nor distinction of meats, nor incensing, nor offerings of sacrifices and burnt offerings.'[59] Loschiavo noticed that at *Didascalia* 6. 19. 5, one can see a similar comparison between Roman law and the law of Moses.[60] Regarding the sixth commandment of Moses, the anonymous compiler of the *Didascalia* writes: '*In Lege dicit: Non occides. Si quis ergo interfecerit, a lege per Romanos condemnatur et sub lege est*' ['In the law he says, you shall not kill. If indeed someone kills, he is condemned by the law by the Romans and is under the law'].[61] So, in the third-century *Didascalia* we can see continued interest in the concept of divine law (but avoidance of dietary laws and other social strictures) in one voice in the Christian community as well as an early attempt to compare Mosaic and Roman law.

Moreover, by the fourth century, it was already a long-established practice for the Christian liturgy to include readings from both the Hebrew and Christian Bibles (a format obviously still followed today).[62] Moses was clearly a revered figure in the fourth-century Church as Eusebius described Constantine as a new Moses.[63] Indeed, it has recently been pointed out that Julian's Christian education led

[59] Translation following Connolly, *Didascalia Apostolorum*, 107–8. For Latin text, see von Funk, *Didascalia* 6. 16. 1: '*Lex ergo est decalogus et iudicia, quae, antequam vitulum faceret populus et idololatriaret, locutus est Dominus. Nam lex vocata est specialiter propter iudicia. 2. Lex autem haec simplex est et levis, non habens onerantes parationes escarum neque sacrificia neque combustionum oblationes.*'

[60] Loschiavo, 'La legge', 81–2.

[61] Latin text from von Funk, *Didascalia*, 6. 19. 5. The same passage occurs in the Syriac version (see Vööbus, *The Didascalia Aposotolorum in Syriac*, II, 254). I would like to thank Hubert Kaufhold for aiding my translation of the Syriac text of this passage.

[62] See Justin Martyr, *First Apology*, 1. 44 and 1. 65–7. See further, J. A. Lamb, 'The place of the Bible in the Liturgy' in Ackroyd and Evans, *The Cambridge History of the Bible*, I, 563–86 at 570–5; more generally, O. Cullmann, *Early Christian Worship*, tr. A. Todd and J. Torrance (London, 1962), 1–33; and, more briefly, Metzger, *Early Versions*, 286.

[63] Eusebius, *Hist. Eccl.* 1. 2; 1. 4. For a study of the importance of Moses in Christian apologetics up to and including Eusebius, see A. Droge, *Homer or Moses? Early Christian interpretations of the history of culture* (Tübingen, 1989). See also, R. Wilken, *Judaism and the Early Christian Mind: A study of Cyril of Alexandria's*

him to recognize the universality of Moses' law in the sixth to tenth commandments (*Contra Galileos*, 152 B–E).[64] Obviously, Jerome would not have gone to the trouble of translating the Hebrew Scriptures (which he called the *Hebraica veritas* or 'Hebrew Truth') afresh for his new Bible if he had not thought they were important. Likewise, the use of the phrase 'Old Testament' by Jerome and Augustine confirms the continued relevance of the sacred Hebrew texts to Christians in the late fourth century.[65] While Ambrose suggested that the need for many of the Hebrew laws was eliminated by Jesus' death, it is now understood that John Chrysostom's late fourth-century sermons *Contra Judaeos* ('Against the Jews') was aimed at Christians who were still interacting with aspects of the Jewish faith.[66] Indeed, the dividing line between Jews and Christians may well have still been blurry in the fourth century.[67] Christians in the post-Roman west continued to value the Ten Commandments and the image of Moses as the divine law-giver.[68] Likewise, in the late antique east (or Byzantine Empire) we also see continued influence

exegesis and theology (New Haven, 1971), 143–61, and, most recently, C. Rapp, 'Comparison, paradigm, and the case of Moses in panegyric and hagiography' in Mary Whitby (ed.), *The Propaganda of Power: The role of panegyric in late Antiquity* (Leiden, 1998), 277–98. E. Becker, 'Konstantin der Grosse, der "neue Moses": Die Schlacht am Pons Milvius und die Katastrophe am Schilfmeer', *Zeitschrift der Kirchengeschichte* 31 (1910), 161–71, is still fundamental.

[64] Humfress, *Orthodoxy and the Courts*, 200–1.

[65] See Jerome, *ep.* 106. 9; *Apol.* 2. 33. Augustine, *Confessions* 5. 14. On Jerome, see further, Sparks, 'Jerome as biblical scholar' in Ackroyd and Evans, *The Cambridge History of the Bible*, I, 510–41. For Augustine, see further G. Bonner, 'Augustine as biblical scholar', in Ackroyd and Evans, 541–63, and, most recently, P. Fredricksen, *Augustine and the Jews: A Christian defense of Jews and Judaism* (New York, 2008).

[66] On Ambrose, see for example *epp.* 72–5. On John Chrysostom, see R. Wilken, *John Chrysostom and the Jews* (Berkeley, 1983). On the similarity to the *Collatio* on this point, see H. A. Drake, 'Socrates' question' in Frakes and Digeser, *Religious Identity in Late Antiquity*, 228–41 at 234–5.

[67] See further, D. Boyarin, *Border Lines: The partition of Judaeo-Christianity* (Philadelphia, 2004).

[68] See, for example, the early seventh-century Isidore of Seville, *Etymologica* 5. 1. On the eighth-century Irish *Liber ex lege Moysi*, see Fournier, 'Le Liber ex Lege Moysi', 221–34, and, more recently, Carella, 'Sources of the Prologue to the Laws of Alfred', 91–118. In general, on Irish interest in Mosaic law, see D. O'Corrain, 'Irish vernacular law and the Old Testament' in P. Ni Chathain and M. Richter (eds.), *Ireland and Christendom: The Bible and the missions* (Stuttgart, 1987), 284–310. Demonstrating late sixth and early seventh-century English and papal interest in Hebrew law, as well as its eighth-century Northumbrian reception, see Bede, *Hist. Eccl.* 1. 27. 5–9 which recounts Augustine of Canterbury's correspondence with Pope Gregory I. Loschiavo, 'La legge', 82–3, points out the importance of the Decalogue for Charlemagne (see MGH, *Capitularia* 1. 170. 33).

of the laws of Moses.[69] Besides, it is important to remember that the Collator chose to use the central laws of the second half of the Ten Commandments, not the 613 Mitzvot or other portions of the Halakhah. Therefore, use of the Old Latin Bible, respect for Hebrew Scriptures, and Hebrew laws do not guarantee Jewish authorship over Christian. Indeed, when keeping Tertullian's similar allusion to the roots of Roman law stemming from divine origin and the comparison of Mosaic and Roman law by the author of the *Didascalia*, the identity of the Collator is more likely to be Christian.[70] Such a conclusion is not surprising as it appears likely that a plurality, if not a majority, of the population of the Roman Empire might have been Christian by the end of the fourth century.[71]

C. THE COLLATOR'S AUDIENCE AND PURPOSE

While some earlier scholars argued that the author of the *Collatio* tried to establish internal Church penalties,[72] for over a century

[69] There are many examples. For instance, see the fifth-century Cyril of Alexandria, *Contra Julian*, 1. 17–18 (an attempted refutation of the fourth-century apostate emperor's *Against the Galilaeans*); on this author and Hebrew learning, see further Wilken, *Judaism and the Early Christian Mind*. See also the prologue affixed to the mid fifth-century *Syro-Roman Lawbook* (pr. 3: 'all people . . . have taken as their basis the law of Moses'). This passage goes on to stress the laws of God. For an excellent recent edition of this work, see W. Selb and H. Kaufhold, *Das Syrisch-Römische Rechtsbuch*, 3 vols. (Vienna, 2002). On the eighth-century Byzantine *Nomos Mosaikos*, see L. Burgmann and S. Troianos in D. Simon (ed.), *Fontes Minores* (Frankfurt, 1979), III, 126–67, as well as the comments of P. Pieler, 'Lex Christiana', in D. Simon (ed.), *Akten des 26. Deutschen Rechtshistorikertages* (Frankfurt, 1987), 485–503. Lastly, for the influence of Mosaic law on Medieval Georgia and Armenia, see Kaufhold, Review of Galbiati and Noja, 266–9.

[70] See Jonathan Price's review of Rutgers in *Journal of the American Oriental Society* 117 (1997), 720–1, where he suggests, 'despite Rutger's vigorous efforts, the strongest argument for the Jewishness of both works [i.e., the *Collatio* and the *Letters of Annas to Seneca*] rests on the possibility that they are not Christian'.

[71] If we accept anything close to the hypothetical conversion rate suggested by Stark, *Rise of Christianity*, 4–13, then by 350 just over half the population of the Roman Empire was Christian and it is possible that the percentage may have continued to increase 3.42 per cent a year (as Stark argued it did from the foundation of Christianity until 350). By the early 390s, this would place the number of Christians well over 90 per cent.

[72] See H. Schmitz, *Die Bussbücher und Bussdisciplin der Kirche nach handschriftlichen Quellen dargestellt* (Mainz, 1883), 194–201, who argued that the *Collatio* was an official Church handbook that set up appropriate punishments for various transgressions.

attention has moved to internal evidence in the work for hints of what the Collator's intended audience might have been. At the beginning of Title 7, in a passage we saw at the beginning of Chapter 1, the Collator emphasized that the 'jurists' who read his work should know how Moses had stated similar things to the law of the Romans (Coll. 7. 1. 1: *scitote iuris consultis*). Jörs and Hyamson translated the term *iuris consultis* here as 'jurists,' and Hyamson even suggested that these might have included legal advisors for bishops involved in mediations in episcopal courts (i.e. the *episcopalis audientia*), as well as Roman advocates.[73] While the phrase could mean simply lawyers in earlier Latin,[74] by this point in Roman history it more likely implies experts of law such as law professors or active lawyers in government circles. Schulz, following his model of viewing the *Collatio* as a series of layers by different compilers, argued that this vocative address in the *Collatio* was unusual and so might be an interpolation, especially since other parts of the sentence are lifted from Cicero, although not the phrase *iuris consulti*.[75] However, since the *Collatio* as a whole is made up of passages from the Bible, the jurists, and Roman law, it is completely in the spirit of the Collator to display some erudition by inserting an allusion to a work of Cicero, especially for an audience of jurists who might thus have included both lawyers in government service as well as some in private practice.[76]

This invocation of the Collator to his intended audience seems to be genuine. However, Rutgers argued that such an audience of lawyers would obviate Christian authorship because he felt an argument for a Christian Collator presupposes that jurists needed assistance in seeing Christianity as an attractive religion. We do not have to be so rigid in accepting such a preclusion. There is evidence of many lawyers who were pagans in the fourth century who converted to Christianity such as Firmicus Maternus and, close to the Collator's

[73] Jörs, 'Collatio', 367–70; Hyamson, xl–xliii, xlix (esp. n. 6). Recently, Loschavio, 'La legge', 79–80, has supported this purpose as well. Since Pugliese, 'A suggestion', 170–1, was convinced that the Collator was Jewish and was writing for a Jewish audience, he argued that the vocative address to the jurists was a rhetorical device.

[74] For instance, Cicero, *De Or.* 1. 48. 212 and *Leg.* 2. 19.

[75] Schulz, 'biblischen Texte', 33–4. See Cicero, *Pro Mil.* 3. 9.

[76] See Humfress, *Orthodoxy and the Courts*, 62–92 ('Legal Experts and Late Roman Courts').

day, Augustine's friend Alypius.[77] However, there were also Christians who became advocates (such as Ambrose).[78] So, in the Collator's day, a lawyer might have had both pagan and Christian colleagues.

Contemplating the context of political events and religious evolution that had recently taken place during the time frame when the *Collatio* was probably being composed (*c*.392–5) can be useful here. Although there had been an array of legislation against traditional divination since the reign of Constantine, Theodosius had only recently made public pagan worship (and state support for it) illegal,[79] but there was no law yet against private individual pagan belief (and, indeed, it is hard to legislate against such Orwellian 'Thought Crime'). The law codes provide solid evidence that many civil administrators in the imperial government were still pagans. In 409, emperors began to reduce the administrative positions that pagans could hold by decreeing in the law that survives as *CJ* 1. 55. 8 that the type of minor judge known as a *defensor civitatis* had to be Christian.[80] Such legislation was expanded upon in 415 when emperors produced a constitution preserved as *CTh* 16. 10. 21 that barred pagans from imperial civil service and gives special emphasis that they should no longer be either administrators or judges. Such legislation would probably not have been drafted unless the number of such pagan judges was regarded as some sort of problem or threat by the Christian emperors and their advisors (and, no doubt if they were serving as judges in 415, many of them had been lawyers for some time before that).

Other evidence shows there were still many pagan lawyers in the Roman west. For instance, it has been argued that the author of the *Historia Augusta*, the famous collection of imperial biographies now securely dated to the late fourth or early fifth century,[81] might

[77] On Firmicus, see H. A. Drake, 'Firmicus Maternus and the politics of conversion' in G. Schmeling and J. Mikalson (eds.), *Qui Miscuit Utile Dulci: Festschrift essays for Paul Lachlan MacKendrick* (Wauconda, 1998), 133–49, and Drake, *Constantine and the Bishops*, 424–6. On Alypius, see Brown, *Augustine of Hippo*, 67–9.

[78] McLynn, *Ambrose of Milan*, 31–44.

[79] See most famously, *CTh* 16. 10. 10.

[80] See discussion in Frakes, *Contra Potentium Iniurias*, 172–3.

[81] Dessau, 'Über Zeit und Persönlichkeit der Scriptores Historiae Augustae', 337–92; R. Syme, *Ammianus and the Historia Augusta* (Oxford, 1968), vi, 72–9; R. Syme, *Emperors and Biography: Studies in the Historia Augusta* (Oxford, 1971), 1–16; B. Pottier, 'L' Histoire Auguste, le consul Aurélien et la réception de la Notitia Dignatatum en occident', *Ant. Tard.* 14 (2006), 225–34; Paschoud, 'Chronique d'historiographie tardive', 349–61.

have been a pagan lawyer who worked as an assessor for the urban prefect of Rome in the 390s (exactly the time when the Collator wrote).[82] This might have been the type of colleague to whom the Collator, quite possible a fellow lawyer in Italy, wrote his work. We know from Ammianus' testimony that the law trade was bustling in exactly this period (probably in both the west and east).[83] So, in the short window from 392–5 when the Collator probably composed his work, Christianity can be arguably perceived as the dominant religion of the state, yet paganism was still fairly widespread throughout large parts of the empire, including Italy, and included many lawyers and judges.

Why would a Christian author aiming his work at pagan jurists have collated religious laws from the Hebrew Bible with Roman laws? The Collator implies throughout his work that the laws of the Romans have Hebrew precedents and it is difficult to escape the conclusion that he is attempting to show pagan jurists that his religion thus has intrinsic worth in that such laws anticipated similar legislation of the Romans. However, would a Christian author with such a plan in the 390s have selected texts from the Hebrew Scriptures? The answer seems to be yes. After all, as Smits noticed, if a Christian were looking for divine legal correlations with Roman law, he would have to turn to the Hebrew Bible. Since we have little in the way of actual distinct laws in the New Testament, a Christian looking to impress an audience of pagan jurists would have to turn to laws in the Hebrew Bible.[84] As we have seen, Tertullian himself took exactly the same approach when he argued that Roman laws stemmed from the same divine laws that Moses organized for the Hebrew Scriptures.[85]

Passages in the Gospel of Matthew show early Christian teaching still valued central aspects of Hebrew law (as we saw at the beginning of this chapter). While this work obviously dates from the first century, it continued to be studied and recited in services up to the end

[82] On the author of the *Historia Augusta*, see Honoré, *Crisis of Empire*, 190–211 as well as his earlier 'Scriptor Historiae Augustae', *JRS* 77 (1987): 156–76. See, however, Paschoud, 'Chronique d'historiographie tardive', 361.

[83] Ammianus, 30. 4. 2–22. It could be that this passage was as influenced by Ammianus' residence in Rome as by experiences in the east. On this passage, see further, Humfress, *Orthodoxy and the Courts*, 15–21.

[84] See comments of Wenger, *Die Quellen*, 547–8, who felt that use of Hebrew law in the *Collatio* did not preclude Christian authorship.

[85] Tertullian, *Apol.* 45. 4.

of the fourth century and, obviously, beyond. After giving the beatitudes in the Sermon on the Mount, Jesus is credited with saying (Matthew 5: 17–19):

> Do not think that I have come to abolish the law or the prophets; I have come not to abolish but to fulfill. 18. For truly I tell you until heaven and earth pass away, not one letter, not one stroke of a letter, will pass from the law until all is accomplished. 19. Therefore, whoever breaks one of the least of these commandments, and teaches others to do the same, will be called least in the kingdom of heaven; but whoever does them and teaches them will be called great in the kingdom of heaven.[86]

Slightly later in the same gospel, as we saw in the story of the rich young man at the beginning of this chapter, Jesus specifically refers to the importance of the Ten Commandments (Matthew 19: 16–19) and suggests that the good person should strive to follow them in his life.[87] If anything, then, the Collator was operating within a Christian tradition of the importance of the Ten Commandments.[88] This approach which would then explain why his work was adopted as part of the library of Western Church councils and bishops in the early Middle Ages, something less likely for a Jewish apologetic work. Indeed, the fact that the work survived suggests that the Collator may have had some sort of official status such as that of a lawyer associated with Roman administration.

[86] Tr. *NRSV*. Matthew 5: 17. *Μὴ νομίσητε ὅτι ἦλθον καταλῦσαι τὸν νόμον ἢ τοὺς προφήτας· οὐκ ἦλθον καταλῦσαι ἀλλὰ πληρῶσαι.* 18. *ἀμὴν γὰρ λέγω ὑμῖν· ἕως ἂν παρέλθῃ ὁ οὐρανος καὶ ἡ γῆ, ἰῶτα ἓν ἢ μία κεραία οὐ μὴ παρέλθῃ ἀπὸ τοῦ νόμου ἕως ἂν πάντα γένηται.* 19. *ὃς ἐὰν οὖν λύσῃ μίαν τῶν ἐντολῶν τούτων τῶν ἐλαχίστων καὶ διδάξῃ οὕτως τοὺς ἀνθρώπους, ἐλάχιστος κληθήσεται ἐν τῇ βασιλείᾳ τῶν οὐρανῶν. ὃς δ' ἂν ποιήσῃ καὶ διδάξῃ, οὗτος μέγας κληθήσεται ἐν τῇ βασιλείᾳ τῶν οὐρανῶν.* Nestle-Aland, *Novum Testamentum Graece*.

[87] Since this story also appears in Mark 10: 17–25 and Luke 18: 18–20, and thus all of the Synoptic Gospels, it may derive from Mark or both Mark and the hypothetical Q Gospel (although the similarity to Mark implies Markan priority here). For a classic study of the interrelationship between the Synoptic Gospels, see Canon B. H. Streeter, *The Four Gospels: A study of origins, treating of the manuscript tradition, sources, authorship, and date* (New York, 1924). See more recently the overview in Ehrman, *New Testament*, 92–100. The story may also have appeared in the hypothetical lost Gospel of the Hebrews. See P. Luomanen, 'Where did another rich man come from? The Jewish-Christian profile of the story about a rich man in the 'Gospel of the Hebrews' (Origen, Comm. In Matth. 15.14)', *Vigiliae Christianae* 57 (2003), 243–75. R. Fuller and D. Westberg, *Preaching the Lectionary: The Word of God for the church today*, 3rd edn (Collegeville, MN, 2006), 364–5, examine the difference between the versions of the story in Matthew and Mark.

[88] See further, John 14: 15.

Why would this anonymous Christian compiler structure his work the way he did? Scholars have wrestled with the purpose of the work for over a century. One scholarly answer is that the Collator meant the work to be helpful in the bishop's court or *episcopalis audientia.*[89] This type of internal Christian arbitration had evolved early on in Christian history (see 1 Corinthians 6: 1–11). In the second and third centuries, bishops had taken on this responsibility and Constantine had given judicial power to bishops in such matters. However, such a purpose will not work for the *Collatio* because the *episcopalis audientia* in the fourth century focused on civil cases and not the types of criminal cases dealt with in many pages of the *Collatio.*[90] If the Collator were a lawyer, he would have known that. And, indeed, it is striking that he would have omitted the name of Christ with such an audience in mind. So, we must look for another purpose.

To help understand the purpose of the work, it is useful to examine the *Collatio* while keeping in mind the Pagan-Christian dialogue (or interaction between traditional pagans and Christians).[91] There had been a trend toward syncretism in paganism since the late second century and of seeing the traditional pagan gods as different representatives of a unified God force.[92] This development seems to have accelerated in the mid to late third century. Many Christians had tried to explain their beliefs to pagans through drawing connections to this monotheistic or monistic trend. And, apparently, late pagans (as we can term those traditional believers in the fourth century) attempted to forge connections with the Christians in believing in a central God force by constructing an ambiguous (though inclusive) rhetoric. For instance, when the pagan civic leaders of Rome dedicated an arch to Constantine after his defeat of Maxentius in 312, they extolled his victories 'by divine inspiration

[89] This theory was originally developed by Bluhme in 1832. See the preface to his edition of the *Collatio*, in Boecking, *Corpus Iuris Romani Anteiustiniani*, 1: 310. It was supported by Hyamson, xl–xlii (and, esp. lvi). See also, more recently, Loschiavo, 'La legge', 79–80.

[90] On types of cases held before bishops, see *CTh* 1. 27. 1 probably of 324; *Con. Sirm.* 1 of 333; and *CJ* 1. 4. 7 of 398. See further Frakes, *Contra Potentium Iniurias*, 195–220.

[91] For framing the interaction as a dialogue, see Dodds, *Pagan and Christian in an Age of Anxiety*, 102–38.

[92] See, for example, Apuleius, *Metamorphosis* 11. 2–5.

and greatness of mind' (*instinctu divinitatis mentis magnitudine*).[93] What one scholar has called 'studied ambiguity' could be useful for both sides of the religious dialogue.[94] Likewise, in a panegyric (*Pan. Lat.* 12) delivered to Constantine, probably in Trier in 313, a pagan orator praises the power of a certain god (12. 2. 4: *quisnam deus*), the divine mind (12. 2. 5, 16. 2, and 26. 1: *divina mens*) and a supreme creator of things (12. 26. 1: *summus rerum sator*) while, again, praising the divine instinct (12. 10. 4: *divino monitus instinctu*).[95] We have already seen that in the Edict of Milan of 313, Constantine used the broad term *divinitatis* to refer to a God force.[96] Ten years later Constantine still tended to refer to God as 'Supreme God', 'God', 'the Divinity', Divine Will', or 'Divine Spirit', as can be seen in his famous Edict to the Palestinians, part of a general edict from 324 (preserved in Eusebius, *VC* 2. 24–42).[97] As late as 335, Eusebius of Caesarea tried to avoid using the name 'Christ' and instead used more vague terms for a monotheistic deity that would also be familiar to pagans from their own usage.[98]

The Collator may well have been doing something analogous with his avoidance of the name 'Christ' and his references to 'God' being open-ended terms such as *deus*.[99] The largest obstacle to this

[93] *CIL* VI. 1139 = *ILS* 694. On this phrase, see Lenski, 'The reign of Constantine', 59–90 at 70–1; L. Jones Hall, 'Cicero's *instinctu divino* and Constantine's *instinctu divinitatis*: The evidence of the Arch of Constantine for the Senatorial view of the 'Vision' of Constantine', *JECS* 6 (1998), 647–71. See also E. Marlowe, 'Framing the sun: The Arch of Constantine and the Roman cityscape', *The Art Bulletin* 88 (2006), 223–42.

[94] Averil Cameron, 'Constantinus Christianus' (Review of Barnes, *Constantine and Eusebius* and *New Empire of Diocletian and Constantine*), *JRS* 73 (1983), 184–90 at 189.

[95] For Latin text, see R. Mynors (ed.), *XII Panegyrici Latini* (Oxford, 1964). See also C. E. V. Nixon and B. S. Rodgers, *In Praise of Later Roman Emperors: The Panegyrici Latini* (Berkeley, 1994), 288–93 for introduction, and 294–333 for translation of *Pan. Lat.* 12.

[96] Lactantius, *De Mortibus Persecutorum*, 48. 2.

[97] See Cameron and Hall, *Eusebius: Life of Constantine*, 239–42 for commentary; Drake, *Constantine and the Bishops*, 243–4, for usage. For date, see Barnes, *Constantine and Eusebius*, 208–9. On authenticity, see A. H. M. Jones and T. C. Skeat, 'Notes on the genuineness of the Constantinian documents in Eusebius' Life of Constantine', *JEH* 5 (1954), 196–200, and B. Warmington, 'The sources of some Constantinian documents in Eusebius' Ecclesiastical History and the Life of Constantine', *Studia Patristica* 18 (1986), 93–8.

[98] See Drake, *Constantine and the Bishops*, 222.

[99] Coll. 1. 1. 1: *Moyses dei sacerdos*; 6. 7. 1: *ex divino nutu, divina . . . sententia, lex divina sic dicit*; 13. 1. 1: *stabunt duo homines ante deum*; 16. 1. 1: *scriptura divina*, 16. 1. 5: *et obtulit Moyses petionem earum coram deo*.

view is the scholarly argument that after the short reign of Julian the Apostate, Christian writers became more aggressive and less interested in conciliatory language toward pagans.[100] That is, many Christian leaders had become more inflexible regarding their religious identity and were now opposed to blurring the distinctions between Christianity and other religions. However, pagans continued to use the open-ended terminology. For instance, the anonymous pagan author of the *De Rebus Bellicis* used terms such as the *caelesti instinctu* (pr. 1) and *providentia divinitatis* (pr. 5 and 21) when he was writing sometime from 364–78.[101] Symmachus, the Prefect of Rome and devotee of traditional Roman religious beliefs, made a direct claim in his *Relationes* of 384 that every pagan temple was 'full of God' (*deus*) and that the 'divine mind' oversaw all religions.[102] Such conceptual inclusive terms were still used by some Christians in the 380s since the Christian Vegetius, a high-ranking civil servant, in his work on the Roman army also stressed the importance of the will of a God force in an ambiguous way terming it 'the Divinity' (2. 18. 4: *Divinitatis nutu*) and 'the Divine instinct' (2. 21.1: *Divinitatis instinctu*).[103]

Analysis of other pagan writers who were contemporaries of the Collator in Italy in the 390s can help shade the religious landscape of his time. As we have seen, the anonymous pagan author of the *Historia Augusta* wrote at about the same time and same place. While divining that author's purpose is difficult and the subject of much debate, he appears to use religiously neutral discourse (whether as an attempt at toleration or an appeal to defend his beliefs) in his narrative (and especially in his life of Severus Alexander where he claims that that third-century emperor included an image of Jesus in

[100] See, among others, Drake, *Constantine and the Bishops*, 434–40.

[101] For traditional dating, see E. A. Thompson, *A Roman Reformer and Inventor* (Oxford, 1952), 1–2. On pagan identity, see Averil Cameron, *Later Roman Empire, AD 284–430* (Cambridge, 1998), 26, who states the author was 'clearly a pagan and blames Constantine for extravagant public spending'.

[102] Symmachus, *Relatio* 3. 5 and 8. See R. H. Barrow, *Prefect and Emperor: The Relationes of Symmachus AD 384* (Oxford, 1973), 36–9.

[103] For Latin text, see M. D. Reeve (ed.), *Vegetius: Epitoma Rei Militaris* (Oxford, 2004). For date, see T. D. Barnes, 'The date of Vegetius', *Phoenix* 33 (1979), 254–7. For religious identity, see F. Mueller, *Vegetius: Abriss des Militärwesens* (Stuttgart, 1997), 11–13, who rightly underscores the importance of 2. 5 where Vegetius stresses the importance of recruits swearing loyalty to God and Christ and the Holy Spirit and the emperor (*Iurant autem per Deum et per Christum et per Sanctum Spiritum et per maiestatem imperatoris*).

his private chapel, along with those of Abraham, Orpheus, and the pagan wonder worker Apollonius of Tyana).[104]

More dramatic pagan use of ambiguous monotheistic vocabulary in Italy in the Collator's day can be seen in one last source. Ammianus, a pagan retired army officer writing in Rome in the early 390s possibly to an administrative audience,[105] several times refers to *deus* (or 'God') in the course of his *Res Gestae* as a way of conveying belief in a central God force.[106] So, in the early 390s Ammianus still used the purposely ambiguous vocabulary of a monistic God force while still saying some positive things about Christians.[107] Thus, it seems likely that pagans involved in aspects of civil and military administration still used open-ended monotheistic vocabulary in an increasingly official Christian state. Possibly they were attempting to

[104] *HA*, *Sev. Alex*, 29. The scholarly literature on religion in the *Historia Augusta* is large and complex. Among others, see H. Mattingly, 'The religious background of the "Historia Augusta"', *HTR* 39 (1946), 213–15; J. Straub, *Studien zur Historia Augusta* (Bern, 1952); J. Straub, *Heidnische Geschichtsapologetik in der christlichen Spätantike: Untersuchungen über Zeit und Tendenz der Historia Augusta* (Bonn, 1963); A. Momigliano, 'Pagan and Christian historiography in the fourth century' in A. Momigliano (ed.), *The Conflict between Paganism and Christianity in the Fourth Century* (Oxford, 1963), 79–99; Syme, *Ammianus and the Historia Augusta*, 137–41; S. A. Stertz, 'Christianity in the Historia Augusta', *Latomus* 36 (1977), 694–715; F. Paschoud, 'Raisonnements providentialistes dans l'Histoire Auguste', *BHAC* 1977/78 (*Antiquitas* IV 14), 163–78; Honoré, 'Scriptor', 164–5; F. Paschoud, 'La Storia Augusta come testimonianza e riflesso della crisi d'identità degli ultimi intellettuali pagani in Occidente' in G. Bonamente and A. Nestori (eds.), *I Cristiani e l'Impero nel IV secolo* (Macopata, 1988), 155–6; C. Bertrand-Dagenbach, *Alexandre Sévère et l' Histoire Auguste* (Brussels, 1990); and, most recently the survey in Paschoud, 'Chronique d' Historiographie Tardive', 349–64.

[105] See R. M. Frakes, '*Graecus* and *Res Gestae*: Ammianus Marcellinus and his intended audience', *Studies in Latin Literature and Roman History* 10 (2000), 392–442. A theory recently supported on the basis of other indicators by F. Wittchow, *Exemplarisches Erzählen bei Ammianus Marcellinus* (Munich, 2001), 365–86.

[106] Ammianus 16. 12. 13; 17. 13. 33; 18. 6. 3; 24. 1. 1; 24. 1. 2; 25. 7. 5. For the scope of the surviving books vs. the probable original length, see Frakes, 'Cross-references to the lost books of Ammianus Marcellinus', *Phoenix* 49 (1995), 232–46 and Frakes, 'Some thoughts on the lost books of Ammianus Marcellinus', *Ancient World* 31 (2000), 48–53 (reprinted in Frakes and Toye, *The Dance of Hippocleides: A Festschrift for Frank J. Frost*, 48–53).

[107] Ammianus, 18. 1. 4; 22. 11. 5; 22. 11. 10; 27. 3. 15. See the comments of Matthews, *Roman Empire of Ammianus*, 435–51. See, more recently, the insightful comments of Barnes, *Ammianus Marcellinus and the Representation of Historical Reality*, 79–94, esp. 80–1 where Barnes argues that the reason some scholars perceive Ammianus as a 'neutral' monotheist sympathetic to paganism and others as polemical against Christianity is that 'there is a deep and irremovable inconsistency in what the historian says about Christianity' that includes both views.

reach out to Christians just as Christians had reached out to their opponents in the third and early fourth century.

D. CONCLUSION: THE CHRISTIAN COLLATOR

It seems plausible, then, that the Collator was a Christian jurist in Italy in the early 390s who was hoping to draw in sensitive pagan colleagues through the use of inclusive vocabulary for the divine. The trend of mainstream Church leaders and theologians since the reign of Julian to move away from such devices to an increasingly more doctrinaire vision might not have percolated down to the level of the Collator whose simpler prose suggests that the author was not someone at the top of the pinnacles of the Church or the imperial civil service. However, he still might have felt a call to spread the word of Christianity in a suitable way to his fellow lawyers of the pagan perspective.

Here keeping the chronological context in mind can be of further help. It is significant that in the time the Collator seems to have worked, the Western Empire saw a serious usurpation under Eugenius (dominated by the *Magister Militum* Arbogast) from 392 to 394. While Eugenius was a Christian, we have seen that as part of an attempt to build support he actively supported individual senators seeking to restore traditional cults and used a rhetorical discourse of toleration toward powerful pagan senators marked symbolically by allowing the restoration of the Altar of Victory. After Theodosius finally defeated Eugenius and Arbogast at the Battle of the Frigidus River in September of 394, many Christian sources become increasingly hostile toward the remnants of the pagan elite in Italy (to the point where some scholars have deemed these Christian works as 'anti-pagan polemic').[108] Scholars of the *Collatio* have noted the chronological synchronicity of Eugenius' 'pagan-friendly' usurpation before and it could be that this event helped motivate the

[108] For the term, see Croke and Harries, *Religious Conflict in Fourth-century Rome*, 73. Under this rubric they include Prudentius's *Contra Symmachum*; the anonymous *Carmen contra Paganos*; Ps. Cyprian, *Carmen ad senatorem ex Christiana religione ad idolorum servitutem conversum*; Ps. Paulinus, *Carmen XXXII: Carmen ad Antonium*; Paulinus of Nola, *Carmen*; Prudentius, *Peristephanon*; and Ambrosiaster, *Quaestiones veteris et novi testamenti*.

Collator at some level to compose his work, perhaps to pagan lawyers who had become more active under Eugenius in Italy.[109]

However, positing this purpose is at odds with the standard scholarly view that increasingly after Julian, and now again after Eugenius, Christian authors would not try to find common ground with pagans, but instead would denounce them.[110] There may be some flaws to this approach. First, we have seen that the Emperors Valentinian and Valens had attempted to follow a tolerant course during their reign (364–78). Moreover, Vegetius' use of the religious *lingua franca* of *instinctu divinatis* shows that a high-ranking civil servant in the west might still use open-ended religious vocabulary in the 380s. The second problem is that such an approach takes the view of powerful emperors and bishops (through the surviving extracts of the law in the codes and the works of major bishops like Ambrose) and accepts that as the total history and *mentalité* of the era. The last few decades of scholarship on later periods in European history have showed us that alternative non-elite sources (such as inquisition records, accounts of lawsuits, and personal journals) can provide us with a more inclusive view of the mentalité of a period.[111] The Christian Collator, probably coming from the middle ranks of Roman town society in the mid and late fourth century, still felt it was possible to reach out to pagans. His more elite co-religionists, on the other hand, had turned more hostile and rigid in their view of paganism.

While some earlier scholars have forced the Collator into a different religion or different date, it is safer to accept that he was a Christian author reaching out to pagan colleagues in the legal and judicial systems of the late empire, trying to build common ground with

[109] Liebs, *Italien*, 170.

[110] See, for example, Fowden, *Empire to Commonwealth*, 56 ('Julian's failure did unique harm to his cause . . . He had given the Christians what they had previously been obliged to invent for themselves—an incarnation of polytheism, a single target to shoot at').

[111] Especially influenced by the third generation of the *Annales* School. See, for example, E. Le Roy Ladurie, *Montaillou: The promised land of error*, tr. G. Braziller (New York, 1978); C. Ginzburg, *The Cheese and the Worms: The cosmos of a sixteenth-century miller* (Baltimore, 1980); N. Z. Davis, *The Return of Martin Guerre* (Cambridge, MA, 1983); and R. Darnton, *The Great Cat Massacre and Other Episodes in French Cultural History* (New York, 1984). See further, P. Burke, *The French Historical Revolution: The Annales School, 1929–89* (Stanford, 1990) and A. Burguière, *L' École des annales: une histoire intellectuelle* (Paris, 2006).

them through his inclusive terminology for the divine. Since such an argument stands against current scholarly opinion, it is important to clarify his purpose. Christian works written before the death of Constantine or the reign of Julian the Apostate are usually labelled as 'apologetic' in that they are defending (from the Greek *apologia*) their minority religious beliefs in a pagan-dominated empire. We might better understand the Collator as a Christian lawyer attempting to explain the Truth of his religion to pagan colleagues in the 390s. While it would be delightful to end this book by stating that finally the enigma of the Collator has now *really* been solved, when dealing with ancient and medieval texts we can only argue in shades of plausibility and probability. On the basis of the surviving evidence of the work and its most plausible context, the most likely probability is that a Christian Collator attempted to draw pagan lawyers to Christianity through demonstrating the connections between the divine laws of Moses and the historic jurisprudence of the Romans. Such a conclusion, if correct, shows we should expand the umbrella of Christian apologetics beyond the reign of Julian to at least the last years of Theodosius' reign.

Part II

The Work (*Collatio Legum Mosaicarum et Romanarum*)

Sigla

Symbols and abbreviations used in Latin text and apparatus:

[ ] = Words supplied, but not in manuscripts
( ) = Words or letters not in the assumed archetype
[. . .] = Spaces exist in manuscripts, but obliterated words and letters are difficult to supply
< > = Words or letters in the manuscripts, but added during the manuscript tradition either by scribal error or by interpolation
B = Berlin manuscript (*Codex Berolinensis*) = 9th Century
V = Vercellli manuscript (*Codex Vercellensis*) = 10th or 11th Century
W = Vienna manuscript (*Codex Vindobonensis*) = Late 9th century

Names of modern scholars, unless otherwise indicated, refer to modern editions of the *Collatio.*

Incipit Lex Dei quam Dominus praecepit ad Moysen[1]

(Titulus 1)
De Sicariis et Homicidis casu vel voluntate[2]

1. 1. 1. MOYSES dei sacerdos haec dicit:
Si quis percusserit hominem ferro et occiderit eum, morte[3] moriatur. 2. si autem manu lapide, quo mori possit, percusserit et mortuus fuerit, homicida est: morte[4] moriatur. 3. si autem per inimicitiam inpulerit eum vel inmiserit super eum aliquod vas ex insidiis et mortuus fuerit, 4. vel per iram percusserit eum manu et mortuus fuerit, morte[5] moriatur.

[1] I follow Huschke, *Lex Dei*, in using no brackets in the title of the work since B, V, and W all bear traces of this beginning. See Mommsen, *Collatio*, for variants (although in my reading of the actual B manuscript in Berlin, I saw traces of a probable 'D', another unreadable letter and then an s, suggesting a reading of 'Dns' as an abbreviation for *Dominus*). V = *incipit legem dei quod precepit dominus ad Moysen*; W = *incipit legem dei quod precoepit dominus ad moysen*. Liebs, *Italien*, 163, suggests the original title may have been *Lex Dei, quam Deus praecepit ad Moysen, et lex Romana* based on Hincmar's citation of the work as *lex Romana*. Mommsen has <*Lex Dei Quam Praecepit Dominus ad Moysen*>. On the next line, Mommsen added *Liber Primus*, followed by Hyamson, Smits, and Spruit and Bongenaar.

[2] B has full title at end of the title, V has *de sicariis et homicidiis*, W has only *de sicariis*. The content of the title would suggest both, since *homicidia* is the main topic and *sicarius* is often used by the jurists. The *casu vel voluntate* is in B, but not in V and W. Mommsen has *De Sicariis* <*et Homicidis casu vel voluntate*>, followed by Hyamson and Smits.

[3] Schulz, 'biblischen Texte', 23–4, suggested *morte puniatur*. See also Huschke. It could be, following Schulz, that *puniatur* follows the text of the Septuagint more closely, but since all three manuscripts have *moriatur*, it must have stood at least in α. The manuscripts do not agree on *mortem* (V has *morte*). Since Schulz, 'biblischen Texte', 23–4, shows *morte* follows the biblical text more closely and is mirrored at Coll. 14. 1. 1, I leave as *morte moriatur*. For use of *morte* with a form of *morior* in classical Latin, see Sallust, *Hist.* 1. 43. Mommsen has *mortem*.

[4] Schulz, 'biblischen Texte', 23–4. Mommsen = *mortem*.

[5] *Ibid.* Mommsen = *mortem*.

1. 2. 1. Paulus quoque libro quinto sententiarum sub titulo ad legem Corneliam de sicariis et veneficis dicit:
Lex Cornelia poenam deportationis infligit ei, qui hominem occiderit eiusque rei causa furtive faciendi cum telo fuerit, et qui venenum hominis necandi causa habuerit vendiderit paraverit, falsumve testimonium dixerit quo quis periret, mortisve causam praestiterit. 2. quae omnia facinora in honestiores poena capitis vindicari placuit: humiliores vero aut in crucem tolluntur aut bestiis subiciuntur.
1. 3. 1. Ulpianus Libro VII de officio proconsulis sub titulo de sicariis et veneficis:
Capite primo legis Corneliae de sicariis cavetur, ut is praetor iudexve quaestionis, cui sorte obvenerit quaestio de sicariis eius quod in urbe Roma propiusve mille passus factum sit, uti quaerat cum iudicibus, qui ei ex lege sorte obvenerint de capite eius, qui cum telo ambulaverit hominis necandi furtive faciendi causa, hominemve occiderit, cuiusve id dolo malo factum erit. et reliqua. 2. Relatis verbis legis modo ipse loquitur Ulpianus:
Haec lex non omnem, qui cum telo ambulaverit, punit, sed eum tantum, qui hominis necandi furtive faciendi causa telum gerit, coercet. conpescit item eum, qui hominem occidit, nec adiecit cuius condicionis hominem, ut et ad servum et peregrinum pertinere haec lex videatur.
1. 4. 1. Item Paulus libro qui supra et titulo dicit:
Homicida est, qui aliquo genere teli hominem occidit mortisve causam praestitit.
1. 5. 1. Item de casualibus homicidis Moyses legaliter dicit:[6]
Si autem subito non per inimicitiam[7] inmiserit super eum aliquod vas non ex insidiis[8] 2. vel lapidem, quo moriatur, non per dolum et ceciderit super eum et mortuus fuerit, si autem non inimicus eius fuerit neque quaesierit male facere ei, 3. iudicabitis inter eum, qui percussit, et proximum mortui secundum iudicia haec, 4. et liberabitis percussorem.

[6] Although B, V, and W read *causalibus*, Mommsen must be correct in emending to *casualibus*. However, Mommsen placed *DE CASUALIBUS HOMICIDIS* as a subtitle before Coll. 1. 5 with no *item*, and was followed by Hyamson, Smits, *FIRA*, and Spruit and Bongenaar. As the phrase appears after the chapter number (Kp dxcvii) in B, I have placed it as an introductory clause of Coll. 1. 5. 1 (as does Scaliger) and perceive it as the Collator's voice.

[7] I accept the emendation of Schulz, 'biblischen Texte', 24–5. Mommsen = *inimicitias*.

[8] Following B and Schulz, 'biblischen Texte', 24–5. Mommsen = *insidians*.

1. 6. 1. Ulpianus libro et titulo qui supra relati:
Distinctionem, casus et voluntatis in homicidio servari rescripto Hadriani confirmatur. 2. verba rescripti: Et qui hominem occidit absolvi solet, sed si non occidendi animo id admisit et qui non occidit, sed voluit occidere, pro homicida damnatur. 3. e re itaque constituendum est: ex quo[9] ferro percussit Epafroditus? nam si gladium instrinxit aut telo percussit, quid dubium est, quin occidendi animo percusserit? si clave[10] percussit aut cucuma aut, cum forte rixaretur, ferro percussit, sed non occidendi mente. 4. ergo hoc exquirite et si voluntas occidendi fuit, ut homicidam servum supplicio summo iure iubete affici.
1. 7. 1. Paulus libro et titulo qui supra:
Qui hominem occidit, aliquando absolvitur et qui non occidit, ut homicida damnatur: consilium enim uniuscuiusque, non factum puniendum est. ideoque si cum vellet occidere, casu aliquo perpetrare non potuit, ut homicida punitur: et is, qui casu [iactu][11] teli hominem inprudenter ferierit, absolvitur. 2. quod si in rixa percussus homo perierit, quoniam ictus quoque ipsos contra unumquemque contemplari oportet, ideo humiliores in ludum aut in metallum damnantur, honestiores dimidia parte bonorum multati relegantur.
1. 8. 1. Item Gregorianus libro IIII [sub titulo] ad legem Corneliam de sicariis et veneficis talem contitutionem ponit:
Imperator Antoninus A. Aurelio Herculano et aliis militibus. Frater vester rectius fecerit, si se praesidi provinciae optulerit: cui si probaverit non occidendi animo Iustam a se percussam esse, remissa homicidii poena secundum disciplinam militarem sententiam proferet. Proposita prid. kal. Febr. Laeto bis cons.
1. 9. 1. Item Gregorianus eodem titulo et libro talem contitutionem ponit:
Imp. Alexander A. Aurelio Flavio et aliis militibus. Si modo pro quo libellum dedistis, non dolo praestitit mortem, minime perhorrescat: crimen quippe ita contrahitur, si et voluntas occidendi intercedat, ceterum ea, quae ex improviso casu potius, quam fraude accidunt, fato plerumque, non noxae inputantur. Prop. XIII kal. Aug. Alexandro cons.

[9] Following the manuscripts. Mommsen = *ecquo*.

[10] Although the manuscripts have forms of *lapis* (stone) here, I follow Mommsen and the variant text in *Dig*. 48. 8. 1. 3 in emending to *clave* as the object would be made of iron and thus fits the sense of the passage.

[11] Mommsen adopted for clarity.

1. 10. 1. Item Gregorianus eodem libro et titulo tale rescriptum dedit: <Quodsi dd. nn.>[12] Have Agatho k(arissime) n(obis). Qualitas precum Iuli Antonini clementiam nostram facile commovit: quippe quod adseveret homicidium se non voluntate, sed casu fortuito fecisse, cum calcis ictu mortis occasio praebita videatur. quod si ita est neque super hoc ambigi poterit, omni eum metu ac suspicione, quod ex admissae rei discrimine sustinet secundum id quod adnotatione nostra conprehensum est, volumus liberari. Dat. prid. k. Decemb.[13] Diocletiano Aug. IIII. et Maximiano conss.

1. 11. 1. Ulpianus libro et titulo qui supra:

Cum quidam per lasciviam causam mortis praebuisset, conprobatum est factum Taurini Egnati proconsulis Baeticae a divo Hadriano, quod eum in quinquennium relegasset. 2. verba consultationis et rescripti ita se habent: Inter Claudium, optime imperator, et Evaristum cognovi, quod Claudius Lupi filius in convivio, dum sago iactatur, culpa Mari Evaristi ita male acceptus fuerit, ut post diem quintum moreretur. atque adparebat nullam inimicitiam cum Evaristo ei fuisse. tamen cupiditatis culpa coercendum credidi, ut ceteri eiusdem aetatis iuvenes emendarentur. ideoque Mario Evaristo urbe Italia provincia Baeticae[14] in quinquennium interdixi et decrevi, ut impendi causa duo milia patri eius persolveret Evaristus, quod manifesta eius fuerat paupertas. 3. Verba rescripti:[15] Poenam Mari Evaristi recte, Taurine, moderatus es ad modum culpae: refert enim et in maioribus delictis, consulto aliquid admittatur an casu. 4. et sane in omnibus criminibus distinctio haec poenam aut iustitiam[16] provocare debet aut temperamentum admittere.

[12] B has *quodsidnm habe agatu KN*, V has *quodsi NN habe agata* and W has *QDsi DNN habe gatu k.n.* At least α must then have had *Quodsi* DD. NN. [that is, *domini nostri*] to refer back to the imperial constitution of the two emperors Diocletian and Maximian along the lines of '[the law of our lords stated thus]: Greetings Agatho, most dear to us.' It is possible that this formulaic phrase stemmed from the Collator who had the *Codex Gregorianus* in front of him or it might have come from scribal error early in the manuscript tradition. See my 'Collatio and the *Codex Gregorianus*', 294–5. Mommsen has '[*Exemplum sacrarum litterarum*]', based upon the version surviving in *CJ* 9. 16. 4 (although he does not include *Dioclietiani et Maximiani AA. Agathoni* that follows).

[13] Following Mommsen. Scaliger has simply 'Dec'. The month appears in a damaged portion of the B manuscript. Elsewhere, at Coll. 3. 4. 1, the Collator uses *Decemb.*

[14] Following B, which thus has the genitive form. Mommsen = *Baetica.*

[15] Following B, W, and Huschke. Mommsen = *V(erba) r(escripti).*

[16] Following Schulz, 'Manuscripts', 316–17. Mommsen = *iustam.*

1. 12. 1. Modestinus libro differentiarum sexto sub titulo de scientibus et ignorantibus generaliter loquitur:
Nonnumquam per ignorantiam delinquentibus iuris civilis venia tribui solet, si modo rem facti quis, non iuris ignoret: quae scilicet consilio delinquentibus praestari non solet. propter quod necessarium est addita distinctione considerare, utrum sciente an ignorante aliquo quid gestum proponatur. et reliqua.
1. 13. 1. Paulus libro et titulo qui supra:
Qui telum tutandae salutis causa gerit, non videtur hominis occidendi causa portare. 2. teli autem appellatione non tantum ferrum continetur, sed omne, quod nocendi causa portatum est.

(Titulus 2)
De Atroci Iniuria

2. 1. 1. Moyses dicit:
Si autem contenderint duo viri et percusserit alter alterum lapide aut pugno et non fuerit mortuus, decubuerit autem in lectulo, 2. et si surgens ambulaverit homo foris in baculo, sine crimine erit ille, qui eum percusserat praeter cessationes eius dabit[17] ei et medico inpensas curationis.
2. 2. 1. Ulpianus libro singulari regularum sub titulo de iniuriis:
Iniuria, si quidem atrox, id est gravis, non est, [non][18] sine iudicis arbitrio aestimatur. atrocem autem aestimare solere praetorem idque colligi ex facto, ut puta si verberatus vel vulneratus quis fuerit. et reliqua.
2. 3. 1. Papinianus libro definitionum secundo sub titulo de iudicatis:
Per hominem liberum noxae deditum si tantum adquisitum sit, quantum damni dedit, manumittere cogendus est a praetore qui noxae deditum accepit: sed fiduciae iudicio non tenetur.
2. 4. 1. Ulpianus libro XVIII<I>[19] ad edictum sub titulo si fatebitur iniuria occisum esse, in simplum et cum diceret:
Rupisse eum utique accipiemus, qui vulneraverit, vel virgis vel loris vel pugnis caedit, vel telo quove alio vis genere sciderit hominis

[17] See Schulz, 'biblischen Texte', 26, and 'Manuscripts', 324, for correction of Mommsen's reading of *praeter ac cessationis eius mercedem dabit* due to corruption creeping in through glosses and from logic of sentence.

[18] Following Huschke. The *non* must have fallen out of the manuscript tradition early (probably due to the previous *non*). See further, Murison, Review of Hyamson, 276; Avenarius, *Pseudo-Ulpianische*, 520–2.

[19] See *Dig.* 9. 2. 27 and Mommsen's apparatus, 144.

corpus vel tumorem fecerit: sed ita demum, si damnum datum est. ceterum si in nullo servum pretio viliorem deterioremve fecerit, Aquilia cessat iniuriarumque erit agendum. ergo et si pretio quidem non sit deterior factus servus, verum sumptus in salutem eius et sanitatem facti sunt, in haec <nec>[20] mihi videri damni Aquilia lege [agi][21] posse.

2. 5. 1. Paulus libro singulari et titulo de iniuriis:

Generaliter dicitur iniuria omne, quod non iure fit: specialiter alia est contumelia, quam Graeci [*ὕβριν appellant, alia culpa, quam Graeci ἀδίκημα dicunt, sicut in lege Aquilia damnum iniuriae accipitur, alia iniquitas et iniustitia, quam Graeci*][22] ἀδικίαν vocant. nam cum praetor non iure adversum nos pronuntiat, iniuriam nos accepisse dicimus: unde apparet non esse verum, quod Labeo putabat, apud praetorem iniuriam ὕβριν dumtaxat significare. 2. commune omnibus iniuriis est quod semper adversus bonos mores fit idque non fieri alicuius interest. 3. hoc edictum ad eam iniuriam pertinet, quae contumeliae causa fit. 4. fit autem iniuria vel in corpore, dum caedimur, vel verbis, dum convicium patimur, vel cum dignitas laeditur, ut cum matronae vel praetextatae comites abducuntur. iniuriarum actio aut legitima est aut honoraria. 5. legitima ex lege duodecim tabularum: qui iniuriam alteri facit, quinque et viginti sestertiorum poenam subito. quae lex generalis fuit: fuerunt et speciales, velut illa: si os fregit libero, CCC[23] servo, CL poenam subito sestertiorum.

2. 6. 1. Idem Paulus eodem libro singulari sub titulo quemadmodum iniuriarum agatur:

Qui autem iniuriarum, inquit, agit, certum dicat, quid iniuriae factum sit et taxationem ponat non minorem quam quanti vadimonium

[20] Although Mommsen follows B in placing *nec* here, this must be an interpolation due to the sense of the passage and *Dig.* 9. 2. 27. 17.

[21] *Agi* is not in the manuscripts, but Mommsen, Smits, and others are likely correct in conjecturing that it stood in the original due to the similarity to the text in *Dig.* 9. 2. 27. 17 and for the clarity of the comprehension of the sentence.

[22] Mommsen supplied from the *Institutes* of Justinian (4. 4 pr.). Something approaching this must have stood in the original due to the logic of the sentence, but it must have already been lost in *α* and is a typical type of scribal error (homoearchon) where the copyist jumped ahead to the next form of a word (in this case, *quam Graeci*).

[23] Mommsen supplied [*si*] here from Gaius, *Institutes* 3. 223. Since it is not in the manuscripts and the sense is clear enough without it, I have deleted it.

fuerit. 2. certum dicit, qui suo nomine demonstrat iniuriam, neque ita, ut per disiunctionem hoc aut illud accidisse conprehendat, sed ut necesse habeat aut unam nomine suo rem designare aut plures ita conplecti, ut omnes eas accidisse cogatur probare. 3. certum autem an incertum dicat, cognitio ipsius praetoris est. demonstrat autem hoc loco praetor non vocem agentis, sed qualem formulam edat. 4. certum non dicit, qui dicit pulsatum se sive verberatum. sed et partem corporis demonstrat et quem in modum, pugno puta an fuste an lapide, sicut formula proposita est: quod Auli Ageri mala pugno percussa est. illud non cogitur dicere, dextra an sinistra, nec qua manu percussa sit. 5. item si dicat infamatum se esse, debet adicere, quemadmodum infamatus sit. sic enim et formula concepta est: quod Numerius Negidius [libe]llum[24] misit Aulo Agerio infamandi causa.

2. 7. 1. Paulus libro sententiarum [quinto][25] sub titulo ad legem Corneliam de sicariis et veneficis:

Causa mortis idonea non videtur, cum caesus homo post aliquot dies officium diurnae vitae retinens decessit nisi forte fuerit ad necem caesus aut letaliter vulneratus.

(Titulus 3)
De Iure et Saevitia Dominorum

3. 1. 1. Moyses dicit:

Si quis percusserit servum [suum][26] aut ancillam virga et mortuus fuerit in manibus eius, iudicio vindicetur. 2. quod si supervixerit die uno aut duobus, non vindicabitur, pretium enim ipsius est.

[24] The manuscripts (and Scaliger) have *illum*. Daube, 'Collatio 2. 6. 5', argued for *capillum*. Although this emendation was ingenuous, it seems simpler that the scribe of α, mistakingly shortened *libellum* to *illum* (as Cornelius Vonck advised Mommsen).

[25] B and W omit this number of the book, and V omits the entire introductory citation. Mommsen = [*quinto*]. The Collator does cite *quinto* elsewhere. Since the clarity of the citation is improved, and since the Collator does stylistically tend to favour giving the book number, I have retained Mommsen's suggestion of the book number in the text here and elsewhere.

[26] Schulz, 'biblischen Texte', 27, argues, on juristic grounds, that *suum* must have fallen out of the text. Since it is missing in B, V, and W, it must have already been missing from α whose scribe must have missed it when copying from proto-α. Mommsen omits.

3. 2. 1. Paulus libro sententiarum [quinto] sub titulo ad legem Corneliam de sicariis et veneficis dicit:
Servus si plagis defecerit, nisi id dolo fiat, dominus homicidii reus non potest postulari: modum enim castigandi et in servorum coercitione placuit temperari.
3. 3. 1. Ulpianus libro octavo de officio proconsulis sub titulo de dominorum saevitia:
Si dominus in servum saevierit vel ad inpudicitiam turpemque violationem conpellat, quae sint partes praesidis, ex rescripto divi Pii ad Aurelium Marcianum proconsulem Baeticae manifestatur. 2. cuius rescripti verba haec sunt: Dominorum quidem potestatem in suos servos inlibatam esse oportet nec cuiquam hominum ius suum detrahi: sed dominorum interest, ne auxilium contra saevitiam vel famen vel intolerabilem iniuriam denegetur his, qui iuste deprecantur. 3. ideoque cognosce de querellis illorum,[27] qui ex familia Iuli[28] Sabini ad statuam confugerunt, et si vel durius habitos, quam aequum est, vel infami iniuria adfectos cognoveris, venire iube, ita ut in potestatem Sabini non revertantur. quod si meae constitutioni fraudem fecerit, sciet me admissum severius executurum. 4. divus etiam Hadrianus Umbram quandam matronam in quinquennium relegavit, quod ex levissimis causis ancillas atrocissime tractaret. 5. item divus Pius ad libellum Alfi Iuli rescripsit [in][29] haec verba: servorum obsequium non solum imperio, sed et moderatione et sufficientibus praebitis et iustis operibus contineri oportet. 6. itaque et ipse curare debes iuste ac temperate tuos tractare, ut ex facili requirere eos possis, ne, si apparverit vel inparem te inpendiis esse vel atrociore dominationem saevitia exercere, necesse habeat proconsul V.C., ne quid tumultuosius contra accidat, praevenire et ex mea iam

[27] Schulz, 'Manuscripts', 323 follows B and V and style of Hadrian's rescripts. Mommsen has *eorum* following W and *Dig.* 1. 6. 2.

[28] I follow Mommsen and the manuscripts in using the republican Latin genitive form of -i for nouns ending in -ius in the nominative, as opposed to the genitive ending of -ii appearing by the end of the classical age. It could be that the Collator, or a scribe at some point in the manuscript tradition, sought to appear to be more juristic or formal by using the older form. I shall follow this convention throughout, except where the manuscripts depart from it.

[29] Mommsen placed in brackets, which Hyamson adopted, and it makes sense on grammatical grounds.

auctoritate[30] ad alienandos eos conpellere. Glabrione et Homullo conss.[31]

3. 4. 1. Gregorianus libro X<V>IIII[32] sub titulo de accusationibus: Impp. Diocletianus et Maximianus Augusti Aurelio Sacrato militi. Cum servum tuum [vi][33] aegritudinis graviter oppressum fati munus implesse proponas, propter inmoderatam castigationem calumniae accusationem emergere innocentiae ratio, cuius fiduciam geris, non permittit. Prop. non. Decemb. Diocletiano A. III. et Aristobulo conss.[34]

(Titulus 4)
De Adulteriis

4. 1. 1. Moyses dicit:[35]

Quicumque[36] moechatus fuerit mulierem[37] proximi sui, morte[38] moriatur qui moechatus fuerit et quae moechata fuerit. 2. quod si aliqui seduxerit virginem non desponsatam et stupraverit eam, dotabit eam sibi in uxorem. 3. quod si rennuerit pater eius et noluerit eam dare illi uxorem, pecuniam inferet patri, in quantum est dos virginis.

4. 2. 1. Paulus libro singulari de adulteris sub titulo:

Brevem interpretationem [legis Iuliae][39] de adulteris coercendis facturus per ipsa capita ire malui ordinemque legis servare. 2. et

[30] Lachmann added *te* here which Mommsen adopted with brackets [*te*], but the meaning is clear enough without it.

[31] Following the convention and style of the Collator (abbreviation for the ablative plural of *consulibus*). This part of B is damaged.

[32] See Rotondi, 'Studi sulle fonti del codice giustinianeo', 157.

[33] Following Mommsen.

[34] Hyamson has *cons.* B has *conss iiii.* Here I have *Conss.* (for the abbreviation of consulships) following B and style of Collator, but leave out *iiii* which probably crept in from a gloss immediately after this subscription where B has *expl titulo de dominorum sevitia cohibenda cons iiii.* This second occurrence might be a scribal error for a transition to the next title (i.e. *tit. iiii*), but in this case it should be Title 3 that is ending and 4 (or iiii) that is starting.

[35] Following Schulz, 'biblischen Texte', 22 and consistency within work. Mommsen = *dixit.*

[36] Following B and style of Collator (Coll. 6. 1. 1; 14. 1. 1).

[37] Schulz, 'biblischen Texte', 27–8, suggested replacing *mulierem* with *uxorem*, but since *mulierem* is in the manuscripts it must have stood in at least α. Mommsen = *mulierem.*

[38] As in Coll. 1. 1, Schulz, 'biblischen Texte', 27–8. V also has *morte* here. Mommsen = *mortem.*

[39] Added by Huschke, but followed by Mommsen, Smits, *FIRA*, and Spruit and Bongenaar. I include due to clarity and to the clear reference that follows at Coll. 4. 2. 2.

quidem primum caput legis Iuliae de adulteris[40] prioribus legibus pluribus obrogat. 3. secundo vero capite permittit patri, [si in][41] filia sua, quam in potestate habet, aut in ea, quae [eo][42] auctore, cum in potestate esset, viro in manum convenerit, adulterum domi suae generive sui deprehenderit isve in eam rem socerum adhibuerit, ut is pater eum adulterum sine fraude occidat, ita ut filiam in continenti occidat. 4. In vidua[43] autem filia qui adulterum deprehensum occiderit et in continenti filiam, licito iure hoc factum Marcellus libro XXXI digestorum scribit. 5. auctoritate quoque [legis][44] patrem posse interficere vel consularem virum vel patronum suum, [si eum][45] in filia adulterum deprehenderit, eodem libro Marcellus probat. 6. sed si filiam non interfecerit, sed solum adulterum, homicidii reus est. 7. et si intervallo filiam interfecerit, tantundem est, nisi persecutus illam interfecerit: continuatione enim animi videtur legis auctoritate fecisse.

4. 3. 1. Idem Paulus eodem singulari libro et titulo:

Certae autem enumerantur personae, quas viro liceat occidere in adulterio deprehensa uxore, quamvis uxorem non liceat. 2. ergo secundum leges viro etiam filiofamilias permittitur domi suae deprehensum adulterum interficere servum, et eum qui auctoramento rogatus est ad gladium, vel etiam illum qui operas suas, ut cum bestiis pugnaret, locavit. 3. sed et iudicio publico damnatum licet interficere in adulterio deprehensum, vel libertinum vel suum vel paternum, et tam civem Romanum quam Latinum. 4. sed et patris et matris et filii et filiae libertum permittitur occidere, quo loco et dediticius habetur. 5. debet autem profiteri apud eum, cuius iurisdictio est eo loco, ubi occidit, et uxorem dimittere. 6. quod si

[40] Mommsen believed this title should be deleted, but *iulia de adult* is in W and V has *iulii de adulteris*; B has a damaged area here, but there is enough space to hold this title which would then make it consistent with the other manuscripts and Scaliger included it.

[41] Mommsen included. This section of B is damaged.

[42] Mommsen added for clarity.

[43] While B and W have *invidia* ('by means of ill will'), I adopt *in vidua* from Triebs, *Studien zur Lex Dei*, 2: 52–4, because it makes more legal sense and is a simple scribal error. Mommsen emended to *in sui iuris* (followed by Hyamson).

[44] Added by Cujas for clarity, followed by Mommsen.

[45] Added by Huschke for clarity, followed by Mommsen.

non fecerit, inpune non interficit. 7. sciendum est autem divum[46] Marcum et Commodum rescripsisse eum qui adulterum inlicite interfecerit, leviori poena puniri. 8. sed et Magnus Antoninus pepercit, si qui adulteros inconsulto calore ducti interfecerunt. et reliqua.

4. 4. 1. Idem Paulus eodem libro singulari et titulo:

Iure[47] mariti vel patris qui accusat, potest et sine calumniae poena vinci: si iure extranei accusat, potest calumniae poena puniri. 2. sed tum post duos menses intra quattuor menses utiles expertus, licet talis sit, qui alias accusare non possit, ut libertinus aut minor viginti quinque annorum, aut infamis, tamen ad accusationem admittitur, ut et Papinianus libro XV scripsit.

4. 5. 1. Papinianus libro XV responsorum sub titulo ad legem Iuliam de adulteris:

Civis Romanus, qui [civem Romanam][48] sine conubio sive peregrinam in matrimonio habuit, iure quidem mariti eam adulteram non postulat, sed ei non opponetur infamia vel quod libertinus rem sesteriorum triginta milium aut filium non habuit, propriam iniuriam persequenti.

4. 6. 1.[49] Paulus libro singulari et titulo qui supra:

In uxorem adulterium vindicatur iure mariti, non etiam sponsam. Severus quoque et Antoninus ita rescripserunt.

4. 7. 1. Papinianus libro singulari de adulteris:

Quaerebatur, an pater emancipatam filiam iure patris accusare possit. respondi: occidendi quidem facultatem lex tribuit eam filiam, quam habet in potestatem, aut [quae][50] eo auctore in manum convenit: sed accusare iure patris ne quidem emancipatam filiam pater prohibetur.

[46] B has *divum*, W has *quod*, and V has *dum*. Mommsen chose to follow B here. Although Commodus was condemned after his death, Septimius Severus rehabilitated his memory and it is possible that this should have read *divos* originally (and *Dig.* 39. 4. 16. 6 reads *divi* for Marcus Aurelius and Commodus).

[47] B, V and W, and Huschke, have *Qui* starting this sentence before *iure*. As this is superfluous, Mommsen omits. I follow Mommsen here since this is the style of Ps. Paulus.

[48] Mommsen added for clarity.

[49] In what must have been an error, Scaliger transposes this quotation after the next passage.

[50] Added by Mommsen for clarity.

4. 8. 1. Papinianus eodem libro singulari et titulo:[51]
Cum patri lex regia dederit in filium vitae necisque potestatem, quod[52] bonum fuit lege conprehendi, ut potestas fieret etiam filiam occidendi, velis mihi rescribere: nam scire cupio. respondit: numquid ex contrario praestat nobis argumentum haec adiectio, ut non videatur lex non habenti dedisse, [sed occidi eam cum adultero iussisse],[53] ut videatur maiore aequitate ductus adulterum occidisse, cum nec filiae pepercerit?
4. 9. 1. Idem:
Si pater qui[54] adulterum occidit et filiae suae pepercit, quaero quid adversus eum sit statuendum? respondit: sine dubio iste pater homicida est: igitur tenebitur lege Cornelia de sicariis. plane si filia non voluntate patris, sed casu servata est, non minimam habebit defensionem pater, quod forte fugit filia. nam lex ita punit homicidam, si dolo malo homicidium factum fuerit, hic autem pater non ideo servavit filiam, quia voluit, sed quia occidere eam non potuit.
4. 10. 1. Idem Papinianus:[55]
Si maritus uxorem suam in adulterio deprehensam occidit, an in legem de sicariis incidat, quaero. respondit: nulla parte legis marito uxorem occidere conceditur: quare aperte contra legem fecisse eum non ambigitur. sed si de poena tractas, non inique aliquid eius honestissimo calori permittitur, ut non quasi homicida puniatur capite vel deportatione, sed usque ad exilium poena eius statuatur.
4. 11. 1. Idem sic:
De mancipiis alterutrius marito vel patre accusante quaestionem habendam palam est: an idem extraneo accusatori permitti debeat, quaero. respondit: potest videri ea ratio fuisse permittendi istis personis de servis quaestionem habere, ut diligentius dolorem animi sui, item iniuriam laesae domus non translaticie

[51] B, W, and V all have as part of manuscript. Mommsen = <*et titulo*>.

[52] Against Huschke and Hyamson who replaced with *quo*, which is not in manuscripts.

[53] Supplied by Mommsen for clarity.

[54] Folllowing B, W, V, and Huschke. Mommsen = *quis*.

[55] B has *Papianus idem*. V again omits introductory formula. W has a gap between chapter number and *Idem* (and then follows with another *idem*), indicating the scribe might have been distracted and missed a word. Based upon B, consistency and gap in W, α probably had *idem papinianus*. Mommsen has *IDEM*.

persequerentur. sed quoniam non facile tale delictum sine ministerio servorum admitti creditum est, ratio eo perduxit, ut etiam extraneo accusante mancipia quaestioni tormentorum subicerentur a iudicibus.

4. 12. 1. Paulus libro sententiarum [secundo] sub titulo de adulteris: Permittitur [patri][56] tam adoptivo quam naturali, adulterum cum filia cuiusque dignitatis domi suae vel generi sui deprehensum sua manu occidere. 2. filius familias pater si filiam in adulterio deprehenderit, verbis quidem legis prope est, ut non possit occidere: permittitur tamen etiam ei, ut occidat. 3. maritus in adulterio deprehensos non alios quam infames et eos qui corpore quaestum faciunt, servos etiam et libertos excepta uxore, quam prohibetur, occidere potest. 4. maritum, qui uxorem deprehensam cum adulterio occidit, quia hoc inpatientia iusti doloris admisit, lenius puniri placuit. 5. occiso adultero dimittere statim maritus debet uxorem atque ita triduo proximo profiteri, cum quo adultero et in quo loco uxorem deprehenderit. 6. inventa in adulterio uxore maritus ita demum adulterum occidere potest, si eum domi suae deprehendat. 7. eum, qui in adulterio deprehensam uxorem non statim dimiserit, reum lenocinii postulari placuit. 8. servi vero tam mariti quam uxoris in causa adulteri torqueri possunt, nec his libertas sub specie impunitatis data valebit.

(Titulus 5)
De Stupratoribus

5. 1. 1. Moyses dicit:
Qui manserit cum masculo mansione muliebri, aspernamentum est: ambo moriantur, rei sunt.

5. 2. 1. Paulus libro sententiarum II sub titulo de adulteris:
Qui masculum liberum invitum stupraverit, capite punietur. 2. qui voluntate sua stuprum flagitiumque inpurum patitur, dimidia parte bonorum suorum multatur nec testamentum ei ex maiore parte facere licet.

5. 3. 1. Hoc quidem iuris est: mentem tamen legis Moysi[57] imperatoris Theodosii constitutio ad plenum secuta cognoscitur. idem

[56] Mommsen supplied from Vs.

[57] Here I follow Mommsen and reject Hyamson's reading of *Moysis*, since B, V, and W have *Moysi* for the genitive as does the Vulgate (Lev. 8: 36).

Theodosius:[58] Impp[p].[59] Valentinianus Theodosius et Arcadius Augg[g].[60] ad Orientium vicarium urbis Romae:

Non patimur urbem Romam virtutum omnium matrem diutius effeminati in viris[61] pudoris contaminatione foedari et agreste illud a priscis conditoribus robur fracta molliter plebe tenuatum convicium saeculis vel conditorum inrogare vel principum, Orienti k[arissime] ac iuc[undissime] nobis. 2. laudanda igitur experientia tua omnes, quibus flagitiosus luxus[62] est virile corpus muliebriter constitutum alieni sexus damnare patientia nihilque discretum habere cum feminis occupatos, ut flagitii poscit inmanitas, atque omnibus eductos, pudet dicere, virorum lupanaribus spectante populo flammis[63] vindicibus expiabit, ut universi intellegant sacrosanctum cunctis esse debere hospitium virilis animae nec sine summo supplicio alienum expetisse sexum qui suum turpiter perdidisset. Prop. pr(idie). id. Maias Romae in atrio Minervae.

(Titulus 6)
De Incestis Nuptiis

6. 1. 1. Moyses dicit:

Quicumque concubuerit cum muliere uxore[64] patris sui, pudenda patris sui detexit, morte<m>[65] moriantur ambo: rei sunt. 2. et quicumque concuberit cum nuru sua, morte<m>[66] moriantur ambo: rei sunt.

[58] See Frakes, 'Item Theodosianus?'. Mommsen = <*item Theodosianus*>.

[59] *Ibid.* Mommsen = *IMPP.*

[60] B has Augg.

[61] Following Huschke's suggestion, Mommsen proposed an emendation of the singular form *viro* for manhood (rare in Latin literature). B and W have *viros.*

[62] Following B and V. Mommsen has *flagiti usus*, following the edited version of the law at *CTh* 9. 7. 6.

[63] Following Huschke as part of an ablative of means. B and V have *flamme*, W has *flammas.* Mommsen proposed *flammae.* The V manuscript of the *Theodosian Code* (Vaticanus reginae 886) has *flammis* for the shortened version of law surviving as *CTh* 9. 7. 6.

[64] Schulz, 'biblischen Texte', 29–30, suggests simply *uxorem.* W has *cum mulierem uxorem* (which is grammatically incorrect). V has *cum muliere uxore* and B has a damaged area, but Scaliger relayed *cum muliere uxore* which Mommsen seems to have followed.

[65] I follow Schulz, 'biblischen Texte', 29–31, who suggested the formula *morte moriantur.* Although the manuscripts have *mortem* here, which Mommsen follows, consistency across the work and the biblical text suggests *morte.*

[66] *Ibid.*

6. 2. 1. Ulpianus libro regularum singulari sub titulo de nuptiis: Inter parentes et liberos, cuiuscumque gradus sint, conubium non est. 2. inter cognatos autem ex transverso gradu olim quidem usque ad quartum gradum matrimonia contrahi non poterant: nunc autem ex tertio gradu licet uxorem ducere, sed tantum fratris filiam, non etiam sororis, nec amitam nec materteram, quamvis eodem gradu sint. 3. eam quae noverca vel privigna, vel quae nurus vel socrus fuit, uxorem ducere non possumus. 4. si quis eam quam non licet uxorem duxerit, incestum matrimonium contrahit: ideoque liberi in potestate eius non fiunt, sed quasi vulgo concepti spurii sunt.

6. 3. 1. Paulus libro sententiarum [secundo] sub titulo de nuptiis: Inter parentes et liberos <iure civili>, matrimonia contrahi non possunt; [iure civili][67] [nec sororem] nec filiam sororis aut neptem uxorem ducere possumus: proneptem aetatis ratio prohibet. 2. adoptiva cognatio impedit nuptias inter parentes ac liberos omnimodo, inter fratres[68] eatenus, quatenus capitis minutio non intervenit. 3. nec socrum nec nurum [nec] privignam nec novercam aliquando citra poenam incesti uxorem ducere licet, sicut nec amitam aut materteram. sed qui [affinem][69] vel cognatam contra interdictum duxerit, remisso mulieri iuris errore ipse poenam adulterii lege Iulia patitur, non etiam ducta.

6. 4. 1. Gregorianus libro quinto sub titulo de nuptiis. Exemplum litterarum Diocletiani et Maximiani impp. talem coniunctionem graviter punire commemorat:

Exemplum edicti[70] Diocletiani et Maximiani [Augg. et Constantii et Maximiani] nobilissimorum Caesarum. Quoniam piis religiosisque

[67] I follow here the word order of Huschke and Hyamson, based on legal grounds. Mommsen has '*Inter parentes et liberos iure civili matrimonia contrahi non possunt*', but allows in his apparatus that Huschke might be correct.

[68] Huschke and Hyamson both include (*ac sorores*) here from Gaius, *Institutes*, 1. 61, but Mommsen more cautiously omits as it is not in B.

[69] Huschke and Hyamson include, but Mommsen omits. Since the *vel* indicates something must have fallen out of the manuscript tradition, I have included [*affinem*] as a possible reading.

[70] Although B, V, and W all have this introductory note, the appearance of the phrase *exemplum litterarum* preceding it raises the possibility that a gloss may have crept into the text by the time of the scribe of α, or a preceding manuscript. The version of the law surviving as *CJ* 5. 4. 17 has only the names of the emperors (*Impp. Diocletianus et Maximianus AA et CC.*) as do most fragments surviving from the *Codex Gregorianus* (such as at Coll. 1. 8; 1. 9; 3. 4; 15. 3). See further, Paul Krüger (ed.), *Codices Gregorianus et Hermogenianus, Collectio Iuris Anteiustiniani* in Paul Krüger, T. Mommsen, and Wilhelm Studemund (eds.), *Collectio Librorum Iuris Anteiustiniani* (Berlin, 1890), III, 221–45; and Frakes, 'Collatio and the "Codex Gregorianus"'.

mentibus nostris ea, quae Romanis legibus caste sancteque sunt constituta venerabilia maxime videntur atque aeterna religione servanda, dissimulare ea, quae a quibusdam in praeteritum nefarie incesteque commissa sunt, non oportere credimus: cum vel cohibenda sunt vel etiam vindicanda, insurgere nos disciplina nostrorum temporum cohortatur. ita enim et ipsos inmortales deos Romano nomini, ut semper fuerunt, faventes atque placatos futuros esse non dubium est, si cunctos sub imperio nostro agentes piam religiosamque et quietam et castam in omnibus mere colere perspexerimus vitam. 2. in quo id etiam providendum quam maxime esse censuimus, ut matrimoniis religiose atque legitime iuxta disciplinam iuris veteris copulatis tam eorum honestati, qui nuptiarum coniunctionem sectantur, quam etiam his, qui inde deinceps nascentur, servata religione incipiat esse consultum et honestate nascendi etiam posteritas ipsa purgata sit. id enim pietati nostrae maxime placuit, ut sancta necessitudinum nomina optineant apud affectus suos piam ac religiosam consanguinitati debitam caritatem. nefas enim credere est [duratura][71] ea, quae in praeteritum a conpluribus constat esse commissa, cum pecudum ac ferarum promiscuo ritu ad inlicita conubia instinctu execrandae libidinis sine ullo respectu pudoris ac pietatis inruerint. 3. sed quaecumque antehac vel inperitia delinquentium vel pro ignorantia iuris barbaricae inmanitatis ritu ex inlicitis matrimoniis videntur admissa, quamquam essent severissime vindicanda, tamen contemplatione clementiae nostrae ad indulgentiam volumus pertinere, ita tamen, ut quicumque in ante actum tempus inlicitis incestisque se matrimoniis polluerunt, hactenus adeptos se esse nostram indulgentiam sciant, ut post tam nefaria facinora vitam quidem sibi gratulentur esse concessam, sciant tamen non legitimos se suscepisse liberos, quos tam nefaria coniunctione genuerunt. ita enim fiet, ut de futuro quoque nemo audeat infrenatis cupiditatibus oboedire, cum et sciant ita praecedentes admissores istius modi criminum venia liberatos, ut liberorum quos inlicite genuerunt successione arceantur, quae iuxta vetustatem Romanis legibus negabatur. Et optassemus quidem nec ante quicquam eius modi esse commissum, quod esset aut clementia remittendum aut legibus corregendum. 4. sed posthac religionem sanctitatemque in conubiis copulandis volumus ab unoquoque

[71] Hyamson, following a suggestion in Mommsen's apparatus.

servari, ut se ad disciplinam legesque Romanas meminerint pertinere et eas tantum sciant nuptias licitas, quae sunt Romano iure permissae. 5. cum quibus autem personis tam cognatorum quam ex adfinium numero contrahi non liceat matrimonium, hoc edicto nostro conplexi sumus: cum filia nepte pronepte itemque matre avia proavia et ex latere amita ac matertera, [sorore,][72] sororis filia et ex ea nepte. itemque ex adfinibus privigna, noverca, socru nuru ceterisque quae antiquo iure prohibentur, a quibus cunctos volumus abstinere. 6. Nihil enim nisi sanctum ac venerabile nostra iura custodiunt et ita ad tantam magnitudinem Romana maiestas cunctorum numinum favore pervenit, quoniam omnes leges suas religione sapienti pudorisque, observatione devinxit. 7. quare hoc edicto nostro volumus omnibus palam fierei, quod praeteritorum venia, quae per clementiam nostram contra disciplinam videtur indulta, ad ea tantum delicta pertineat, quae in diem III kal. Ian. Tusco et Anullino conss.[73] videntur esse commissa. 8. si qua autem contra Romani nominis decus sanctitatemque legum post supra dictum diem deprehendentur admissa, digna severitate plectentur. nec enim ullam in tam nefario scelere quisquam aestimet veniam se consequi posse, qui in[74] tam evidenti[75] crimini et post edictum nostrum non dubitabit inruere. Dat. kal. Mai. Damasco Tusco et Anullino conss.[76]

6. 5. 1. Hermogenianus sub titulo de nuptis:

Impp. Diocletianus et Maximianus Augg. Fl. Flaviano. His qui incestas nuptias per errorem contrahunt, ne poenis subiciantur, ita demum clementia principum subvenit, si postea quam errorem suum rescierint, ilico nefarias nuptias diremerint. Prop. id. Mart [Tiberiano][77] et Dione conss.[78]

[72] Huschke following *CJ* 5. 4. 17, adopted by Mommsen = [*sorore*]. The scribe of α, or an earlier manuscript in the tradition, may have left out due to fear of committing dittography.

[73] Mommsen suggested *cons.* but B and W have *conss.* which fits style of Collator better.

[74] Huschke, following W and V.

[75] Here I follow Mommsen, B, and V, although Huschke proposes *evidens*. W has *evidentur*.

[76] B and V had *damasco*. Mommsen has *cons*, but *conss.* fits the style of Collator better. On the place name and date, see Barnes, 'Damascus or Demessus', *Zeitschrift für Papyrologie und Epigraphik* 151 (2005), 266–8 and Commentary.

[77] Proposed by Huschke and followed by Mommsen. A first consul's name must have fallen out of the manuscript tradition and Dio (corrected from Diogene in B) shared the consulship with Tiberianus in 291. Hyamson inaccurately states that this reading follows V and W, when the subscription survives in B.

[78] Following style of the Collator.

Hanc quoque constitutionem Gregorianus titulo de nuptiis inservit, quae est tricesima et secunda, aliis tamen et die [et cons.],[79] id est: constitutio prop. V id. Iun. Diocletiano ter et Maximiano Augustis.

6. 6. 1.[80] Papinianus libro singulari de adulteris:

Qui sororis filiam uxorem duxerat per errorem, antequam praeveniretur a delatore, diremit coitum: quaero an adhuc possit accusari? respondit: ei qui coitu sororis filiae bona fide abstinuit, poenam remitti palam est, quia qui errore cognito diremit coitum, creditur eius voluntatis fuisse, ut, si scisset se in eo necessitudinis gradu positum, non fuisset tale matrimonium copulaturus.

6. 7. 1. Idem dicitur in eos, qui incestas nuptias contraxerunt. 1. maledicti tamen sunt omnes incesti per legem, cum adhuc rudibus populis ex divino nutu condita isdem adstipulantibus sanciretur. et utique omnes maledicti puniti sunt, quos divina et humana sententia consona voce damnavit. lex divina sic dicit:

Maledictus, dicit[81] Moyses, qui concubuerit cum uxore patris sui: et dicit omnis populus: fiat, fiat. 2. Maledictus, qui concubuerit cum sorore sua de patre aut de matre: et dicit omnis populus: fiat, fiat. 3. maledictus, qui concubuerit cum nuru sua: et dicit omnis populus: fiat, fiat. 4. maledictus, qui concuberit cum socra[82] sua: et dicit omnis populus: fiat, fiat. 5. maledictus, qui concuberit cum sorore patris sui: et dicit omnis populus: fiat, fiat. 6. maledictus, qui concubuerit cum sorore matris suae: et dicit omnis populus: fiat, fiat. 7. maledictus, qui concubuerit cum sorore uxoris suae: et dicit omnis populus, fiat, fiat. 8. maledictus, qui dormierit cum uxore fratris sui: et dicit omnis populus: fiat, fiat. 9. maledictus, qui dormierit cum omni pecore: et dicit omnis populus: fiat, fiat.

[79] Following Mommsen.

[80] While Mommsen placed this section number at the end of the preceding sentence, it fits better with the style of the Collator here. All three manuscripts also place a chapter division (*Kp*) here also.

[81] The manuscripts have *inquid dixit*, as does Scaliger. This is redundant and not consistent with the Collator's style. I have emended to *dicit* (and the historical present). The revision of Huschke by Seckel and Kübler has only *inquit Moyses*. Huschke and Mommsen have *inquit, dixit Moyses*. I have left the rest of the forms of *dicere* in this section as *dicit*, following B and W as well as Mommsen.

[82] Following Schulz, 'biblischen Texte', 30. Mommsen = *socru*.

(Titulus 7)
De Furibus et de Poena eorum

7. 1. 1. Quod si duodecim tabularum nocturnum furem[, quoquo modo, diurnum][83] autem si se audeat telo defendere, interfici iubent, scitote, iuris consulti, quia Moyses prius hoc statuit, sicut lectio manifestat. Moyses dicit:

Si perfodiens nocte parietem inventus fuerit fur et percusserit eum alius et mortuus fuerit hic, non est homicida is qui percusserit eum. 2. si autem sol ortus fuerit super eum, reus est mortis percussor: et ipse morietur.

7. 2. 1. Paulus libro sententiarum V [sub titulo][84] ad legem Corneliam de sicaris et veneficis:

Si quis furem nocturnum vel diurnum cum se telo defenderet occiderit, hac quidem lege non tenetur, sed melius fecerit, qui eum conprehensum transmittendum ad praesidem magistratibus optulerit.

7. 3. 1. Ulpianus libro [X]VIII[85] ad edictum sub titulo si quadrupes pauperiem dederit:

Iniuria occisum esse merito adicitur: non enim sufficit occisum, sed oportet iniuria id esse factum. proinde si quis servum latronem occiderit, lege Aquilia non tenetur, quia [iniuria][86] non occidit. 2. sed et quemcumque alium ferro se petentem qui occiderit, non videbitur iniuria occidisse. proinde si furem nocturnum, quem lex duodecim tabularum omnimodo permittit occiderit, aut diurnum, quem aeque lex permittit, sed ita demum, si se telo defendat, videamus, an lege Aquilia teneatur. et Pomponius dubitat, num haec lex non sit in usu. 3. et si quis noctu furem occiderit, non dubitamus, quin lege Aquilia [non] teneatur: sin autem, cum posset adprehendere, maluit occidere, magis est, ut iniuria fecisse videatur: ergo etiam lege Cornelia tenebitur. 4. iniuriam autem accipere hic nos oportet non, quemadmodum et circa iniuriarum actionem, contumeliam quandam, sed quod non iure factum est, hoc est contra ius, id est si culpa quis occiderit. et reliqua.

[83] Added by Mommsen.

[84] I have added for consistency since every other citation of the *Sententiae* in the *Collatio* has this phrase. Mommsen omits.

[85] See Commentary.

[86] Added by Bluhme, followed by Huschke and Mommsen.

7. 4. 1. Ulpianus libro octavo de officio proconsulis sub titulo de furibus:
Fures ad forum remittendi sunt diurni, nocturnique extra ordinem audiendi et causa cognita puniendi, dummodo in poena eorum sciamus operis publici temporarium[87] modum non egrediendum. 2. idem et in balneariis furibus. sed si se telo fures defendunt vel effractores vel ceteri similis[88] nec quemquam percusserunt, metalli poena humiliores, honestiores vero relegatione adficiendi erunt.
7. 5. 1. Paulus libro sententiarum II sub titulo de furibus:
Furti quocumque genere damnatus famosus efficitur. 2. fur est qui rem alienam contrectat. 3. furtorum genera sunt quattuor, manifesti, nec manifesti, concepti et oblati. manifestus fur est, qui in faciendo deprehensus est, et qui intra terminos eius loci, unde furatus est, conprehensus est, vel antequam ad eum locum, quo destinaverat, pervenerit. nec manifestus est fur, qui in rapiendo quidem conprehensus non est, sed eum fecisse negari non potest. 4. concepti actione tenetur, apud quem furtum est inventum. oblati actione is tenetur, qui rem furtivam ali optulit, ne apud se inveniretur. 5. furti actione is agere potest, cuius interest rem non perisse. 6. conceptiva autem agere potest, qui rem concepit et invenit. oblati agere potest, penes quem res concepta inventa est.

(Titulus 8)
De Falso Testimonio

8. 1. 1. Moyses dicit:
Si steterit testis iniustus adversus hominem accusans[89] eum impietatis, 2. stabunt duo homines, quibus est invicem contentio, ante deum et ante sacerdotes et ante iudices, quicumque fuerint in illis diebus. 3. cum inquisierint iudices diligenter et inventus fuerit testis iniustus testificans iniusta, insurgens[90] adversus eum 4. facietis ei, sicut voluit malefacere et delebitis malum de medio vestrum: 5. et ceteri

[87] Following B and V and Seckel and Kübler. W has *temporalium*, which is similar. Mommsen has *temporari*, following *Dig.* 47. 17. 1.

[88] Following W and Schulz, 'Manuscripts', 322–3. Mommsen = *ceteri his similis*, following *Dig.* 47. 17. 1. Scaliger has *ceteri similes.*

[89] Schulz, 'biblischen Texte', 34–6, argues persuasively that this passage suffers from a gloss that crept into the text at some point in the manuscript tradition (α or before). Mommsen = *accusandum accusans.*

[90] See Schulz, 'biblischen Texte', 34–6. Unfortunately, this passage appears in a damaged part of the Berlin manuscript. Mommsen and Scaliger = *insurgentes.*

audientes timebunt nec audebunt haec mala [verba][91] facere inter vos.

8. 2 1. Paulus libro singulari de poenis omnium legum sub titulo ad legem Iuliam de adulteris:

Qui falsum testimonium dixerit, proinde tenebitur, ac si lege Cornelia testamentaria damnatus esset.

8. 3. 1. Paulus libro sententiarum quinto sub titulo de testibus et de quaestionibus:

Hi, qui falso vel varie testimonia dixerunt vel utrique parti prodiderunt, aut in exilium aguntur aut in insulam relegantur aut curia submoventur.

8. 4. 1. Idem libro [sententiarum quinto sub titulo] ad legem Corneliam de sicaris et veneficis:

Lex Cornelia poenam deportationis infligit ei qui hominem occiderit eiusque rei causa furtive faciendi cum telo fuerit, et qui venenum hominis necandi causa habuerit vendiderit paraverit, falsumve testimonium dixerit quo quis periret, mortisve causam praestiterit. 2. quae omnia facinora in honestiores poena capitis vindicari placuit: humiliores vero aut in crucem tolluntur aut bestiis subiciuntur.

8. 5. 1. Paulus libro sententiarum quinto sub titulo ad legem Corneliam testamentariam:

Hi,[92] qui ob falsum testimonium perhibendum[93] pecuniam acceperit dederit, iudicemve ut sententiam ferat vel non ferat corruperit corrumpendumve curaverit, humiliores capite puniuntur, honestiores publicatis bonis cum ipso iudice in insulam deportantur.

8. 6. 1. Idem eodem libro et titulo:

Falsum est quidquid in veritate non est, sed pro vero adseveratur.

8. 7. 1. Ulpianus libro octavo [de officio proconsulis] sub titulo de poena legis Corneliae testamentariae:

Praeterea factum est senatusconsultum Statilio et Tauro consulibus, quo poena legis Corneliae inrogatur ei, qui quid aliud quam

[91] Schulz, 'biblischen Texte', 34–6, argued this word had fallen out of the manuscript tradition by accident and a form of the phrase [*verbum malum*] is in the Lyons manuscript of the Latin Bible. It certainly clarifies the sentence. Mommsen omits.

[92] Following V and style of Coll. 8. 3. 1. W has *his*, B has *hii*, Huschke prefers *is*. Mommsen omits.

[93] Huschke and Hyamson supplied [*vel verum non*] from Ps. Paulus before this. Mommsen rightly omits.

testamentum sciens[94] signaverit signarive curaverit, item qui ad falsas testationes faciendas testamentave falsa invicem dicenda aut consignanda dolo malo coierint<, Licinio V et Tauro conss.>[95] 2. item qui ob instruendam advocationem testimoniave pecuniam acceperit pactusve fuerit societatem[ve][96] coierit aut aliquam de ea [re pac][97]tionem interposuerit, item si quis coierit ad occisionem innocentium senatus consulto quod Cotta et Messalla factum est coercetur. 3. sed et si quis ob denuntiandum vel non denuntiandum remittendumve testimonium pecuniam acceperit, senatus consulto quod duobus Geminis conss. factum est poena legis Corneliae adficitur. et reliqua.

(Titulus 9)
De Familiaris Testimonio Non Admittendo

9. 1. 1. Moyses dicit:[98]
Falsum testimonium non dabis adversus proximum tuum.
9. 2. 1. Ulpianus libro VIII<I>[99] de officio proconsulis [sub titulo][100] ad legem Iuliam de vi publica et privata:
Eadem lege quibusdam testimonium omnino, quibusdam interdicitur invitis capite octogesimo septimo et capite octogesimo octavo[101] in haec verba his hominibus: 2. Hac lege in reum testimonium dicere ne liceto, qui se ab eo parenteve eius libertove cuius eorum libertive libertave liberaverit, quive inpubes erit, quive [*iudicio*

[94] I have deleted Mommsen's emendation here of [*dolo malo falsum*] supplied from *Dig.* 48. 10. 9. 3.

[95] Huschke is persuasive, contra Hyamson, that this is a gloss. See also Wieacker, *Textstufen*, 396.

[96] Mommsen added for clarity.

[97] Clarification by Mommsen.

[98] Mommsen has *Item Moyses*, following B, W. This completely breaks the pattern of the *Collatio* beginning each title with *Moyses dicit*. Here I follow V which has *Moyses dicit*, which might have been a 'happy conjecture', to borrow Schulz's phrase, on that scribe's part based on usage of the Collator. Schulz, 'biblischen Texte', 36–7, argues that *item*, which must have stood in α, crept in from a gloss, which seems likely.

[99] Following Lenel, *Paling.*, II, col. 978. See Commentary.

[100] Not in B. Following Collator's style, Huschke, and Mommsen.

[101] I have deleted [*capite octogesimo octavo*] following *octavo*, which was added by Karl Lachmann ('Verbesserungen des Textes der Collatio', *Zeitschrift für geschichtliches Rechtswissenschaft* 10 (1842), 309–14) and adopted by Huschke, Mommsen, and editors dependant upon Mommsen. If this conjecture of Lachmann remains, the whole sentence seems awkward and smacks of a gloss creeping into the text.

publico damnatus est, qui][102] eorum in integrum restitutus non est, quive in vinculis custodiaque publica erit quive depugnandi causa auctoratus erit, quive ad bestias depugnare se locavit locaverit, praeterquam qui iaculandi causa ad urbem missus est erit, palamve corpore quaestum faciet feceritve, quive ob testimonium dicendum[103] pecuniam accepisse iudicatus erit. nec vo[lens][104] quis eorum hac lege in reum testimonium dicit. 3. capite octogesimo septimo: his[105] inviti in reum testimonium ne dicunto qui sobrinus est ei reo propioreve cognatione coniunctus, quive socer gener vitricus privignusve eius erit. et reliqua.

9. 3. 1. Paulus libro sententiarum [V] sub titulo de testibus et quaestionibus:

Suspectos testes et eos vel maxime, quos accusator de domo eduxit vel vitae humilitas infamaverit, interrogari non placuit: in testibus enim et vitae qualitas spectari debet et dignitas. 2. in adfinem vel cognatum inviti testes interrogari non possunt. 3. adversus se invicem parentes et liberi itemque[106] liberti nec volentes ad testimonium admittendi sunt, quia rei verae testimonium necessitudo personarum plerumque corrumpit.

(Titulus 10)
De Deposito</1>

10. 1. 1. Moyses dicit:

Si aliquis dabit proximo suo argentum aut vas servare et furatum fuerit de domo hominis, si invenitur qui furatus est, reddet duplum. quod si non fuerit inventus fur, accedet is qui commendatum susceperat ante dominum et iurabit nihil se nequiter egisse de omni re commendata proximi sui et liberabitur.

[102] This phrase was supplied by Pithou from *Dig.* 22. 5. 3. 5, and was followed by Mommsen, but does not stand in the manuscripts. Due to the legal sense of the passage, it must have originally stood here and dropped out of the manuscript tradition by the scribe of *α* or a proto-*α*.

[103] I have deleted [*vel non dicendum*] which was inserted by Huschke (based on *Dig.* 22. 5. 3. 5) and followed by Hyamson, but not by Mommsen.

[104] Clarification by Mommsen.

[105] I have placed after the colon as part of the quotation, following Huschke against Mommsen.

[106] I have deleted [*patroni et*] which Huschke inserted here based on *Dig.* 22. 5. 4.

10. 2. 1. Modestinus libro differentiarum secundo [sub titulo][107] de deposito vel[108] commodato:
Commodati iudicio conventus et culpam praestare cogitur: qui vero depositi convenitur, de dolo, non etiam de culpa condemnandus est. commodati enim contractu, quia utriusque contrahentis utilitas intervenit, utrumque praestatur: in depositi vero causa sola deponentis utilitas vertitur et ibi dolus tantum praestatur. 2. sed in ceteris quoque partibus iuris ista regula custoditur: sic enim et in fiduciae iudicium et in actionem rei uxoriae dolus et culpa deducitur, quia utriusque contrahentis utilitas intervenit. 3. in mandati vero iudicium dolus, non etiam culpa deducitur. quamvis singulariter denotare liceat in tutelae iudicium utrumque deduci, cum solius pupilli, non etiam tutoris utilitas in administratione versetur. 4. depositi damnatus infamis est: qui vero commodati damnatur, non fit infamis: alter enim propter dolum, alter propter culpam condemnatur. 5. actione depositi conventus cibariorum nomine apud eundem iudicem utiliter experitur: at is cui res commodata est inprobe cibariorum exactionem intendit. inpensas tamen necessarias iure persequitur, quas forte in aegrum vel alias laborantem inpenderit. 6. res deposita si subripiatur, dominus dumtaxat habet furti actionem quamvis eius apud quem res deposita est intersit ob inpensas in rem factas rem retinere. is vero cui res commodata sit furti experiri debebit, si modo solvendo fuerit. 7. actio commodati semper in simplum competit, depositi uero nonnumquam in duplum, scilicet si ruinae vel naufragii vel incendii aut tumultus causa res deponatur.
10. 3. 1. Hermogenianus sub titulo de deposito[109] huiusmodi inserit constitutiones:
Idem Augg. [et][110] Caess. Fl. Munatio. Eum qui suscepit depositum dolum, non etiam casum praestare certi iuris est. cum itaque proponas ignis vi quaedam cremata de his quae tibi fuere commendata nec ullum dolum in subtrahendis rebus adhibitum, rector provinciae nihil contra iuris rationem fieri patietur. et quoniam necti quereris

[107] Added by Huschke, but accepted by Mommsen.

[108] Mommsen, following manuscripts. Huschke and Hyamson emended to *et commodato.*

[109] Following B and Huschke. Mommsen has *sub titulo depositi.*

[110] Although B leaves out (V and W have idem), the *et* must have stood in the archetype and is supplied by Huschke and Mommsen. The augusti alluded to here and in Coll. 10. 4, 5, and 6 are Diocletian and Maximian and the caesars are Constantius I and Galerius.

moras adhibita varietate, negotium inter vos ortum secundum iuris ordinem sua ratione decidetur. Subscripta VIII k. Iul. Serdica Augustis conss.[111]

10. 4. 1. Idem Augg. et Caess. Fl. Aurelio Altenico Andronico.

Eos penes quos vestem et argenti materiam deposuisse proponis apud rectorem provinciae convenit interrogari, qui eos, sive teneant sive dolo fecerint quominus possint restituere, secundum bonam fidem tibi satisfacere conpellet. Subscripta VI k. April. Sirmi. Caess. conss.[112]

10. 5. 1. Idem Augg. et Caess. Aurelio et Eustathio et Diosimo.

Is, qui depositum suscepit, ultra dolum, si non aliud specialiter convenit, praestare nihil necesse habet. cuius memor iuris rector provinciae partium allegationibus auditis pro repertorum[113] qualitate suam ordinabit sententiam. Subscripta XIV k. Nov. Appiaria.

10. 6. 1. Idem Augg. et Caess. Septimiae Quadratillae.

Qui dolo malo depositum non restituit, suo nomine conventus ad eius restitutionem cum infamiae periculo urguetur. Subscripta prid. idus Decembres Nicomedia, CC. conss.

10. 7. 1. Paulus libro secundo sententiarum sub titulo de deposito:

Deponere possumus apud alium id quod nostri iuris est vel alieni. 2. depositum est quasi diu positum. servandum est, quod[114] breve tempus custodiendum datur. 3. deponere videtur, qui in metu ruinae incendii naufragii apud alium custodiae causa deponit. 4. deponere videtur et is, qui suspectam habens vel minus idoneam custodiam domus vel vim latronum timens apud aliquem rem custodiendam commendat. 5. si sacculum vel argentum[115] deposuero et is penes quem depositum fuit me invito contrectavit, et depositi et furti actio mihi in eum conpetit. 6. ob res depositas dolus tantum praestari solet. 7. in iudicio depositi ex mora et fructus veniunt et usurae rei depositae praestantur. 8. si quis rem penes se depositam apud alium deposuerit, tam ipse directam quam is qui apud eum deposuit utilem actionem depositi habere possunt. 9. si pecuniam deposuero eaque uti[116] tibi permisero, mutua magis videtur quam deposita ac per hoc

[111] Following Collator's style. [112] Following B and Collator's style.

[113] Following Huschke and Hyamson. Mommsen = *ereptorum*.

[114] I have deleted [*ad*] which Mommsen inserted here because it is not in the manuscripts and the clause could still be rendered without it.

[115] I have deleted the emendation of [*signatum*] supplied from *Dig.* 16. 3. 29 because it is not in the manuscripts and the sentence is still clear enough without it.

[116] Following Bluhme, Huschke, and Hyamson. Mommsen = *eamque*.

periculo tuo erit. 10. si rem apud te depositam vendideris eamque redemeris, post perdideris, semel admisso dolo perpetua depositi actione teneberis. 11. ex causa depositi lege duodecim tabularum in duplum actio datur, edicto praetoris in simplum.

10. 8. 1. Gregorianus libro IV sub titulo de deposito:

Imp. Alexander A. Mestrio militi: Incursu latronum ornamenta deposita apud interfectum ab eis perierunt: detrimentum ad heredes eius qui depositum accepit, qui dolum tantum praestare debuit, non pertinet. quod si praetextu latrocinii commissi res, quae in potestate heredis sunt, non restituuntur, tam depositi quam [ad][117] exhibendum actio, sed et in rem vindicatio conpetit. Prop. VII kal. Iul. Maximo bis et Urbano conss.[118]

10. 9. 1. Paulus libro responsorum V sub titulo ex locato et conducto:

Imp. Antoninus Iulio Agrippino. Dominus horreorum periculum vis maioris vel effracturae latronum praestare non cogitur. his cessantibus si quid ex depositis rebus inlaesis extrinsecus horreis perit, damnum depositorum sarciri debet. Prop. IV non. Nov. Antonino IV cons. Paulus respondit: satis praepositam constitutionem declarare his, qui horrea locant, maiorem vim inputari non posse.

(Titulus 11)
De Abactoribus

11. 1. 1. Moyses dicit:

Si quis involaverit vitulum aut ovem et occiderit aut vendiderit, quinque vitulos restituet pro vitulo uno, quattuor oves pro ove una. 2. quod si non habet unde reddat, venundetur pro furto.

11. 2. 1. Paulus libro sententiarum V sub titulo de abactoribus:

Atroces pecorum abactores plerumque ad gladium vel in metallum, nonnumquam autem in opus publicum dantur. atroces autem sunt, qui equos et greges ovium de stabulo vel de pascuis abigunt vel si id saepius aut ferro aut conducta manu faciunt.

11. 3. 1. Idem Paulus eodem libro et titulo:

Abactores sunt, qui unum equum vel duas equas totidemque boves[119] vel capras decem porcos quinque abegerint. quidquid vero

[117] Mommsen added from *CJ* 4. 34. 1.

[118] Following CC in B and the Collator's style.

[119] I have deleted [*oves*] which Mommsen adopted from Huschke since it is missing from all three manuscripts.

intra hunc numerum fuerit ablatum, in poenam[120] furti pro qualitate eius aut in duplum aut in triplum convenitur aut fustibus caesus in opus publicum unius anni datur aut sub poena vinculorum domino restituetur.

11. 4. 1. Idem Paulus eodem libro et titulo:

Si ea pecora, de quibus quis litigaverat, abegerit, ad forum remittendus est atque ita convictus in duplum vel in triplum furis more damnatur.

11. 5. 1. Idem Paulus eodem libro et titulo:

Qui bovem vel equum errantem quodve aliud pecus abduxerit, furem magis eum quam abactorem constitui placuit.

11. 6. 1. Paulus libro singulari de poenis paganorum sub titulo de abigeis dixit:

Cum durius abigei damnantur, et ad gladium traduntur. itaque divus Pius ad concilium Baeticae rescripsit. 2. qui pecora, de quibus litagabat, abegit, ad forum remittendus est et si victus fuerit, in duplum vel quadruplum condemnandus.

11. 7. 1. Ulpianus libro octavo de officio proconsulis sub titulo de abigeis:

De abigeis puniendis ita divus Hadrianus rescripsit concilio Baeticae: Abigei cum durissime puniuntur, ad gladium damnari solent. puniuntur autem durissime non ubique, sed ubi frequentius est hoc genus maleficii: alioquin et in opus et nonnumquam temporarium damnantur. 2. ideoque puto apud vos quoque sufficere genus poenae, quod maximum huic maleficio inrogari solet, ut ad gladium abigei dentur: aut si quis tam notus et tam gravis in abigendo fuit, ut prius ex hoc crimine aliqua poena affectus sit, hunc in metallum dari oportere. 3. rescriptum divi Hadriani sic loquitur, quasi gravior poena sit metalli: nisi forte hoc sensit divus Hadrianus gladii poenam dicendo ludi damnationem. 4. est autem differentia inter eos qui ad gladium et eos qui ad ludum damnantur: nam ad gladium damnati confestim consumuntur vel certe intra annum debent consumi: hoc enim mandatis continetur. enimvero qui in ludum damnantur, non utique consumuntur sed etiam pilleari et rudem accipere possunt

[120] The manuscripts all have *inponat* which then must have been in α. While Cujas suggested emending this to *in poena*, followed by Mommsen, it seems more likely that the scribe of α, or the manuscript preceding it, committed dittography by writing two a's, but then put a macron or stroke over the second one as an abbreviation indicating the ending should be *-am*, as indeed *ablatum* is so written immediately before in all manuscripts (and thus Huschke). This can seen most clearly in the B manuscript where *a* with macron is discernable.

post intervallum, si quidem post quinquennium pilleari, post triennium autem rudem induere eis permittitur. 5. eodem rescripto divi Hadriani diligentissime expressum est non ubique parem esse poenam abigeorum.

11. 8. 1. Idem Ulpianus libro et titulo qui supra:

Abigei autem proprie hi habentur, qui pecora ex pastu et ex armentis subtrahunt et quodammodo depraedantur et abigei studium quasi artem exercent equos de gregibus vel boves de armentis abducentes. ceterum si quis bovem aberrantem vel equum in solitudine abduxerit, non est abigeus, sed fur potius. 2. sed et qui porcum vel capram vel vervecem[121] abducunt, non tam graviter ut hi qui maiora animalia abigunt plecti debent. 3. quamquam autem Hadrianus metalli poenam, item operis[122] vel etiam gladii praestituerit, attamen qui honestiore loco nati sunt non debent ad hanc poenam pertinere, sed aut relegandi erunt aut removendi ordine. 4. Romae tamen etiam bestiis subici abigeos videmus: et sane qui cum gladio abigunt, non inique hac poena adficiuntur.

(Titulus 12)
De Incendiariis

12. 1. 1. Moyses dicit:

Si exierit ignis et invenerit spinas et conprehenderit areas vel spicas aut campum, aestimationem restituet ille qui succendit ignem.

12. 2. 1. Paulus libro sententiarum [quinto] sub titulo de incendiariis:

Qui casam aut villam inimicitiarum gratia incenderunt, humilores in metallum aut in opus publicum damnantur, honestiores in insulam relegantur. 2. fortuita incendia, quae casu venti furentis vel incuria ignem supponentis ad usque vicini agros evadunt, si ex eo seges vel vineae vel olivae vel fructiferae arbores concrementur, datum damnum aestimatione sarciatur.

12. 3. 1. Idem Paulus eodem libro et titulo:

Commissum vero servorum, si domino videatur, noxae deditione sarcitur. 2. messium sane per dolum incensores vinearum olivarumve aut in metallum humiliores damnatur aut honestiores in insulam relegantur.

[121] The manuscripts have *berbicem*. I supply *vervecem* as the regularized form for the English word 'wether' (a castrated ram). Mommsen emended to *verbecem* (due to concern with betacism).

[122] I find Schulz, 'Manuscripts', 331–2, persuasive. The manuscripts have *item operibus*. Mommsen has *temporari*.

12. 4. 1. Idem Paulus libro et titulo qui supra:
Incendiarii, qui quid in oppido praedandi causa faciunt, facile capite puniantur.[123]
12. 5. 1. Ulpianus libro octavo de officio proconsulis [sub titulo][124] de naufragis et incendiariis:
Incendiariis lex quidem Cornelia aqua et igni interdici iussit, sed re varie sunt puniti. nam qui data opera in civitate incendium fecerunt, si humillimo loco sunt, bestiis subici solent, si in aliquo gradu et Romae id fecerunt, capite puniuntur: aut certe adficiendi sunt qui haec committunt. 2. sed eis qui non data opera incendium fecerint plerumque ignoscitur, nisi in lata et incauta neglegentia vel lascivia fuit.
12. 6. 1. Paulus libro <singulari> [sententiae] <de poenis pagano> sub titulo de <abigeis> [incendiariis] dicit:[125]
Incendiarii, qui in oppido praedae causa id admiserint, capite puniantur: qui casu insulam aut villam, non ex inimicitiis incenderint, levius. fortuita enim incendia ad forum remittenda sunt, ut damnum vicinis sarciatur.
12. 7. 1. Ulpianus libro XVIII ad edictum, sub titulo si fatebitur iniuria occisum esse, in simplum et cum diceret:
Item si insulam meam adusseris vel incenderis, Aquiliae actionem habebo, idemque est, et si arbustum meum vel villam meam. 2. quod si dolo quis insulam exusserit, etiam capitis poena plectitur, quasi incendiarius. 3. Item si quis insulam voluerit exurere et ignis etiam ad vicini insulam pervenerit, Aquilia tenebitur lege vicino etiam, non minus inquilinis ob res eorum exustas, et ita Labeo libro XV responsorum refert. 4. sed si stipulam in agro tuo incenderis ignisque evagatus ad praedium vicini pervenerit et illud exusserit, Aquilia lex locum habeat an in factum actio sit, fuit quaestio. 5. sed plerisque Aquilia lex locum habere non videtur, et ita Celsus libro XXXVII

[123] I follow B here which has this form of the hortatory subjunctive instead of Mommsen's *puniuntur*. Interestingly, Hyamson misread this in his apograph text of B and wrote *puniuntur* when the manuscript itself seems to read *puniantur* (as suggested by an anonymous hand in the copy of Hyamson's book housed in the Leopold Wenger Institute at the University of Munich).

[124] Following Mommsen and Collator's style. B is damaged here.

[125] While Mommsen followed the manuscripts here, Hyamson, 116, noticed that this title reference to Paulus must be a mistake, since Title 11 deals with cattle rustlers, not Title 12. Since this appears in all our manuscripts, the error must have been made at least in α. See further, R. M. Frakes, 'A note on *Collatio* 12. 6. 1 and Paulus', *Roman Legal Tradition* 3(2) (2006), 1–5, and Commentary at Coll. 12. 6. 1.

digestorum scribit. ait enim si stipulam incendentis ignis effugit, Aquilia lege eum non teneri, sed in factum agendum, quia non principaliter hic exussit, sed dum aliud egit, sic ignis processit. 6. Cuius sententia et rescripto divi Severi conprobata est in haec verba: profitere propter ignem, [qui][126] pabuli gratia factus culpa servorum Veturiae Astiliae evagatus agrum tuum, ut proponis, depopulatus est, ad exemplum legis Aquiliae noxali iudicio actura: si litis aestimatio permittitur, iudicium consistere[127] potest. videlicet non est visa Aquilia sufficere. 7. si forte servus, qui idem conductor est, coloni[128] ad fornacem obdormisset et villa fuerit exusta, Neratius scribit ex locato conventum praestare debere, si neglegens in elegendis ministeriis fuit. ceterum si alius ignem subiecerit fornaci, alius neglegenter custodierit,[129] tenetur? namque qui non custodit, nihil fecit: qui recte ignem subiecit, non peccavit: quemadmodum si hominem medicus recte secuerit, sed neglegenter vel ipse vel alius curaverit, Aquilia cessat. quid ergo est? et hic puto ad exemplum Aquiliae dandam actionem tam in eum, qui ad fornacem obdormivit vel neglegenter custodit quam in medicum qui neglegenter curavit, sive homo periit sive debilitatus est. Nec quisquam dixerit in eo qui obdormivit rem eum humanam et naturalem passum, cum deberet vel ignem extinguere vel ita munire, ut non evagaretur. 8. item libro VI ex Viviano[130] relatum est: si furnum secundum parietem communem haberes, an damni iniuria teneris? et [Proculus][131] ait agi non posse Aquilia lege, quia nec cum eo qui focum haberet: et ideo aequius putat in factum actionem dandam. sed non proponit exustum parietem. sane enim quaeri potest, [si][132] nondum mihi damnum dederis et ita ignem habeas, ut metuam ne mihi des, an aequum sit me interim actionem, id est in factum inpetrare? fortassis

[126] Scalinger supplied as a marginal note, but not in manuscripts. I keep because it helps clarity of sentence. Mommsen = [*qui*].

[127] Following Mommsen's suggestion. B and V have *cum adire*, but that does not construe.

[128] Here I follow Mommsen and reject Hyamson's emendation of this sentence based on Huschke and *Dig.* 9. 2. 27. 9.

[129] Here I delete the [*an*] supplied from *Dig.* 9. 2. 27. 9 and accepted by Mommsen.

[130] Following B and W (V omits). Mommsen emended to *Vibiano* probably due to concern with betacism.

[131] Mommsen accepted [*Proculus*] here supplied from *Dig.* 9. 2. 27. 10. It is missing from all the manuscripts of the *Collatio*, but the sense of the sentence is difficult without it as the subject of *ait*. See Commentary.

[132] Mommsen accepted [*si*] from *Dig.* 9. 2. 27. 10. Although it is not in the manuscripts, the sense of the sentence works better with it.

enim de hoc senserit Proculus, nisi quis dixerit damni non facti sufficere cautionem.[133] 9. sed et si qui servi inquilini insulam exusserint, libro X Urseius refert Sabinum respondisse lege Aquilia servorum nomine dominum noxali iudicio conveniendum: ex locato autem dominum teneri negat. Proculus autem respondit, cum coloni servi villam exusserint, colonum vel ex locato vel lege Aquilia teneri, ita ut colonus servos posset noxae dedere et si uno iudicio res esset iudicata, altero amplius non agendum. 10. item Celsus libro XXVII digestorum scribit: si, cum apes meae ad tuas advolassent, tu eas exusseris, quosdam negare conpetere legis Aquiliae actionem, inter quos et Proculum, quasi apes domini mei non fuerint. sed id falsum esse Celsus ait, cum apes revenire soleant et fructui mihi sint.[134] sed Proculus eo movetur, quod nec mansuetae nec ita clausae fuerint. ipse autem Celsus ait nihil inter has et columbas interesse, quae, si manum refugiunt, domi tamen fugiunt.

(Titulus 13)
De Termino Amoto

13. 1. 1. Moyses dicit:

Non transmovebis terminos proximi tui, quos constituerunt patres tui <vel principes>[135] possessioni<s>[136] tuae.

13. 2. 1. Paulus libro sententiarum [primo] sub titulo finium regundorum:

In eum, qui per vim terminos deiecit vel amovit, extra ordinem anima advertitur.

13. 3. 1. Ulpianus libro octavo de officio proconsulis sub titulo de termino moto:

Eos qui terminos moverunt non inpune id facere debere divus Hadrianus Terentio Gentiano XVII k. Sept. se III consule rescripsit, quo rescripto poenam variam statuit. 2. verba rescripti ita se habent: pessimum factum eorum, qui terminos finium causa positos abstulerunt, dubitari non potest. poenae tamen modus ex condicione personae et mente facientis magis statui potest: nam si splendidiores

[133] Mommsen followed B, V, and W but notes that *Dig.* 9. 2. 27. 10 has alternate text here. See Commentary.

[134] Following Mommsen's correction of the mood. The manuscripts have *sunt.*

[135] Schulz, 'biblischen Texte', 38–9, makes a strong argument that this crept into the manuscript tradition.

[136] *Ibid.*

sunt personae, quae convincuntur, non dubito quin occupandorum aliorum finium causa id admiserint, et possunt in tempus, ut cuiusque patitur aetas, relegari [id est si iuvenior in longius, si senior recisius: si vero alii negotium gesserunt et ministerio functi sunt, castigari][137] et sic in biennium aut triennium ad opus publicum dari. quod si per ignorantiam aut fortuito lapides usus causa furati sunt, sufficit eos verberibus coerceri.

(Titulus 14)
De Plagiariis

14. 1. 1. Moyses dicit:

Quicumque plagiaverit quemquam Israhel et vendiderit eum, morte moriatur.[138]

14. 2. 1. Paulus libro sententiarum V sub titulo ad legem Fabiam:

Lege Fabia tenetur, qui civem Romanum ingenuum libertinumve servumve alienum celaverit vendiderit vinxerit comparaverit. 2. et olim quidem huius legis poena nummaria fuit, sed translata est cognitio in praefectum urbis, itemque praesidis provinciae extra ordinem meruit animadversionem. ideoque humiliores aut in metallum dantur aut in crucem tolluntur, honestiores adempta dimidia parte bonorum in perpetuum relegantur. 3. si servus sciente domino alienum servum subtraxerit vendiderit celaverit, in ipsum dominum animadvertitur: quod si id domino ignorante commiserit, in metallum datur.

14. 3. 1. Ulpianus libro nono de officio proconsulis sub titulo ad legem Fabiam:

Frequens est etiam legis Fabiae cognitio in tribunalibus praesidum, quamquam quidam procuratores Caesaris usurpaverint quam Roma etiam in provinciis.[139] 2. sed enim iam eo perventum est constitutionibus, ut Romae quidem praefectus urbis solus super ea re cognoscat, si intra miliarium centesimum sit iniuria commissa: enimvero si ultra centesimum, praefectorum praetorio erit cognitio.

[137] Mommsen supplied from *Dig.* 47. 21. 2. Although the phrase is not in the manuscripts and the sentence is at one level clear enough without it, I have included Mommsen's restoration because it is legally correct in that *splendidiores* would be relegated.

[138] Note that here the text must be correct (B and V) as Schulz, 'biblischen Texte', 23–4, suggested as the same construction for Coll. 1. 1 and elsewhere.

[139] Here I have rejected Mommsen and Huschke in favour of a reading closer to the manuscripts (B = *quam rome tam in puintiis*, V = *quam roma etiam in puincus*, W = *quam romae tam prouintpr*). Mommsen = *tam in provinciis quam Romae.*

in provincia est praesidum provinciarum, nec aliter procuratori Caesaris haec cognitio iniungitur, quam si praesidis partibus in provincia fungatur. plane post sententiam de Fabia latam procuratoris partes succedunt huiusce rei. 3. attamen procurator qui illam[140] provinciam regit licet de capitalibus causis cognoscere nec soleat, tamen ut de lege Fabia possit cognoscere, imp. Antoninus constituit. idem legis Iuliae de adulteris coercendis constitutione imperatoris Antonini quaestionem accepit. 4. lege autem Fabia tenetur, qui civem Romanum eumve, qui in Italia liberatus sit, celaverit vinxerit vinctumve habuerit, vendiderit emerit, quive in eam rem socius fuerit: cui capite primo eiusdem legis poena iniungitur. si servus quis sciente domino fecerit, dominus eius sestertiis quinquaginta milibus eodem capite punitur. 5. eiusdem legis capite secundo tenetur, qui alieno servo persuaserit, ut dominum fugiat quive alienum servum invito domino celaverit vendiderit emerit dolo malo, quive in ea re socius fuerit: iubeturque populo sestertia[141] quinquaginta milia dare. et reliqua. 6. Sciendum tamen est ex novellis constitutionibus capitali sententia plagiatores pro atrocitate factis puniendos: quamvis et Paulus relatis supra speciebus crucis et metalli poenam[142] huiusmodi reis inrogaverit poenam.

(Titulus 15)

De Mathematicis, Maleficis et Manichaeis

15. 1. 1. Moyses dicit:

Non inveniatur in te qui lustret filium <t>[s]uum aut filiam <t>[s]uam,[143] nec divinus apud quem sortes tollas: nec consentias venenariis inpostoribus, qui dicunt, quid conceptum habeat mulier, quoniam fabulae seductoriae sunt.[144] nec intendas prodigia, nec interroges mortuos. 2. non inveniatur in te auguriator nec inspector

[140] Following manuscripts. Mommsen = *nullam*.

[141] Following W and Mommsen. Schulz, 'Manuscripts', 323, argued that the scribe of *α* made a mistake here and had *populos extertiam* which B and V followed, but W emended to the correct reading based upon conjecture.

[142] I have inserted following manuscripts. Mommsen omits.

[143] Schulz, 'biblischen Texte', 39–40, argues persuasively that *tuum* . . . *tuam* are errors for *sum* . . . *suam*. This correction also follows the Hebrew, Septuagint, and Vulgate versions. The *te* is in the singular because it is referring to the people of Israel (invoked at Dt. 6. 4) as a collective singular. Mommsen = *tuum* and *tuam*.

[144] Schulz, 'biblischen Texte', 39–40, argued this clause was a gloss that crept into the text, since it does not stem from the Septuagint. This is possible, but it could also stem from the Collator's voice (see Commentary).

avium nec maleficus aut incantator nec pythonem habens in ventrem nec haruspex nec interrogator mortuorum nec portenta inspiciens.[145] 3. omnia namque ista a domino deo tuo damnata sunt et qui fecerit haec. propter has enim abominationes deus eradicabit Chaldaeos[146] a facie tua. 4. tu autem perfectus eris ante dominum deum tuum: 5. gentes enim istae, quas tu possides, auguria et sortes et divinationes audiebant.

15. 2. 1. Ulpianus libro VII de officio proconsulis sub titulo de mathematicis et vaticinatoribus:

Praeterea interdictum est mathematicorum callida inpostura et obstinata persuasione. nec hodie primum interdici eis placuit, sed vetus haec prohibitio est: denique extat senatus consultum Pomponio et Rufo conss. factum, quo cavetur, ut mathematicis Chaldaeis ariolis et ceteris, qui simile inceptum fecerunt, aqua et igni interdicatur omniaque bona eorum publicentur, et si externarum gentium quis id fecerit, ut in eum animadvertatur. 2. sed fuit quaesitum, utrum scientia huiusmodi hominum puniatur an exercitio et professio. quidem[147] apud veteres dicebatur professionem eorum, non notitiam esse prohibitam: postea variatum. nec dissimulandum est nonnumquam inrepsisse in usum, ut etiam profiterentur et publice se praeberent. quod quidem magis per contumaciam et temeritatem eorum factum est, qui visi erant vel consulere vel exercere, quam quod fuerat permissum. 3. saepissime denique interdictum est fere ab omnibus principibus, ne quis omnino huiusmodi ineptiis se inmisceret, et varie puniti sunt hii[148] qui id exercuerunt,[149] pro mensura scilicet consultationis. nam qui de principis salute, capite puniti sunt vel qua alia poena graviore adfecti: enimvero si qui de sua suorumque, levius. inter hos habentur vaticinatores, quamquam hii[150] quoque plectendi sunt, quoniam nonnumquam contra

[145] Mommsen adopted this clause following advice from the famous biblical scholar Julius Wellhausen, although he acknowledged it was probably an interpolation. Since it is in all three manuscripts, it must have stood in α and, if it was an interpolation, probably crept into the manuscript tradition very early on. See further Schulz, 'biblischen Texte', 40.

[146] Although Schulz, 'biblischen Texte', 40, was unsure as to whether this should just read *eos*, I have left as *Chaldaeos*, as it is in all three manuscripts. Hyamson translated this as 'Canaanites', although he left as *Chaldaeos* in his Latin text.

[147] Pithou suggested [*et*] as an emendation before *quidem* and this has been followed by Huschke, Mommsen, and Hyamson. As it does not stand in the manuscripts and the sense is clear enough without it, I have deleted it.

[148] Following B (V = *hi*, W = *id*). Mommsen = *ii*.

[149] Following B.

[150] Following B again (V = *hi*, W omits). Mommsen = *ii*.

publicam quietem imperiumque populi Romani inprobandas artes exercent. 4. extat denique decretum divi Pii ad Pacatum legatum provinciae Lugudunensis, cuius rescripti verba quia multa sunt, de fine eius ad locum haec pauca subieci. 5. denique divus Marcus eum, qui motu Cassiano vaticinatus erat et multa quasi instinctu deorum dixerat, in insulam Syrum relegavit. 6. et sane non debent inpune ferre huiusmodi homines, qui sub obtentu ex monito deorum quaedam vel enuntiant vel iactant vel scientes confingunt.

15. 3. 1. Gregorianus libro VII[151] sub titulo de maleficis et Manichaeis:

Impp. Diocletianus et Maximianus AA [et Constantius] et Maximianus nobilissimi [CC.][152] Iuliano proconsuli Africae. Otia maxima interdum homines in communione[153] condicionis naturae humanae modum excedere hortantur et quaedam genera inanissima ac turpissima doctrinae superstitionis inducere suadent, ut sui erroris arbitrio pertrahere et alios multos videantur, Iuliane karissime. 2. sed dii inmortales providentia sua ordinare et disponere dignati sunt, quae bona et vera sunt ut multorum et bonorum et egregiorum virorum et sapientissimorum consilio et tractatu inlibata probarentur et statuerentur, quibus nec obviam ire nec resistere fas est, neque reprehendi a nova vetus religio debet.[154] maximi enim criminis est retractare quae semel ab antiquis statuta et definita suum statum et cursum tenent ac possident. 3. unde pertinaciam pravae mentis nequissimorum hominum punire ingens nobis studium est: hi enim qui novellas et inauditas sectas veterioribus religionibus obponunt, ut pro arbitrio suo pravo excludant quae divinitus concessa sunt quondam nobis, 4. de quibus sollertia tua serenitati nostrae retulit Manichaeos;[155] audivimus eos nuperrime veluti nova [et][156] inopinata prodigia in hunc mundum de Persica adversaria nobis gente progressa vel orta esse et multa facinora ibi committere populos namque quietos perturbare nec non et civitatibus maxima

[151] Following Mommsen and B (W omits and V has VI).

[152] This is the heading proposed by Mommsen, but it seems logical because V and W have *imperatoribus maximianus diocletianus et maximimus* [V = *maximus*] *nobilissimi AAA*, probably following β. It also follows the style of the imperial constitution quoted from the *Codex Gregorianus* at Coll. 6. 4.

[153] Following Mommsen and manuscripts as opposed to Bluhme and Hyamson.

[154] Following Pithou. The manuscripts have *debere*. Mommsen has *deberet*.

[155] Following B (V and W have *manicheus*, which is a close enough mistake). Mommsen = *Manichaei*.

[156] Following Mommsen for clarity. Huschke suggested *ac*.

detrimenta inserere: et verendum est, ne forte, ut fieri adsolet, accedenti tempore conentur [per][157] execrandas consuetudines et saevas leges Persarum innocentioris naturae homines, Romanam gentem modestam atque tranquillam et universum orbem nostrum veluti venenis de suis malivolis inficere. 5. et quia omnia, quae pandit prudentia tua in relatione religionis illorum, genera maleficiorum statutis evidentissimorum[158] exquisita et inventa commenta, ideo aerumnas atque poenas debitas et condignas illis statuimus 6. iubemus namque auctores quidem ac principes una cum abominandis scripturis eorum severiori poenae subici, ita ut flammeis ignibus exurantur: consentaneos vero et usque adeo contentiosos capite puniri praecipimus, et eorum bona fisco nostro vindicari sancimus. 7. si qui sane etiam honorati aut cuiuslibet dignitatis vel maioris[159] personae [ad][160] adhuc inauditam et turpem atque per omnia infamem sectam, vel ad doctrinam Persarum se transtulerint, eorum patrimonia fisco nostro adsociari facies ipsos quoque Phaenensibus vel Proconnensibus metallis dari. 8. ut igitur stirpitus amputari mala[161] haec nequitiae de saeculo beatissimo nostro possit, devotio tua iussis ac statutis tranquillitatis nostrae maturet obsecundare. Dat. prid. k. April. Alexandriae.

(Titulus 16)
De Legitima Successione

16. 1. 1. Scriptura divina sic dicit:
Filiae Salfad adstantes ante Moysen et Eleazarum sacerdotem et principes omnemque senatum filiorum Israhel in foribus tabernaculi testimonii dixerunt: 2. pater noster mortuus est et filii non fuerunt ei <sed filiae>[162] 3. et ideo non deleatur nomen patris nostri de medio tribus suae. non[163] est ei masculus: date nobis possessionem in medio fratrum patris nostri. 4. et obtulit Moyses petitionem earum coram

[157] Added by Pithou for clarity, followed by Mommsen.

[158] Following manuscripts and Scaliger (in damaged part of B manuscript). Mommsen = *evidentissime sunt.*

[159] Following manuscripts. Mommsen = *maiores.*

[160] Following Mommsen. I keep for clarity.

[161] Following Huschke. B has *malis*; V and W have *mali.* Mommsen suggested *lues.*

[162] Schulz, 'biblischen Texte', 41–2, deletes *sed filiae* because it is not in the biblical text. Mommsen includes because it is in the manuscripts. It seems likely that it crept into the manuscript tradition early on, before α, as a gloss.

[163] Schulz, 'biblischen Texte', 41–2, suggested inserting *quia* before *non*, basing his emendation on the Vulgate. However, since the Collator edited this scriptural passage in several places, Schulz's emendation is not necessary.

deo. 5. et locutus est dominus [ad][164] Moysen dicens: 6. recte filiae Salfad[165] locutae sunt: et ideo debitis eis possessionem hereditatis in medio fratrum patris earum. 7. et dices haec filiis Israhel: homo si decesserit et filium non habuerit, [dabitis hereditatem eius filiae eius. 8. Si filiam non habuerit, dabitis fratribus eius. 9. Si fratres non habuerit, dabitis patruis eius. 10. Si patruos non habuerit,][166] dabitis hereditatem proximo eorum de tribu eius: et possidebit omnia eius: et erit haec filiis Israhel iustificatio iudiciorum secundum quae constituit dominus Moysi.

16. 2. 1. Gaius institutionum libro III legitimas sic ordinat successiones:

Intestatorum hereditates lege[167] duodecim tabularum primum ad suos heredes pertinent. 2. sui autem heredes existimantur liberi qui in potestate morientis fuerunt, veluti filius filiave, nepos neptisve [ex filio],[168] pronepos proneptisve ex nepote filio nato prognatus prognatave. nec interest naturales[169] liberi an adoptivi. ita demum tamen nepos neptisve et pronepos proneptisve suorum heredum numero sunt, si praecedens persona desierit [in potestate parentis esse, sive morte id acciderit][170] sive alia ratione, veluti emancipatione. nam si per id tempus, quo quisque morietur, filius in potestate eius sit, nepos ex eo suus heres esse non potest. idem et in ceteris deinceps liberorum personis dictum intellegimus. 3. uxor quoque, quae in manu est,[171] sua heres est, quia filiae loco est: item nurus quae in

[164] Here I follow Schulz, 'biblischen Texte', 41, who suggests adding *ad* since it follows the biblical text and W has *Moysen* (in the accusative as the object of the preposition *ad* which must have dropped out of the manuscript tradition). W has *Moyses*, indicating that β must not have had *Moysi.* Of course the title of the work itself has the phrase *ad Moysen.* Mommsen, following B, has *dominus Moysi.*

[165] B has *salpade*, W has *salphad* (which Mommsen followed). I have adjusted to agree with *Salfad* in 16. 1. 1.

[166] A brief look at Numbers 27: 1–11, and indeed at the state of the text as it stands, reveals that a large part of the biblical citation is missing and must have fallen out of the manuscript tradition before α. The above approximation was suggested by Huschke.

[167] *Institutes* of Justinian (3. 1. 1) has *ex lege*, but, since no manuscript has this reading, Mommsen avoids.

[168] Mommsen has *ex filio* drawn from *Institutes* of Justinian, 3. 1. 2, although this phrase is absent from the manuscripts of the *Collatio.*

[169] Mommsen follows with [*sint*] drawn from *Institutes* of Justinian, 3. 1. 2 (which has *sunt*), but this word is also absent from the manuscripts.

[170] Mommsen supplied from *Institutes* of Justinian, 3. 1. 2b, for clarity which must be correct.

[171] Mommsen also suggested adding [*ei cuius in manu est*], but it is absent from the manuscripts.

filii manu est, nam et haec neptis loco est. sed ita demum erit sua heres, [si][172] filius, cuius in manu sit cum pater moritur, in potestate eius non sit. idemque dicimus et de ea, quae [in][173] nepotis manu matrimonii causa sit, quia proneptis loco est. 4. postumi quoque,[174] si vivo parente nati essent, in potestate eius futuri essent,[175] sui heredes sunt. 5. Idem iuris est de his, quorum nomine ex lege Aelia Sentia vel ex senatus consulto post mortem patris causa [probatur: nam et hi vivo patre causa][176] probata in potestate eius futuri essent. 6. et[177] de eo filio, qui ex prima secundave mancipatione post mortem patris manumittitur, intellegemus. 7. cum[178] filius filiave et ex altero filio nepotes neptesve extant, pariter ad hereditatem vocantur nec qui gradu propior est, ulteriorem excludit. aequum enim videtur nepotes neptesve in patris sui locum portionemque succedere. pari ratione et si nepos neptisve sit ex filio et ex nepote pronepos proneptisve, simul vocantur. 8. Et quia placebat nepotes neptesve, item pronepotes proneptesve in patris sui locum succedere, conveniens esse visum est non in capita, sed in stirpes hereditates dividi, [ita][179] ut filius dimidiam partem hereditatis ferat [et][180] ex altero filio duo pluresve nepotes alteram dimidiam: item si ex duobus filiis nepotes extent, ex altero filio unus forte vel [duo],[181] ex altero tres aut quattuor, [ad unum aut ad duos dimidia pars pertineat et ad tres aut quattuor],[182]

[172] Mommsen's emendation, accepted by Hyamson. Although not in the manuscripts, I keep for clarity.

[173] Following Mommsen. V had *de*. B and W omit. I keep for clarity.

[174] Mommsen supplied [*qui*] here from *Institutes* of Justinian, 3. 1. 2b, but I delete since the meaning is clear enough without it and it is not in the manuscripts.

[175] I follow B here. Mommsen had *forent* which he drew from the *Institutes* of Justinian 3. 2b, but the corresponding section of Gaius' work is lost. Gaius certainly used the expression *futuri essent* several times.

[176] Mommsen supplied from Gaius (*Institutes*, 3. 5). This phrase likely stood in the archetype, but then fell out of the manuscript tradition due to a simple scribal error by the time of α.

[177] Mommsen had instead [*quod*] from Gaius (*Institutes*, 3. 6, who replaces the *et* with *etiam*), but the manuscripts omit.

[178] Mommsen supplied [*igitur*] from Gaius (*Institutes*, 3. 7), but the manuscripts omit.

[179] Supplied from Gaius (*Institutes*, 3. 8), and accepted without brackets by Mommsen. Since it is not in the manuscripts, I have placed in brackets.

[180] Mommsen supplied from Gaius (*Institutes*, 3. 8). I keep for clarity.

[181] Mommsen supplied from Gaius (*Institutes*, 3. 8) which must be correct.

[182] Mommsen drew this phrase from Gaius (*Institutes*, 3. 8). Although the manuscripts omit, I have kept for clarity. Either it fell out of the manuscript tradition or it was not in the Collator's copy of the *Institutes* of Gaius.

altera dimidia. 9.<De Agnatis>[183] si nullus sit suorum heredum, tunc hereditas pertinet ex eadem lege duodecim tabularum ad agnatos. 10. Vocantur autem agnati, qui legitima cognatione iuncti sunt. legitima autem cognatio <hoc>[184] est quae per virilis sexus personas coniungitur: itaque [qui][185] eodem patre nati sunt fratres agnati sibi sunt, qui etiam consanguinei vocantur, nec requiritur, an matrem eandem habuerint. Item patruus fratris filio et invicem is illi agnatus est. eodem numero sunt fratris patrueles inter se, id est qui ex duobus fratribus progenerati sunt, quos plerique etiam consobrinos vocant: qua ratione scilicet etiam ad plures gradus agnationis pervenire poterimus. 11. non tamen omnibus simul agnatis dat lex duodecim tabularum hereditatem, sed his, qui tum cum certum est aliquem intestatum[186] decessisse, proximo gradu sunt. 12. Nec in eo iure successio est: ideoque si hereditatem proximus omiserit vel antequam hereditatem adierit decesserit, sequentibus nihil iuris ex lege competit. 13. ideo autem non mortis tempore, quis proximus erit, requirimus, sed eo tempore, quo certum fuerit aliquem intestatum decessisse, quia si quis testamento facto decesserit, melius esse visum est tunc requiri proximum, cum certum esse coeperit neminem ex [eo][187] testamento heredem fore.[188] 14. quod ad feminas tamen adtinet[189] hoc iure aliud in ipsarum hereditatibus capiendis placet,[190] aliud in ceterorum ab his capiendis. nam[191] feminarum hereditates proinde[192] agnationis iure redeunt atque masculorum:

[183] The subtitle *De agnatis* appears in B and W (and Mommsen and other editions, but not *FIRA*). This subheading is not present in Gaius (*Institutes*, 3. 9) and is not in V (which omits this paragraph). Since it is in B and W, it must have stood in α. It is most likely a gloss that crept into the text by the scribe of α or proto-α.

[184] The manuscripts have *hoc*. Gaius (*Institutes*, 3. 10) has *est ea*, Mommsen has *est*.

[185] Mommsen's suggestion. Not in the manuscripts or in Gaius or the *Institutes* of Justinian. I include for clarity.

[186] The manuscripts have *intestato*, but Gaius (*Institutes*, 3. 11) and clarity demand *intestatum* (which Mommsen follows).

[187] The manuscripts omit, Mommsen supplied from Gaius (*Institutes*, 3. 13). I include for clarity.

[188] Another 'happy conjecture' of W, to use Schulz's phrase, that approaches the text of Gaius (who has *fore heredem* at *Institutes*, 3. 13).

[189] Gaius (*Institutes*, 3. 14) follows with *in*, the manuscripts and Mommsen omit.

[190] Gaius (*Institutes*, 3. 14) has *placuit*. Mommsen and the manuscripts have *placet*, although Mommsen suspects Gaius may be correct here.

[191] The manuscripts follow with *et*, Gaius and Mommsen omit.

[192] Gaius (*Institutes*, 3. 14) has *ad nos* following *proinde*. The manuscripts and Mommsen omit.

nostrae vero hereditates ad feminas ultra consanguineorum gradum non pertinent. itaque soror fratri sororive legitima heres est, amita vero et fratris filia[193] heres esse non potest. sororis autem nobis loco est etiam mater aut noverca, quae per in manum conventionem apud patrem nostrum ius filiae nancta est. 15. Si [ei][194] qui defunctus erit sit frater et alterius fratris filius, sicut ex superioribus intellegitur, frater potior est, quia gradu praecedit: sed alia facta [est][195] iuris interpretatio inter suos heredes. 16. quod si defuncti nullus frater extet, sed sint liberi fratrum, ad omnes quidem hereditas pertinet, sed quaesitum est, si dispari numero sint, forte nati ex uno unus vel duo et ex altero tres aut quattuor, utrum in stirpes dividenda sit hereditas, sicut inter suos heredes iuris est an potius in capita. iam dudum autem placuit in capita dividendam[196] hereditatem: itaque quotquot erunt ab utraque parte personae, in tot portiones hereditas dividetur et singuli singulas portiones ferunt. 17. si nullus agnatus sit, eadem lex duodecim tabularum gentiles ad hereditatem vocat. qui sint autem gentiles, primo commentario retulimus et cum illic admonuerimus[197] gentilicium ius in desuetudinem abisse, supervacuum est hoc quoque loco de ea re curiosius tractare.

16. 3. 1. Paulus libro sententiarum IV[198] sub titulo de intestatorum successionibus:[199]

Intestati dicuntur, qui testamentum facere non possunt[200] vel ipsi linum ut intestati decederent abruperunt vel hii[201] quorum hereditas

[193] Gaius (*Institutes*, 3. 14) follows with *legitima*. The manuscripts and Mommsen omit.

[194] Mommsen supplied from Gaius (*Institutes*, 3. 15). Although the manuscripts have *quis*, for clarity I follow Mommsen.

[195] *Est* supplied from Gaius (*Institutes*, 3. 15).

[196] Gaius (*Institutes*, 3. 16) follows with *esse*, but here Mommsen rightfully omits as it is not in the manuscripts and is not necessary for the sense of the sentence.

[197] Gaius (*Institutes*, 3. 17) follows with *totum*. Mommsen omits as it is not in the manuscripts.

[198] B has VII, Mommsen corrected to IIII. I have regularized to IV.

[199] Ps. Paulus, *Sententiae* 4. 8. 1–13 is restored from this passage. See further, Krüger, *Sententiae*.

[200] Mommsen here supplies [*vel iure non fecerunt cum possent*] as a clarification (Hyamson followed, but accidentally left out the *non*). While Mommsen is legally correct, since the manuscripts omit the clause, as does Krüger, in his edition of the fragments of the *Sententiae* (99), I omit.

[201] Supplied from B (V and W have *hic*). Mommsen omits.

repudiata est cuiusve[202] condicio defecerit, sane[203] iure praetorio[204] factum testamentum obiecta doli exceptione optinebit. 2. eorum[205] quorum testamenta rumpuntur aut inrita fiunt, ipso quidem iure testati decedunt, sed per consequentias sublato testamento intestati decedunt. 3. intestatorum hereditas lege duodecim tabularum primum suis heredibus, deinde agnatis et aliquando quoque gentilibus deferebatur. sane consanguinei, quos lex non adprehenderat, interpretatione prudentium primum inter agnatos locum acceperunt. 4. sui heredes sunt primo loco filius filia[ve][206] in potestate patris constituti: nec interest, si adoptivi sint an naturales et secundum legem Iuliam Papiamve quaesiti, modo maneant in potestate. 5. qui sui heredes sunt, ipso iure heredes etiam ignorantes constituuntur, ut furiosi aut infantes et peregrinantes: quibus bonorum possessio nisi propter praetoriam actionem non erat necessaria. 6. suis heredibus adeo a morte testatoris rerum hereditariarum[207] dominium continuatur, ut nec tutoris auctoritas pupillis nec furiosis curator sit necessarius, nisi forte[208] solvendo sit hereditas: quamvis etiam furiosus, si resipuerit, et pupillus, si adoleverit, abstinere possint. 7. post mortem patris natus vel ab hostibus reversus aut ex primo secundove mancipio manumissus cuiusve erroris causa probata,[209] licet non fuerint in potestate, sui tamen patri heredes efficiuntur. 8. post filios filias ad intestatorum successionem inter suos veniunt[210] nepotes neptes, pronepotes proneptes ac deinde masculino sexu post[211] filium descendentes, si nullo parentum

[202] B = *cuius nec*, V = *cuiusvel*, W = *cuiusve*. Mommsen = *quibusve*.

[203] Although Huschke suggested *nisi*, and was followed by Mommsen; the manuscripts have *sine*. Cujas, cited in Mommsen's apparatus, suggested this was an error for *sane* and I accept this emendation.

[204] Mommsen adds here [*non iure*].

[205] Following manuscripts. Mommsen = *horum*.

[206] I have added for clarity.

[207] The manuscripts have in error here *hereditariorum*, which then must trace back to at least α.

[208] Krüger, *Sententiae*, 100, suggested here [*in hoc ut abstineant*] which Mommsen adapted to [*ut abstineant, si minus forte*] to fill what he felt was a hiatus in the text.

[209] Huschke added *est* here to complete the verb, followed by Mommsen with [*est*]. Since it is not in the manuscripts and is not necessary grammatically as it can be assumed, I have deleted it.

[210] Following Mommsen. The manuscripts have *veniant*.

[211] The manuscripts have *post*. Conrad Rittershusius proposed *per* which Mommsen and Hyamson follow, but not Krüger's edition of the *Sententiae*. The sense is clear enough from either word—that is, males descended from the son's line.

inpedimento ipsi in avi potestate vel proavi familia remanserint: parentes enim liberis suis, cum quibus in potestate fuerint ipsi, ordine successionis obsistunt. 9. filii, si cum nepotibus ex alio filio susceptis in familia retinentur, ad intestati patris successionem cum fratris filiis vocantur: quibus in patris sui partem venientibus hereditas in stirpes, non in capita dividitur, ita ut unus filius et plures nepotes singulos semisses habeant. idemque evenit, si avo ex duobus filiis inpari numero nepotes successerint. 10. ex filia nepotes sui heredes non sunt: in avi enim materni potestate alienam familiam sequentes ipsa ratione esse non possunt. 11. eo tempore suus heres constituendus est, quo certum est aliquem intestatum decessisse: quod ex eventu deficientis condicionis et ortu nepotis, qui vivo avo post mortem patris[212] natus, finiri potest. 12. quem[213] filius emancipatus suscepit vel adoptavit, sui heredis locum in avi successione sic ut ipse pater obtinere non potest:[214] adoptivus, tamen nec quasi cognatus bonorum possessionem eius petere potest. 13. si sui heredes non sunt, ad agnatos legitima hereditas pertinebit,[215] inter quos primum locum consanguinei optinent. agnati autem sunt cognati virilis sexus per virilem[216] descendentes, sicut filius fratris et patruus et deinceps tota successio. 14. inter agnatos et cognatos hoc interest:[217] in agnatis etiam cognati continentur, inter cognatos vero agnati non conprehenduntur. et ideo patruus agnatus est et[218] cognatus, avunculus autem cognatus tantummodo est. 15. consanguinei sunt eodem patre nati, licet diversis matribus, qui in potestate fuerunt mortis tempore: adoptivus quoque frater, si non sit

[212] Here Mommsen inserted [*conceptus sit et post mortem avi*] based on the *Institutes* of Justinian (3. 1. 8). Since it is not in the manuscripts and the sense is clear enough without it, I have deleted it.

[213] B has *cum*, V has what appears to be *idem qui*, W has *cuius*. Mommsen admitted uncertainty on the reading here and proposed *idem cum*. However, the *idem* here is simply the normal way the V scribe began a new capital. I propose a reading of *quem*.

[214] Mommsen added an additional [*potest*] after this *potest* to accompany *adoptivus*.

[215] End of V manuscript.

[216] Bluhme supplied *sexum* here and was followed by Mommsen [in brackets] and Hyamson who mistakenly put the *virilem* in brackets also. Since it is missing in all three manuscripts and since the sense is clear enough without it, I omit it.

[217] Mommsen follows with [*quod*], supplied from *Dig*. 38. 7. 5. B and W omit, but the Visigothic summary of the *Sententiae* supplies (following Seckel and Kuebler). Since it is not critical for the sense of the passage, I delete it.

[218] Also supplied from the Visigothic summary of the *Sententiae*.

emancipatus, et hi qui post mortem patris nati sunt vel causam probaverunt. 16. soror iure consanguinitatis tam ad fratris quam ad sororis hereditatem admittitur. 17. consanguineis non existentibus agnatis defertur hereditas, prout quis alterum gradu praecesserit. quod si plures eodem gradu consistunt, simul admittuntur. 18. si sint fratris defuncti[219] et filius et nepos fratre non existente, filius fratris nepoti praefertur. 19. sed si duorum fratrum sint liberi, non in stirpes, sed in capita hereditas distribuitur, scilicet ut pro numero singulorum viritim distribuatur hereditas. 20. feminae ad hereditates legitimas ultra consanguineas[220] successiones non admittuntur: id quod iure civili Voconiana ratione videtur effectum: ceterum lex duodecim tabularum sine ulla discretione sexus admittit.

16. 4. 1. Ulpianus libro singulari [regularum] sub titulo de legitimis hereditatibus:

Intestatorum gentiliciorum[221] hereditates pertinent primum ad suos heredes, id est liberos qui in potestate sunt ceterosque qui liberorum loco sunt: si sui heredes non sint,[222] ad consanguineos, id est fratres et sorores ex eodem patre: si nec hi sunt, ad reliquos agnatos[223] virilis sexus per mares descendentes eiusdem familiae. id enim cautum est lege duodecim tabularum hac: si intestatus moritur, cui suus heres nec escit, agnatus proximus familiam habeto. 2. si agnatus defuncti non sit, eadem lex duodecim tabularum gentiles ad hereditatem vocat his verbis: si agnatus nec escit, gentiles familiam [habento. nunc nec ullus est][224] heres hinc nec gentilicia iura in usu sunt.

16. 5. 1. Idem [libro] institutionum ... [sub titulo de successionibus][225] ab intestato:

Ab intestato quoque hereditas defertur aut per ius civile aut per praetoris beneficium: per ius civile suis heredibus vel liberis, qui in

[219] Following closer to the order of B. Mommsen has *si sint defuncti fratris et filius et nepos fratre non existente*, based on an emendation of Krüger in his edition of the fragments of the *Sententiae*.

[220] Following B. Huschke and Mommsen emended to *consanguineorum*.

[221] Following B and Mommsen. Hyamson follows Ps. Ulpian (*Liber singularis Regularum*, 26.1) with *ingenuorom*.

[222] Here I follow Seckel and Kuebler. Mommsen has *sunt*, following Ps. Ulpian (*Liber singularis Regularum*, 26. 1).

[223] Mommsen inserts here [*proximus, id est cognatos*] from the text of Ps. Ulpian (*Liber singularis Regularum*, 26. 1). Not in the manuscripts, V. Arangio-Ruiz, 'Sul liber singularis Regularum', *BIDR* 30 (1921), 178–219 at 216, convincingly argues this section is an interpolation as it appears to be a gloss that crept into the text.

[224] Added by Mommsen for clarity.

[225] B has *Item ab intestato*, but Mommsen must be correct here.

potestate fuerunt,[226] filii filiae et deinceps qui in locum defuncti parentis, quia ex eodem nati sunt, succedunt.

16. 6. 1. Idem eodem libro:

Post suos ab intestato legitimi admittuntur, primum consanguinei. [consanguinei][227] sunt frater et soror, qui in eiusdem potestate patris fuerunt, etsi ex diversis matribus nati sunt. 2. consanguineos et adoptio facit et adrogatio [et][228] causae probatio et in manum conventio.

16. 7. 1. Idem eodem libro:

1. De[ficientibus][229] consanguineis legitimi vocantur. hi sunt agnati qui nos per patris cognationem contingunt virilis sexus: nam sciendum feminis ultra consanguineas hereditates legitimas non deferri. 2. suis praetor solet emancipatos liberos itemque civitate donatos coniungere data bonorum possessione,[230] ita tamen, ut bona si qua propria habent, his qui in potestate manserunt conferant. nam aequissimum putavit neque eos bonis paternis carere per hoc, qui[231] non sunt in potestate neque praecipua bona propria habere, cum partem sint ablaturi suis heredibus.

16. 8. 1. Idem libro qui supra [sub titulo][232] de suis heredibus:

Post agnatos praetor vocat cognatos: cognati autem sunt, qui nos per patrem aut matrem contingunt: post cognatos virum et uxorem. 2. et haec, si qui decessit non fuit libertinus vel stirpis libertinae: ceterum si libertinus est vel libertina, patrono eius legitima hereditas patronaeve lege duodecim tabularum defertur.[233]

16. 9. 1. Idem eodem libro:

Post familiam patroni vocat praetor patronum et patronam, item liberos et parentes patroni et patronae, deinde virum et uxorem, mox cognatos patroni et patronae. 2. quod si is qui decessit liber

[226] Mommsen inserted [*qui sunt*] after the comma. Since the phrase is not in the manuscripts, and the meaning is clear enough, I have deleted it.

[227] Added by Lenel, adopted by Mommsen for sense of the sentence, although it could be assumed from *sunt*.

[228] Huschke and Mommsen add [*et*] here for clarity.

[229] End of word added by Mommsen for clarity. Seckel and Kuebler prefer *post consanguineis*.

[230] End of W.

[231] Following B (and Scaliger). Mommsen has *quod*, following a suggestion of Boecking.

[232] Omitted by B, but Mommsen kept for sense of citation and style.

[233] B has *refertur*, but clarity and Collator's style supports reading of *defertur*.

fuit [nec][234] ex remancipatione manumissus, lex quidem duodecim tabularum manumissori legitimam hereditatem detulit, sed praetor aequitate motus decem personas cognatorum ei praetulit has: patrem matrem, filium filiam, avum aviam, nepotem neptem, fratrem sororem, ne quis occasione iuris sanguinis necessitudinem vinceret. 3. sed imperator noster in hereditatibus quae ab intestato deferuntur eas solas personas voluit admitti, quibus decimae inmunitatem ipse tribuit.[235]

[234] Supplied by Mommsen, followed by Hyamson. Huschke has *liber fuit ex (mancipatione citra) remancipationem manumissus.* B has *libero fuit ex remacipatione[m] manumissus.*

[235] End of B. Mommsen added '(*reliqua desunt*)' since he believed there was originally a large part of the work after Title 16 that was lost in the manuscript tradition.

The Law of God that the Lord gave to Moses begins

(Title 1)

Concerning Assassins and Murderers (by chance or by design)

1. 1. 1. Moses the Priest of God says this:

If someone strikes a person with an iron weapon and kills him, let him die. 2. Moreover, if someone strikes a person by hand with a stone by which he might die and he dies, he is a murderer: let him die. 3. And if through hostility someone strikes him or throws an implement at him from an ambush and he dies, 4. or strikes him by hand through anger and he dies, let him die.

1. 2. 1. Paulus also in the fifth book of *Opinions* under the title 'With regard to the Cornelian Law concerning Assassins and Poisoners' says:

The Cornelian law inflicts the punishment of deportation on someone who kills a person, or who has a weapon for the purpose of murder or of committing a theft, or who has possession of, sells, or prepares poison for the purpose of killing a person, or who gives false testimony by which someone dies, or is responsible for any cause of death. 2. It is resolved that all these crimes are to be punished by capital punishment for *honestiores*; *humiliores*, on the other hand, are to be killed either by crucifixion or by being thrown to the wild beasts.

1. 3. 1. Ulpian in the seventh book of *Concerning the Office of Proconsul* under the title 'Concerning Assassins and Poisoners':

In the first chapter of the Cornelian law concerning assassins, it is prescribed that he who is praetor or the judge of the court to whom has been allotted the investigation concerning assassinations which have been committed in the city of Rome or within one mile should investigate (together with the judges allotted to him according to the law concerning capital cases) anyone who walks with a weapon for the purpose of killing a person or committing a robbery, or who kills a person, or who does this with malice aforethought. And the rest. 2. Having related the words of the law, Ulpian himself says thus:

'This law does not punish everyone who walks with a weapon, but punishes only someone who carries a weapon for the purpose of killing a person or of committing a robbery. Likewise, it restrains someone who has killed a person, not adding which condition of person, so that the law may be seen to pertain also to a slave and to a foreigner.'

1. 4. 1. In the same way Paulus in the same book and title as above says:

A murderer is someone who has killed a person with any kind of weapon or has been responsible for the cause of death.

1. 5. 1. In the same way concerning accidental homicides Moses says according to the law:

If, however, someone neither through hostility nor from an ambush suddenly throws an implement or a stone at someone, 2. by which someone might die (not through intention), and it strikes someone and makes him dead, but he was not his enemy nor sought to do evil to him, 3. you shall judge between the person who struck and the relative of the dead man according to these judgments, 4. and you shall free the person who struck.

1. 6. 1. Ulpian in the book and title related above:

That a distinction between accident and intention is maintained for homicide is confirmed by a rescript of Hadrian. 2. The words of the rescript: 'And someone who has killed a person is generally absolved if he committed it not with the intention of killing, and someone who has not killed, but wished to kill, should be condemned for homicide. 3. It is therefore to be determined from the circumstance: with what kind of iron implement did Epafroditus strike someone? For if he drew a sword or struck with a spear, what doubt is there but that he struck with the intent of killing? But if he struck someone with a key or a cooking pot, or, when he was brawling by chance, struck with an iron weapon, it was not with the intent of killing. 4. Therefore, investigate this and, if there was intent to kill, order that the slave be sentenced with the highest penalty by law as a murderer.'

1. 7. 1. Paulus in the book and title as above:

Someone who has killed a person is sometimes absolved and someone who has not killed is sometimes condemned as a murderer: for each and every one the deliberation, and not the deed, is to be punished. And for that reason if someone wished to kill, and by some chance was not able to follow through, he is punished as a murderer. And he who by chance unknowingly attacked a person by a [thrown] weapon is absolved. 2. But if a person struck in a brawl dies, since it is proper that the blows themselves against each and every one also be evaluated, for that reason *humiliores* are condemned to the games or the mines; *honestiores* are fined half of their goods and sentenced to relegation.

1. 8. 1. In the same way the *Gregorian Code* in the fourth book [under the title] 'With Regard to the Cornelian Law concerning Assassins and Poisoners' lays out the following constitution:

The Emperor Antoninus Augustus to Aurelius Herculanus and other soldiers. Your comrade acts more properly if he gives himself up to the governor of the province. If he proves to him that Justa was not struck by him with the intent of killing, the punishment of homicide is remitted and he will pronounce a sentence following military discipline. Posted on the day before the Kalends of February in the second consulship of Laetus.

1. 9. 1. In the same way the *Gregorian Code* in the same title and book provides the following constitution:

The Emperor Alexander Augustus to Aurelius Flavius and other soldiers. If he for whom you have just now given the petition was not responsible for the death by malice, let him not fear. For a crime is committed if intent to kill is also involved, but those things which occur by unexpected chance, rather than by wrongdoing, are charged for the most part to fate, and not to wrongdoing. Posted on the thirteenth day before the Kalends of August in the consulship of Alexander.

1. 10. 1. In the same way the *Gregorian Code* in the same book and title gives the following rescript:

Greetings Agatho, most dear to us. The quality of the supplication of Julius Antoninus promptly moved Our Clemency. For he asserted that he committed the homicide not intentionally but by chance, since it seems that the circumstance of death was provided by a kick of the heel. If this is the case, and there is not able to be any doubt about it, we desire that he be freed from all fear and suspicion that he might have faced by the risk of his commission of the act, following that which is included in our annotation. Issued the day before the Kalends of December in the consulship of the Augusti Diocletian (for the fourth time) and Maximian.

1. 11. 1. Ulpian in the same book and title as above:

When someone was responsible for the cause of another person's death through mischievousness, it was decided by Taurinus Egnatus,

Proconsul of Baetica, and approved by the Divine Hadrian, that he be sentenced to relegation for five years. 2. The words of the consultation and the rescript read thus: 'Oh best emperor, I have investigated the case between Claudius and Evaristus, and discovered that Claudius the son of Lupus, while being tossed in a military cloak at a party, by the fault of Marius Evaristus was so badly treated that after five days he died. And it was clear that there had been no hostility between him and Evaristus. However, I believed that he needed to be punished because of the fault of high spirits, so that young men of the same age might be corrected. And I thus banished Marius Evaristus for five years from the city and Italy and the province of Baetica and decreed that Evaristus pay out two thousand [sesterces] to Claudius' father due to expenses, because his poverty was manifest.' 3. The words of the rescript: 'You have adjusted, Oh Taurinus, the punishment of Marius Evaristus rightly to the manner of the crime: for it is important even in quite great transgressions whether something is committed by design or by chance. 4. And this distinction in all crimes rightly ought to provoke punishment or inspire justice or allow moderation.'

1. 12. 1. Modestinus in the sixth book of *Distinctions* under the title 'Concerning Those Knowing or Ignorant' says generally:

Sometimes it is the custom to grant pardon to those who committed a crime of civil law through ignorance, but only if there was ignorance of the facts of the matter, not of the law. Of course, it is not customarily provided to those who commit crimes by deliberate design. On account of this, it is necessary to consider, by means of an added distinction, if something is stated to have been done by someone knowing or not knowing. And the rest.

1. 13. 1. Paulus in the same book and title as above:

Someone who bears a weapon for self-defence is not to be seen as carrying it for the cause of homicide. 2. Weapons by definition, moreover, include not only iron weapons, but all that are carried to cause injury.

(Title 2)
Concerning Severe Injury

2. 1. 1. Moses says:

If two men fight and one strikes the other with a stone or with a fist and the man does not die, but lies in bed, 2. and if the man, rising, walks outside upon a staff, he who struck him will not be guilty of a crime, except he will compensate him for his disability and his doctor for the costs of treatment.

2. 2. 1. Ulpian in his single book of *Rules* under the title 'Concerning Injuries':

An injury, if it is not frightful, that is to say serious, is [not] to be estimated for damages without the decision of a judge [i.e. a *iudex*]. If it is a severe injury, however, it is customary that the praetor estimate damages and that it be computed from the deed, such as if, for example, someone is beaten or wounded. And the rest.

2. 3. 1. Papinian in the second book of *Definitions* under the title 'Concerning Judgments':

If as much has been acquired by a free man surrendered as chattel in a noxal action as the amount for which he was liable, he who accepted him in chattel status through the noxal action is to be forced by the praetor to free him: but he is not to be held liable for a fiduciary judgment.

2. 4. 1. Ulpian in the eighteenth book of *On the Edict* under the title 'If accepted that an injury killed, for simple damages' when he also says:

We accept 'to damage' includes: someone who wounds (whether he strikes by means of rods, or by whips, or with fists), or who cuts the body of a person by a weapon or in any other way, or makes a swelling: but only, if loss has been caused. However, if the striking makes a slave lower in value or worse in no way, an action by means of the Aquilian law will not apply and the case will be for injury [i.e. *iniuria*]. Therefore, even if the slave has not been made lower in value, but expenditures were made for his health and safety, in these cases it does seem to me that one is able [to make an action] for damages by the Aquilian law.

2. 5. 1. Paulus in his single book and under the title 'Concerning Injuries':

Injury [i.e. *iniuria*] is generally said to be all things that have been done unjustly [i.e. *non iure*]: specifically, one form of injury is *contumelia* which the Greeks call [ὕβρις, another kind of wrongdoing, which the Greeks call ἀδίκημα, like *damnum iniuriae* accepted in the Aquilian law, and other iniquities and injury, which the Greeks call] ἀδικία. For when the praetor pronounces against us unjustly, we say that we have suffered injury: from whence it is clear that what Labeo thought is not true, that ὕβρις signified only injury at the praetor's court. 2. It is common to all injuries that they are always against good morals and it is in someone's interests that they not be done. 3. This edict pertains to that injury, made for the sake of insult. 4. We suffer injury either in body, when we are beaten, or in words, when we suffer verbal abuse, or when dignity is violated, as when the companions of a matron or of a girl are abducted. An action of injuries is either prescribed by law or by honour. 5. In accord with a law of the Twelve Tables: 'Let he who makes injury to another be punished immediately by 25 sesterces.' This law was a general law. There were also individual laws such as this: 'If someone has broken a bone, let him suffer a penalty of 300 sesterces for the bone of a free man, or 150 sesterces for that of a slave.'

2. 6. 1. The same Paulus in the same single book under the title of 'How cases of *Iniuria* should be conducted':

He said: 'Someone who makes an action regarding injuries must state exactly what kind of injury was committed and must put down an amount not less than the amount of what the security is.' 2. Someone 'states exactly', who describes the injury under its own name, and not so that he understands disjunctively that either this or that happened, but so that he considers it necessary that he either designate one thing under its own proper name or include more things in such a way that he is compelled to prove that all these things happened. 3. The determination as to whether he 'states exactly' or not is for the praetor himself. The praetor does not in this place designate the (exact) words of the plaintiff, but (only) which formula he should use. 4. He does not 'state exactly,' who states merely that he was struck or beaten. But he must also show which part of the body and in what way, for example by fist, club, or rock, just as is set out in the formula: 'Because Aulus Agerius was struck on the cheek by a fist.' He is not compelled to state on the right or left cheek, nor which hand struck him. 5. Likewise, if he says he was defamed, he ought to add in what way he was defamed. For thus also was the formula conceived: 'Because Numerius Negidius sent a pamphlet to Aulus Agerius with the intent of defaming.'

2. 7. 1. Paulus in the [fifth] book of *Opinions* under the title 'With regard to the Cornelian Law concerning Assassins and Poisoners':

It is not seen as a sufficient cause of death, when a beaten person dies after several days while retaining the functions of daily life, unless he was beaten to death or fatally wounded.

(Title 3)
Concerning the Law and Cruelty of Masters

3. 1. 1. Moses says:
If someone strikes his [own] male or female slave by means of a rod and he or she dies at his hands, let him be punished by a judgment. But if he or she survives one or two days, he will not be punished, for the value lost is his own.
3. 2. 1. Paulus in the [fifth] book of *Opinions* under the title 'With regard to the Cornelian Law concerning Assassins and Poisoners' states:
If a slave dies because of beating, the master is not able to be charged with homicide, unless it was done with intent: for it is decided that even in the punishment of slave there is to be propriety.
3. 3. 1. Ulpian in the eighth book of *Concerning the Office of the Proconsul* under the title 'Concerning the Cruelty of Masters':
If a master vents his rage upon a slave or compels him or her to lewdness and shameful violation, the duties of a *praeses* are clearly shown by the rescript of the Divine Pius to Aurelius Marcianus, Proconsul of Baetica. 2. The words of this rescript are these: 'It is certainly proper that the power of masters over their own slaves is to be undiminished nor should any person's rights be taken away: but it is in the interest of masters not to deny to help those who are justly pleading against savagery or hunger or intolerable injury. 3. For that reason, examine the case of the complaints of those who fled from the family of Julius Sabinus to the statue, and, if you will have found either more harsh conditions than is fair, or they are affected by disgraceful injury, then order them to be sold, so that they are not returned into the power of Sabinus. But if he makes fraudulent evasion of my constitution, let him learn that I will even more severely prosecute the crime.' 4. The Divine Hadrian even ordered the relegation of a certain matron Umbra for five years, because she had handled her female slaves most outrageously on account of the pettiest of causes. 5. In a similar way, the Divine Pius replied [in] these words to the petition of Alfius Julius: 'The obedience of slaves ought to be preserved not only by command, but also by moderation and by providing necessities and by just works. 6. Therefore, you ought to be careful to treat your slaves in a just manner and with moderation, so that you are able to look after them easily, lest, if it appears that you are unequal to the costs or exercise domination by rather outrageous cruelty, the most famous proconsul might

consider it necessary, in order that a large tumult might not occur in response, to take the initiative and compel you to sell them on my authority. In the consulship of Glabrio and Homullus.'

3. 4. 1. The *Gregorian Code* in book fourteen under the title 'Concerning Accusations':

The Emperors Diocletian and Maximian Augusti to the soldier Aurelius Sacratus: 'Since you propose that your slave, oppressed gravely by the force of sickness, died a natural death, the account of your innocence, to which you bear assurance, does not allow a false accusation on account of immoderate punishment to emerge.' Posted on the Nones of December in the consulship of Diocletian (for the third time) and Aristobolus.

(Title 4)
Concerning Adultery

4. 1. 1. Moses says:

Whoever is an adulterer with the wife of his neighbour, let that person die: he who is the adulterer and she who is the adulteress. 2. But if anyone seduces a virgin who is not betrothed and defiles her, he must marry her himself without dowry. 3. But if her father refuses and does not desire to give her to him as wife, he shall pay money to the father, in the amount of the dowry of a virgin.

4. 2. 1. Paulus in his single book *Concerning Adultery* under the title:

In making a brief interpretation [of the Julian law] concerning the punishment of adulterers, I have chosen to go through the chapters themselves and to observe the order of the law. 2. And, indeed, the first chapter of the Julian law concerning adultery repeals many previous laws. 3. In the second chapter it permits to a father, if, in the case of a daughter whom he has in power or in the case of a daughter who passed into the *manus* of her husband with his [the father's] authority, when he had (her) in his power, he catches an adulterer at his own house or his son-in-law's house, or he involves his father-in-law in this matter, that the father may kill the adulterer with impunity, provided that he kills the daughter on the spot. 4. However, in the cases of a widowed daughter, he who kills a man caught in adultery and kills the daughter on the spot is permitted by his legal right to do so Marcellus writes in the thirty-first book of his *Digests*. 5. By the authority also of this law, Marcellus, in the same book, approves that a father is able to kill even a man of consular rank or his own patron, if he catches the adulterer with his daughter. 6. But if he does not kill the daughter, but only the adulterer, he is guilty of homicide. 7. And if he kills his daughter after an interval of time, it is the same, unless he kills her after hot pursuit: for, by continuation of intent, it is seen to have been done with authority of the law.

4. 3. 1. The same Paulus in the same single book and title:

Certain persons, moreover, are enumerated whom it is allowed for the husband to kill when caught in adultery with his wife, although it is not allowed to kill the wife. 2. Therefore, following the laws, a man (even if a *filius familias*) is permitted in his own home to kill a slave caught in adultery, or someone contracted to gladiatorial service, or also someone who hires himself out to fight with beasts. 3. But it is also allowed to kill a person who was convicted by a criminal court when caught in adultery; for instance, a freedman (whether his own or his father's), and a Roman citizen as well as a Latin. 4. But it is also permitted to kill the freedman of the father and of the mother and of the son and of the daughter; he who surrendered in war [i.e. a *dediticius*] is also considered to be in this category. 5. He ought, however, to declare before the man with jurisdiction in that place where he killed, and he ought to divorce his wife. 6. But, if he does not do that, he does not kill with impunity. 7. It should be known, however, that the Divine Marcus and Commodus wrote in a rescript that he who kills an adulterer unlawfully is to be punished with a lighter punishment. 8. But Antoninus the Great even pardoned those who had killed adulterers if they were overwhelmed by the ill-advised heat of passion. And the rest.

4. 4. 1. The same Paulus in the same single book and title:

He who accuses by the right of a husband or father, if defeated, is not liable to the punishment of a false charge. If he accuses by the right of an outsider, he is liable to be punished with the punishment of a false charge. 2. But, in these circumstances, after two months, but without passing beyond the four months in which an action may be brought, if someone brings an action, although he be someone who is not otherwise able to accuse (such as a freedman or a minor under twenty-five years of age, or a disreputable person) he is, nevertheless, allowed to make an accusation, as Papinian also wrote in book fifteen.

4. 5. 1. Papinian in the fifteenth book of *Responses* under the title 'With regard to the Julian Law concerning Adultery':

A Roman citizen, who is with a Roman female citizen without marriage or has married a foreign woman, cannot accuse her as an adulteress by the right of a husband, but *infamia* or the fact that he is a freedman who does not have property worth 30,000 sesterces or a son will not be impediments to him seeking the appropriate damages.

4. 6. 1. Paulus in the single book and title as above:

Adultery can be avenged by the right of a husband in respect of a wife, but not a betrothed. Severus and Antoninus have also thus written.

4. 7. 1. Papinian in the single book *Concerning Adultery*:

It was asked if a father was able to accuse his emancipated daughter by means of the legal power of the father. I responded: 'Indeed, the law grants the power of killing a daughter who he has in his power, or who married on his authority: but the father is also not prohibited to accuse even his emancipated daughter by the legal power of the father.'

4. 8. 1. Papinian in the same single book and title:

Since a law from the period of the monarchy gave to the father the power of life and death over his son, what good was it that it be included in the law, that there might also be the power of killing the daughter? Please reply to me, for I wish to know. He responded: 'Does this addition not, on the contrary, present to us the argument, that it should not be seen as having given to one not (already) having [but to have ordered that she be killed with the adulterer], so that he should be seen as being directed by greater justice to kill the adulterer, since he did not even spare the daughter?'

4. 9. 1. The same author:

If a father kills an adulterer and spares his own daughter, I ask what should be the decision against him? He responded: 'Without a doubt that father is a murderer: therefore he will be held by the Cornelian law concerning assassins. Plainly, if the daughter is saved, not by the desire of the father, but by chance because the daughter fled, the father will have a substantial defence. For the law punishes a murderer thus, if a homicide is committed with malice aforethought; here, however, the father did not save the daughter on that account, because he desired it, but rather because he was not able to kill her.'

4. 10. 1. The same Papinian:

If a husband kills his own wife caught in adultery, I ask whether it falls under the law concerning assassins. He responded: 'In no part of that law is it permitted to a husband to kill a wife: therefore, it is not doubtful that he has committed something openly against the law.

But if you are discussing punishment, it is not unfair that something be permitted to his most honourable anger, so that he is not punished as if he was a murderer by execution or deportation, but let his punishment be established as exile.'

4. 11. 1. The same author thus:

It is well known that if a husband or father makes an accusation [of adultery], slaves of either are to be tortured: I ask whether the same ought to be permitted if the accuser is an outsider? He responded: 'It is clear that the reason that it was permitted for these persons to have the slaves tortured was so that they might more diligently seek restitution for the pain of their mind and likewise not carelessly seek restitution for the injury to their damaged household. But since it is believed that such an offence is not easily committed without the assistance of slaves, the reason extends to the point that even in cases where an outsider accuses the slaves should be subjected to inquiry under torture by judges.'

4. 12. 1. Paulus in the [second] book of *Opinions* under the title 'Concerning Adultery':

It is permitted to a father (either adopted or natural) to kill with his own hand an adulterer, no matter what his rank, caught with his daughter in his own house or that of his son-in-law. 2. If the father is a *filius familias* who catches his daughter in adultery, although in the words of the law it is almost the case that he is not able to kill, it is nevertheless permitted even to him that he may kill. 3. The husband is able to kill only those caught in adultery who are of ill repute and those who make money with their bodies, slaves also and freedmen, excepting his wife who is prohibited. 4. It is decided that a husband who has killed his wife caught in adultery committed this because of his inability to endure his righteous pain, and thus he should be punished more lightly. 5. The adulterer having been killed, the husband ought to divorce his wife at once and make a public statement within the next three days, regarding in which place he had caught his wife and with what adulterer. 6. The husband is thus only able to kill the adulterer found in adultery with his wife if had caught him in his own house. 7. He who does not at once divorce his wife who had been caught in adultery, it is acceptable to charge with pandering. 8. Slaves, indeed, of the husband and of the wife are able to be tortured in a case of adultery, nor will freedom given those on the pretext of impunity be valid.

(Title 5)
Concerning Those Engaged in Illicit Sexual Intercourse

5. 1. 1. Moses says:
He who spends the night with a male in the role of a female, it is an abomination: let them both die, they are guilty.
5. 2. 1. Paulus in the second book of *Opinions* under the title 'Concerning Adultery':
He who commits illicit sexual intercourse with a free male against his will, let him be punished with death. 2. He who willingly allows illicit sexual intercourse and an impure disgraceful act is fined the half part of his own goods and is not allowed to make a testament for more than half of the remainder.
5. 3. 1. This is indeed law. However, a constitution of the Emperor Theodosius is known to have followed to the full the meaning of the law of Moses. The same Theodosius: the Emperors Valentinian, Theodosius, and Arcadius Augusti, to Orientius, Vicar of the City of Rome:
We no longer allow the city of Rome, the mother of all virtues, to be defiled for so long by the contamination of the womanish shame in men and that rustic strength of the ancient founders, diminished by the effeminately enervated people, to inflict insult against the ages of the founders and of the emperors, Oh Orientus, most dear and pleasant to Us. 2. Your praiseworthy skill, therefore, will purge by means of the flames of vengeance with the people watching, as the immensity of the outrage demands, all those caught and dragged out of all the brothels of men (it is shameful even to say the term) whose disgraceful sensuality led them to use the male body in a female manner so to damn it to the passive role of the other sex and to have nothing differentiated from women, so that all may comprehend that the shelter of the spirit of man ought to be sacrosanct nor shall those who have foully thrown away their own sex and sought to be the other be without the highest punishment. Posted on the day before the Ides of May at Rome in the atrium of Minerva.

(Title 6)
Concerning Incestuous Marriages

6. 1. 1. Moses says:
Whoever lies with a woman who is the wife of his own father uncovers the private parts of his own father, let them both die: they

are guilty. 2. And whoever lies with his own daughter-in-law, let them both die: they are guilty.

6. 2. 1. Ulpian in his single book of *Rules* under the title 'Concerning Marriages':

Between parents and children, whatever the degree might be, there can be no legal capacity to marry. 2. Between cognates, however, once, long ago, marriages could not be made from the transverse degree all the way to the fourth degree. Now, however, it is allowed to marry a wife from the third degree, but only a daughter of a brother, not also that of a sister, nor a father's sister nor a mother's sister, although they are of the same degree. 3. We also are not able to marry a woman who has been a step-mother or step-daughter, or a daughter-in-law or mother-in-law. 4. If someone marries a woman whom he is not allowed to, he has made an incestuous marriage: and for this reason the children will not be in his power, but are of illegitimate birth as if they were conceived promiscuously.

6. 3. 1. Paulus in the [second] book of *Opinions* under the title 'Concerning Marriages':

Between progenitors and children, marriages are not able to be made; [by civil law] we are not able to marry [a sister] nor a daughter of a sister, nor a granddaughter: the basis of age prohibits a great-granddaughter. 2. Adoptive relationship impedes marriages between progenitors and children in all cases and between siblings also to such a degree, up to the point where ending family membership does not stop it. 3. Nor is it ever allowed to marry a mother-in-law nor a daughter-in-law nor a step-daughter nor a step-mother without the punishment of incest, just as not with a paternal aunt or a maternal aunt. But he who marries [a relation by marriage] or a blood relation against the prohibition, will suffer the punishment of adultery from the Julian law, but not also the woman married, the error about the legal principle having been forgiven to the woman.

6. 4. 1. The fifth book of the *Gregorian Code* under the title 'Concerning Marriages': a copy of the letter of the Emperors Diocletian and Maximian reminding that such a union is to be gravely punished:

Copy of the edict of Diocletian and Maximian [Augusti and Constantius and Galerius] most noble Caesars. Since it seems to Our pious and religious minds that those things established by Roman laws in a pure and holy manner are most venerable and must be guarded by the eternal religion, We believe it behooves Us not to ignore those things, which have been committed abominably and incestuously in the past by certain people: since they are to be either restrained or even punished, the discipline of Our times calls Us to rise up. For it is not to be doubted that the immortal gods themselves will always be, as they always have been, favourable and propitiated toward the Roman glory, if We will ensure those joined under Our rule lead a life which is pious and religious and quiet and wholly chaste in all matters. 2. In which We also order that it be provided, as much as possible, that of marriages made religiously and legitimately according to the discipline of ancient law then, that with religious practice preserved We begin to consult the interests both of the honour of those who seek the conjunction of marriage and also of those will be born from it, and that posterity itself be cleansed by the honourableness of birth. For it is greatly pleasing to Our piety, that the sacred name of kinship should obtain among its relatives the dutiful and religious dearness that is owed to consanguinity. For it is sinful to trust a continuation of those acts which it is agreed were committed by very many in the past when, by the goading of accursed lust, they rushed into illicit marriages in the promiscuous fashion of cattle and wild animals without any respect for decency and piety. 3. But whatever seems to have been admitted from illicit marriages in the manner of barbaric monstrosity before this either by the inexperience of the wrongdoers or by ignorance of law, although they should be punished most severely, nevertheless, by the contemplation of Our clemency, We wish that they come within the scope of this indulgence, provided that whoever have defiled themselves before by illicit and incestuous marriages should know that the things obtained up to this point are Our indulgence, so that after such shameful deeds they should rejoice that life has been granted to them. They should know, however, that children who were born by means of such shameful unions are themselves not legitimate. For it will be so, that in the future no one might dare to obey such unbridled lusts, since they should know that those who had earlier committed this type of crime were freed by grace, but the children they bore illicitly were prohibited from inheritance, which was denied to those joined by Roman laws of the distant past. And We might have indeed wished that no such act had been committed in this way before, which would need to be either abated by Our clemency or corrected by laws. 4. But after this We wish that religion and sanctity in the joining of marriages be guarded by one and all, so that they will always remember they belong to the Roman discipline and laws and they should know that only such marriages are valid which are permitted by Roman law. 5. In this Our edict We have included with which persons, either by blood kinship or of relation by marriage, it is not allowed to contract marriage: with a daughter, granddaughter, great-granddaughter, and likewise with a mother, grandmother, great-grandmother, and, laterally, a paternal aunt and a maternal aunt, [a sister,] a daughter of a sister and a sister's granddaughter. And likewise, we wish all to abstain from relatives by marriage, a step-daughter, step-mother, mother-in-law, daughter-in-law, and the rest who are prohibited by ancient law. 6. For Our legal principles guard nothing unless it is old and venerable and the Roman majesty has come to such magnitude by the favour of all the gods, since it bound up all its laws in wise religious practices and the preservation of *pudor*. 7. Therefore, We wish by this Our edict that it become well known to all, that the pardon of past deeds, which through Our clemency is seen to be granted counter to *disciplina*, pertains only to violations seen to have been committed up to the third day before the Kalends of January in the consulship of Tuscus and Anullinus. 8. If, however, any crimes are caught which were committed against the glory of the Roman name and the sanctity of the laws after the above spoken day, let them be punished by worthy severity. For in the case of such a nefarious crime, let no one who in so evident a crime and after Our edict does not hesitate to rush in think he is able to acquire any pardon. Issued on the Kalends of May at Damascus in the consulship of Tuscus and Anullinus.

6. 5. 1. Hermogenianus under the title 'Concerning Marriages':
The Emperors Diocletian and Maximian Augusti to Flavius Flavianus. To those who contract incestuous marriages through error, lest they be subjected to punishments, the clemency of the emperors gives succour if, after they ascertain the error, they sunder the shameful marriage on the spot. Posted on the Ides of March in the consulship of [Tiberianus] and Dio. 2. Gregorianus also inserted this constitution in the title 'Concerning Marriages', which is the thirty-second [title], however with another day [and consulship], that is: the constitution posted on the fifth day before the Ides of June in the consulship of the Augusti Diocletian (for the third time) and Maximian.

6. 6. 1. Papinian in his single book *Concerning Adultery*:
He who marries the daughter of his sister through error, [and] sunders the union before it is reported by an informer: is he able to be accused for it? He responded: 'To him who abstained in good faith from a union with the daughter of his sister, it is clear that the punishment is remitted, because it is believed that for one who sundered the union once the error is recognized, it was his wish that, if he had known that he was placed in the degree of close relationship, he would not have intended to join such a marriage.'
6. 7. 1. The same is said against those who contracted incestuous marriages.
Cursed by the law, however, are all those engaged in incest, although it was ordained by the Divine Will for the still primitive people, and sanctioned by them making a covenant. And the cursed certainly are punished, who divine and human judgment have condemned by a harmonious voice. The Divine Law states thus: 'Cursed', says Moses, 'is he who lies with the wife of his father': and all the people say: 'So be it, so be it.' 2. 'Cursed, is he who lies with his own sister, the daughter of his father or of his mother': and all the people say: 'So be it, so be it.' 3. 'Cursed, is he who lies with his own daughter-in-law': and all the people say: 'So be it, so be it.' 4. 'Cursed is he who lies with his own mother-in-law': and all the people say: 'So be it, so be it.' 5. 'Cursed is he who lies with the sister of his father': and all the people say: 'so be it, so be it'. 6. 'Cursed is he who lies with the sister of his own mother': and all the people say: 'So be it, so be it.' 7. 'Cursed is he who lies with the sister of his own wife': and all the people say: 'So be it, so be it.' 8. 'Cursed is he who sleeps with the wife of his own brother': and all the people say: 'So be it, so be it.' 9. 'Cursed is he who sleeps with any beast': and all the people say: 'So be it, so be it.'

(Title 7)
Concerning Thieves and their Punishment

7. 1. 1. Just as the Twelve Tables order a thief in the night to be killed in any case[, or a thief in the daytime] if he dares to defend himself with a weapon, know oh Jurists, that Moses ordained this earlier, just as a close reading shows. Moses says: 'If a thief is found digging through a wall by night and someone strikes him and he dies, he who struck him is not a murderer. 2. If, however, the sun rises on him, he who struck is responsible for death; and he himself will die.'

7. 2. 1. Paulus in the fifth book of *Opinions* [under the title] 'With regard to the Cornelian Law concerning Assassins and Poisoners':
If someone kills a thief by night or during the day when he defended himself with a weapon, he is not liable by this law. But he would have acted better if he brought the captured thief to the magistrates to be transmitted to the provincial governor.
7. 3. 1. Ulpian in the eighteenth book of *To the Edict* under the title 'If a four-footed animal has damaged property':
'Unlawfully' is rightfully added to 'killed': for killing does not suffice, but it is necessary that it was done unlawfully. Accordingly, if someone killed a slave who is a robber, he is not liable by the Aquilian law, because he did not kill unlawfully. 2. But someone who kills any type of person seeking to kill him with a sword will not be seen as having killed unlawfully. Accordingly, if he kills a thief coming at night, which the law of the Twelve Tables permits in every way, or during the day, which the law equally permits, but only if the thief defends himself with a weapon, we should see whether he is liable under the Aquilian law. And Pomponius doubts whether this law would apply. 3. And if he kills a thief at night, we do not doubt that he is [not] liable under the Aquilian law. But if, when he was able to apprehend, he chose instead to kill, it is more likely that he might be seen to have done it unlawfully: therefore he is liable under the Cornelian law. 4. It is not proper that we accept as unlawfully here a certain *contumelia* (as in an *actio inuriarum*), but that which is done not by law (that is against legal principles), that is if someone kills with fault. And the rest.
7. 4. 1. Ulpian in the eighth book of *Concerning the Office of Proconsul* under the title 'Concerning Thieves':
Thieves of the day are to be sent to the forum, and those of the night are to be heard and to be punished on conviction by a trial before the governor, provided we understand that their punishment is not to exceed a term in the public works. 2. And the same is for thieves in the baths. But if thieves defend themselves with a weapon, or are breaking and entering, or do similar things [even if] they have not struck anyone, they are to be sentenced to the mines as a punishment if they are *humiliores*, if *honestiores* they are to be sentenced to relegation.

7. 5. 1. Paulus in the second book of *Opinions* under the title 'Concerning Thieves':
Someone who is convicted of any sort of theft whatsoever is made infamous. 2. A thief is someone who handles another's property unlawfully. 3. There are four types of theft: manifest, not manifest, *conceptum*, and transference. A manifest thief is someone who is caught in the act, and who is apprehended inside the bounds of the place from whence he stole, or before he came to the place to which he resolved to go. A thief is not manifest who is not arrested in the act, but is not able to deny that he did it. 4. Someone is liable to an action of *conceptum*, among whose things stolen property is found. One who transfers stolen property to another, lest it be found among his property, is liable to an action for transference. 5. One is able to sue by means of an action of theft, in whose interest it is not to have lost the property. 6. He who searched for and found the property is able to sue by an action for detected theft. The one who is able to sue for transference is the person in whose possession the detected property was found.

(Title 8)
Concerning False Testimony

8. 1. 1. Moses says:
If an unfair witness rises up against a person accusing him of wrong-doing, 2. the two men, between whom there is dispute, shall stand before God and before the priests and before the judges, whoever they will be in those days. 3. When the judges have inquired diligently and the witness will have been found to be testifying unjust things, you, rising up against him, 4. will do to him just as he wished to injure and you will take away the evil from your midst. 5. And the others hearing will fear and they will not dare to make these evil [words] among you.
8. 2. 1. Paulus in his single book *Concerning Punishments of All Laws* under the title 'On the Julian Law Concerning Adultery':
Someone who speaks false testimony will be held in the same manner as if he had been condemned under the Cornelian law concerning Testaments.
8. 3. 1. Paulus in the fifth book of *Opinions* under the title 'Concerning Witnesses and Investigations':
Those who speak falsely, or change their testimony, or proffer their testimony to either party, are to be driven into exile or sentenced to relegation to an island or removed from the *curia*.

8. 4. 1. The same book [the fifth book of *Opinions* under the title] 'With Regard to the Cornelian Law Concerning Assassins and Poisoners':
The Cornelian law inflicts the punishment of deportation on someone who kills a person, or who has a weapon for the purposes of murder or theft, or who sells or prepares poison for the sake of killing a person, or speaks false testimony through which a person perishes or is responsible for the cause of death. 2. It is commanded that all these crimes shall be punished with the penalty of death for *honestiores*; *humiliores* are to be crucified or thrown to the beasts.
8. 5. 1. Paulus in the fifth book of *Opinions* under the title 'With Regard to the Cornelian Law concerning Testaments':
Those who accept money or give money for the sake of bringing forward false testimony, or corrupt a judge or arrange for his corruption so that he proposes a verdict or does not propose a verdict, if *humiliores* will be punished with capital punishment, if *honestiores* will be deported with the judge himself to an island with their goods being given to the people.
8. 6. 1. The same author in the same book and title:
False is anything that is not in truth, but is asserted to be true.
8. 7. 1. Ulpian in the eighth book of [*Concerning the Office of the Proconsul*] under the title 'Concerning the Punishment of the Cornelian Law of Testaments':
Furthermore, a *senatusconsultum* was passed in the consulship of Statilius and Taurus, in which the punishment of the Cornelian law is imposed on anyone who knowingly seals, or arranges to be sealed, something other than a testament. The same to those who conspire with malice aforethought to make false attestations, or make a false will or authenticate wills on each other's behalf<, in the consulship of Licinus (for the fifth time) and Taurus>. 2. Likewise, he who accepts money for the sake of arranging legal advice or testimony or makes a contract or conspires or pledges himself in any kind of bargain, likewise if someone conspires to kill innocent people, is to be punished by the *senatusconsultum* that was made in the consulship of Cotta and Messalla. 3. But also, if someone accepts money for the sake of denouncing or not denouncing or renouncing testimony, by the *senatusconsultum* made in the consulship of the two Gemini he is to be visited with the punishment of the Cornelian law. And the rest.

(Title 9)
Concerning Not Admitting the Testimony of Family Members

9. 1. 1. Moses says:
You will not give false testimony against your neighbour.

9. 2. 1. Ulpian in the eighth book of *Concerning the Office of the Proconsul* under the title 'With regard to the Julian Law Concerning Public and Private Violence':
In the eighty-seventh chapter and in the eighty-eighth chapter, by this same law in these words to these people: some are forbidden to give testimony under any circumstances and others if they are unwilling. 2. By this law these are not allowed to speak testimony against a defendant: someone who is freed by the party in the lawsuit himself or by his father or by the freedman of either of them or by the freedman's freedman or freedwoman, or who is under the age of puberty, or someone [condemned by a criminal court] who is not restored to his former condition, or who was in chains or public custody, or who engaged himself for the sake of fighting, or who has hired himself out for fighting wild beasts, or will do so (except someone who is sent or will be sent to the city for the cause of throwing javelins), or he who has made or will make a profit by using his body publicly, or who is judged to have accepted money because of giving testimony. None of these, even if they are willing, can give testimony against a defendant by this law. 3. The eighty-seventh chapter says: 'Anyone who is a cousin of the person in the lawsuit, or joined by closer connection, or who is a father-in-law or son-in-law or stepfather or stepson will not give testimony against their will in a lawsuit.' And the rest.

9. 3. 1. Paulus in the [fifth] book of *Opinions* under the title 'Concerning Witnesses and Investigations':
It is resolved that suspect witnesses and especially those whom the accuser brought from his home or whose lowness of life defames them are not to be interrogated: for one ought to look at the quality and dignity of life in witnesses. 2. Witnesses are not able to be interrogated unwillingly against relatives by marriage or cognates. 3. Parents and children (and, in like manner, freedmen) are not admitted to testimony against each other even if they are willing, because people's relationship for the most part corrupts the testimony of the true matter.

(Title 10)
Concerning Deposit

10. 1. 1. Moses says:
If someone gives silver or a vessel to his neighbour to hold and it is stolen from the house of the person, if the person who stole it is found, he will return twofold. But if the thief not be found, he who undertook the protection will swear before the Lord that he has done nothing wrong concerning that of his neighbour which was committed to his care and he will be released.

10. 2. 1. Modestinus in the second book of *Distinctions* [under the title] 'Concerning Deposits or Loans for Use':
Someone who is sued by means of a trial for loaned things is also considered to be responsible for negligence: but he who is sued regarding a deposit, is to be condemned for fraud, but not also for negligence. For, by a contract of loan for use, because the interest of both parties of the contract comes into play, he is responsible for both things: but in a case of deposit, the interest only of the depositor is in play and in that matter he is responsible for fraud alone. 2. But this rule is also guarded in other parts of law: for both in an action of trust and in action of *rei uxoriae*, fraud and fault are taken into account in this way, because the interest of both parties of the contract comes into play. 3. But in an action for the non-performance of a commission, fraud, but not also fault, can be taken into account. However, it should be pointed out that in the unique situation of an action of guardianship both are taken into account, although the interest of the minor alone, not also of the guardian, comes into play. 4. One condemned in an action for deposit is infamous: but one condemned in an action of loan for goods, is not rendered infamous: for the former is condemned on account of fraud, the latter on account of negligence. 5. Someone sued for an action of deposit can claim before the same judge in an *actio utilis* for the sake of subsistence: but he who borrows for use makes a request for subsistence wrongly. However, by law he pursues necessary expenses which he made for someone sick or otherwise in difficulties. 6. If the object deposited has been stolen, only the owner has the action for theft, although the person with whom it was deposited has an interest in retaining the thing on account of expenses made for it. But someone who borrowed for use must sue for theft, for the sake of paying back the loan. 7. In an action of loan for use, it is always equal to the value of the goods, but in an action of deposit it is sometimes double, to

whit, if the thing was deposited because of a collapse of a building or a shipwreck or a fire or a riot.

10. 3. 1. Hermogenianus under the title 'Concerning Deposit' inserts constitutions of this kind:

The same Augusti [and] Caesars to Flavius Munatius. It is clear by law that someone who undertakes a deposit is responsible for a fraud, but not also for an accident. Since, therefore, as you set forth, some of the things commended to you were burned by the force of fire, nor was any fraud applied in removing the things, the governor of the province will not allow anything to be done against the rule of law. And since you complain that delays are added by various additional matters, the case that has arisen between you will be decided following the ordinary course of law on its own merit. Subscribed the eighth day before the Kalends of July in Serdica, in the consulship of the Augusti.

10. 4. 1. The same Augusti and Caesars to Flavius Aurelius Altenicus Andronicus.

Those in whose charge you relate you deposited clothing and an amount of silver, it is fitting to interrogate before the governor of the province who will compel them to give satisfaction to you in accordance with good faith as to whether they might retain it or whether they, by fraud, have made it that they are unable to make restitution. Subscribed the sixth day before the Kalends of April in Sirmium, in the consulship of the Caesars.

10. 5. 1. The same Augusti and Caesars to Aurelius and Eustathius and Diosimus.

He who undertook a deposit, if he does not specifically agree to otherwise, does not have to be responsible for anything beyond fraud. The governor of the province remembering this legal principle having heard the allegations of the parties will order his judgment according to his findings. Subscribed the fourteenth day before the Kalends of November at Appiaria.

10. 6. 1. The same Augusti and Caesars to Septimia Quadratilla.

He who, with malice aforethought, does not restore a deposit is sued in his own name and pressed to restore it with the danger of becoming infamous. Subscribed the day before the Ides of December at Nicomedia, in the consulship of the Caesars.

10. 7. 1. Paulus in the second book of *Opinions* under the title 'Concerning Deposit':

We are able to deposit with someone else that which is ours by law or another's. 2. Depositing is like placing for a long time [i.e. *diu positum*]. Something that is to be guarded for a short time is said to be in safekeeping. 3. Something is considered to be deposited which in fear of a collapse of a building, or a fire, or shipwreck, someone places in the care of another. 4. It is also considered to be a deposit, when someone commends something to the guardianship of another because of having questionable or less than appropriate guard of his house or fearing the power of thieves. 5. If I deposit a purse or silver, and the person with whom it has been deposited handles it without my approval, an action is possible for me against him for both deposit and theft. 6. In cases of deposited things, he is usually only responsible for fraud. 7. In a case of deposit, both profits from the time spent in deposit and interest of the deposited article hold good. 8. If someone has deposited the article deposited with him with someone else, he is able to have a direct action for deposit and the one who deposited it with him is able to have an *actio utilis*. 9. If I deposit money and I permit you to use it, it is seen more as a loan than as a deposit and, because of this, it will be at your own risk. 10. If you sell the object deposited with you and you buy it back, and you lose it afterwards, you are always liable, fraud having once been committed, by the action of deposit. 11. In an action for deposit, damages are set at double the value by a law of the Twelve Tables, but at the value of the goods by the praetor's edict.

10. 8. 1. The *Gregorian Code* in the fourth book under the title 'Concerning Deposit':

The Emperor Alexander Augustus to the soldier Mestrius: 'By an attack of brigands, items deposited with a man killed by them disappeared: the loss does not pertain to the heirs of the person who accepted the deposit, who ought only be responsible for fraud. But if, by the pretext of a theft having been committed, the articles, which are in the power of the heirs, are not restored, then an action both of deposit and *ad exhibendum* is allowed as is also a *vindicatio in rem*.' Posted on the seventh day before the Kalends of July in the consulship of Maximus (for the second time) and Urbanus.

10. 9. 1. Paulus in the fifth book of *Responses*, under the title 'Concerning Leasing and Hiring':

The Emperor Antoninus to Julius Agrippinus. The owner of warehouses is not considered to be responsible for the risk of superior force or by the breaking and entering of brigands. These things being absent, if there is loss from the deposited items but the warehouses are undamaged on the outside, the loss of the deposited items must be restored. Posted on the fourth day before the Nones of November in the fourth consulship of Antoninus. Paulus responded: 'It is declared sufficiently by the preceding constitution that those who lease warehouses are not responsible for superior force.'

(Title 11)
Concerning Cattle Rustlers

11. 1. 1. Moses says:
If someone seizes a bull calf or a sheep and kills it or sells it, he must restore five bull calves for one calf, four sheep for one sheep. 2. But if he does not have that which he must repay, he is to be sold for theft.

11. 2. 1. Paulus in the fifth book of *Opinions* under the title 'Concerning Cattle Rustlers':
Cattle rustlers of hardened hearts are generally to be sentenced to the sword or to the mines; sometimes, however, they are sentenced to the public works. They are 'hardened' who steal horses and flocks of sheep from the stable or from pastures, or if they do it quite often, or use a weapon, or lead a gang of men.

11. 3. 1. The same Paulus in the same book and title:
Rustlers are those who take away one stallion or two mares and just as many cows or ten goats or five pigs. But whenever the number of those led away is less, he will be sued for the punishment of theft according to his quality either for double or triple the value or be beaten by clubs and given to the public works for one year or he will be restored under the punishment of chains to the owner.

11. 4. 1. The same Paulus in the same book and title:
If someone rustles from herds about which he has litigated, he shall be sent to the forum and, thus convicted, be sentenced in the manner of a thief for twice or three times the value.

11. 5. 1. The same Paulus in the same book and title:
Someone who leads away a straying cow or horse or some other domestic animal is, by standard agreement, more a thief than a rustler.

11. 6. 1. Paulus in his single book *Concerning the Punishment of Peasants* under the title 'Concerning Rustlers' says:
When cattle rustlers are sentenced more harshly, they are even handed over to the sword. Therefore the Divine Pius wrote in a

rescript to the council of Baetica: 2. 'He who has raided herds about which he was litigating is to be sent to the forum and, if he is found guilty, is sentenced to pay double or quadruple the value.'

11. 7. 1. Ulpian in the eighth book of *Concerning the Office of Proconsul* under the title 'Concerning Rustlers':

Concerning the punishment of rustlers, the Divine Hadrian wrote in a rescript to the council of Baetica: 'When rustlers are punished most severely, they are usually sentenced to the sword. They are not, however, punished most severely everywhere, but where this type of crime is more frequent: otherwise they are sentenced to the public works and sometimes for a limited time. 2. And, therefore, I think that the maximum type of penalty that is generally imposed on this crime, namely that the rustlers be given to the sword, is appropriate also for your area: or, if someone is so well-known and so serious in rustling that he has been punished for this crime before, he ought to be given to the mines.' 3. The rescript of the Divine Hadrian states thus, as if the punishment of the mines would be more severe: unless by chance the Divine Hadrian by speaking of punishment 'of the sword' meant sentencing to the games. 4. There is, however, a difference between those who are condemned to the sword and those to the games: for those sentenced to the sword are to be done away with immediately or certainly ought to be done away with within a year: for this is contained in the orders. To be sure, those who are sentenced to the games are not at any rate done away with, but are, after a period of time, even able to be freed and to receive the staff of the discharged gladiator, since it is permitted to be freed after five years, and to receive the staff after three years. 5. In the same rescript of the Divine Hadrian it is expressed most diligently that the punishment of rustlers is not everywhere the same.

11. 8. 1. The same Ulpian in the same book and title as above:

Specifically considered as rustlers are those who take flocks away from pasture and from herds and, in a certain way, make spoils of them and exercise the practice of rustling as if an art by leading off horses or cows. On the other hand, if someone leads away a stray cow or a horse in an uninhabited area, he is not a rustler, but rather a thief. 2. But those who abduct a pig or goat or wether ought not to be punished as severely as those who steal larger animals. 3. Although Hadrian presented the punishment of the mines, the public works, or even the sword, but yet those who are born in the station of *honestiores* ought not to have this kind of punishment, but will be sentenced to relegation or removed from their order. 4. For all that, at Rome we also see rustlers thrown to the beasts: and, indeed, it is not unjust for those who raid cattle with a sword to be inflicted with this punishment.

(Title 12)
Concerning Arsonists

12. 1. 1. Moses says:
If a fire breaks out and it comes upon brush and engulfs threshing floors or grain or fields, he who set the fire must restore the estimated value.
12. 2. 1. Paulus in the [fifth] book of *Opinions* under the title 'Concerning Arsonists':
Those who set fire to a house or farmhouse because of hostility, if they are *humiliores* are sentenced to the mines or to the public works, if *honestiores* they are sentenced to relegation to an island. 2. If accidental fires, which by the chance occurrence of fierce winds or the carelessness of the person tending the fire, spread all the way to the fields of a neighbour, burn sown fields or vines or olives or fruit trees, the damage given, through an assessment, must be made good.
12. 3. 1. The same Paulus in the same book and title:
But that committed by slaves, if it seems appropriate to the master, is made good by their being handed over. 2. To be sure, deliberate arsonists of harvests, vines, or olive trees are condemned to the mines if *humiliores* or sentenced to relegation to an island if *honestiores*.
12. 4. 1. The same Paulus in the same book and title as above:
Let arsonists who commit the act in a town for the purpose of ill-gotten gains be indisputably punished with death.
12. 5. 1. Ulpian in the eighth book of *Concerning the Office of Proconsul* [under the title] 'Concerning Shipwrecks and Arsonists':
Indeed, the Cornelian law ordered that arsonists be banned from water and fire, but in actuality, they are punished variously. For those who have deliberately made a fire in a city, if they are *humiliores*, are usually thrown to the beasts. If they are in any grade and they set the fire in Rome, they are punished with death: or certainly those who commit this ought to be so punished. 2. But those who set a fire by accident are for the most part to be forgiven, unless there was wide and incautious negligence or irresponsible mischief.

12. 6. 1. Paulus in the [fifth] book of *Opinions* under the title 'Concerning Arsonists' says:
Let arsonists, who committed the act in a town for the cause of gain, be punished with death: those who burned down an apartment house or farmhouse not out of hostility, but by chance, should be punished more lightly. For [cases of] accidental fires are to be sent to the forum, so that the damage to the neighbours might be made good.
12. 7. 1 Ulpian in the eighteenth book of *Concerning the Edict*, under the title 'If accepted that one was killed unjustly, for simple damages' when he also said:
Likewise, if you set fire or burn my apartment house, I will have an Aquilian action, and the same holds if you burn my vineyard or my farmhouse. 2. But if someone burns down an apartment house intentionally, he is to be punished with death as an arsonist. 3. In the same way, if someone wishes to burn down an apartment house and the fire also spreads to the apartment house of his neighbour, he will be liable by the Aquilian law also to his neighbour, not less so to the tenants on account of the burning up of their goods, and the fifteenth book of Labeo's *Responses* relates this. 4. But if you burn the stubble in your field and the fire wanders to the land of your neighbour and burns it, there has been a debate as to whether the Aquilian law has a place or if it is a matter for an *actio in factum*. 5. But most believe that the Aquilian law does not have a place here, and Celsus writes thus in the thirty-seventh book of his *Digests*. For he says 'If a fire of someone burning stubble gets out of control, he is not liable by the Aquilian law, but an *actio in factum* is to be made, because he did not directly burn down things, but while he did something else, the fire thus spread.' 6. His legal opinion is also confirmed by a rescript of the Divine Severus in these words: 'You propose that you will sue for a noxal surrender modelled on the example of the Aquilian law on account of a fire which was made for the purpose of fodder which then spread through the fault of the slaves of Verturia Astillia and, you assert, laid waste your field. If the assessment of damages is allowed, a trial can take place.' Clearly, it was seen that the Aquilian law did not suffice by itself. 7. If, by chance, a hired slave of a tenant had fallen asleep at an oven and a farmhouse was burned down, Neratius writes that the person who hired ought to make good by the contract, if he was negligent in the selection of his assistants. But, if one lit the fire of the furnace, and another negligently tended

it, is he held liable? For he who did not tend [the fire] did nothing: he who properly lit the fire did not commit a fault: just as if a doctor rightly operated on a human being, but either he or another cared for the patient negligently, the Aquilian law is not in force. What therefore is it? And here I think an action modelled on the Aquilian law is to be given against the person who fell asleep at the furnace or tended it negligently just as it is to be given against the doctor who cared for his patient negligently, whether the human being perished or was disabled. Nor can anyone say about the person who fell asleep that he suffered a thing human and natural, since he ought to have either extinguished the fire or to have built it so that it would not spread. 8. Thus, it is related in the sixth book of Vivianus: 'If you have a bake oven next to a common wall, then are you responsible for wrongful damage? And [Proculus] says an action is not possible by the Aquilian law, because this action is not also possible against a man who has a fireplace: and, on that account, he thinks it is more just that an *actio in factum* be given. But in the case proposed by him the common wall is not burned down. For it may sensibly be asked, 'If you have not yet caused me damage and you keep the fire in such a way that I fear that you might cause me damage, might it be fair for me to make an interim action, that is to make an *actio in factum*?' Perhaps Proculus had perceived such a thing, unless one could argue that a guaranty [i.e. *cautio*] that no damage will occur is sufficient.' 9. Moreover, if some slaves of a tenant burn down an apartment house, in the tenth book Urseius relates that Sabinus responded that the master is to be sued in the name of the slaves for a noxal judgment by the Aquilian law: by the lease, however, the master is not liable. Proculus however responded, when the slaves of a tenant burn down a farm house, the tenant is to be held either by the lease or by the Aquilian law, so that the tenant may be able to give the slaves as recompense, and if the trial has been adjudicated in one way, a further action is not to be brought in the other way. 10. In the same way, Celsus in the twenty-seventh book of his *Digests* writes: 'If when my bees flew to yours you burned them out, some (and among them is Proculus) deny that an action by the Aquilian law can take place, as if the bees were not my property.' But this is false, Celsus says, since the bees are accustomed to return and are a source of profit for me. But Proculus was moved by the fact that they are neither tamed nor shut in. Celsus, however, says that there is no difference between them and doves, which, if they fly away from the hand, nevertheless fly home.

(Title 13)
Concerning a Moved Boundary Marker

13. 1. 1. Moses says:
You shall not move the boundary markers of your neighbours that your fathers set up for your property.
13. 2. 1. Paulus in the [first] book of *Opinions* under the title 'Of the Adjustments of Boundaries':
Extraordinary punishment is inflicted on someone who threw down or removed boundary markers through force.
13. 3. 1. Ulpian in the eighth book of *Concerning the Office of the Proconsul* under the title 'Concerning the Moving of Boundary Markers':
The Divine Hadrian issued a rescript on the seventeenth day before the Kalends of September in the third year he was consul to Terentius Gentianus that those who moved boundary markers ought not to be unpunished, by which rescript he set up various punishments. 2. The words of the rescript state: 'It is impossible to doubt that the deed of those who carry away boundary markers placed for the sake of setting boundaries is most wicked. However, the mode of punishment is best established by the condition and intention of the person committing it: For if those who are convicted are people of high rank, I do not doubt that they did it to seize the lands of others, and they are to be sentenced to relegation for the period as their age permits, [that is, if they are younger for a longer period, if older for a shorter term. If others actually committed the act and indeed executed a service, they are to be punished] and thus they are given for two years or three years to the public works. But if they are stolen through ignorance or for the sake of using the boundary stones, it suffices for them to be beaten with whips.'

(Title 14)
Concerning Kidnappers

14. 1. 1. Moses says:
Whoever abducts someone in Israel and sells him, let him die.
14. 2. 1. Paulus in the fifth book of *Opinions* under the title 'Concerning the Fabian Law':
Someone who conceals, sells, imprisons, or purchases a free-born Roman citizen or a freedman or another's slave, is liable by the Fabian law. 2. Indeed, the punishment by this law was earlier monetary, but the legal investigation has been transferred to the urban

prefect, and merits the extraordinary punishment of the governor of the province. And on that account *humiliores* are either sentenced to the mines or crucified, *honestiores* are deprived of half of their property and sentenced to relegation forever. 3. If a slave steals, sells, or hides the slave of another with the knowledge of his master, the master himself will be punished: but if he did it with no knowledge of his master, he is to be sentenced to the mines.

14. 3. 1. Ulpian in the ninth book of *Concerning the Office of Proconsul* under the title 'With regard to the Fabian Law':

An investigation of the Fabian law is frequently at the tribunal of a governor, although some of the procurators of Caesar have usurped them at Rome and also in the provinces. 2. But now it has reached the point by means of imperial constitutions that the prefect of Rome alone investigates the matter if the injury is committed within the hundredth milestone: for if beyond this distance, the investigation will be for the praetorian prefect. In a province it is for the governors of the provinces, nor will it otherwise be imposed on the procurator of Caesar, unless he is taking the role of the governor in the province. Plainly, after the sentence passed under Fabian law, the duties of the procurator take power over the matter. 3. But a procurator who governs that province, although it is not customary for him to judge capital cases, however the Emperor Antoninus decided that he could judge concerning the Fabian law. In the same way, he received the power to conduct the investigation in cases of the Julian law concerning adultery by a constitution of the Emperor Antoninus. 4. Someone is liable under the Fabian law, however, who conceals, binds, holds captive, buys, or sells a Roman citizen or someone freed in Italy, or was an accomplice in this matter: the punishment is imposed in the first chapter of this law. If a slave does it with the knowledge of his master, the master is to be punished by 50,000 sesterces by the same chapter. 5. Someone is liable under the second chapter of this law, who persuades another man's slave to flee his master or, against his master's wishes, hides, sells, or buys the slave of another with malice aforethought, or who was an accomplice in such a matter: and he is ordered to pay 50,000 sesterces to the public treasury. And the rest. 6. Nevertheless, it is to be known from recent constitutions that kidnappers are to be punished for the atrocity of their deeds by the sentence of death: although Paulus related in the specific cases above that the punishment imposed for such things is crucifixion or the mines for guilty parties of this sort.

(Title 15)

Concerning Astrologers, Sorcerers, and Manichees

15. 1. 1. Moses says:

Let there not be found among you someone who purges his son or his daughter by sacrifice, nor a fortune teller with whom you cast lots: nor should you agree to the poisons of imposters who say what a woman might have conceived (since these are seductive tales). Nor should you direct thoughts to prodigies, nor should you ask the dead questions. 2. Let there not be found among you an *augur*, nor an inspector of birds, nor a sorcerer, nor an enchanter, nor a snake charmer, nor a *haruspex*, nor a medium, nor an inspector of portents. 3. For all these things and the person who does them, are condemned by the Lord your God. For, on account of these abominations, God will eradicate the Chaldeans from your sight. 4. You, however, will be perfect before the Lord your God: 5. For those peoples, who you will control, used to listen to auguries and lots and divinations.

15. 2. 1. Ulpian in the seventh book of *Concerning the Office of Proconsul* under the title 'Concerning Astrologers and Soothsayers':

Besides, the cunning imposture and obstinate persuasion of the astrologers is forbidden. Nor is it decided to forbid these things today for the first time, but this prohibition is ancient: indeed, a *sentusconsultum* given in the year Pomponius and Rufus were consuls still exists, in which provision is made that sorcerers, Chaldeans, soothsayers and others who have undertaken something similar, are interdicted from water and fire and all their goods confiscated, and if the person who did it is of a foreign nation, he should be punished with death. 2. But it has been questioned whether a man should be punished for this sort of knowledge or the exercise and practice of such a thing. Indeed, among the ancients it was said that the profession of these things, not the knowledge of them, was to be prohibited: later this was changed. Nor is it to be ignored that sometimes they have crept into use, so that they were even professed and offered publicly. But this was done more through the insolence and boldness of those who had been seen either to consult or to practice these things, rather than because it was permitted. 3. It has been forbidden by nearly all the emperors again and again for anyone to meddle at all in inappropriate things of this sort, and that those who practice them be variously punished, namely by the measure of the consultation. For those who did it concerning the health and safety of the emperor are punished by death or by some other more serious punishment: to be sure, if someone does it about his own or his family's health, he should be punished more lightly. Among these are held soothsayers, although these also are to be punished, since they sometimes practice their improper arts against the public peace and the empire of the Roman people. 4. Finally, there exists a decree of the Divine Pius to Pacatus, legate of the province of Lugdunensis. Because the words of the rescript are so many, I have appended these few words from its end to this place. 5. And indeed, the Divine Marcus sentenced someone to relegation to the island of Syrus who was a soothsayer in the movement of Cassius and said many things as if by the inspiration of the gods. 6. And, clearly, people should not be allowed to conduct things of this sort with impunity, who, under the pretence of a warning of the gods, either make or spread pronouncements or feign knowledge.

15. 3. 1. Gregorianus in the seventh book, under the title 'Concerning Sorcerers and Manichees':

The most noble Emperors Diocletian and Maximian Augusti to Julian, Proconsul of Africa. Oh most dear Julian, the greatest leisure occasionally urges people in the common condition to exceed the proper form of human nature and persuades them to introduce the most inane and wicked types of superstitious doctrine, so that they are seen to entice many others also by the will of their errors. 2. But the immortal gods, by their providence, deemed it worthy to ordain and to arrange that the things which are good and true would be approved and established in an undiminished state by the counsel and handling of many good and outstanding and very wise men, things which it is evil to obstruct or to resist, and that the old religion should not be refuted by a new belief. For it is the greatest crime to retract those things that, being set up and defined by the ancients, hold and possess standing and precedent. 3. From whence We are extremely eager to punish the obstinacy of the perverse mind of good-for-nothing men: for these are men who set new and unheard sects against the older religions, so that they exclude (the authority) which was once divinely granted to Us in exchange for their own depraved authority, 4. out of whom, Your Resourcefulness has reported to Our serenity are the Manichees; We have heard that they, as a new and unexpected monstrosity, have recently arisen and progressed into this world from Persia (an enemy nation to Us) and have committed there many crimes and disturb the quiet peoples and introduce the greatest damage to the cities: and it is to be feared, lest by chance, as is accustomed to happen, in the course of time they attempt through their cursed usages and the savage laws of the Persians to corrupt persons of more innocent nature, the modest and tranquil Roman people, and Our entire world just as with the poison of their own malevolent ones. 5. And because all the varieties of the most evident crimes which your prudence exposes in the report of their religious practice have been discovered by the ordinances and their lies found out, therefore We establish for them toils and well-earned and fitting penalties. 6. For We order that the founders and leaders are to be subjected to more severe punishment together with their abominable writings so that they be consumed entirely by the fiery flames. However, We order that their followers and those constantly obstinate ones be punished with death, and We order their goods be claimed by the public treasury. 7. If those who transfer themselves to this unheard of, wicked, and entirely infamous sect, or to the doctrine of the Persians, are also in high office or of any dignified rank or persons of greater status, you shall arrange that their patrimony be made part of Our treasury and the persons themselves also be sentenced to the mines of Phaeno or Proconnesus. 8. So that, therefore, this evil of worthlessness might be completely cut off at the stem from Our most blessed age, let your devotion hasten to comply with the orders and statutes of Our tranquility. Issued the Pridies of April at Alexandria.

(Title 16)
Concerning Legitimate Succession

16. 1. 1. The Divine Scripture says thus:

The daughters of Salfad standing before Moses and the Priest Eleazar and the princes and all the senate of the sons of Israel in the doorway of the tabernacle of testimony said: 2. 'Our father is dead, and there were no sons to him<, but only daughters>. 3. And, on that account, let not the name of our father be deleted from the midst of his tribe. [Because] there is no male to him: give to us the possessions before the midst of the brothers of our father.' And Moses offered their petition before God. 5. And the Lord spoke to Moses saying: 6. 'The daughters of Salfad have spoken rightly: And, on that account, you ought to give to them possession of the inheritance before the midst of the brothers of their father. 7. And you shall say this to the sons of Israel: If a man dies and he has no son, [you will give the inheritance to his daughter. 8. If he has no daughter, you will give it to his brothers. 9. If he has no brothers, you shall give to his father's brothers. 10. If he has no paternal uncles,] you will give the inheritance to the most closely related of those of his tribe: and he shall possess all of his things: and this shall be to the sons of Israel a righteous decision of the judges following that which the Lord established for Moses.'

16. 2. 1. Gaius in the third book of his *Institutes* lays out legitimate succession in this way:

Inheritances of those who are intestate belong first by the law of the Twelve Tables to their immediate heirs. 2. Now, immediate heirs are deemed children who were in the power of the person when he died, such as a son or a daughter, a grandson or a granddaughter [from the son], a great-grandson or a great-granddaughter born from a grandson born from a son. It does not matter if the children are born or adopted. But, nevertheless, only a grandson or granddaughter and a great-grandson or great-granddaughter is to be numbered among immediate heirs, if the person preceding them ceased [to be in the power of a father, whether by death] or for another reason, such as emancipation. For, if at the time someone dies, a son should be in his power, the grandson by him is not able to be an immediate heir. And we think the same refers to other persons of such children in the order of succession. 3. A wife, also, who is in *manus*, is an immediate heir, because she is in the place of a daughter: it is the same for a daughter-in-law who is in the *manus* of a son, for she is also in the place of a granddaughter. But she will only be an immediate heir if the son, in whose *manus* she was when the father died, was not himself in his power. And we say the same also concerning she who is in the *manus* of a grandson because of marriage, because she is in the place of a great-granddaughter. 4. Posthumous children also, if they would have been born when the parent had been living and would have been in his power, are immediate heirs. 5. The same legal principle holds concerning those under whose name a case was proved [i.e. *causae probatio*] by means of the Aelian Sentian law or the *Senatusconsultum* after the death of the father[: for if the case was proved when the father was living,] they would have been in his power. 6. And we think this also concerning a son, who was manumitted by a first or second mancipation after the death of his father. 7. When there lives a son or a daughter and, from another son, grandsons and granddaughters, they are called equally to the inheritance, nor does he who is closer in grade exclude the more distant. For it seems just that grandsons and granddaughters succeed in the place of their father. By a similar reason also, if there is a grandson or granddaughter from a son and great-grandsons or great-granddaughters from a grandson, they are called simultaneously. 8. And because it was pleasing that grandsons or granddaughters, likewise great-grandsons or great-granddaughters, succeed in the place of their father, it is seen to be appropriate that the inheritances be divided not by individuals, but by branches, so that a son might bear a half part of the inheritance [and] the two or more grandsons from the other son the other half. Likewise, if there are grandchildren from two sons, from one son, by chance, one or [two], and from the other three or four, [the half part pertains to the one or two and] the other half [to the three or four]. 9. If there is no immediate heir, then the inheritance belongs to the agnates, according to the same law of the Twelve Tables. 10. Now, agnates are those who are linked by legitimate kinship. Legitimate kinship is that of persons joined together through the male sex: therefore, those who are born brothers to the same father are agnates to each other, who also are called consanguinous, nor is it asked whether they have the same mother. Likewise, a paternal uncle is agnate to the son of his brother and, alternately, he to him. In the same condition are numbered among themselves *patrueles* descended from brothers, that is those who are descended from two brothers, those that many also call *consobrinos*: by this reasoning we are naturally able to come to many grades of agnates. 11. However, the law of the Twelve Tables does not give inheritance to all agnates simultaneously, but to those who are of the nearest grade when it is certain that someone dies intestate. 12. Nor is there succession in this right: Therefore, if the nearest lays aside the inheritance or dies before he comes to the inheritance, those following in order have no right by law. 13. Therefore, we ask who will be next in line not at the time of death, but at that time when it is certain that someone has died intestate, because if someone has died after the testament has been made, it seems to be better then to search for the nearest when it begins to be certain that no one by chance is heir by that testament. 14. As to women, however, by legal right one thing is decided in cases of taking their own inheritances, another in the taking of other inheritances by them. For inheritances of women flow in the same manner by the right of agnates as those of men: but our inheritances do not extend to women beyond the grade of consanguinity. And so, a sister is a lawful heir to a brother or a sister, but an aunt and a daughter of a brother is not able to be a lawful heir. However, a mother or step-mother is also in the place of a sister to us who through the convention of being in the *manus* of our father obtains the legal right of daughter. 15. If for someone who dies there is a brother and the son of another brother, the brother is preferable, just as is thought in the preceding, because he is prior in grade: But the interpretation of this legal principle is made another way among immediate heirs. 16. But if no brother to the deceased exists, but there are children of brothers, the inheritance, indeed, extends to all. But it is questioned, if the numbers are disparate (by chance, one or two born from one and three or four from the other), whether the inheritance should be divided into branches, just as it is the legal right among immediate heirs, or whether it is better to divide individually. It long ago has been determined that the inheritance be divided individually: therefore, however many persons there are from each part, the inheritance will be divided in so many portions and every single person carries a single portion. 17. If there is no agnate, by the same way, the law of the Twelve Tables calls the members of the clan to the inheritance. Who the members of the clan might be, we have related in the first commentary and since we admonished there that the legal right of members of the clan has fallen into disuse, it is unnecessary to treat this also in great detail in this place concerning this matter.

16. 3. 1. Paulus in the fourth book of *Opinions* under the title 'Concerning Intestate Successions':

Those are called intestate who are not able to make a will, or cut the cord [that sealed up the will] themselves so that they might die intestate, or those of whom the inheritance was rejected or whose condition failed; to be sure, he obtains a testament made by praetorian law by an objection of the *doli exceptio*. 2. Indeed, those whose testaments are broken or become invalid die testate under this legal principle, but when the testament has been overturned consequently, they die intestate. 3. By the law of the Twelve Tables, inheritances of intestates defer first to immediate heirs, then to agnates and, occasionally, also to members of the clan. To be sure, consanguinous relatives, whom the law had not taken care of, first received a place among agnates by the interpretation of the jurists. 4. Immediate heirs are, in the first place, a son or daughter standing in the power of the father: nor is it important if they are adopted or are natural children sought according to the Julian and Papian laws, provided they remain in the power [of the father]. 5. They who are immediate heirs are designated heirs by law even if they do not know it, such as insane people, young children, or those travelling in foreign lands: for these possession of goods was not necessary except on account of a praetorian action. 6. Ownership of the things of inheritance is taken up by immediate heirs from the moment of the death of the testator, so that the authority of a guardian is not necessary for minors nor a curator for insane people, unless by chance the inheritance might be discharged through payments: although an insane person also, if he recovers, and a minor, if he matures, might be able to renounce it. 7. Someone born after the death of his father, or who returned from enemies, or was manumitted by a first or second mancipation, or whose cause of error was proved [i.e. *erroris causae probatio*], although they were not in the power [of the father], are, however, made heirs of the father. 8. After sons and daughters, [then] grandsons, granddaughters, great-grandsons, great-granddaughters and, finally, descendants of the male sex after sons, come to the succession of a person who died intestate, if no father impedes them and they remain in the power of the grandfather or great-grandfather: for fathers stand in the way of their own children in the order of succession, since they were themselves in the power [of the male ancestor]. 9. Sons, if they are retained in the family with grandsons begotten by another son, are called with the sons of their brother to the succession of an intestate father: to those coming into the goods of the father, the heredity is to be divided in branches, not individually, so that the one son and several grandsons might have half each. And the same happens if grandsons from two sons in unequal number inherit from a grandfather. 10. Grandsons from a daughter are not immediate heirs: for they are not able to be in the power of their maternal grandfather by the reason that they are in another family. 11. Who an immediate heir is must be decided at the time when it is certain that someone has died intestate: this is able to be concluded when the conditions fail and by the birth of a grandson who was born after the death of the father while the grandfather lived. 12. He whom an emancipated son begot or adopted, is not able to be in the place of heir in the succession of the grandfather as the father himself is not able to inherit: an adopted person is able to seek possession of the goods, but not if he was a cognate. 13. If there are no immediate heirs, the legitimate inheritance falls to the agnates, among whom the consanguinous ones obtain the first place. Agnates, moreover, are those who are cognates of the male sex descending through the male line, just as a son of a brother and a brother of the father and, one after another, the entire succession. 14. There is this difference between agnates and cognates: cognates are certainly contained among agnates, but agnates are not included among the cognates. On that account, a father's brother is an agnate and a cognate, a mother's brother, however, is only a cognate. 15. Consanguineous ones are those born to the same father—it is allowed that they have different mothers—who were in the power of the father at the time of his death: an adopted bother is also, if he is not emancipated, and those who are born after the death of the father, or have proved cause [i.e. *causae probatio*]. 16. A sister is admitted by the legal principle of consanguinity both to the inheritance of a brother and to the inheritance of a sister. 17. When consanguinous relatives do not exist, the inheritance defers to the agnates, according as one precedes another in grade. But if there are many of the same grade, they are admitted simultaneously. 18. If there should be a son of a deceased brother and a grandson by a brother who is now also not alive, the sons of the brother is preferred to the grandson. 19. But if there might be children of two brothers, the inheritance is to be distributed not in branches, but individually, just as the inheritance should be distributed individually for each single person. 20. Women are not admitted to legitimate inheritances beyond consanguinous successors: this is seen to have been effected by civil law by reason of the Voconian law: but, the law of the Twelve Tables admits without any distinction of sex.

16. 4. 1. Ulpian in his single *Book [of Rules]* under the title 'Concerning Legitimate Inheritances':

The inheritances of intestate members of particular clans belong first to immediate heirs, that is children who are in the power [of a father] and others who might be in the place of children: if there should be no immediate heirs, the inheritances belong to consanginous ones, that is brother and sisters from the same father: if there are none of those, they belong to the remaining agnates of the male sex descending through the males of the same family. For it is provided by a law of the Twelve Tables in this way: 'If someone dies intestate for whom there is no immediate heir, let the nearest agnate have the household.' 2. If there should be no agnate of the deceased, the same law of the Twelve Tables calls members of the clan to the inheritance with these words: 'If there is no agnate, let the clansmen [have the] household.' [Now, there is neither any] heir here nor are legal rights of clansmen in customary use.

16. 5. 1. The same author [in the book of the *Institutes* . . . under the title 'Concerning Successions] from an Intestate Person':

The inheritance is also conveyed from an intestate person either through civil law or through the benefice of the praetor: by civil law to immediate heirs or to children who were in power: sons, daughters, and, finally, those who succeed in the place of a deceased parent, because they were born from him.

16. 6. 1. The same author in the same book:

After immediate heirs, legal heirs are admitted to an intestate estate, and first consanginous ones. [Consanginous ones] are brother and sister, who were in the power of the same father, even if they were born from different mothers. 2. Consanginuinity is also made by adoption, adrogation, proving cause [i.e. *causae probatio*], and having come under *manus*.

16. 7. 1. The same author in the same book:

When there are no consanginous ones, legal heirs are called. Agnates are those of the male sex who are connected to us through the relationship with the father: for it is to be known that inheritances are not to be carried to female heirs beyond consanginous female relatives. 2. To immediate heirs, the praetor is accustomed to join, once possession of goods has been given, emancipated children and likewise those granted citizenship, in such a way however, that if they have goods as their own, they must hand them over to those who remained in power. For [the praetor] thought it most fair that neither those who are not in power should be deprived of the goods of their father because of this, nor that they have their own individual goods, since they are about to take away a part (of the inheritance) from the immediate heirs.

16. 8. 1. The same author in the book as above [under the title] 'Concerning Immediate Heirs:'

After agnates, the praetor calls the cognates. Cognates, moreover, are those who are connected to us through a father or mother: after cognates [he calls] husband and wife. 2. And these things exist if the person who died was not a freedman or offspring of a freedman: But, if the deceased was a freedman or freedwoman, the legal inheritance passes to his patron or a patroness by a law of the Twelve Tables.

16. 9. 1. The same author in the same book:
After the family of a patron, the praetor calls the patron and patroness, and also the children and parents of the patron and patroness, finally the husband and wife, then the cognates of the patron and patroness. 2. But if he who died was a freeman [not] manumitted after remancipation, a law of the Twelve Tables passed the legal inheritance to the manumitter. But the praetor, moved by fairness, preferred these ten types of relatives to him: father, mother, son, daughter, grandfather, grandmother, grandson, granddaughter, brother, and sister, lest anyone defeat the close connection of blood by an accident of legal principle. 3. But, in the case of inheritances which pass from an intestate man, our emperor wished that only those persons to whom he himself granted immunity of the ten percent succession payment [i.e. *decima*] be admitted to succession.

Commentary

The following commentary attempts to serve several masters. It provides additional information not only for specialists in Roman law, but is always constructed for historians, classicists, and scholars of religion interested in passages in the *Collatio*. To reach these multiple audiences I have deliberately cast a wide net that yields both broad and specific information (including brief articles from Adolf Berger's *Encyclopedic Dictionary of Roman Law* for non-specialists in Roman law). For comparative purposes, I have provided the standard modern English translation from the *New Revised Standard Version* (*NRSV*) as well as the Latin text of the Stuttgart Vulgate for the biblical passages. While Mommsen, *Collatio*, 131–4 and Hyamson, *Mosaicarum et Romanarum Legum Collatio*, 153–8, attempted brief commentaries on the biblical citations, more recent work by Smits, *Collatio*, 44–71; Schulz, 'biblischen Texte'; and an array of work on the Old Latin Bible makes this task much easier. Since the *Collatio* is arguably one of the first works of comparative law,[1] I have also given comparative examples from the Ancient Near Eastern *Code of Hammurabi* of *c.*1700 BCE (cited as *LH)* and the *Laws of Eshnunna* of *c.*1850 BCE (cited as *LE*) for the biblical strictures quoted by the Collator. For more information on the jurists cited in the *Collatio*, please turn to the chapter on the sources of the *Collatio*. A note at the beginning of each title will offer some standard bibliography on relevant topics in the scholarly literature on Roman law.

[1] While it is tempting to make a case for the third-century Syriac *Book of the Laws of the Countries* attributed to Philip, follower of Bardaisan, only five pages deal with laws and the rest of the work develops the role of Fate. See further, H. J. W. Drijvers (ed. and tr.), *The Book of the Laws of Countries: Dialogue on Fate of Bardaisan of Edessa* (Assen, 1965) and his *Bardaisan of Edessa* (Assen, 1966).

TITLE 1: CONCERNING ASSASSINS AND MURDERERS (*DE SICARIIS ET HOMICIDIIS*)[2]

1. 1

Numbers 35: 16, 17, 20, 21:

[*NRSV*] 16. But anyone who strikes another with an iron object, and death ensues, is a murderer; the murderer shall be put to death. 17. Or anyone who strikes another with a stone in hand that could cause death, and death ensues, is a murderer; the murderer shall be put to death . . . 20. Likewise, if someone pushes another from hatred, or hurls something at another, lying in wait, and death ensues, 21. or in enmity strikes another with the hand, and death ensues, then the one who struck the blow shall be put to death; that person is a murderer; the avenger of blood shall put the murderer to death when they meet.

[Stuttgart Vulgate] *16. si quis ferro percusserit et mortuus fuerit qui percussus est reus erit homicidii et ipse morietur 17. si lapidem iecerit et ictus occubuerit similiter punietur . . . 20. si per odium quis hominem inpulerit vel iecerit quippiam in eum per insidias 21. aut cum esset inimicus manu percusserit et ille mortuus fuerit percussor homicidii reus erit cognatus occisi statim ut invenerit eum iugulabit.*

This section of Numbers treats the difference between premeditated murder and accidental homicide. The Collator seems to have used the Old Latin Bible as his source for this passage. Moreover, comparing this passage from the *Collatio* with the corresponding section in the Lyons Codex of the Old Latin Bible, the Vulgate, and the original Hebrew text, shows that the Collator edited and condensed the text. For instance, he left out Numbers 35: 18 which deals with wood weapons because it was so similar to the other sections. Also, he excised the section in Numbers 35: 21 about the 'avenger of the blood' (who is also mentioned at Numbers 35: 19), a family member who had the right to kill the murderer. On this facet of ancient

[2] On homicide in Roman law, see A. Berger, 'Homicidium', *Encyclopedic Dictionary*, 487–8; Eva Cantarella, *Studi sull'omicidio in diritto greco e romano* (Milan, 1976); Emil Brunnenmeister, *Das Tödtungsverbrechen im altrömischen Recht* (Leipzig, 1887); Dieter Nörr, *Causa Mortis* (Munich, 1986); O. F. Robinson, *The Criminal Law of Ancient Rome* (London, 1995), 41–6. Most recently, see D. Cloud, 'Leges de Sicariis: The first chapter of Sulla's *lex de sicariis*', *ZRG (R.A.)* 126 (2009), 114–55. I am grateful to Professor Cloud for sharing a draft of this article with me in the autumn of 2007.

Hebrew law, see further Baruch A. Levine, *Numbers 21–36: A new translation with introduction and commentary*, The Anchor Bible Commentary 4.A (New York, 2000), 547–8, 555–6, and 561–5 ('Requiting the Debit of Blood').

In the preface to this quotation, the Collator refers to Moses with the title *dei sacerdos* (or 'Priest of God'). Hyamson, 56, pointed out that this title is unusual as he is normally called the servant of God. Traditionally, Aaron (Moses' brother) and the line descending from him were traditionally termed priests. Hyamson, 56, posits that the Collator may have used the term *dei sacerdos* as an explicit comparison to *iustitiae sacerdos* ('priest of justice') which Ulpian used to describe Roman jurists (*Institutes* 1, preserved in *Dig.* 1. 1). If valid, then here we should see this description as an example of the Collator's voice which appears throughout the *Collatio.*

1. 2

Ps. Paulus, *Sententiae*, Book 5 (Krüger, 5. 23. 1; Liebs, 5. 29. 1). Hereafter, the first *Sententiae* reference will be to Krüger's edition, the second to Liebs' revised version ('Die pseudopaulinischen Sentenzen II'). The passage also survives in the *Lex Romana Visigothorum* (or *LRV*) at 5. 25. 1 (with several minor variants). For a text of *LRV*, see G. Haenel, *Lex Romana Visigothorum* (Berlin, 1849). The Collator quotes this passage again at Coll. 8. 4. 1 (see also comments on that passage).

The *Lex Cornelia de Sicariis et Veneficis* was originally passed in 81 BCE under the Dictator Sulla and survives in fragments. For a collection of the fragments, see M. Crawford, *Roman Statutes*, II, 749–53. For a discussion that suggests this law initially dealt with gangsters, but then over time was viewed as treating homicide in general, see J. Duncan Cloud, 'The primary purpose of the lex Cornelia de Sicariis', *ZRG (R.A.)* 86 (1969), 258–86, and, more recently, his 'Leges de Sicariis'. See also J.-L. Ferrary, 'Lex Cornelia de sicariis et veneficis', *Athenaeum* 79, n.s. 69 (1991), 417–34, and Harries, *Law and Crime*, 118–21.

Deportation (*deportatio*) was permanent banishment and loss of citizenship rights and property. See further, Berger, 'deportatio', *Encyclopedic Dictionary*, 432; Garnsey, *Social Status and Legal Privilege*, 112–15; and E. Grasmück, *Exilium: Untersuchungen zur Verbannung in der Antike* (Paderborn, 1978), 101–2, 129–31.

1. 3

Ulpian, *De officio proconsulis*, Book 7. Lenel, *Paling.*, II, col. 976. Nogrady, *Ulpian*, 155 n. 708, proposes that this quotation was taken from the Title *Ad legem Corneliam de sicariis et veneficiis* of Ulpian's work, which may well be correct. For a detailed study of the importance of this passage of Ulpian, see further Nogrady, *Ulpian*, 155–65. The Collator ends this quotation with *et reliqua*, indicating that he was working from a longer passage. Since he quotes so often from Ulpian's *De officio proconsulis*, and often uses the formula *et reliqua* when ending his quotations from this work (e.g., Coll. 7. 3; 8. 7), the Collator probably had the entire work in front of him while he was compiling the *Collatio*. I translate the legal phrase *dolo malo* in Coll. 3. 1 with the English common law 'malice aforethought' which can refer to actions (including fraud) that are committed with malicious intent. See Berger, *Encyclopedic Dictionary*, 440, on *dolo malo* and *dolus* in Roman criminal offences. The prefatory formula *relatis verbis legis modo ipse loquitur* before Ulpian's name at Coll 1. 3. 2 provides another example of the Collator's voice. The *Quaestio de sicariis* was one of the *Quaestiones Perpetuae* (standing commissions or courts) in Classical Roman law.

1. 4

Ps. Paulus, *Sententiae*, Book 5 (Krüger, 5. 23. 2; Liebs, 5. 29. 2). Liebs suggests adding *enim* and thus rendering *homicida enim est . . .* ('for a murderer is he . . .').

1. 5

Numbers 35: 22–5:

[*NRSV*] 22. But if someone pushes another suddenly without enmity, or hurls any object without lying in wait, 23. or, while handling any stone that could cause death, unintentionally drops it on another and death ensues, though they were not enemies, and no harm was intended, 24. then the congregation shall judge between the slayer and the avenger of blood, in accordance with these ordinances; 25. and the congregation shall rescue the slayer from the avenger of blood. Then the congregation shall send the slayer back to the original city of refuge. The slayer shall live in it until the death of the high priest who was anointed with the holy oil.

[Stuttgart Vulgate] *22. quod si fortuito et absque odio 23. et inimicitiis quicquam horum fecerit 24. et hoc audiente populo fuerit conprobatum atque inter percussorem et propinquum sanguinis quaestio ventilata 25. liberabitur innocens de ultoris manu et reducetur per sententiam in urbem ad quam confugerat manebitque ibi donec sacerdos magnus qui oleo sancto unctus est moriatur.*

In this passage, the Collator shifts to developing the concept of accidental homicide. Comparing the Collator's text with the Vulgate and the Lyons Codex of the Old Latin Bible again shows his dependance on the Old Latin Bible. Further, examining other versions of this text (whether the Vulgate, the Greek Septuagint, or the original Hebrew) in comparison with that in the *Collatio* shows that the Collator condensed the biblical text at the end of this passage (as he did at Coll. 1. 1). Here, however, the Collator must more aggressively edit the text as the biblical strictures provided for exile to an asylum town for someone who had killed with no malice. After the death of the high priest, the killer would be granted an amnesty, but if he left the asylum earlier, he could be killed by a blood avenger of the family. On this practice, see further, Levine, *Numbers 21–36*, especially 547–8 and 561–5. Since the later Roman Empire had no such legal equivalent, the Collator must have trimmed off this part to make the comparison between the biblical law and Roman law clearer to his audience.

This passage is one of the rare times that the Collator inserts a biblical passage into the middle of a title. His normal practice was to start each title with a statement from the 'Law of God'. This aberration may have led the scribe of the B manuscript to interpret Coll. 1. 5–13 as a second title (and can thus explain why he later numbered Title 5 as Title 6). On this development, see further Frakes, 'Manuscript tradition', 297–8. For the older view that there were actually two titles here, see Triebs, *Studien sur Lex Dei*, I, 97. It is more likely that the Collator broke apart the respective sections of Numbers 35 that dealt with premeditated versus accidental homicide for organizational purposes and to clarify the similarities between biblical and Roman law for his readers.

1. 6

Ulpian, *De officio proconsulis*, Book 7. Lenel, *Paling.*, II, col. 976. Marcian (a jurist from the early to mid third century) in his *Institutes* (Book 14) also cites this rescript of Hadrian (preserved in *Dig.* 48. 8. 1. 3). However, this variant text leaves out the example of Epafroditus that survives in the *Collatio*. For the interrelationship of the texts, see Wieacker, *Textstufen*, 402–4 and, more recently, Nogrady, *Ulpian*, 167–73, who feels the text in the *Collatio* is close to the original (although he suspects, 170, that the *aut* before *cum forte rixaretur ferro percussit* was not originally in Ulpian's text). It is possible that a final clause fell out of Coll. 1. 6. 3. On this passage, see recently Johannes Platschek, Review of Nogrady's *Ulpian* in *TR* 76 (2008), 396–9. The dramatic example of Epafroditus may have been more useful in a didactic environment such as the Collator envisioned for his work than in the *Digest* and so Tribonian's staff excised it. 'Epaphroditus' was a conjecture of Bluhme as the manuscripts have forms of *ipsa fonditus*, but it seems quite likely to be correct as Epaphroditus was a fairly common slave name, according to H. Solin, *Die Stadtrömischen Sklavennamen: Ein Namenbuch* (Stuttgart, 1996), 281–3. Scaliger's Apograph is useful for reading this damaged portion of the B manuscript (as Mommsen noticed).

At Coll. 1. 6. 4, *iure* (the ablative of *ius*) is used to denote the collective law of the Romans or Roman law. Forms of *ius* can have that meaning, or denote an individual legal right, or a legal principle. Throughout this translation I will use the English meaning that best fits the context. See further, Berger, *Encyclopedic Dictionary*, 523 (on *iure*) and 525–6 on *ius*.

1. 7

Ps. Paulus, *Sententiae*, Book 5 (Krüger, 5. 23. 3–4; Liebs, 5. 29. 3–4). Although B and V have *libro tertio quinto*, Mommsen suggested this was an error and proposed an emendation of *libro et titulo in qui supra* which I have accepted. This error must have already stood in α. The first part of this passage also survives in *LRV* 5. 25. 2, with a few variants. The second part of this passage survives in *Dig.* 48. 8. 17. For its possible relation to the text of Ulpian cited above, see Nogrady, *Ulpian*, 168–71, where he plausibly suggests that the anonymous author of the *Sententiae* had access to Ulpian's *De officio proconsulis* as a sources for this passage since it is so similar to the preceding quotation.

For relegation as a form of exile, see, Berger, 'Relegatio', *Encyclopedic Dictionary*, 673; S. Bingham, 'Life on an island: A brief study of places of exile in the first century AD', *Studies in Latin Literature and Roman History* 12 (2003), 376–400; Garnsey, *Social Status and Legal Privilege in the Roman Empire*, 111–22; Grasmück, *Exilium*, 100–2 and 122–32; and G. Kelly, *A History of Exile in the Roman Republic* (Cambridge, 2006), 65–8.

1. 8

Codex Gregorianus, Book 4, under the Title *Ad legem Corneliam de sicariis et veneficis*. The manuscripts give a reading of IIII (a variant of the Roman numeral 4). Pithou had argued that the citation should read XIIII (i.e. 14) for the book number instead (and this view was adopted by Haenel and Huschke). If so, this error must have crept into the tradition in at least α, since all three surviving manuscripts have it. Krüger, *Codices Gregorianus et Hermogenianus*, in *Collectio Librorum Iuris Anteiustiniani*, III, 242, lists it under 14 in his skeleton outline of the contents of the *Codex Gregorianus*, probably following Huschke. We have so few attested title names and book numbers in citations from the *Codex Gregorianus* that reconstructing its correct order is difficult (and it is probably safer to go with the reading in the manuscripts of the *Collatio* for this citation).

The version of the constitution surviving in Coll. 1. 8 is quoted through the first half of *CJ* 9. 16. 1. The remainder of the constitution that survives as *CJ* 9. 16. 1 (with the same subscription) is probably drawn from the original full constitution that might have stood in the *Codex Gregorianus*. Interestingly, the masculine form Justus (instead of the feminine Justa) appears as the victim of the crime in *CJ* 9. 16. 1.

The passage cites a rescript of the Emperor Caracalla that dates to 31 January 215. Honoré, *Emperors and Lawyers*, 92, attributes this rescript to the hypothetical secretary number 5 and hypothesizes, 190, that he might have been Marcus Ofellius Theodorus.

1. 9

This citation must also be actually to *Codex Gregorianus*, Book 4 (IIII), and was to the same title in that work as cited above at Coll. 1. 8. See Krüger, *Codices Gregorianus et Hermogenianus*, 242. This passage cites a constitution of Severus Alexander from 20 July 222. Honoré, *Emperors and Lawyers*, 95, hypothetically attributes this rescript to secretary number 6. The odd thing is, as hinted at above, that this imperial law as it appears in the *Collatio* at Coll. 1. 9 shows up in the second half of *CJ* 9. 16. 1. The most likely explanation is that Tribonian's staff conflated the two laws, coming from slightly different times, from Book 14 of the *Codex Gregorianus* into one constitution in the *Code of Justinian* and gave it the subscription of the first constitution. The two laws probably originally stood one after the other in the *Codex Gregorianus*.

1. 10

This citation should also be to *Codex Gregorianus*, Book 4, and was to the same title as above at Coll. 1. 8. This passage preserves a legal decision from the two Emperors Diocletian and Maximian from 30 November 290 sent to an official named Agatho. *PLRE*, I, 28 suggests the form of address implies he held senatorial rank and argues he might have held a judicial office, but see the comments of Corcoran, *Empire of the Tetrarchs*, 335 cautioning against this view. Another version of this text survives as *CJ* 9. 16. 4 (where Krüger conjectured that the addressee's name in the dative case was Agathoni) and relates that it was released at Sirmium. The version in the *Collatio* is somewhat longer, especially at the beginning and probably preserves a bit more of the original document as presented in the *Codex Gregorianus*. Since the three quotations from Book 4 of the *Codex Gregorianus* which are preserved at Coll. 1. 8–10 stand in chronological order, they probably represent the original order in that late Roman law code. See further, Frakes, 'The *Collatio* and the *Codex Gregorianus*', 293–300.

The *adnotatione* mentioned at the end of the passage refers to an imperial decision that had the force of law usually responding to a petition addressed to the emperor requesting a legal exemption of special favor. On this type of document, see recently R. Mathisen, '*Adnotatio* and *Petitio*: The emperor's favor and special exceptions in the early Byzantine Empire' in D. Feissel and J. Gascou (eds.), *La pétition à Byzance* (Paris, 2004), 23–32.

1. 11

Ulpian, *De officio proconsulis*, Book 7. Lenel, *Paling.*, II, cols. 976–7. This passage preserves a rescript of the Emperor Hadrian (who reigned 117–38) about Evaristus and Claudius. A slight variant survives in *Dig.* 48. 8. 4. 1, which also gives more of the original passage from Ulpian. See also, the rescript formula cited in *Dig.* 48. 19. 5. 2. For the text from which the Collator worked, see Wieacker, *Textstufen*, 391–2 and, more recently, Nogrady, *Ulpian*, 173–7. On relegation, see commentary above at Coll. 1. 7.

1. 12

Modestinus, *Liber differentiarum*, Book 6, allegedly under the title *De Scientibus et Ignorantibus*. See Lenel, *Paling.*, I, col. 704. The quotation is introduced with the prefatory phrase *generaliter loquitur*, indicating that in the Collator's time this was often cited in legal education and thus confirming that the Collator came from the legal milieu. On forms of *ius* denoting the collective law or law in general, see above at Coll. 1. 6. The Collator ends his quotation with *et reliqua*, indicating he was working from a longer text. For more on this work of Modestinus, see Schulz, *History of Roman Legal Science*, 183 and the hypothetical similarity with chancery secretary number 8 suggested by Honoré, *Emperors and Lawyers*, 2nd edn, 101–7.

1. 13

Ps. Paulus, *Sententiae*, Book 5 (Krüger 5. 23. 7; Liebs, 5. 29. 7). *Dig.* 48. 6. 11 preserves a slightly fuller quotation of this quotation, the first part of which was not used by the Collator.

TITLE 2: CONCERNING SEVERE INJURY (*DE ATROCI INIURIA*)[3]

2. 1

Exodus 21: 18–19:

[*NRSV*] 18. When individuals quarrel and one strikes the other with a stone or fist so that the injured party, though not dead, is confined to bed, 19. but recovers and walks around outside with the help of a staff, then the assailant shall be free of liability, except to pay for the loss of time, and to arrange for full recovery.

[Stuttgart Vulgate] *18. si rixati fuerint viri et percusserit alter proximum suum lapide vel pugno et ille mortuus non fuerit sed iacuerit in lectulo. 19. si surrexerit et ambulaverit foris super baculum suum innocens erit qui percussit ita tamen ut operas eius et inpensas in medicos restituat.*

The text of the Old Latin Bible that the Collator used has some clear verbal differences to the Vulgate of Jerome and is again closer to the Lyons Codex of the Old Latin Bible. The sense however is the same. The biblical stricture here clarifies that such an injury that results from a verbal argument escalating into a fight is not the same as from malice aforethought. If someone becomes disabled as a result of the fight, the perpetrator must support him financially. The implication seems to be that if the victim does not rise out of bed, but instead dies, the perpetrator might be guilty of accidental homicide, but not premeditated murder. On this, see further, William H. C. Propp, *Exodus 19–40: A new translation with introduction and commentary*, The Anchor Bible Commentary V.2A (New York, 2006), 214–17. The

[3] *Iniuria* could include a wrongful act, a physical injury, and the Greek concept of hubris (in this case, arrogant statements against someone's reputation). *Iniuria Atrox*, a severe or outrageous injury, could be defined by the severity of the injury, the class standing of the person being injured, and the place where the person was injured. In general, on *iniuria* and *iniuria atrox* in Roman law, see Berger, *Encyclopedic Dictionary*, 502; E. Polay, *Iniuria Types in Roman Law* (Budapest, 1986); Robinson, *Criminal Law*, 49–51; A. Völkl, *Die Verfolgung der Körperverletzung im frühen Römischen Recht* (Vienna, 1984); and R. Wittmann, *Die Körperveletzung an Freien im klassischen römischen Recht* (Munich, 1972). For the *Lex Aquilia* and *Iniuria*, see M. F. Cursi, *Iniuria cum damno: antigiuridicità e colpevolezza nella storia del danno Aquiliano* (Milan, 2002); Harries, *Law and Crime*, 46–9; F. La Rosa, 'Il valore originario di' "iniuria" nella "lex Aquilia"', *Labeo* 44 (1998), 366–76; and Zimmerman, *The Law of Obligation*, 953–1094.

strictures contained in Exodus 20: 22 – 3: 33 are very ancient since the 'Book of the Covenant' is arguably the oldest part of Hebrew law, predating E (the Elohist) who included the Book of the Covenant in his text (following the documentary hypothesis). See further, *The Book of Exodus* with introduction and notes by S. R. Driver, *The Book of Exodus* (Cambridge, 1911), 202–5. More recently, see Calum M. Carmichael, *The Origin of Biblical Law: The Decalogues and the Book of the Covenant* (Ithaca, 1992).

Laws regarding severe injury have a long history in the Near East and may have influenced biblical law. From Mesopotamia, see *LH* 196–223 on various situations where the punishments vary due to gender and social class. See especially *LH* 206 and 207 (the former of which has a similar situation to that described in Exodus 21: 18–19).

2. 2

The quotation is from Ps. Ulpian, *Liber singularis regularum* from the Title *De Inuriis* ('Concerning Injuries'). Only four fragments of this work survive, of which three come from the *Collatio* (see Lenel, *Paling.*, II, col. 1016). On the nature of this work, see further, Avenarius, *Pseudo-Ulpianische* (especially 520–22 on this passage), and, more briefly, Wieacker, *Textstufen*, 435, and Liebs, *HLL4*, 207–8. Murison, 272, pointed out, the second *non* must have been lost early in the manuscript tradition. As this citation ends with the formula *et reliqua*, the Collator was working from a longer text of Ps. Ulpian than he gives, quite possibly the entire work.

2. 3

The statement comes from Papinian, *Liber definitionum*, Book 2, under the Title *De Iudicatis*. This passage is one of twenty-three fragments from the work that has survived; the rest are known from the *Digest*. See Lenel, *Paling.*, I, col. 813. On the contents and authorship of this work, see Wieacker, *Textstufen*, 373–5.

The statement quoted here does not at first glance appear to pertain to the topic of 'Severe Injury' stated in the title of this section of the *Collatio*. Perhaps the Collator felt that the action of not freeing an enslaved man acquired in a noxal action who had accumulated the value of his purchase price through labour for his master was an injury of a severe kind, in so far as the Roman legal concept of *iniuria* denotes a wrongful act. Triebs, *Studien*, I, 154–5, suggested that another part of the Papinian passage that was not used by the Collator, and has since been lost, developed the connection further to *iniuria atrox*. The noxal action described was a type of reimbursement as a penalty for damages in Roman law. On *noxa*, see further D. Daube, 'Nocere and Noxa', *Cambridge Law Journal* 7 (1939), 23–54; Berger, 'Noxa' and 'Noxae datio, deditio', *Encyclopedic Dictionary*, 600–1; G. Pugliese, 'Noxia', *Law Quarterly Review* 88 (1972), 543–8 and V. Spagnuolo, '*Actio iniuriarum noxalis*', *Labeo* 15 (1969), 33–76. For further development of the legal problems and possible interpolations in this passage, see Solazzi, 'Per la data', 494; Masi, 'Contributi ad una Datazione', 300–7.

2. 4

Ulpian, *Liber ad edictum*, Book 18. A much longer version survives in *Dig.* 9. 2. 27. 1–35 with the section quoted in the *Collatio* appearing at *Dig.* 9. 2. 27. 17 (see Lenel, *Paling.*, II, col. 529). The Collator added the prefatory *et cum diceret* at the beginning of his quotation. O. Lenel, 'Kritisches und Exegetisches', *ZRG (R.A.)* 8 (1887), 195–206 at 195–8, offers an ingenious attempt to explain this expression as a result of at least three layers of corruption by scribes in the manuscript tradition. While possible, the Collator did occasionally use forms of *dicit* to introduce quotations from the jurists (Coll. 3. 2; 12. 6). Although the manuscripts certainly have some variants here, they are close enough to indicate that we have here, instead, an occurrence of the Collator's voice, which also occurs at Coll. 12. 7, remarking on the similarity of Ulpian's comments to those of other jurists.

Presumably, the Collator was more interested in the basic definition of the legal problem in Ulpian's text than in the more detailed description in the larger passage. On the interrelationship of these texts, see Wieacker, *Textstufen*, 233–4 and Wittmann, *Die Körperverletzung*, 100–1. The last sentence of the fragment in Coll. 2. 4 which adds the negation *nec* is different, and indeed opposite, from that in the *Digest* which makes more legal sense (and so I have deleted *nec*). See further, Wieacker, *Römische Rechtsgeschichte* (Munich, 1988), I, 157 (especially note 14: 'Auch die . . . einfach Umkehrung durch blosse Negationspartikeln (*non*, *nec*) wird immerhin nicht gescheut').

The *Lex Aquilia* was originally passed sometime after 287 BCE and treated liability due to damage. For a recent collection of the fragments of the *Lex Aquilia*, see Crawford, *Roman Statutes*, II, 723–6. The damage in this case is to the slave as property. Triebs, *Studien*, I, 158 argued that a Roman author of the pre-Christian age would never have seen whipping a slave as a category of *iniuria atrox*. While slaves did have some protection in the empire, the Collator's inclusion of this passage under *Iniuria Atrox* is problematic.

2. 5

Ps. Paulus, *Liber singularis de iniuriis* under the Title *De Iniuriis*. See Lenel, *Paling.*, I, cols. 1112–13. On this book being a post-classical revision of Book 55 of Paulus' commentary on the edict, see Wieacker, *Textstufen*, 136 and Liebs, *HLL4*, 156–7. Since no fragments or testimony of this work appear elsewhere, it is remotely possible that this may actually be a citation from *Sententiae* 5. 4 (also conveniently titled *de iniuriis*). Mommsen supplied text from the *Institutes* of Justinian, 4. 4 pr. which might have been based on either of the two works (see discussion by Wieacker, *Textstufen*, 272–7). Marcus Antistius Labeo, who is cited in the passage, was a senatorial Roman jurist from the early first century CE. For a discussion of Labeo's view of *iniuria* and the role of earlier Greek models, see H. F. Hitzig, *Iniuria. Beiträge zur Geschichte der Injuria im griechischen und römischen Recht* (Munich, 1899) and Wittmann, *Die Körpverletzung*, 23–5, 36–7.

2. 6

Ps. Paulus, *Liber singularis de iniuriis* under the Title *Quemadmodum iniuria agatur*. See above, especially Liebs, *HLL4*, 156–7. 'Aulus Agerius' was the standard fictitious name for a plaintiff and 'Numerius Negidius' for a defendant. See further, M. Wlassak, 'A. Agerius', *RE* (Stuttgart, 1895), I, col. 794. It must be admitted that the style of this passage, with its didactic quotation, makes it less likely to have come from the *Sententiae* then the passage quoted in Coll. 2. 5. On the legal issues, see Wittmann, *Die Körperverletzung*, 49–50 and Dieter Nörr, 'Zur Taxatio bei der Actio Iniuriarum', *Collatio Iuris Romani: Études dédiées à Hans Ankum* (Amsterdam, 1995), II, 389–401. Although it is artful, I am not persuaded by the argument of Daube, 'Collatio 2. 6. 5', 107–22, that *illum* should be read as *capillum* instead of *libellum* (i.e. 'if someone wears messy hair').

2. 7

Ps. Paulus, *Sententiae*, Book 5 (Krüger, 5. 23. 5; Liebs, 5. 29. 5). On this passage and its relation to the *Lex Cornelia*, see the comments of Nörr, *Causa Mortis*, 116–20.

TITLE 3: CONCERNING THE LAW AND CRUELTY OF MASTERS (*DE IURE ET SAEVITIA DOMINORUM*)[4]

3. 1

Exodus 21: 20–1:

[*NRSV*] 20. When a slave-owner strikes a male or female slave with a rod and the slave dies immediately, the owner shall be punished. 21. But if the slave survives for a day or two, there is no punishment; for the slave is the owner's property.

[Stuttgart Vulgate] *20. qui percusserit servum suum vel ancillam virga et mortui fuerint in manibus eius criminis reus erit 21. sin autem uno die supervixerit vel duobus non subiacebit poenae quia pecunia illius est.*

While the Collator's passage is somewhat similar to the Vulgate, it seems more closely related to the Old Latin Bible as seen in the Lyons Codex (especially the verbatim *duobus non vindicabatur pretium enim* at the end). The fifth-century Ps. Augustine seems to have used the same (or a closely related) text in his *Speculum*, c.58. In ancient Hebrew law, only a master who beats a slave to immediate death is

[4] Note that I translate the form of *ius* here as denoting the collected body of Roman law (see above at Coll. 1. 6). On the limits of the use of violence toward slaves in Roman law and society, see, in general, W. W. Buckland, *The Roman Law of Slavery* (Cambridge, 1908); M. I. Finley, *Ancient Slavery and Modern Ideology* (London, 1980); K. R. Bradley, *Slaves and Masters in the Roman Empire: A study on social control* (Brussels, 1984); Peter Garnsey, *Ideas of Slavery from Aristotle to Augustine* (Cambridge, 1996); A. Watson, *Roman Slave Law* (Baltimore, 1987); L. Schumacher, *Sklaverei in der Antike* (Munich, 2000); F. Lucrezi, *L'uccisione dello schiavo in diritto ebraico e romano* (Turin, 2001) and his 'L'uccisione del proprio Schiavo nella Collatio' in *Iuris Vincula: Studi in Onore di Mario Talamanca* (Naples, 2001), 21–92.

directly punished. Since the owner would have lost the value of the slave if he dies after several days, he has already been punished by that pecuniary loss (see further, Propp, *Exodus 19–40*, 220).

3. 2

Ps. Paulus, *Sententiae*, Book 5 (Krüger, 5. 23. 6; Liebs, 5. 29. 6). There has been much debate about the mechanics of Roman law in this passage: see further, Masi, 'Contributi', 313–17; Cervenca, 'Ancora sul Problema della Datazione', 267–72; De Francisci, 'Ancora intorno alla Collatio', 100–1; Lucrezi, *L'uccisione*, 86–92; and Lucrezi, 'Sulla data di redazione della "Collatio" alla luce di due costituzioni Constantiniane', 599–613. The arguments revolve around a constitution of Constantine surviving as *CTh* 9. 12. 1 (and *CJ* 9. 14. 1) and whether such legislation influenced possible fourth-century interpolations of the texts that were excerpted by the Collator. See discussion in chapter 2 above.

3. 3

Ulpian, *De officio proconsulis*, Book 8 under the Title *De Dominorum Saevitia*. See Lenel, *Paling*., II, col. 981. A shorter version of this rescript to Marcianus survives in *Dig.* 1. 6. 2 which does not include the quotation after the sentence of Hadrian regarding Umbricia's banishment. Justinian, *Institutes*, 1. 8. 2, also preserves a variant of this passage. On the differences between the three surviving versions, see Wieacker, *Textstufen*, 392–4. See also recently, Lucrezi, *L'uccisione*, 64–73 and Nogrady, *Ulpian*, 256–60.

Presumably, the emphatic nature of the example of Sabinus and Umbra, while useful in a didactic context, might not have been needed in the *Digest*. The consulship mentioned in the rescript to Alfius Iulius occurred in 152 CE. Such laws guarding against forced prostitution of some slaves are not uncommon in Roman law as seen in the *ne prostituatur* clause (see *CJ* 4. 5. 6; *Dig.* 1. 10, 2. 4. 1, 11. 3; and T. A. J. McGinn, '"Ne Serva Prostituatur": Restrictive covenants in the sale of slaves', *ZRG (R.A.)* 107 (1990), 315–53). On Roman prostitution, see T. A. J. McGinn, *Prostitution, Sexuality, and the Law in Ancient Rome* (Oxford, 1998).

3. 4

Although the text reads *Codex Gregorianus*, Book 19, under the Title *De Accusationibus*, G. Rotondi, 'Studi sulle fonti del Codice giustiniano' in *Scritti Giuridici* (Milan, 1922), I, 110–283 at 157 proposed that the citation should be to Book 14 (i.e. XIIII), not 19 (XVIIII). The Collator had already used Book 4 of the *Codex Gregorianus* at Coll. 1. 8, 1. 9, and 1. 10. The rescript preserved here directed to the soldier Aurelius Sacratus dates to 5 December 285 CE, based upon the consulship in the subscription, although *PLRE*, I, 1042, lists this as Diocletian's second consulship, not his third. This rescript of the *Codex Gregorianus* does not appear in Krüger's attempted reconstruction. Honoré, *Emperors and Lawyers*, 148 n. 47, attributes this rescript to the alleged chancery secretary number 17 and hypothesizes, 190, that this might have been Gregorius (or Gregorianus), the compiler of the *Codex Gregorianus*. However, at 180–1, Honoré also hypothesizes the author of the rescript might have been Arcadius.

TITLE 4: CONCERNING ADULTERY (*DE ADULTERIIS*)[5]

4. 1

Leviticus 20: 10 and Exodus 22: 16–17:

[*NRSV*: Leviticus 20:] 10. If a man commits adultery with the wife of his neighbour, both the adulterer and the adulteress shall be put to death.

[Vulgate Leviticus 20:] *10. si moechatus quis fuerit cum uxore alterius et adulterium perpetrarit cum coniuge proximi sui morte moriantur et moechus et adultera.*]

[5] On adultery in Roman law, see Berger, 'Adulterium', *Encyclopedic Dictionary*, 352; Judith Evans Grubbs, *Law and Family in Late Antiquity: The Emperor Constantine's marriage legislation* (Oxford, 1995), 203–60; Imre Molnár, 'Das adulterium als ein das Ansehen der römischen Familie verletzendes Verbrechen' in Hans-Georg Knothe (ed.), *Status Familiae: Festschrift für Andreas Wacke* (Munich, 2001): 345–64; G. Rizzelli, '"Stuprum" e "adulterium" nella cultura augustea e la "Lex Iulia de adulteriis"', *BIDR* 90 (1987), 355–88; S. Treggiari, *Roman Marriage: Iusti Coniuges from the time of Cicero to the time of Ulpian* (Oxford, 1991), esp. 262–319; and Triebs, *Die Lex Iulia de adulteriis coercendis auf Grundlage der sog. Lex Dei.*

[*NRSV*: Exodus 22:] 16. When a man seduces a virgin who is not engaged to be married, and lies with her, he shall give the bride-price for her and make her his wife. 17. But if her father refuses to give her to him, he shall pay an amount equal to the bride-price for virgins.

[Vulgate Exodus 22:] *16. si seduxerit quis virginem necdum desponsatam et dormierit cum ea dotabit eam et habebit uxorem 17. si pater virginis dare noluerit reddet pecuniam iuxta modum dotis quam virgines accipere consuerunt.*]

The Collator's Latin Bible again has some differences from the Vulgate and again is more similar to versions of the Old Latin Bible surviving in Ps. Augustine, *Speculum*, *c*.45 and the Würzburger Codex. On the similarity, see further Schulz, 'biblischen Texte', 27–39. The Collator makes a connection between these two biblical passages by placing them both under the title *De Adulteriis*. The first passage does indeed treat adultery where a man has sexual intercourse with another man's wife (while *proximus* in Latin could mean neighbour or relative, the Hebrew and Greek Septuagint texts confirm the translation must mean neighbour). On the intricacies of the original Hebrew grammar, see Jacob Milgrom, *Leviticus 17–22: A new translation with introduction and commentary* (New York, 2000), 1747–8. The passage from Exodus treats the seduction of a virgin that actually fell under the category of theft in Hebrew law. Propp, *Exodus*, 253–4, points out that a non-virgin such as a widow would not have the cash value of a virgin for a family (which was 50 shekels). By connecting the passages here under this title, the Collator saw all extramarital intercourse as adulterous when in Roman law only extramarital intercourse involving a married woman was properly adultery. For the importance of adultery laws in the ancient Near East, see *LH* 129–36 (similar strictures are described in *LH* 129 and 130).

4. 2

Ps. Paulus, *Liber singularis de adulteriis*. On this work of Ps. Paulus and its connection to the *Collatio*, see Wieacker, *Textstufen*, 421–2. The passage is noteworthy in that it preserves material from the late second-century jurist Marcellus (from his *Digest*, Book 31). See also, Lenel, *Paling*., I, cols. 953–4, who adopts at Coll. 4. 2. 4 the reading of Pithou and Huschke of *in vidua* instead of *invidia* found in B and W. Mommsen emended this to *sui iuris* to make it fit his understanding of Roman law. Triebs, *Studien zur Lex Dei*, II, 52–4 argued for *in vidua* ('in the case of a widow') and repeated this argument in his *Die Lex Iulia de adulteriis coercendis auf Grundlage der sog. Lex Dei*, 28–32. His reading makes the most sense because a father had the legal right (*ius*) to kill his widowed *filiafamilias* if he finds her with a lover.

The *Lex Iulia de adulteriis coercendis* was created under Augustus in 18 BCE. For a recent collection of the fragments of this law, see Crawford, *Roman Statutes*, II, 781–6 and for a recent overview, see Harries, *Law and Crime*, 95–101. It was part of a broad legislative program of the first emperor that included his slightly earlier *Lex Iulia de maritandis ordinibus* (see further McGinn, *Prostitution, Sexuality, and the Law*, 140–215). *Potestas* or physical power in this passage refers to the legal power of the eldest male ascendant who was the head of the household or *paterfamilias*. Traditionally, a daughter left the power of her father when she married and passed into the hand (*manus*) of her husband, although marriage with *manus* was already becoming rare in the time of Augustus and was long obsolete by the Collator's day in the late fourth century.

4. 3

Ps. Paulus, *Liber singularis de adulteriis*. Lenel, *Paling.*, I, col. 954. On the Collator's use of this work, see Wieacker, *Textstufen*, 421–2. The passage refers to a rescript of Marcus Aurelius and Commodus, joint augusti from 177–80. The Collator ends his quotation with *et reliqua*, again indicating he was working from a longer quotation. This rescript is also discussed in a long quotation from Papinian's *Liber quaestionum* in *Dig.* 48. 5. 39. 8. It is possible that Paulus in his longer three-book commentary *De Adulteriis* had consulted Papinian. Likewise, it is possible that the anonymous author of the spurious text took this information from Papinian (see below at Coll. 4. 4).

A *filius familias* ('son of the family') was a son still under the *potestas* (or power) of his father, grandfather, or other male ancestor who stood as *paterfamilias*. A *dediticius* was a member of the class of freedmen formed of conquered enemies of Rome who lacked citizenship. See further, Gaius, *Inst.* 1. 13–15 and Sherwin-White, *Roman Citizenship*, 280–94. 'Antoninus Magnus' ('Antoninus the Great') is the title used by the Emperor Caracalla (r. 211–17).

4. 4

Ps. Paulus, *Liber singularis de adulteriis.* Lenel, *Paling.*, I, col. 954. In this citation, the author cites Papinian's *Liber responsorum.* On the connection between these works, see further Wieacker, *Textstufen*, 421–2. It may well be that Paulus originally did cite Papinian in his three-volume work on adultery from which Ps. Paulus drew. For the two-month limit for a husband or father to make an accusation at Coll. 4. 4. 2 (*menses . . . utiles*), see *Dig.* 48. 12. 6, 48. 15. 2. For the concept of *actio utiles* in general, see R. Sotty, *Recherche sur les utiles actiones: la notion d'action utile en droit romain classique* (Grenoble, 1977); R. Stolmar, *Actio Utiles: Grundlagen, Wesen, Voraussetzungen, Andwendungen, Wirkungen* (Sindelfingen, 1984); and E. Valiño, *Actiones utiles* (Pamplona, 1974).

4. 5

Papinian, *Liber responsorum*, Book 15 under the Title *Ad legem Iuliam de adulteriis.* Lenel, *Paling.*, I, col. 942. Seeing that this citation comes immediately after the Ps. Paulus recounting of a text in this work of Papinian, it is remotely possible that the Collator transformed a passage from Papinian contained within Ps. Paulus into a direct citation. However, since we then have a string of citations from 'Papinian' from Coll. 4. 5–11, it is more likely that the reference to Papinian in Coll. 4. 4 turned the Collator's mind to what he thought were the works of this author.

4. 6

Ps. Paulus, *Liber singularis de adulteriis.* Lenel, *Paling.*, I, col. 954. On this passage, see further, Wieacker, *Textstufen*, 421–2. The 'Antoninus' mentioned in the rescript is most likely the 'Antoninus Magnus' (i.e. Caracalla) cited at Coll. 4. 5. 8 (see also Coll. 14. 3. 3). He served as co-augustus with his father Septimius Severus from 198–211. Two of their surviving laws treating adultery are preserved in *CJ* 9. 9. 1 and 2 dated in their subscriptions to 197 and 199. On this passage, see Triebs, *Die Lex Iulia*, 22–3. For some reason, perhaps a scribal error, Scaliger moved this passage to after the next Papinian quotation, although it clearly stands here in the B manuscript. There is a large damaged area here in B that probably held the capital number ('KP dcxxviiii').

4. 7

Ps. Papinian, *Liber singularis de adulteriis*. Lenel, *Paling*., I, col. 808. See Wieacker, *Textstufen*, 419–21. The quotations appearing in Coll. 4. 7–11 are probably from successive parts of Ps. Papinian's work. On this passage, see also Triebs, *Die Lex Iulia*, 22–8, and J. Gardner, *Family and Familia in Roman Law and Life* (Oxford, 1998), 121–2. I translate the form of *ius* here as 'legal power'. For further on this famous 'law of the father' (*ius patris*, *vitae necisque potestas*, or *ius vitae necisque*), see comments at Coll. 4. 8.

4. 8

Ps. Papinian, *Liber singularis de adulteriis*. Lenel, *Paling*., I, col. 808. Wieacker, *Textstufen*, 419–21. The quotations in Coll. 4. 7–11 are probably from successive parts of Ps. Papinian's work, but which title is meant is unclear. On this passage, see also Triebs, *Die Lex Iulia*, 22–8. The 'law of the father' cited at Coll. 4. 8. 1 is attested by Dionysius of Halicarnassus, *Roman Antiquities*, 2. 26, as coming from the reign of Romulus (traditionally 753–715 BCE). If it actually existed, it may have been enshrined in the Twelve Tables (*Tabula* IV. 2, following *FIRA*, I, 35), but for an opposing view, see Crawford, *Roman Statutes*, II, 562. On the scholarly debate over this power, see W. V. Harris, 'The Roman father's power of life and death' in R. S. Bagnall and W. V. Harris (eds.), *Studies in Roman Law in Memory of A. Arthur Schiller* (Leiden, 1986), 81–95; R. Saller, *Patriarchy, Property, and Death in the Roman Family* (Cambridge, 1994), 115–17; and, most recently, Brent Shaw, 'Raising and killing Roman children: Two Roman myths', *Mnemosyne* 54 (2001), 31–77 at 56–77 (especially 64–5 on Coll. 4. 8. 1) on the conflation by the jurists of the alleged *vitae necisque potestas* of the monarchy with the right of killing an adulterer.

4. 9

Ps. Papinian, *Liber singularis de adulteriis*. Lenel, *Paling*., I, col. 808. Wieacker, *Textstufen*, 419–21. The quotations appearing in Coll. 4. 7–11 probably derive from successive parts of Ps. Papinian's work, but again which title meant is unclear. On this passage, see also

Triebs, *Die Lex Iulia*, 22–8. On 'malice aforethought', see comments on *dolo malo* above at Coll. 1. 3.

4. 10

Ps. Papinian, *Liber singularis de adulteriis.* Lenel, *Paling.*, I, col. 809. Wieacker, *Textstufen*, 419–21. The quotations from Coll. 4. 7–11 probably stem from successive parts of Ps. Papinian's work. Which title is meant is again unclear. On this passage, see also Triebs, *Die Lex Iulia*, 22–8. This passage seems to vary from the previous quoted views in Coll. 4. 2 regarding the punishment of the wife.

Exile (*exilium*) evolved as a Roman concept from voluntary withdrawal to a category of punisment that could be completed or limited in the sentence. See further Garnsey, *Social Status and Legal Privilege*, 111–15; Grasmück, *Exilium*, 62–127; Kelly, *History of Exile*, throughout (and 40 on *deportatio*). A still influential work on the history of exile in the Roman Republic is G. Crifò, *Ricerche sull' 'exilium' nel periodo repubblicano* (Milan, 1961).

4. 11

Ps. Papinian, *Liber singularis de adulteriis.* Lenel, *Paling.*, I, col. 809. Wieacker, *Textstufen*, 419–21. The quotations excerpted in Coll. 4. 7–11 probably derive from successive parts of Ps. Papinian's work, but which title is meant is unclear. On the torture of slaves as witnesses, see *Dig.* 68. 18; Triebs, *Die Lex Iulia*, 23–4; and Alan Watson, 'Roman slave law and Romanist ideology', *Phoenix* 37 (1983), 53–65. For an overview of the torture of slaves in antiquity, see Schumacher, *Sklaverei*, 276–91. See especially the law surviving as *CTh* 9. 7. 4 (dated to 385 in subscription) that stipulated the interrogation and torture of household slaves in charges of adultery. For a discussion of the possible influence of this law on an interpolation in either this passage from Ps. Papinian or directly on the Collator, see Masi, 'Contributi ad una Datazione', 294–300 and, above, chapter 2 on dating the work.

4. 12

Ps. Paulus, *Sententiae*, Book 2 (Krüger, *Sententiae*, 2. 26. 1–9; Liebs 2. 37. 1–2, 4–9). Parts of this passage also survived in *LRV* 2. 27. 1, in the so-called *Codex Vesontinus* that Cujas used for his 1586 edition of the *Sententiae* of Paulus and is now lost (hereafter Vs.), and the epitomes to *LRV* that are known as *LRVS* and are included in Haenel's edition of *LRV*.

There is a long history to laws allowing a husband to kill an adulterer. See *LH* 129 for an ancient Mesopotamian law allowing a husband to kill both his wife and the adulterer (but allowing him the chance to save his wife's life). On the legal concept discussed in Coll. 4. 12, see Gardner, *Family and Familia*, 122. For further on the scholarly debate on possible influence of the constitution of 385 mentioned above (part of which survives as *CTh* 9. 7. 4) as leading to an interpolation for this passage, see Masi, 'Contributi ad una Datazione', 295–300; Cervenca, 'Ancora sul Problema', 263–7; De Francisci, 'Ancora', 99–100; and De Dominicis, 'Ancora Sulla Collatio', 339–40.

TITLE 5: CONCERNING THOSE ENGAGED IN ILLICIT SEXUAL INTERCOURSE (*DE STUPRATORIBUS*)[6]

5. 1

Leviticus 20: 13.

[*NRSV*] If a man lies with a male as with a woman, both of them have committed an abomination; they shall be put to death; their blood is upon them.

[Vulgate Leviticus] *qui dormierit cum masculo coitu femineo uterque operati sunt nefas morte moriantur sit sanguis eorum super eos.*

The Collator's biblical text has several differences from the Vulgate. Schulz, 'biblischen Texte', 29, and Smits, *Collatio*, 53, cite Sabatier

[6] Although the Latin word *stuprum* includes all kinds of illicit sexual intercourse, the Collator examines only male homosexual sexual relations in this title (*stuprum cum masculo*). On *stuprum cum masculo* in Roman law, see D. Dalla, *Ubi Venus mutatur: Omosessualità e Diretto nel mondo Romano* (Milan, 1987); S. Lilja, *Homosexuality in Republican and Augustan Rome* (Helsinki, 1983); and Rizzelli, '"Stuprum" e "adulterium" nella cultura augustea'. For a radical work that has not been fully accepted, see J. Boswell, *Christianity, Social Tolerance, and Homosexuality: Gay people in Western Europe from the beginning of the Christian era to the fourteenth century* (Chicago, 1980).

directly for a closer corresponding passage from the Old Latin Bible (*Quicumque manserit cum masculo concubito muliebri ... ambo moriantur*). Ultimately, this fragment of the Old Latin Bible seems to derive from the *Capitularium S. Pauli et Petr.* 62–3 (see further, J. N. Ott, Review of C. Paucker, *Spicilegium addendorum lexicis latinis composuit adnotavit, Zeitschrift für die oesterreichischen Gymnasien* 26 (1875), 517–18 and H. Rönsch, *Semasiologische Beiträge zum lateinischen Wörterbuch* (Leipzig, 1887), 58).

The Leviticus passage is, of course, famous for its condemnation of male homosexuality and has received great attention during the recent gay-marriage debate in the United States of America. The passage is insightful for showing the different view of homosexuality in Hebrew vs. Greek or Roman culture. It is revealing that the Collator chose this passage and not one from Paul's epistle to the Romans 1: 26–7 (*NRSV*: 'For this reason God gave them up to degrading passions. Their women exchanged natural intercourse for unnatural, 27. and in the same way also the men, giving up natural intercourse with women, were consumed with passion for one another. Men committed shameless acts with men and received in their own persons the due penalty for their error') which condemned both male and female homosexuality. Nor did the Collator choose another passage from Paul (1 Corinthians 6: 9: 'Do not be deceived! Fornicators, idolators, adulterers, male prostitutes, Sodomites ... none of these will inherit the Kingdom of God'). Apparently, drawing from the Ten Commandments was more consistent with the Collator's plan for the *Collatio*.

While some have argued that this Hebrew rule against male homosexuality was meant to increase the population of ancient Israel, its placement in a section of the book of Leviticus against various sexual crimes would suggest the ancient Hebrews saw such acts as moral outrages in the eyes of God (see further, Milgrom, *Leviticus 17–22*, 1749–50). For a comparison with Assyrian law, see David Daube, 'The Old Testament prohibitions of homosexuality', *ZRG (R.A.)* 103 (1985), 447–8.

5. 2

Ps. Paulus, *Sententiae*, Book 2 (Krüger, 2. 26. 12–13; Liebs, 2. 37. 12–13). Since this section of the *Sententiae* was just used at Coll. 4. 12, we can see how the Collator must have kept the book open and at hand when he moved to his Bible. The connecting sentences between the *Sententiae* (Krüger, 2. 26. 10–12; Liebs, 2. 37. 10–12) were preserved in Vs. and LRVS. See further, Krüger, *Sententiae*, 44 and Liebs, 'pseudopaulinischen Sentenzen', 167.

This passage may be a reference to the *Lex Scantin(i)a* of uncertain dating (perhaps mid second century BCE) during the republic, although this is uncertain because the law itself is lost. Most of the testimony regarding the law seems to refer to non-consensual homosexual sex with a young Roman male citizen. Tertullian, *De Monogamia* 12. 3, indicates that the *Lex Scantinia* was still known in the third century CE. On this law, see further, Lilja, *Homosexuality in Republican and Augustan Rome*, 112–21; Dalla, *Ubi Venus mutatur*, 71–99; F. X. Ryan, 'The *Lex Scantinia* and the prosecution of censors and aediles', *CP* 89 (1994), 159–62; McGinn, *Prostitution, Sexuality, and the Law*, 140–1; and J. Duncan Cloud, 'A "philologist" looks at the "Lex Scantinia"' in *Iuris Vincula: Studi in Onore di Mario Talamanca* (Naples, 2001), II, 201–25. The lost first-century *Lex Iulia de adulteriis coercendis* may have also punished those engaged in male homosexual acts, but the testimony is late (Justinian, *Institutes*, 4. 18. 4).

5. 3

A constitution of Valentinian, Theodosius, and Honorius. See further, Frakes, '*Item Theodosianus*?', 163–8. This constitution against homosexual prostitution survives in a severly-edited form at *CTh* 9. 7. 6 which gives the year as 390. The grammar of the text of this constitution as it stands in the *Collatio* is extremely complicated (to some degree due to the rhetorical prose). Honoré, 'The making of the Theodosian Code', 221, and *Law in the Crisis of Empire*, 194, proposes that Virius Nicomachus Flavianus might have been the quaestor who drafted this constitution. He also suggests, 124, that there is an echo of this law in the biography of the emperor Carus (6. 1) in the *Historia Augusta* (a view elaborated by Ratti, 'Nicomaque Flavien Seniore auteur de L'Histoire Auguste', 311–12, but effectively rebutted by Paschoud, 'Chronique d'historiographie tardive', 361). For more on the implications of this law for an understanding of attitudes toward homosexuality, see Dalla, *Ubi Venus mutatur*, 170–5. The Collator may have well used the entire constitution which he might have found in Rome. See Liebs, *Jurisprudenz im Italien*, 165–70.

The shortened version of the constitution in the *Theodosian Code* (*CTh* 9. 7. 6) would later, in the fifth and early sixth century, receive an interpretation attached to it that briefly stated *haec lex interpretatione non indiget* ('This law does not require Interpretation'), implying that, at that point, this law was clear and possibly still being enforced. Constantius II and Constans had already created a law in December 342 against homosexual marriage, surviving as *CTh* 9. 7. 3 (= *CJ* 9. 9. 30). See Dalla, *Ubi Venus mutatur*, 167–70. In this earlier constitution, the fraternal emperors had ordered the 'statutes to arise' (*iubemus insurgere leges*) against homosexual marriage, implying that there may have been earlier lost legislation against homosexuality. It is puzzling, or perhaps ironic, that the law of 342 was issued at Milan in the part of the empire controlled by Constans who was reputed to live openly as a homosexual emperor (see Eutropius, *Breviarium* 10. 9; Aurelius Victor, *Caes.* 41. 24; Zosimus, *Historia Nova*, 2. 42. 1; Zonaras, 13. 5. 15, 6. 7–9). Such legislation in combination with the biblical strictures continued in the east for some time (see *Syro-Roman Lawbook*, 76b and comments of Selb and Kaufhold, *Syrisch-Römische Rechtsbuch*, III, 150).

The appearance of the Collator's voice in the prefatory formula at the beginning of this passage ('This is indeed law. However, a constitution . . . is known to have followed to the full the meaning of the law of Moses') is revealing by its elegant juxtaposition of *ius* as the objective sense of Roman law in general with the *lex* of Moses and the *constitutio* of the emperors. The preface also shows that in the Collator's eyes at least, the imperial constitution of Theodosius was based on the stricture in Leviticus. Of course, this constitution, while condemning male homosexuality, only punishes male homosexual prostitutes who take a passive role in receiving anal intercourse. It does not actually follow fully the law of Leviticus which would kill both the male prostitutes and their male clients (as well as any other male homosexuals). For more evidence of late fourth-century hostile attitudes toward homosexuality, see Ammianus, 31. 9. 5 and Augustine, *De civitate dei*, 6. 8. For the argument that this constitution was the basis for Butheric's jailing of the charioteer that led to the crisis in Thessalonika (Sozomen, 7. 25. 1–9), see Hohenlohe, *Ursprung*, 11–12, and Ensslin, *Religionspolitik*, 67 (while intriguing, the chronology of the event is not clear enough to completely accept this ingenous argument). It is tempting to see the anti-homosexual attitude displayed in Ps. Cyprian, *Carmen ad Senatorem ex Christiana religione ad idolorum servitutem conversum*, 9–14 as related to this constitution of Theodosius also.

TITLE 6: CONCERNING INCESTUOUS MARRIAGES (*DE INCESTIS NUPTIIS*)[7]

6. 1

Leviticus 20: 11–12:

[*NRSV*] 11. The man who lies with his father's wife has uncovered his father's nakedness; both of them shall be put to death; their blood is upon them. 12. If a man lies with his daughter-in-law, both of them shall be put to death; they have committed perversion; their blood is upon them.

[Vulgate Leviticus] *11. qui dormierit cum noverca sua et revelaverit ignominiam patris sui morte moriantur ambo sanguis eorum sit super eos 12. si quis dormierit cum nuru sua uterque moriantur quia scelus operati sunt sanguis eorum sit super eos.*

The Collator's text has several differences from the Vulgate. Presumably he drew from the Old Latin Bible here also, although this corresponding passage has not survived in any of the manuscripts of the *Vetus Latina* (although Sabatier relates the text '*cum uxore patris qui dormierit . . . ambo mariantur*', he does not cite a source). The Collator condensed the text somewhat (as can be seen from contrasting with the Vulgate and original Hebrew text) and removed references to blood and perversion. Again, he may have done this to make the connection between biblical law and Roman laws against incest clearer to the audience of the *Collatio*. The biblical stricture, of

[7] On incest in Roman law, see Berger, 'Incestus', *Encyclopedic Dictionary*, 497; P. Bonte (ed.), *Épouser au plus proche, inceste, prohibitions et stratégies matrimoniales autour de la Méditerranée* (Paris, 1994); P. E. Corbett, *The Roman Law of Marriage* (Oxford, 1930); A. Guarino, 'Studi sull' "incestum"', *ZRG (R.A.)* 63 (1943), 175–267; Harries, *Law and Crime*, 90–5; P. Moreau, *Incestus et prohibitae nuptiae* (Paris, 2002); S. Puliatti, *Incesti Crimina: Regime Giuridico da Augusto a Giustiniano* (Milan, 2001); Brent Shaw and R. P. Saller, 'Close-kin marriage in Roman society?', *Man: Journal of the Royal Anthropological Institute*, n. s. 19 (1984), 432–44; Treggiari, *Roman Marriage*, esp. 37–9. For an overview of the etymology of *incestum*, see Triebs, *Studien zur Lex Dei*, II, 80–110.

course, implies incest because the wife of the father would typically be the mother of the male involved (see Milgrom, *Leviticus 17–22*, 1749). For a recent study of the incest strictures in Leviticus, see Calum M. Carmichael, *Law, Legend, and Incest in the Bible: Leviticus 18–20* (Ithaca, 1997). For comparison with ancient Mesopotamian law, see *LH* 154, 155, and, especially, 157.

6. 2

Ps. Ulpian, *Liber regularum singularis* under the Title *De Nuptiis.* One of five total citations to this book in Lenel, *Paling.*, II, col. 1016. When Ps. Ulpian mentions, at Coll. 6. 2. 2, that Roman law had changed to allow marriage to a brother's daughter, he is referring to the Emperor Claudius' legislation that enabled his marriage to his niece Agrippina. On this passage, see further Avenarius, *Der Pseudo-Ulpianische*, 242–4.

6. 3

Ps. Paulus, *Sententiae*, Book 2 (Krüger, 2. 19. 3–5; Liebs, 2. 21. 3–5). On the debate over the inclusion of the *nec sororem* clause in 6. 3. 1, see Triebs, *Studien*, II, 102–3 n. 1. The *capitis minutio* clause at 6. 3. 2 refers to the allowance of adopted siblings to marry each other after they have become emancipated (see Gaius, *Inst.*, 1. 61). The *Lex Iulia* cited at Coll. 6. 3. 3 must be the *Lex Iulia de adulteriis* cited fully at Coll. 4. 2. 2. See *Dig.* 48. 5. 39. 4 and 23. 2. 57 for specific cases where women in incestuous relationships were granted leniency. At 6. 3. 3, for *ius* as legal principle, see above at Coll. 1. 6.

6. 4

Codex Gregorianus, Book 5, under the Title *De Nuptiis.* On the text see Frakes, 'Collatio and the Codex Gregorianus' and note in apparatus above. It is noteworthy that we see the Collator's voice in the prefatory statement. On the usage of *exemplum*, see recently S. Corcoran, 'The heading of Diocletian's prices edict at Stratonicea', *Zeitschrift für Papyrologie und Epigraphik* 166 (2008), 295–302. The edict as preserved in the *Collatio* (via the *Codex Gregorianus*) seems to represent the length of many late Roman constitutions and is similar in length to those surviving in the Sirmondian Constitutions.

Of course, rescripts tended to be shorter. This law survives in much shortened form in *CJ* 5. 4. 17, which takes only the resumé of the constitution offered at Coll. 6. 4. 5 although it interpolates the phrase *praeterea fratris filia et ex ea nepte* ('or with the daughter of a brother or a granddaughter by her') which must have been influenced by *CTh* 3. 12. 1 of 342). See further, S. Corcoran, 'The sins of the fathers: A neglected constitution of Diocletian on incest', *Legal History* 21 (2000), 1–34 at 13–14.

This legal pronouncement of the tetrarchs is traditionally held to be issued in Damascus on 1 May 295, but see T. D. Barnes, 'Damascus or Demessus?', *Zeitschrift für Papyrologie und Epigraphik* 151 (2005), 266–8, who argues that the site name should read Demessus (a Danubian town that is probably to be identified as modern Stojnik in Serbia) and the date should be sometime from 14–30 April 295 (since he suggests a number may have originally stood in the text before the accusative form of Maias). The caesars since 293 were Constantius I and Galerius Maximianus. Honoré, *Emperors and Lawyers*, 154–5, attributes this constitution to the hypothetical secretary 17/18 and posits, 190, that he might have been the compiler of the *Codex Gregorianus*. Corcoran, *Empire of the Tetrarchs*, 173–4 and 'Sins of the fathers', 9–11, links this constitution to anti-Persian rhetoric. See further, Judith Evans Grubbs, *Law and Family*, 97–101, who analyses it as an example of marriage legislation before Constantine. This law of 295 (or, indeed, the statement of Ps. Ulpian cited in Coll. 6. 2) may have influenced the later constitution of 396 preserved as *CTh* 3. 12. 1 (and *CJ* 5. 5. 6) which was probably issued shortly after the *Collatio* was compiled.

At 6. 4. 2 and 3, for forms of *ius* as the collective law of the Romans, see above at Coll. 1. 6. At 6. 4. 6, I use 'legal principles' for *iura* to make the contrast with *leges* later in the sentence clearer.

6. 5

Codex Hermogenianus under the Title *De Nuptiis.* See Krüger, 'Codicis Gregoriani Fragmenta', 243. The *Codex Hermogenianus* apparently only had titles and was not long enough to be divided into separate books like the slightly earlier *Codex Gregorianus.* The *clementia principum* ('clemency of the emperors') that Diocletian and Maximian refer to was an existing law discussed already by Papininian (*Liber Quaestionum* 36), excerpted in *Dig.* 48. 5. 38. 7. It could be that Diocletian's chancery secretary (number 19, according to Honoré, *Emperors and Lawyers*, 156–8) read this passage of Papinian when he drafted the rescript.

In a rare comparative passage, the Collator states in his own voice (with certainty) that his copy of the *Codex Hermogenianus* gives a date of 15 March 291 for the rescript by stating it was posted on the Ides of March in the consulship of Dio (*PLRE*, Cassius Dio) and Tberianus (*PLRE*, C. Iunius Tiberianus 8), although most of the firmly dated material in the *Codex Hermogenianus* ranges in dating from 293–4. However, he also states, at Coll 6. 5. 2, that the same text is dated to 287 in the *Codex Gregorianus*. Following Honoré's stylistic analysis, it might date to 291. There is epigraphic evidence for Flavius Flavianus as *praeses* of Numidia sometime in a window of 286–93 (see *PLRE*, Flavius Flavianus 9). On the problematic nature of the two codes having copies of the same rescript, see Rotondi, 'Studi sulle fonti del codice giustinianeo', 127 and Corcoran, *Empire of the Tetrarchs*, 34 and 125 and 'Sins of the fathers', 8–9 and 28 n. 58. For an argument supporting the inclusion, see Frakes, 'The *Collatio* and the *Codex Gregorianus*'. The problem is difficult. The subscription at the end of Coll. 6. 5. 1 and the following comparison to the *Codex Gregorianus* survive only in the B manuscript. However, B is the oldest manuscript (and usually the best) and the copyist of β might have slipped here and not included this comparison (which thus explains its absence from V and W). This is an easier explanation than having the copyist of B make an interpolation, since it is unlikely that the *Codex Gregorianus* would have survived into the ninth century. It is even possible that the Collator's copy of either the *Codex Gregorianus* or the *Codex Hermogenianus* might have already suffered from a scribal error.

It is interesting that, while the Collator made use of the *Codex Hermogenianus* and *Codex Gregorianus* for legal material on incestuous marriages, he did not cite the constitution of Constantius II and Constans banning marriage between uncle and niece, earlier allowed by the Emperor Claudius (*CTh* 3. 12. 1 of 342) or another of their constitution (*CTh* 3. 12. 2 of 355) banning the marriage between a man and his former sister-in-law, although it would seem that such legislation would have fit well. This absence further suggests that the Collator had imperfect access to fourth-century laws.

6. 6

Ps. Papinian, *Liber singularis de adulteriis*. Lenel, *Paling*., I, col. 809. This passage from Ps. Papinian may have influenced the constitution that survives as *CJ* 5. 5. 4 (of *c*.392, following *PLRE*, I, 63). On this passage, see Wieacker, *Textstufen*, 419–21, 426.

6. 7

This is a rare case where the Collator put a second biblical passage at the end of a title, prefaced by a personal observation in his voice. The biblical text is woven from Deuteronomy 27: 20, 22, 23; Leviticus 18: 12, 13, 18, 16; and then Deuteronomy, 27: 21:

[*NRSV*: Deuteronomy 27:] 20. 'Cursed be anyone who lies with his father's wife, because he has violated his father's rights.' All the people shall say, 'Amen!' 22. 'Cursed be anyone who lies with his sister, whether the daughter of his father or the daughter of his mother.' All the people shall say, 'Amen!' 23. 'Cursed be anyone who lies with his mother-in-law.' All the people shall say, 'Amen!'

[Vulgate: Deuteronomy 27:] *20. maledictus qui dormit cum uxore patris sui et revelat operimentum lectuli eius et dicet omnis populus amen 21. maledictus qui dormit cum omni iumento et dicet omnis populus amen 22. maledictus qui dormit cum sorore sua filia patris sui sive matris suae et dicet omnis populus amen 23. maledictus qui dormit cum socru sua et dicet omnis populus amen.*

[*NRSV*: Leviticus 18:] 12. You shall not uncover the nakedness of your father's sister; she is your father's flesh. 13. You shall not uncover the nakedness of your mother's sister, for she is your mother's flesh. 14. You shall not uncover the nakedness of your father's brother, that is, you shall not approach his wife; she is your aunt. 15. You shall not uncover the nakedness of your daughter-in-law: she is your son's wife; you shall not uncover her nakedness. 16. You shall not uncover the nakedness of your brother's wife; it is your brother's nakedness. 17. You shall not uncover the nakedness of a woman and her daughter, and you shall not take her son's daughter or her daughter's daughter to uncover her nakedness; they are your flesh; it is depravity. 18. And you shall not take a woman as a rival to her sister, uncovering her nakedness while her sister is still alive.

[Vulgate: Leviticus 18:] *12. turpitudinem sororis patris tui non discoperies quia caro est patris tui. 13. turpitudinem sororis matris tuae non revelabis eo quod caro sit matris tuae. 14. turpitudinem patrui tui non revelabis nec accedes ad uxorem eius quae tibi adfinitate coniungitur. 15. turpitudinem nurus tuae non revelabis quia uxor filii tui est nec discoperies ignominiam eius. 16. turpitudinem uxoris fratris tui non revelabis quia turpitudo fratris tui est. 17. turpitudinem uxoris tuae et filiae eius non revelabis filiam filii eius et filiam filiae illius non sumes ut reveles ignominiam eius quia caro illius sunt et talis coitus incestus est. 18. sororem uxoris tuae in pelicatum illius non accipies nec revelabis turpitudinem eius adhuc illa vivente.*

[*NRSV*: Deuteronomy 27:] 21. 'Cursed be anyone who lies with any animal.' All the people shall say, 'Amen!'

[Vulgate: Deuteronomy 27:] *21. maledictus qui dormit cum omni iumento et dicet omnis populus amen.*

There are stylistic differences between the corresponding passages in the Vulgate and the Collator's Bible. Again, the Collator's Bible seems to be a version of the Old Latin Bible (see the Lyons Codex and Augustine, *Quaestiones in Heptateuchum* 5 (*Locutiones de Deuteronomio*), 59, which Hyamson, 155, mistakenly listed as being in Book 6). Hyamson, 92, correctly pointed out that the Collator altered the texts in Leviticus to make them parallel to those from Deuteronomy (as can be seen by examining the Vulgate, Septuagint, and Hebrew texts). For further on the Dodecalogue of Shechem, see von Rad, *Deuteronomy: A commentary*, 166–9. On the Collator's voice here, see Harries, 'How to make a law code', 68.

The 'still primitive people' at Coll. 6. 7. 1 refers to the ancient Hebrews (before the time of Moses). Early patristic authors had to wrestle with why the Hebrew Bible portrayed the early Hebrews apparently engaging in unusual forms of marriage, such as marrying relatives (e.g. Gen. 8: 15–9: 1 implying that Noah's grandchildren married their first cousins and even mentions a covenant at Gen. 9: 9–17; Gen. 19: 33–36 on Lot and his daughters; Gen. 20: 12 on Abraham and his half-sister Sarah) and having multiple wives, when such practices were later condemned by God. The late third–early fourth-century Methodius of Olympus, *Symposium*, Logos 1. 2 related that these two forms of marriage had been necessary long ago in order to populate the world, but were later ended. Just a few years after the Collator, Augustine (*c.*401), *De bono coniugali*, 1. 17–20, echoed Methodius in that plural marriages had served an important function in the early history of increasing the world's population (but condemned incest altogether). The Collator thus follows what must have been an accepted line of patristic thought in this manifestation of his voice.

The fact that the Collator moved from the cursing liturgy in Deuteronomy to Leviticus and then back to Deuteronomy is revealing because the Collator deliberately broke the chain of references to Deuteronomy after 27: 20, shifted to Leviticus 18: 12–18 (but played freely with the order of those verses), and then finally returned at Deuteronomy 27: 21. It seems he wanted to end this passage with the anti-bestiality rule. Since that is the last stricture that the reader would see, it could be that the Collator felt a special drive to bring that rule to his audience's attention. This conclusion seems to be strengthened by the fact that none of the Roman sources he cites in this title have to do with bestiality. As we have seen, the Collator often trimmed off parts of biblical law that did not have parallels with Roman laws or jurisprudence in the titles of the *Collatio*. Here he seems to do the opposite by adding a passage that does not link to the Roman material. It seems that this editorial handling, when taken together with his deliberate inclusion of Theodosius' constitution at Coll. 5. 3. 1, stems from a special concern of the Collator's with what he perceived as sexual deviance.

TITLE 7: CONCERNING THIEVES AND THEIR PUNISHMENT (*DE FURIBUS ET DE POENA EORUM*)[8]

7. 1

The unusual prefatory clause in the Collator's voice regarding the Twelve Tables, considering the normal style of the Collator, originally comes from Cicero, *Pro Mil.* 3. 9 (but not the command *scitote iuris consulti* that the Collator inserted). See further, Schulz, 'biblischen Texte', 33–4. Crawford, *Roman Statutes*, II, 608–13, lists these articles from the Twelve Tables as I. 17 and 18. For the use of the Collator's

[8] On theft in Roman law, see E. Albertario, *Animus furandi, contributo alla dottrina del furto nel diritto romano e nel diritto bizantino* (Milan, 1923); F. De Robertis, *La Legittimazione attiva nell'actio furti* (Bari, 1950); J. Gaudemet, 'A propos du "furtum" a l'epoque classique' in A. Gaurino and M. Bretone (eds.), *Mnemeion Siro Solazzi* (Naples, 1964), 141–53; Harries, *Law and Crime*, 43–58; J. M. Kelly, *Roman Litigation* (Oxford, 1966), 140–8, 161–3; L. Pepe, *Richerche sul furto nelle XII tavole e nel diritto attico* (Milan, 2004); W. Pika, *Ex causa furtiva condicere im klassichen römischen Recht* (Berlin, 1988); and Zimmerman, *The Law of Obligations*, 922–52.

voice here, see Harries, 'How to make a law code', 68. Mommsen, *Collatio*, 165, correctly supplies three words (*quoquo modo diurnum*) for the reading in the *Collatio* from Cicero. While it is possible that the Collator read Cicero himself, it might also be possible that he took this quotation from some kind of legal manual. The quotation from Cicero's speech appears in Quintilian's *Institutio Oratoria* in a long section dependant upon Cicero's *Pro Milone* (5. 14. 18) and it seems more likely that the Collator either obtained the quote directly from Quintilian or from a source dependant on Quintilian. It is quite possible that Quintilian's examples were common school rhetorical exercises.

Exodus 22: 2–3:

[*NRSV*] 2. If a thief is found breaking in, and is beaten to death, no blood-guilt is incurred; 3, but if it happens after sunrise, blood-guilt is incurred.

[Stuttagart Vulgate] *2. si effringens fur domum sive suffodiens fuerit inventus et accepto vulnere mortuus fuerit percussor non erit reus sanguinis 3, quod si orto sole hoc fecerit homicidium perpetravit et ipse morietur si non habuerit quod pro furto reddat venundabitur.*

The prefatory clause *sicut lectio manifestat* ('just as a close reading shows') confirms that the Collator was familiar with reading the Latin text of the Hebrew Bible and was working with that text directly at hand. The Collator's Latin Bible had some clear differences from the Vulgate text and again is much closer to the Old Latin Bible (see Augustine, *Questionum in Heptateuchum*, 2. 84). This type of crime and response is universal where a homeowner has the right to defend his home (from ancient Mesopotamia, see *LH* 21). See also more generally on theft, *LH* 8 and 22. For the continuation of the influence of both the Twelve Tables and Mosaic law, see the fifth-century *Syro-Roman Lawbook* 76a (see also, comments of Selb and Kaufhold, *Syrisch-Römische Rechtsbuch*, III, 148–50). For debate over whether Alfred the Great was influenced by this passage of the *Collatio* in the prologue to his ninth-century legal code, see Wormald, *The Making of English Law*, 418–20 and the cautious rejection of Carella, 'Sources of the Prologue to the Laws of Alfred', 91–118.

7. 2

Ps. Paulus, *Sententiae*, Book 5 (Krüger, 5. 23. 9; Liebs, 5. 29. 9). While the Cornelian law was not surprisingly influenced by the law in the Twelve Tables (see Crawford, *Roman Statutes*, II, 610–12), it is striking that the 'thief in the night' clause is so similar to the biblical text cited at Coll. 7. 1. This response may be due to the universality of greater anxiety at night. On arguments that this passage may suffer from interpolation in the fourth century, see Masi, 'Contributi', 307–13; De Francisci, 'Ancora', 97–101; Cervenca, 'Ancora sul Problema', 258–63; and De Dominicis, 'Ancora', 338–9.

7. 3

Although a simple scribal error in B and W cites Book 8 or VIII (the V manuscript does not list any book number), the passage probably comes from Ulpian, *Liber ad edictum*, Book 18 (or XVIII) in the Title *Si quadrupes pauperiem dederit*. This is a normal enough type of scribal error, the dropping of the X from XVIII, that we see elsewhere in the *Collatio*. For the remains of this book, see Lenel, *Paling.*, II, col. 522. Other parts of this passage from Ulpian, some of which overlap with that in the *Collatio* at Coll. 7. 3, appear in *Dig.* 9. 2. 3 and 9. 2. 5. For the citation from the Twelve Tables, see Crawford, *Roman Statutes*, II, 609–13. The Collator ends his quotation with *et reliqua*, showing that he had more material at hand. On the textual variants between the version in the *Collatio* and that excerpted in the *Digest*, see Wieacker, *Textstufen*, 234–56 (including stemma on 237). For arguments regarding possible fourth-century interpolation, see Masi, 'Contributi', 307–13; Cervenca, 'Ancora sul Problema', 258–63; De Francisci, 'Ancora', 97–101; and De Dominicis, 'Ancora', 338–41. The reference to Sextus Pomponius (a jurist of the mid second century BCE and author of a handbook on Roman legal history) does not appear in the *Digest*. On the connection between *contumelia* and *iniuria*, see Triebs, *Studien zur Lex Dei*, I, 133–5 and, more recently, M. F. Prieto, *La difamación en el derecho romano* (Valencia, 2002). For meanings of forms of *ius* at 7. 3. 4, see above at Coll. 1. 6.

7. 4

Ulpian, *De officio proconsulis*, Book 8 under the Title *De Furibus*. See Lenel, *Paling.*, II, col. 983. For a variant of this passage, see *Dig.* 47. 17. 1. On the interrelationship of these passages, see Wieacker, *Textstufen*, 393–6 and, more recently, Nogrady, *Ulpian*, 273–7, who feels the Collator's text is close to the original. The phrase *ad forum* ('to the forum') at Coll. 7. 4. 1 means the case is sent to the appropriate court for a civil action. The *cognitio extraordinaria* or *extra ordinem* (a newer type of legal proceeding that operated under special rules and usually under imperial officials) evolved in the early empire. On the scholarly debate over this concept, see W. Turpin, '*Formula*, *Cognitio*, and proceedings *extra ordinem*', *RIDA* 46 (1999), 499–574 and, more recently, Harries, *Law and Crime*, 9 and 29–33. In this passage in the *Collatio*, the *cognitio extra ordinem* as described by Ulpian refers to a trial before a governor which had become the usual kind of legal procedure by the second century CE (and the only kind in the provinces). *Effractores* are engaged in 'breaking and entering' which could be translated with the older English label of 'housebreaker' or 'burglars' since 'burglary' as a crime in the modern USA has expanded from earlier treating only nocturnal thieves who break into a house to now including all thieves who enter a structure to commit a felony. On relegation, see above at Coll. 1. 7.

7. 5

Ps. Paulus, *Sententiae*, Book 2 (Krüger, 2. 31. 1–5; Liebs, 2. 43. 1–5). This passage also survived in Vs. and *LRV* 2. 32. 1–9 with minor variants. For instance, *LRV* has *concepti is agere potest.* While the sense is clear enough, there are extra letters in B (possibly the result of confusion with several forms of the same words in successive lines), although V and W have *conceptiva.* The form of theft denoted by *conceptum* means that someone had stolen goods in their possession that were discovered by an official search (and so had received stolen property). On *furtum conceptum*, see Gaius, *Inst.*, 3. 183–6, 191, and Pepe, *Richerche sul furto.* On the Roman legal concept of *infamia*, see recently McGinn, *Prostitution, Sexuality, and the Law*, 65–9.

TITLE 8: CONCERNING FALSE TESTIMONY (*DE FALSO TESTIMONIO*)[9]

8. 1

Deuteronomy 19: 16–20:

[*NRSV*] 16. If a malicious witness comes forward to accuse someone of wrongdoing, 17. then both parties to the dispute shall appear before the Lord, before the priests and the judges who are in office in those days, 18. and the judges shall make a thorough inquiry. If the witness is a false witness, having testified falsely against another, 19. then you shall do to the false witness just as the false witness had meant to do to the other. So you shall purge the evil from your midst. 20. The rest shall hear and be afraid, and a crime such as this shall never again be committed among you.

[Stuttgart Vulgate] *16. si steterit testis mendax contra hominem accusans eum praevaricationis 17. stabunt ambo quorum causa est ante Dominum in conspectu sacerdotum et iudicum qui fuerint in diebus illis 18. cumque diligentissime perscrutantes invenerint falsum testem dixisse contra fratrem suum mendacium 19. reddent ei sicut fratri suo facere cogitavit et auferes malum de medio tui 20. ut audientes ceteri timorem habeant et nequaquam talia audeant facere.*

There are noticeable differences here between the Collator's Latin Bible and the Vulgate and clear similarities to the Old Latin Bible in the Lyons Codex and Lucifer of Cagliari, *De Athanasio* 1. 7. This passage in Deuteronomy is a clarification of the ninth commandment against bearing false witness (found at Exodus 20: 16 and cited at Coll. 9. 1). Anthony Phillips, *Deuteronomy: Commentary* (Cambridge, 1973), 132–3, rightly points out that the clause at Deuteronomy 19: 19 is one of the rare examples of the *lex talionis* (or law of direct retaliation) in the Hebrew Bible and may stem from Near Eastern influence. For a similar type of retribution in ancient Mesopotamia, see *LH* 1–4. While some of the Roman laws have status differences in punishments, the Collator no doubt wanted his

[9] On perjury in Roman law, see Berger, 'Falsum', *Encyclopedic Dictionary*, 467; J. A. Crook, 'Lex Cornelia de falsis', *Athenaeum* 65 (1987), 163–71; A. D'Ors, 'Contribuciones a la historia del crimen falsi', in *Studi in onore di Edoardo Volterra* (Milan, 1977), II, 527–58; M. Piazza, *La disciplina del falso nel diritto romano* (Padua, 1991); Rilinger, *Humiliores-Honestiores*; O. F. Robinson, 'An aspect of *Falsum*', *TR* 60 (1992), 29–38; and R. Taubenschlag, 'Testimonium Falsum', *RE* (Stuttgart, 1934), supp. 5a, col. 1061.

audience to notice the absolute condemnation of false testimony in both Hebrew and Roman law.

8. 2

Ps. Paulus, *Liber singularis de poenis omnium legum* under the Title *Ad Legem Iuliam de Adulteris.* Lenel, *Paling.*, I, col. 1178. The *Lex Cornelia testamentaria* (also called the *Lex Cornelia de falsis*) was created in 81 BCE by Sulla. On *Falsum*, see further *CTh* 9. 19. 1–4.

8. 3

Ps. Paulus, *Sententiae*, Book 5 (Krüger, 5. 15. 5; Liebs, 5. 19. 10). A variant shortened text survives as *Dig.* 22. 5. 16. Another version survives in *LRV* 5. 17. 5. Mommsen's text of the *Digest* reproduces the section from the *Collatio* that is missing in the *Digest* (see 328, n. 17), but cites Paulus as the source (after stating in note 15 that this passage from Paulus' *Sententiae* comes from Coll. 8. 3). On relegation, see above at Coll. 1. 7.

8. 4

Ps. Paulus, *Sententiae*, Book 5 (Krüger, 5. 23. 1; Liebs, 5. 29. 1). The passage also survives in *LRV* 5. 25. 1. The Collator here cites the quotation as coming from *Idem libro*, and at Coll. 8. 3 the citation had been to *Sententiae* 5. Strangely enough, the Collator had already quoted the exact passage that he cites here at Coll. 1. 2. 1. This stands in all the manuscripts, although in W the first part of the citation to Paulus is missing, but since it is in V and B, it must have stood in α. So, we must suppose that the Collator had originally put the quotation in twice. It is possible that he could have forgotten at this point in his collection that he had already cited it or perhaps he believed it was such an essential definition that it could be used twice.

8. 5

Ps. Paulus, *Sententiae*, Book 5 (Krüger, 5. 25. 2; Liebs, 5. 31. 3). This passage also survives in *LRV* 5. 27. 2. For *honestiores* and *humiliores*, see Garnsey, *Social Status and Legal Privilege*, 221–76; Bauman, *Crime and Punishment in Ancient Rome*, 124–36; and, generally, Rilinger, *Humiliores-Honestiores*. On *deportatio*, see above at Coll. 1. 2.

8. 6

Ps. Paulus, *Sententiae*, Book 5 (Krüger, 5. 25. 3; Liebs, 5. 31. 4). This type of definition is typical of the jurists. The continuous run of usage of the *Sententiae* here is common in the *Collatio*.

8. 7

Ulpian, *De officio proconsulis*, Book 8 under the Title *De poena legis Corneliae testamentariae*. Lenel, *Paling.*, II, col. 978. A variant of this quotation survives as *Dig.* 48. 10. 9. 3, but leaves out the fuller details that the quotation in the *Collatio* preserves from Ulpian. On the interrelationship between these two passages, see Wieacker, *Textstufen*, 396–7 and, more recently, Nogrady, *Ulpian*, 217–21, who feels the *Collatio* text is the relatively best version of the text from Ulpian. The Collator ended his quotation with *et reliqua*, implying that he was working from a substantial part of *De officio proconsulis* (including at least Books 7–9).

The *senatusconsultum* was a frequently used tool of law-making in the early principate. For *dolo malo*, see above at Coll. 1. 3. The conflicting identification of the consuls as Statilius and Taurus in the first line of Coll. 8. 7. 1 and then Licinus and Taurus at the end of the same passage seems to result from scribal error. It should read Statilius and Taurus at the beginning and the second appearance is probably a gloss that crept in from the margins. Moreover, the first citation is itself an error as the consulship was shared by Sisenna Statilius Taurus and Lucius Scribonius Libo in 16 CE. Somewhere in the tradition either of Ulpian or of the *Collatio*, a fuller citation must have been given which was reduced over time to that error. The consulship of Marcus Aurelius Cotta and Marcus Valerius Messalla dates to 20 CE while that of Gaius Fufius Geminus and Lucius Rubellius Geminus dates to 29 CE. For the consular datings, see A. Degrassi, *I Fasti Consolari dell'Impero Romano* (Rome, 1952).

TITLE 9: CONCERNING NOT ADMITTING THE TESTIMONY OF FAMILY MEMBERS (*DE FAMILIARIS TESTIMONIO NON ADMITTENDO*)[10]

9. 1

Exodus 20: 16:

[*NRSV*] You shall not bear false witness against your neighbour.

[Stuttgart Vulgate] *non loqueris contra proximum tuum falsum testimonium.*

The Collator's Latin Bible has only minor differences from the Vulgate such as *contra* as opposed to *adversus* which is also used in the Old Latin Bible. Again, he probably drew from the Old Latin Bible (see Augustine, *Quaestionum in Heptateuchum* 2. 71; Ps. Augustine, *Speculum*, c.42; and Lucifer, *De Athanasio* 1. 3). In general, on this biblical stricture, see Propp, *Exodus*, 179–80. What is immediately noticeable is that the Collator could have cited this stricture at the beginning of Title 8, but chose instead to use the passage from Deuteronomy there (perhaps because of its greater specificity). Likewise, this passage here does not mention family members. It could be that the Collator noticed that the following Roman laws did not fit under the rubric of false testimony and so manufactured this other title and desperately looked for a biblical stricture to tie to it. This could imply some planning ahead of time before he actually composed the *Collatio*. That is, the Collator could have used Exodus 20: 16 at the beginning of Title 8 but knew he had to use it for Title 9, so he turned to Deuteronomy 19: 16–20 instead.

9. 2

Ulpian, *De officio proconsulis*, Book 8. Although B gives a reading of 9 (or VIIII) and V and W omit, Lenel, *Paling.*, II, col. 978, suggests this fragment actually belongs in Book 8 or VIII of the *De officio proconsulis* because a scribe made the simple mistake of VIIII for

[10] On the testimony of family members in Roman law, see Berger, 'Testimonium Domesticum', *Encyclopedic Dictionary*, 735; M. Kaser, 'Testimonium', *RE* (Stuttgart, 1934), supp. 5a, cols. 1021–61; C. Paulus, 'Testimonium', *Der Neue Pauly* (Stuttgart, 2002), XII, cols. 189–91; M. Radin, 'The privilege of confidential communication between lawyer and client', *California Law Review* 16 (1928), 487–97.

VIII. On this passage, see Nogrady, *Ulpian*, 231–4. Nogrady, 231, argues this was really from Book 9, but since so many of the Collator's fragments of this work come from Book 8, Lenel's argument seems more attractive.

Ulpian was dependant here upon the work of the early third-century jurist Callistratus, whose name must have dropped out of the manuscript tradition, although the citation to the eighty-eighth chapter comes from his work. A much longer variant text that allegedly comes directly from Callistratus survives as *Dig.* 22. 5. 3. The section introducing the passage at Coll. 9. 2. 1 probably derives from Ulpian. The passage in the *Collatio* appears at *Dig.* 22. 5. 3. 5 where Callistratus was commenting upon the *Lex Iulia de Vi*, on which see the comments of J. D. Cloud in Crawford, *Roman Statutes*, II, 789–92 as well as his earlier 'Lex Iulia de vi: Part I', *Athenaeum* 76, n. s. 66 (1988), 578–95 and 'Lex Iulia de vi: Part II', *Athenaeum* 77, n. s. 67 (1989), 427–65. While Cloud in *Roman Statutes*, II, 790, argues the *et reliqua* clause at Coll. 9. 2. 3 was actually part of the eighty-seventh chapter of Callistratus' work, since the Collator so often uses that phrase, it more likely indicates he was working from a longer text himself (in this case, Ulpian's *De officio proconsulis*).

The phrase *palamve corpore quaestum faciet feceritve* ('or he who has made or will make a profit by using his body publicly') at Coll. 9. 2. 2 is a euphemism for someone acting as a prostitute. Hyamson, 103, translates this as 'one who for profit shall act or shall have acted as a public performer'. Hyamson was no doubt influenced by the propriety of his time to avoid frank use of sexually explicit terms, as can be seen in a few other passages in the *Collatio*. For discussion of the exclusion of the testimony of prostitutes, see McGinn, *Prostitution, Sexuality, and the Law*, 61–4.

9. 3

Ps. Paulus, *Sententiae*, Book 5 (Krüger, 5. 15. 1–3; Liebs, 5. 19. 6–8). A much shorter version appears as *Dig.* 22. 5. 24. It also survives in *LRV* 5. 17. 1–3. On the influence of this part of Ps. Paulus on the Council of Carthage in 419, see Humfress, *Orthodoxy and the Courts*, 209 n. 52. Obviously, the idea of not having family members testify against each other survives in the common law concept of spousal privilege.

TITLE 10: CONCERNING DEPOSIT (*DE DEPOSITO*)[11]

10. 1

There is some dispute regarding this passage. Mommsen felt this biblical passage came only from Exodus 22: 7–8, Hyamson, 102, suggested it also came from Exodus 22: 11 or was perhaps a summary of 7–11.

[*NRSV*] 7. When someone delivers to a neighbour money or goods for safe keeping, and they are stolen from the neighbour's house, then the thief, if caught, shall pay double. 8. If the thief is not caught, the owner of the house shall be brought before God, to determine whether or not the owner had laid hands on the neighbour's goods. 9. In any case of disputed ownership involving ox, donkey, sheep, clothing, or any other loss, of which one party says, 'This is mine', the case of both parties shall come before God; the one whom God condemns shall pay double to the other. 10. When someone delivers to another a donkey, ox, sheep, or any other animal for safekeeping, and it dies or is injured or is carried off, without anyone seeing it, 11. an oath before the Lord shall decide between the two of them that the one has not laid hands on the property of the other; the owner shall accept the oath, and no restitution shall be made.

[Stuttgart Vulgate] *7. si quis commendaverit amico pecuniam aut vas in custodiam et ab eo qui susceperat furto ablata fuerint si invenitur fur duplum reddet 8. si latet dominus domus adplicabitur ad deos et iurabit quod non extenderit manum in rem proximi sui 9. ad perpetrandam fraudem tam in bove quam in asino et ove ac vestimento et quicquid damnum inferre potest ad deos utriusque causa perveniet et si illi iudicaverint duplum restituet proximo suo 10. si quis commendaverit proximo suo asinum bovem ovem et omne iumentum ad custodiam et mortuum fuerit aut debilitatum vel captum ab hostibus nullusque hoc viderit 11. iusiurandum erit in medio quod non extenderit manum ad rem proximi sui suscipietque dominus iuramentum et ille reddere non cogetur.*

Upon closer examination of the biblical text, it would appear that Hyamson is correct. The Collator is loosely summarizing the content

[11] On the Roman law of deposit, see Berger, 'Depositum', *Encyclopedic Dictionary*, 432; A. Bürge, *Retentio im römischen Sachen und Obligationenrecht* (Zurich, 1979); G. Gandolfi, *Il Deposito nella problematica della giurisprudenza romana* (Milan, 1976); M. Kaser and R. Knütel, *Römische Privatrecht*, 18th edn (Munich, 2005), 196–8; W. Litewski, 'Dei Personen des römischen Verwahrungsverhältnisses', *RIDA* 3, série 47 (2000), 235–349; and Zimmerman, *The Law of Obligations*, 205–20.

of Exodus 22: 7–11. Again, the Collator's biblical passage has some differences from the Vulgate and some similarities to the Old Latin Bible (surviving for this passage in the Würzburger Codex). On this biblical stricture, see Propp, *Exodus*, 246–9. The example of silver (as opposed to the biblical donkey, ox, or sheep) was probably chosen by the Collator because it would seem similar to the statements from the Roman jurists in this title. For comparison with similar Near Eastern laws regarding deposit, see *LE* 36–7 and *LH* 112, 120–6.

10. 2

Modestinus, *Liber differentiarum*, Book 2. Lenel, *Paling.*, I, col. 702. One sentence (Coll. 10. 2. 5) survives independently as a short quotation in *Dig.* 16. 3. 23. On the selection in the *Digest*, see Wieacker, *Textstufen*, 218–19. On the debate over whether there is an interpolation in this passage, see G. Beseler, 'Confestim-Continuo', *ZRG (R.A.)* 51 (1931), 188–202 at 198; Schulz, *History of Roman Legal Science*, 183; F. Pastori, *Il commodato in diritto romano* (Bologna, 1995), 289–99; and C. Cannata, *Richerche sulla risponsabilità contrattuale nel diritto romano* (Milan, 1996), 133 n. 43, who all argue it is interpolated and F. De Robertis, *Risponsibilita contrattuale nel diritto romano* (Bari, 1994), 314–20, who argues it is not. For further on the validity of the quotation from Modestinus, see D. Daube, 'Utiliter agere', *Iura* 11 (1960), 69–148, especially at 126–7 and, more recently, M. Navarra, 'Note in tema di "utilitas": Modestino e Coll. 10. 2', *Labeo* 50 (2004), 84–134. For meaning of forms of *ius* as collective Roman laws at 10. 2. 2 and 10. 2. 5, see above at Coll. 1. 6. For more on the Roman laws of deposit, see Bürge, *Retentio im römischen Sachen und Obligationenrecht*, 179–81.

10. 3

The Collator begins to cite a series of laws from the *Codex Hermogenianus*, under the Title *De Deposito* ('Concerning Deposit'). The Collator writes that Hermogenianus 'inserted constitutions of this kind' (*huiusmodi inserit constitutiones*) thereby giving us testimony of how Hermogenianus' lost work would have appeared. Since the laws run in chronological order, Corcoran, *Empire of the Tetrarchs*, 39, has suggested this may have been their original order in the *Codex Hermogenianus*.

The first of these constitutions leads off with 'Idem Augg. Caes.' probably because it was lifted directly from the *Codex Hermogenianus*. Normally, laws with just the abbreviations *augg.* and *caes.* from a Diocletianic law code are probably citing Diocletian and Maximian (similarly on the subscripts, see Corcoran, *Empire of the Tetrarchs*, 26–7) and the caesars are Constantius I and Galerius. Note that Corcoran, 'The Tetrarchy: Policy and image as reflected in imperial pronouncements' in D. Boschung and W. Eck (eds.), *Die Tetrarchie: eine neues Regierungssystem und seine mediale Präsentation* (Wiesbaden, 2006), 31–61 at 44–8 now suggests that the original *Codex Hermogenianus* did not have the emperors' names in its headings. However, to be fair to the Collator, the last law he quoted which also came from the *Codex Hermogenianus*, cites Diocletian and Maximian (Coll. 6. 5). It seems likely that the Collator had the *Codex Hermogenianus* close at hand, perhaps even open, from Coll. 6. 5–Coll. 10. 3. The constitution as it stands is addressed to one Flavius Munatius and it was subscribed at Serdica, in June of 293. From the content, Munatius appears to have been not a provincial governor, but rather a complainant in a legal proceeding. *PLRE*, I, 345, describes a Munatius Flavianus who was apparently a large landowner in Numidia (*AE* 1903, 243), but this may not have been the same person.

The three appearances of forms of *ius* can all be taken as the collective body of earlier Roman laws on these topics. See above at Coll. 1. 6.

10. 4

Also from the *Codex Hermogenianus*, this constitution of Diocletian and Maximian is directed to one Flavius Aurelius Altenicus Adronicus, about whom we have no further information, except that from the content of the rescript he had lost goods that he had deposited with people. The emperors advise him to go to the provincial governor. It dates to March of 294. For *ius* as a specific legal principle, see above at Coll. 1. 6.

10. 5

Another law from the *Codex Hermogenianus*, this constitution of Diocletian and Maximian is addressed to Aurelius, Eustathius, and

Diosimus. Because the first name Aurelius is so common (due to the Antonine Constitution of 212 which spread Roman citizenship), it could be that either the cognomen fell out of this passage over time or perhaps we should combine these three names into one or two. Indeed, the manuscript tradition records variants here with B giving *idem augustus et cesares a. et eustatio et diosimo*, W giving only *idem*, and V omitting the name. Regardless, there is not enough information to know who the addressees may have been. The law dates to October 294.

10. 6

Also from the *Codex Hermogenianus*, this rescript of Diocletian and Maximian dates to December of 294 and was subscribed at Nicomedia. We must assume that Septimia Quadratilla was a wealthy woman whose complaint made it way up the chain of command to catch the eye of the imperial chancery. Presumably, the law cited here is given as ammunition for Septimia's lawyer in a lawsuit. This constitution also survives in *CJ* 4. 34. 10, with some minor textual variants. For *dolo malo*, see above at Coll. 1. 7.

10. 7

Ps. Paulus, *Sententiae*, Book 2 (Krüger, 2. 12. 1–11; Liebs, 2. 14. 1–13). Parts of this quotation survive in the *Digest* in variant texts. *Dig.* 16. 3. 29 preserves a variant of the passage in Coll. 10. 7. 5 with some differences, for instance the version in the *Collatio* leaves out the statement regarding the interest owed to the depositor. Although Longo, 'Appunti', 125–7, argued this part of the citation in the *Digest* was added by Justinian's compilers, it is possible that it may have been originally been part of this passage. The Collator might have left out that part because his intention in this title seems to be to guard against the theft or loss of deposited goods or money (in keeping with the biblical passage at the beginning of the title). While Krüger and Liebs suggest that the principle discussed at *Dig.* 50. 16. 223 pr. which preserves a short statement on *lata culpa* ('gross negligence') may be another part of the Ps. Paulus quotation (6a) that was not used by the Collator, the content does not make the association secure. Likewise, see F. Schultz, 'Das Ediktsystem in den Paulus-Sentenzen', *ZRG (R.A.)* 47 (1927), 39–52 at 46. Parts of the passage

(Coll. 10. 7. 5 and 7) also survive in *LRV* 2. 12. 1–2. The form of *ius* at 10. 7. 1 refers to the general principles of Roman law (see above at Coll. 1. 6). On the *diu positum* at Coll. 10. 7. 2, see comments of Montemayor Aceves, *Mosaicarum*, 30, n. 51. For a similar construction to Coll. 10. 7. 2 on *quasi diu positum*, see Isidore of Seville, *Etymologies* 5. 25. The Twelve Tables reference at Coll. 10. 7. 11 may have been to Table VIII. 8 (see Crawford, *Roman Statutes*, II, 687). On the scholarly dispute over this part of the Twelve Tables, see R. Evans-Jones, 'The action of the Twelve Tables "ex causa depositii"', *Labeo* 34 (1988), 188–208. For *actiones in simplum*, see Berger, *Encyclopedic Dictionary*, 346.

10. 8

Codex Gregorianus, Book 4, under the Title of *De Deposito*. Here we can see how the Collator had several different works at hand. This citation preserves a rescript from Severus Alexander (r. 222–35) to the soldier Mestrius that was posted on 14 July 234. Honoré, *Emperors and Lawyers*, 111–14, attributes this rescript to the hypothetical secretary number 11. This law also survives in variant form as *CJ* 4. 34. 1 which preserves several differences, such as the addition of the clause *et latam culpam*. Such differences were either caused by the Collator (who, again, may have wanted to make the connection to the biblical passage at Coll. 10. 1 more clear) or by interpolations made by the compilers of the *Code of Justinian*.

The *actio ad exhibendum* refers to the legal right to demand to produce the item of dispute in court during a lawsuit. The phrase *rei vindicatio* refers to the legal mechanism to regain the item that was taken and so was a formal laying claim to property. See further, Berger, 'Exhibere', *Encyclopedic Dictionary*, 463 and, more fully, G. Demelius, *Die Exhibitionspflicht in ihrer Bedeutung für das classische und heutige Recht: juristische Untersuchung* (Graz, 1872).

10. 9

Paulus, *Liber responsorum*, Book 5, under the Title *Ex Locato et Conducto*. Here the Collator preserves a quotation from Paulus of a rescript of Caracalla dated to 213 to one Julius Agrippinus. A variant text of Caracalla's law survives as *CJ* 4. 65. 1 which includes some more words than the version in the *Collatio*, perhaps due to editorial handling on the part of the compilers of the Code. Honoré, *Emperors and Lawyers*, 88, attributes the rescript to secretary number 4, whom he hypothesizes might have been Arrius Menander. While Paulus felt this law pertained to the concept of *locatio conductio* (lease and hire), the Collator saw the connection to the protection of items being deposited and so included it in Title 10. For further development of the Roman concept of *locatio conductio*, see P. Du Plessis, 'Subletting and the Roman law of letting and hiring: Interpreting C. 4.65.6', *RIDA* 52 (2005), 131–44; 'Between theory and practice: New perspectives on the Roman law of letting and hiring', *Cambridge Law Journal* 65 (2006), 423–37; and 'The Roman concept of *lex contractus*', *Roman Legal Tradition* 3 (2006), 79–94. The Roman legal concept of *vis maior* ('superior force' or *force majeure*) refers to an action that cannot be stopped by human activity and survives in the modern concept of 'an act of God'. On *vis maior*, see D. Behrens, *Die vis maior und das klassische Haftungssystem* (Giessen, 1936); J.-F. Gerkens, '*Vis maior* and *vis cui resisti non potest*' in R. van den Bergh *et al.* (eds.), *Ex iusta causa traditum: Essays in honour of Eric H. Pool* (Pretoria, 2005), 109–20; and F. Sitzia, 'D. 19.2.15.2: "vis maior" e "vitia ex ipsa re"' in C. Cascione (ed.), *Fides humanitas ius: studi in onore di Luigi Labruna*, 7 (Naples, 2007), 5211–27.

TITLE 11: CONCERNING CATTLE RUSTLERS (*DE ABACTORIBUS*)[12]

11. 1

Exodus 22: 1 and 3:

[*NRSV*] 1. When someone steals an ox or a sheep, and slaughters it or sells it, the thief shall pay five oxen for an ox, and four sheep for a sheep . . . 3. The thief shall make restitution, but if unable to do so, shall be sold for the theft.

[12] On cattle rustling in Roman law, see S. Bello Rodriguez, 'Un rescripto de Adriano sobre el crimen de abigeatus: civiliter vel criminaliter agere?' in A. Murillo Villar (ed.), *La responsibilidad civil de Roma al derecho moderno* (Burgos, 2001), 93–104; A. Berger, 'Some remarks on cattle-stealing in Roman law', *Seminar* 2 (1944), 23–40; Berger, 'Abigeatus', *Encyclopedic Dictionary*, 338; L. M. Hartmann, 'Abigeatus', *RE* 1 (Stuttgart, 1893), col. 97; Robinson, *Criminal Law*, 25–6.

[Stuttgart Vulgate]: *1. si quis furatus fuerit bovem aut ovem et occiderit vel vendiderit quinque boves pro uno bove restituet et quattuor oves pro una ove . . . 3 . . . si non habuerit quod pro furto reddat venundabitur.*

The *NRSV* translation has rearranged the verses of the Hebrew, Septuagint, and Vulgate texts to move the sale of the thief as a slave if he cannot pay restitution earlier (and push the lawful killing of such a thief later). The Collator's Latin Bible has only minor differences from the Vulgate as the passage is fairly straightforward. Nonetheless, there are some clear verbal similarities to the Old Latin Bible (see Augustine, *Quaestionum in Heptateuchum*, 4. 10 and, especially, Ps. Augustine, *Speculum*, c.74). On this passage in general, see Propp, *Exodus*, 239–42. The Collator's decision not to include Exodus 22: 2 and the first part of 22: 3 may be to avoid the issue of blood guilt treated there. As elsewhere in the *Collatio*, his decision makes the biblical passage more similar to the Roman laws treated in this title. For comparison with ancient Mesopotamian law (which has compensation as tenfold for commoners or thirtyfold for the god or priest-king), see *LH* 8.

11. 2

Ps. Paulus, *Sententiae*, Book 5 (Krüger, 5. 18. 2; Liebs, 5. 24. 2). The harsher punishment of repeat offenders was probably meant as a deterrent.

11. 3

Ps. Paulus, *Sententiae*, Book 5 (Krüger, 5. 18. 1; Liebs, 5. 24. 1). This passage also survives in *LRV* 5. 20. 1. Hyamson took *pro qualitate eius* to denote the animals being stolen. It more likely refers to the class status of the rustler (see further, Garnsey, *Social Status and Legal Privilege*, 228, n. 3). The passage describing more than the amount being returned is similar to the passage in Exodus quoted at Coll. 11. 1 (and also to Mesopotamian law, see *LH* 8). See further, Berger, 'Actiones in simplum', *Encyclopedic Dictionary*, 346.

11. 4

Ps. Paulus, *Sententiae*, Book 5 (Krüger, 5. 18. 3; Liebs, 5. 24. 3). This passage also survives in *LRV* 5. 20. 2. Again, note that Roman law states the compensation must be double or triple the value (see above at Coll. 11. 3). The formula *ad forum* ('to the forum') indicates this will be settled in a civil court (above at Coll. 7. 4).

11. 5

Ps. Paulus, *Sententiae*, Book 5 (Krüger, 5. 18. 4; Liebs, 5. 24. 4). Here we again see the necessary juristic habit of specification.

11. 6

Ps. Paulus, *Liber singularis de poenis paganorum*, under the Title *De Abigeis*. This passage cites a rescript of the Emperor Antoninus Pius (r. 138–61) to the Council of the Province of Baetica (in southern Spain).

11. 7

Ulpian, *De Officio Proconsulis*, Book 8, under the Title *De Abigeis*. Lenel, *Paling.*, II, col. 982. A variant of this text survives in *Dig.* 47. 14. 1. pr. On the relationship between these texts, see Wieacker, *Textstufen*, 396–401, including a stemma. See also, more recently, Nogrady, *Ulpian*, 277–9, who stresses how the Collator probably stuck to the original text. The passage cites a rescript of the Emperor Hadrian to the Council of the Province of Baetica. The stipulation at Coll. 11. 7. 2 that that a first offender is executed, but a repeat offender is sentenced to life in the mines strikes a modern reader, and indeed apparently Ulpian, as bizarre. Ulpian hedges that perhaps the formula *ad gladium* might mean not execution, but rather sentencing to gladiatorial combat. Of course, it is possible that being sentenced to life imprisonment in the mines might have been considered worse than death. On this passage, see Bauman, *Crime and Punishment*, 158–9, and D. Nörr, *Rechtskritik in der römischen Antike* (Munich, 1974), 125, 131. On condemnation to the mines, see F. Millar, 'Condemnation to hard labour in the Roman Empire from the Julio-Claudians to Constantine', *PBSR* 52 (1984), 124–47, and M. Gustafson, 'Condemnation to the mines in the later Roman Empire', *HTR* 87 (1984), 421–33. In general, on mining in the Roman world, see J. Healy, *Mining and Metallurgy in the Greek and Roman World* (London, 1978) and J. C. Edmondson, 'Mining in the later Roman Empire and beyond: Continuity or disruption', *JRS* 79 (1989), 84–102.

The clause at 11. 7. 4 on the difference between three years and five years suggests that a gladiator might be discharged from fighting (and given a symbolic staff or wooden sword) after three years but could still be enslaved for two more years and might work as a trainer (*lanista*) or referee (such as a *summa rudis*). On gladiators and the games, see K. Hopkins, *Death and Renewal* (Cambridge, 1983); T. Wiedemann, *Emperors and Gladiators* (New York, 1992); and A. Futrell, *Blood in the Arena: The spectacle of Roman power* (Austin, 1997). The 'orders' mentioned are the imperial *mandata* to the governor. On *mandata*, see Millar, *Emperor in the Roman World*, 313–17.

11. 8

Ulpian, *De officio proconsulis*, Book 8, under the Title *De Abigeis*. Lenel, *Paling.*, II, cols. 982–3. The passage in the *Collatio* survives in a variant text in *Dig.* 47. 14. 1. 2–3. On the relationship of these texts, see Wieacker, *Textstufen*, 397–401, including a stemma. See also, more recently, Nogrady, *Ulpian*, 279–82. On the mines, see above at Coll. 11. 7. On relegation, see above at Coll. 1. 7.

TITLE 12: CONCERNING ARSONISTS (*DE INCENDIARIIS*)[13]

12. 1

Exodus 22: 6:

[*NRSV*] 6. When fire breaks out and catches in thorns so that the stacked grain or the standing grain or the field is consumed, the one who started the fire shall make full restitution.

[13] On arson in Roman law, see Berger, 'Incendiarius', *Encyclopedic Dictionary*, 496; S. Johnstone, 'On the uses of arson in classical Rome', *Studies in Latin Literature and Roman History* 6 (1992), 41–69; G. MacCormack, 'Criminal liability for fire in early and classical Roman law', *Index* 3 (1972), 382–96; Robinson, *Criminal Law*, 35–6. On the connection between arson and the *Lex Cornelia*, see Cloud, 'Leges Sicarii'.

[Stuttgart Vulgate] 6. *si egressus ignis invenerit spinas et conprehenderit acervos frugum sive stantes segetes in agris reddet damnum qui ignem succenderit.*

Again the Collator's Latin Bible has some clear minor differences from the Vulgate text, but leaves the sense of the passage as can be seen through the Septuagint and Hebrew text. Unfortunately, no corresponding portion of the Old Latin Bible survives. It is conceptually very similar to the passage immediately preceding it (Exodus 22: 5) dealing with damage of foreign animals to crops (see further, Driver, *Exodus*, 225–6). This passage from Exodus would also influence a twelfth-century Armenian law book. See R. W. Thomson (tr.), *The Lawcode (Datastangirk') of Mxit'ar Gos* (Amsterdam, 2000), 167–8.

12. 2

Ps. Paulus, *Sententiae*, Book 5 (Krüger, 5. 20. 2–3; Liebs, 5. 26. 2–3). This passage also survived in Vs., following Liebs, 'pseudopaulinischen Sentenzen', 228. Arson was naturally prohibited early on in Rome, as in all civilizations. For the Twelve Tables citation for arson, see further Crawford, *Roman Statutes*, II, 685–6 on Tabula VIII. 6. For relegation, see above at Coll. 1. 7.

12. 3

Ps. Paulus, *Sententiae*, Book 5 (Krüger, 5. 20. 4–5; Liebs, 5. 26. 4–5). This passage survived in Vs., following Liebs, 'pseudopaulinischen Sentenzen', 228. For relegation, see above at Coll. 1. 7.

12. 4

Ps. Paulus, *Sententiae*, Book 5 (Krüger, 5. 20. 1; Liebs, 5. 26. 1). This passage also survives in Vs., following Liebs, 'pseudopaulinischen Sentenzen', 228.

12. 5

Ulpian, *De officio proconsulis*, Book 8, under the Title *De Naufragis et Incendiariis*. Lenel, *Paling.*, II, cols. 981–2. The passage survives in a variant text in *Dig.* 47. 9. 12. The *Digest* passage keeps a sentence at the beginning that the version in the *Collatio* does not have and the *Collatio* has perhaps two extra sentences at the end (including the reference to the penalty for a fire in Rome). Mommsen, *Collatio*, 177, felt some of the text of the passage in the *Collatio* had fallen out of the manuscript tradition. On the interrelationship of these texts, see Wieacker, *Textstufen*, 401–2. See also, more recently, Nogrady, *Ulpian*, 202–10. Ulpian in this passage was treating topics from one of the laws associated with the Dictator Sulla, possibly the *Lex Cornelia de sicariis et veneficiis*.

12. 6

Allegedly from Ps. Paulus, *Liber singularis de poenis paganorum*, under the Title *De Abigeis*, but there is a problem with the citation here. Title 11 of the *Collatio* dealt with rustlers (*De Abigeis*) not Title 12 which deals with arson (*De Incendiariis*). The quotation itself does treat arson and is very similar to a section surviving as Ps. Paulus, *Sententiae* (Krüger, 5. 20; Liebs, 5. 26). It is likely that the citation here at Coll. 12. 6 is a scribal error and it should instead be to *Sententiae* Book 5 (or V), the same title as above. See further, Frakes, 'A note on *Collatio* 12. 6. 1 and Paulus', 1–5.

12. 7

Ulpian, *Liber ad edictum*, Book 18 under the Title *Si fatebitur iniuria occisum esse*. Lenel, *Paling.*, II, cols. 528–9. This section dealt with losses due to fire. On the prefatory statement *et cum diceret* after the title, see comments above at Coll. 2. 4 as well as Lenel, 'Kritisches und Exegetisches', 195–8. Variants of this quotation survive in the *Digest* at 9. 2. 27. 7–12. On the interrelationship between the version in the *Collatio* and in the *Digest*, see Wieacker, *Textstufen*, 237–48. The Collator had earlier quoted another part of this passage at Coll. 2. 4.

The noxal surrender mentioned at 12. 7. 6 refers to a penalty arising from the potential liability of a master for his/her slaves actions. The master could either pay the amount of the damage or surrender the slave(s). See Gaius, *Inst.*, 4. 75–7 (and above at Coll. 2. 3).

At 12. 7. 7, I translate the *aquilia* as an ablative of means. Hyamson instead took it as a nominative. The third-century BCE *Lex Aquilia* dealt with damages resulting from a wrongful act. Later, conceptually similar cases (where some of the specifics of the *Lex Aquilia* did not hold) could be made as part of an *actio in factum*. See Berger, 'Lex Aquilia', *Encyclopedic Dictionary*, 547–8, and 'Formula in ius concepta', *Encyclopedic Dictionary*, 475 (for the *actio in factum*); F. De Robertis, *Damnum Iniuria Datum*, 2 vols. (Bari, 2000–2); P. Gröschler, *Actiones in factum: eine Untersuchung zur Klage-Neuschöpfung im nichtvertraglichen Bereich* (Berlin, 2002); G. MacCormack, 'Juristic interpretation of the *Lex Aquilia*', *Studi in onore di Cesare Sanfilippo* 1 (Milan, 1982), 253–83; and G. Valditara, *Damnum iniuria datum*, 2nd edn (Turin, 2005). On the legal concept of *locatio conductio*, see Du Plessis, 'Subletting and the Roman law of letting and hiring'; 'Between theory and practice'; and 'The Roman concept of *lex contractus*'.

Scholars have long noticed that the text at Coll. 12. 7. 8 is problematic. The version surviving in the *Digest* has some interesting differences (Proculus is mentioned by name, the *si* in the third sentence is present, and the *non* in the last sentence is missing). So, either the version in the *Collatio* is in error (through scribal error or otherwise), or that in the *Digest*, or that in either of their sources for Ulpian's text. Ulpian's description itself is open to complexity with its citation to the sixth book of Vivianus (or perhaps to an extract of it) where that work cites an earlier interpretation by Proculus (on Proculus, see A. M. Honoré, 'Proculus', *TR* 30 (1962), 472–509). The *cautio* mentioned at the end of 12. 7. 8 refers to a guarantee against feared potential damage (see further, Berger, 'Cautio', *Encyclopedic Dictionary*, 384). Since the text in the *Digest* is missing the final *non*, it reads (using Alan Watson's translation at the end of *Dig.* 9. 2. 27. 10) 'I think your giving security against threatened damage will suffice.' The *non* in the version in the *Collatio* (whether stemming from the original Collator or an early scribe) is difficult. It could be part of what might have originally been an ablative absolute construction with *damno non facto* ('the damage not having been done'), but a manuscript error by the time of α had changed *facto* to *facti*. Or, somewhere in the manuscript tradition of the *Collatio* (or his copy of Ulpian) someone might have attempted to suggest that perhaps Proculus meant that when someone did not make a *cautio damni infecti* and then later damage did indeed arise, the injured party could sue as part of an *actio in factum* (see further, Berger, 'Cautio damni infecti', *Encyclopedic Dictionary*, 384). For a small sample of some scholarly work on this passage, see C. H. Monro (tr.), *Digest IX. 2: Lex Aquilia* (Cambridge, 1898), 37–41; Schulz, *History of Roman Legal Science*, 200; F. Lawson, *Negligence in the Civil Law* (Oxford, 1950), 105; Wieacker, *Textstufen*, 242–5; A. Watson, 'Two studies in textual history', *TR* 209 (1962), 209–42; Liebs, 'Rechtsschulen und Rechtsunterricht', 200; and Nörr, *Causa Mortis*, 171–2.

At 12. 7. 10, the reference to the loss of bees due to fire is complex. It seems to treat a situation where a neighbour used fire to destroy stray bees that swarmed to his property, rather than a case of a neighbour smoking them out (and thus dulling the release of the phermone isopentyl acetate) to harvest the honey since the verb is a form of *exuro* and not a form of *fumo*. Nevertheless, the owner suffered financial loss. This passage has received conflicting modern interpretations. See, for instance, B. Frier, 'Bees and lawyers', *Classical Journal* 78 (1982), 105–14, who suggests that the word *aedes* dropped out of the manuscript tradition after *tuas*; Nörr, *Cause Mortis*, 192–3, suggests smoke generated by the fire was used to drive off an unwelcome swarm; B. Frier, 'Why did the jurists change Roman law? Bees and lawyers revisited', *Index* 22 (1994), 135–49, uses this passage as a lens through which to view change in Roman law. While elegantly constructed, I am not convinced by A. Pretto-Sakmann, '"You never can tell with bees": Good advice from Pooh for students of the *Lex Aquilia*', in A. Burrows and A. Rodger (eds.), *Mapping the Law: Essays in honour of Peter Birks* (Oxford, 2006), 475–96, who suggests that kept bees were perceived as conceptually similar to cultivated fruit in Roman law. On apiculture in antiquity, see J. Klek and L. Armbruster, *Die Bienenkunde des Altertums*, 3 vols. (Leipzig, 1919–21) and, more recently, E. Crane, *The World History of Beekeeping and Honey Hunting* (New York, 1999). On the Roman perception of bees and doves occupying a status between domesticated and wild animals, see Pliny, *NH* 8. 220 and 11. 12. On dove and pigeon keeping in antiquity, see Varro, *Rerum rusticarum*, 3. 7–8.

Ulpian mentions many earlier jurists in this passage (which no doubt impressed the Collator). They include: Labeo (first century BCE/CE), Celsus (second century CE), Vivianus (perhaps early second century CE),[14] Neratius (end first/beginning of second

[14] See Kunkel, *Die Römischen Juristen*, 146.

century CE),[15] Proculus (first century CE), Urseius (first century CE), and Sabinus (first century CE). At Coll. 12. 7. 9, Hyamson, 121, in an apparent mistake names Proculus instead 'Paulus'. The 'Divine Severus' (Coll. 12. 7. 6) refers to the Emperor Septimius Severus.

TITLE 13: CONCERNING A MOVED BOUNDARY MARKER (*DE TERMINO AMOTO*)[16]

13. 1

Deuteronomy 19: 14:

[*NRSV*] 14. You must not move your neighbour's boundary marker, set up by former generations, on the property that will be allotted to you in the land that the Lord your God is giving you to possess.

[Stuttgart Vulgate] *14. non adsumes et transferes terminos proximi tui quos fixerunt priores in possessione tua quam Dominus Deus tuus dabit tibi in terra quam acceperis possidendam.*

The Collator's passage again has clear differences from the Vulgate and clear similarities to the Lyons Codex of the Old Latin Bible. This stricture is the same as that stressed in the Shechem Dodecalogue at Deuteronomy 27: 17 (see further Hyamson, 120, and von Rad, *Deuteronomy*, 129). Of course, moving property markers is a form of land theft (condemned by both Hebrew law and Roman law). The Collator edited out the allusion to God granting the land, perhaps following his pattern of slightly editing his biblical texts to help the comparison to the Roman laws.

[15] See *ibid.*, 144–5.

[16] On moving property markers in Roman law, see Berger, 'Terminum movere', *Encyclopedic Dictionary*, 732; G. MacCormack, 'Terminus motus', *RIDA* 26 (1979), 239–60; Robinson, *Criminal Law*, 40 (who contemplates a link to sacrilege); R. Taubenschlag, 'Terminus Motus', *RE* (Stuttgart, 1934), supp. 5a, cols. 784–5. Taubenschlag cites a work by G. H. Trotz, *De Termino Moto* (Trai., 1730) that I have unfortunately not yet been able to find.

13. 2

Ps. Paulus, *Sententiae*, Book 1 (Krüger, *Sententiae*, 1. 16. 1; Liebs, 1. 27. 1). This passage also survives in *LRV* 1. 16. 1. Property ownership is, of course, important in agricultural societies. This was naturally a concern to the Romans already in the Twelve Tables. See further, Crawford, *Roman Statutes*, II, 667–71 on Tabula VII. 2–5.

13. 3

Ulpian, *De officio proconsulis*, Book 8, under the Title *De Termino Moto*. The book number should perhaps be VIIII (i.e. IX), but one of the Roman numerals was lost during the manuscript tradition, following the argument of Lenel, *Paling.*, II, cols. 984–5. The passage preserves a rescript of the Emperor Hadrian from the year 119 to one Terentius Gentianus. This rescript is also cited by the jurist Callistratus (Lenel, *Paling.*, II, 984 n. 4 labels it Callistr., Frg. 19) and his citation survives in *Dig.* 47. 21. 2 (where it is cited as coming from his *liber tertio de cognitionibus*). Although Ulpian does not cite Callistratus by name here (Honoré, *Ulpian*, 128–38), this passage must represent usage by Ulpian of Callistratus. On the textual variants between the two versions, see Wieacker, *Textstufen*, 404–5. See also, more recently, Nogrady, *Ulpian*, 270–3 who feels that the Collator fairly accurately reproduced the original text. At Coll. 13. 3. 1, Hyamson, 123 (and, indeed, throughout his entire text) translates the Latin *divus* as either 'the emperor' or 'the late emperor' possibly to avoid the pagan implication of 'divine'.

Mommsen suggested adding a clause in 13. 3. 2 introducing the punishment of those lower in status (adopted from *Dig.* 47. 21. 2) that he felt had been lost in the manuscript tradition. As the error stands in all our manuscripts, it must have stood in α (and possibly may even be an error in the archetype). For a discussion of the connection between motives, status, and penalty in this passage, see Harries, *Law and Empire*, 144. On relegation, see above at Coll. 1. 7.

TITLE 14: CONCERNING KIDNAPPERS (*DE PLAGIARIIS*)[17]

14. 1

There is dispute among scholars over the source for this biblical stricture. Mommsen cites Exodus 21: 17 (which must actually be 21:16 as 21: 17 deals with the punishment for a child cursing his/her parents). Hyamson suggests Exodus 21: 16:

[*NRSV*] 16. Whoever kidnaps a person, whether that person has been sold or is still held in possession, shall be put to death.

[Stuttgart Vulgate] *16. qui furatus fuerit hominem et vendiderit eum convictus noxae morte moriatur.*

However, Hyamson also noted the similarity of the stricture in Exodus 21: 16 to Deuteronomy 24: 7:

[*NRSV*] 7. If someone is caught kidnapping another Israelite, enslaving or selling the Israelite, then that kidnapper shall die. So you shall purge the evil from your midst.

[Stuttgart Vulgate] *7. si deprehensus fuerit homo sollicitans fratrem suum de filiis Israhel et vendito eo accipiens pretium interficietur et auferes malum de medio tui.*

There seem to be parts of both these passages from Exodus and Deuteronomy in the Collator's quotation (the latter has a reference to Israel in it and the Collator just cited from Deuteronomy at Coll. 13. 1). It could even be possible that the Collator combined them. Even allowing for conflation, the Collator's passage is quite different from the Vulgate and is more similar to the Lyons Codex of the Old Latin Bible. Schulz, 'biblischen Texte', 39, suggests the Collator replaced *involaverit* with *plagiaverit* because it was the Roman legal term for kidnapping.

On Deuteronomy 24: 7, see Phillips, *Deuteronomy*, 161. For comparison with ancient Mesopotamian law, see *LH* 14. See also the

[17] On kidnapping in Roman law, see Bauman, *Crime and Punishment*, 110–12; Berger, 'Plagium', *Encyclopedic Dictionary*, 632; Berger, 'Lex Fabia', *RE* (Stuttgart, 1940), supp. 7, cols. 386–94; R. Lambertini, *Plagium* (Milan, 1980); G. Longo, 'Crimen plagii', *Annali della facoltà giuridica dell' università di Genova* 13 (1974), 381–482; Robinson, *Criminal Law*, 32–5.

comparative discussion regarding Mesopotamia and Greece in Driver, *Exodus*, 216–17.

14. 2

Ps. Paulus, *Sententiae*, Book 5 (Krüger, 5. 30b. 1–2; Liebs, 5. 37. 1–2). On the possible influence of a constitution of Constantine of 315 (surviving as *CTh* 9. 18. 1) on the Collator, see Masi, 'Contributi', 320–1; Cervenca, 'Ancora sul Problema', 253–8; De Francisci, 'Ancora', 97–101; and De Dominicis, 'Ancora', 337–42. On relegation, see above at Coll. 1. 7.

14. 3

Ulpian, *De officio proconsulis*, Book 9, under the Title *Ad legem Fabiam*. Lenel, *Paling.*, II, col. 985. On the importance of this passage, see Wieacker, *Textstufen*, 406–7 and, more fully, Nogrady, *Ulpian*, 299–305 (who makes use of *Dig.* 48. 15. 1, 2, 6, and 7). In this passage, the Collator preserves Ulpian's citation of a law of Caracalla (Antoninus Magnus). The Collator ends his quotation with *et reliqua*, confirming that he probably had the entire *De officio proconsulis* in front of him. The late republican *Lex Fabia* laid out punishments for kidnapping and aiding and abetting kidnapping. See further, Crawford, *Roman Statutes*, II, 755 and Bauman, *Crime and Punishment*, 110–12 (although Bauman adapts the text of this passage rather aggressively).

For *dolo malo* at 14. 3. 5, the meaning is that the buyer is intentionally procuring the slave through fraud (see above comments at Coll. 1. 7). At Coll. 14. 3. 6, we see the Collator's voice comparing the various juristic citations in this title to more recent constitutions (*novellis constitutionibus*). There has been scholarly argument over which constitutions these might have been. They might include those that were preserved as *CJ* 9. 20. 7 (287 CE) and *CTh* 9. 18. 1 (315 CE). See further, Dirksen, 'Über die Collatio', 122–3; Liebs, *Jurisprudenz im spätantiken Italien*, 164–6; and Corcoran, 'Sins of the fathers', 28 n. 59. While the Collator might have been referring to the law surviving as *CJ* 9. 20. 7, some might argue that he would have had access to that text via the *Codex Gregorianus*. However, we have seen that when the Collator used that collection as a source, he usually cited it explicitly. On the relationship between the imperial law preserved as *CTh* 9. 18. 1 and the Collator, there has been much debate over whether the Collator (or the scribe of Ulpian's work that the Collator used) may have made an interpolation. See further, Masi, 'Contributi', 317–21; Cervenca, 'Ancora', 253–8; De Francisci, 'Ancora', 97–101; and De Dominicis, 'Ancora', 337–42. The Collator ends this passage at Coll. 14. 3. 6 with a reflection on a passage from Paulus that he cited at Coll. 14. 2. 2, implying that we do have one voice throughout the *Collatio.*

TITLE 15: CONCERNING ASTROLOGERS, SORCERERS, AND MANICHEES (*DE MATHEMATICIS, MALEFICIS, ET MANICHAEIS*)[18]

15. 1

Deuteronomy 18: 10–14:

[*NRSV*] 10. No one shall be found among you who makes a son or daughter pass through fire, or who practises divination, or is a soothsayer, or an augur, or a sorcerer, 11. or one who casts spells, or who consults ghosts or spirits, or who seeks oracles from the dead. 12. For whoever does these things is abhorrent to the Lord; it is because of such abhorrent practices that the Lord your God is driving them out before you. 13. You must remain completely loyal to the Lord your God. 14. Although these nations that you are about to dispossess do give heed to soothsayers and diviners, as for you, the Lord your God does not permit you to do so.

[Stuttgart Vulgate] *10. nec inveniatur in te qui lustret filium suum aut filiam ducens per ignem aut qui ariolos sciscitetur et observet somnia atque auguria ne sit maleficus 11. ne incantator ne pythones consulat ne divinos et quaerat a mortuis veritatem 12. omnia enim haec abominatur Dominus et propter istiusmodi scelera delebit eos in introitu tuo 13. perfectus eris et absque macula cum Domino Deo tuo 14. gentes istae quarum possidebis terram augures et divinos audiunt tu autem a Domino Deo tuo aliter institutus es.*

[18] On astrology and sorcery in Roman law, see T. Barton, *Ancient Astrology* (London and New York, 1994); Berger, 'Magia', *Encyclopedic Dictionary*, 570; F. Cramer, *Astrology in Roman Law and Politics* (Philadelphia, 1954); Dickie, *Magic and Magicians in the Greco-Roman World*; Lotz, *Magiekonflikt*; and Luck, *Arcana Mundi.* On Manichaeism, see Brown, 'Diffusion of Manichaeism in the Roman Empire', 92–103; Gardner and Lieu, 'Manichaean documents from Roman Egypt', 146–69; Lieu, *Manichaeism in the Later Roman Empire and Medieval China*; and Lieu, *Manichaeism in Mesopotamia and the Roman East.*

In general, on this passage see von Rad, *Deuteronomy*, 122–5 and Phillips, *Deuteronomy*, 124–5. The Collator's text has several clear differences to that of the Vulgate. However, the Collator's Bible also has some differences from corresponding surviving passages of the Old Latin Bible (of the surviving texts, the Collator's passage is closest to Ps. Augustine, *Speculum*, c.55). Moreover, there are substantial differences between the text of Deuteronomy 18: 10–14 in the Vulgate text (and, in the main, the Hebrew text, Greek Septuagint, and the English translation of the *NRSV*) on the one hand and the text cited by the Collator on the other. Schulz, 'biblischen Texte', 39–40, argued that the clause added at Coll 15. 1. 2 (which adds the goal of discovering the gender of an unborn child as well as an evaluative comment upon all such divination) was a gloss that crept into the manuscript during the transmission process in the Middle Ages. Certainly, a curiosity about the gender of an unborn child is very normal (leading to invasive procedures in the modern age). While it is possible this was a gloss, augury is certainly already mentioned at the beginning of the biblical passage. It would appear that the Collator, or a scribe early in the manuscript tradition, desired to elaborate upon these different types of sorcery (and it seems to have stood in α). Likewise, the sentence at 15. 1. 3 (on various types of forbidden divination) that Mommsen felt was a gloss (following the advice of Julius Wellhausen) might also have already stemmed from the Collator elaborating upon forbidden practices and also probably stood in α. Moreover, the reference to the snake charmer and necromancy are also in the Vulgate version. The two references to necromancy in the Collator's version may have been influenced by the legend of the Witch of Endor (1 Samuel: 28. 7–25) and her raising the ghost of the prophet Samuel for King Saul that resonated in early Church history. On this legend, see K. A. D. Smelik, 'The Witch of Endor: I Samuel 28 in rabbinic and Christian exegesis till 800 AD', *Vigiliae Christianae* 33 (1979), 160–79, and, more recently, R. Greer and M. Mitchell (tr.), *The 'Belly-Myther' of Endor: Interpretations of 1 Kingdoms 28 in the early Church* (Atlanta, 2007).

There are other differences in the Collator's text also such as the reference to the Chaldeans (which appears in all three manuscripts of the *Collatio*). What is more interesting is that there is a reference to Chaldeans in the following passage from Ulpian. By the Collator's day, many laws from pagan and, more recently, Christian emperors had banned divination (as we have seen in legislation of Constantine and Constantius II). So, some of these variants in the biblical passage may stem from the Collator shaping his biblical passage to align with religious interests of his day and to compare with anti-magic aspects of the text of Ulpian that follows.

15. 2

Ulpian, *De Officio Proconsulis*, Book 7, under the Title *De Mathematicis et Vaticinatoribus*. Lenel, *Paling*., II, col. 975. On this passage, see, briefly, Wieacker, *Textstufen*, 407 n. 89 and, more fully, Nogrady, *Ulpian*, 187–98, who supports the authenticity of the citation. *Sententiae* 5. 21 is also entitled *De Vaticinatorbus et Mathematicis*. Although the Collator certainly made great use of the *Sententiae*, especially Book 5, he must have preferred the fuller nature of Ulpian's coverage.

The consulship of Pomponius and Rufus was in the latter part of 16 CE under the emperor Tiberius. It should be noted that this law banned the use of astrology for political purposes. *Divus* Pius refers to the emperor Antoninus Pius. Pacatus was governor of Lugdunensis sometime between 140 and 143 (Nogrady, *Ulpian*, argues for a date of *c*.140–1). On the dating, see further, H. Dohrmann, *Anerkennung und Bekämpfung von Menschenopfern im römischen Strafrecht der Kaiserzeit* (Frankfurt, 1995), 122–6, who hypothesizes that Pacatus might have arrested a Druid and was asking the emperor for instruction on how to proceed. The sedition of Avidius Cassius was in 175 CE during the reign of Marcus Aurelius. On relegation, see above at Coll. 1. 7. In general, on the Roman view of the political uses of astrology, see Cramer, *Astrology in Roman Law and Politics*, 232–81. On the puzzle of death as opposed to more serious punishments alluded to at 15. 2. 3, 'by death' (*capite*) denoted simple execution by the sword whereas 'by more serious punishment' (*alia poena graviore*) would include crucifixion, condemnation to the beasts, and burning alive. Some death penalties were clearly more serious than others.

15. 3

Codex Gregorianus, Book 7 (or VII), under the Title *De Maleficis et Manichaeis*. The B manuscript gives the book number as VII, the

V manuscript as VI, and W omits. Krüger, *Codicis Gregoriani Fragmenta*, 242, proposed instead Book XIV. The text in all three manuscripts gives *de maleficis et Manichaeis*, so this must have stood at least in α. And the beginning of the title in B reads reads 'INCIP XV. DE MATHEMATICIS et manicheis.' However, the end of the Title reads 'Expl. TITULUS de MATHEMATICS MALEFICIS ET MANICHEIS.' The combination of *Mathematicis* and *maleficis* occurs also in *CJ* 9. 18 and *CTh* 9. 16, so it probably stood in the *Codex Gregorianus* which was to a large extent the model for these later imperial law codes (see the comments of Rives, 'Magic in Roman law', 334 n. 65). The compiler of the *Codex Gregorianus* might have included Manichees in this title due to the hostility in Diocletian's rescript. It could be that Diocletian's legitimacy was threatened equally by astrology and by a new religion such as Manichaeism (and, indeed, Christianity). Likewise, the biblical stricture cited at the beginning of this title mentions foreigners as does the reference to Chaldeans at Coll. 15. 2. The Collator may have chosen to include the law against Manichees because he saw the connection between *mathematicis* and *maleficis* and Manichaeism in the *Codex Gregorianus* and because of the presence of Manichees in Italy in the late fourth century (see Augustine, *Confessions* 5. 3–11 and Brown, *Augustine of Hippo*, 46–60).

This passage presents a long rescript of Diocletian and Maximianus regarding the dangers of Persian Manichaeism to Julian, Proconsul of Africa, dating possibly to 31 March 302. Some have argued for a dating to 297 (see Barnes, *New Empire*, 55 n. 41). On this rescript, see further, Pharr, 'Interdiction of magic', 290–1; Corcoran, *Empire of the Tetrarchs*, 135–6 and 'Sins of the father', 11–12; and Humfress, *Orthodoxy and the Courts*, 245–6. Since the standard view of the compilation of the *Codex Gregorianus* is *c.*291, this rescript must have been added later, perhaps by the original compiler or by a later editor who felt it was a significant addition. This constitution is useful in gauging Diocletian's views of newer religions that challenged traditional Roman pagan beliefs (which would soon result in his general Edict of Persecution in 303). Liebs, 'pseudopaulinischen Sentenzen', 228, hypothesizes that the compiler of the *Sententiae* might have been dependant on this passage from the *Codex Gregorianus* for Ps. Paulus, *Sententiae* (Krüger, 5. 21. 2; Liebs, 5. 27. 2).

TITLE 16: CONCERNING LEGITIMATE SUCCESSION (*DE LEGITIMA SUCCESSIONE*)[19]

16. 1

Numbers 27: 1–11

[*NRSV*] 1. Then the daughters of Zelophehad came forward. Zelophehad was son of Hepher son of Gilead son of Machir son of Manasseh son of Joseph, a member of the Manassite clans. The names of his daughters were: Mahlah, Noah, Hoglah, Milcah, and Tirzah. 2. They stood before Moses, Eleazar the priest, the leaders, and all the congregation, at the entrance of the tent of meeting, and they said, 3. 'Our father died in the wilderness; he was not among the company of those who gathered themselves together against the Lord in the company of Korah, but died for his own sin; and he had no sons. 4. Why should the name of our father be taken away from his clan because he had no son? Give to us a possession among our father's brothers.' 5. Moses brought their case before the Lord. 6. And the Lord spoke to Moses, saying: 7. The daughters of Zelophehad are right in what they are saying; you shall indeed let them possess an inheritance among their father's brothers and pass the inheritance of their father on to them. 8. You shall also say to the Israelites, 'If a man dies, and has no son, then you shall pass his inheritance on to his daughter. 9. If he has no daughter, then you shall give his inheritance to his brothers. 10. If he has no brothers, then you shall give his inheritance to his father's brothers. 11. And if his father has no brothers, then you shall give his inheritance to the nearest kinsman of his clan, and he shall possess it. It shall be for the Israelites a statute and ordinance, as the Lord commanded Moses.'

[19] On inheritance in Roman law, see, among others, Berger, 'Succedere (successio)' and 'Testamentum' in *Encyclopedic Dictionary*, 722 and 733; Gardner, *Family and Familia*; F. Lucrezi, *La Successione intestata in diritto ebraico e romano. Studi sulla Collatio* (Turin, 2005), III; J. Merkel, *Die Lehre von der successio graduum unter Intestaterben* (Tübingen, 1876); G. Oliviero, 'A proposito di succcessio ordinum nell'eredità in testata della Dodici Tavole', *SDHI* 68 (2002), 625–31; R. Saller, 'Family and household' in A. K. Bowman, P. Garnsey, and D. Rathbone (eds.), *Cambridge Ancient History*, XI: *The High Empire, AD 70–192*, 2nd edn (Cambridge, 2000), 855–74; A. Sanguinetti, *Dalla querela alla portio legitima: aspetti della successione necessaria nell' epoca tardo imperiale e giustinianea* (Milan, 1996); P. Voci, *Diritto ereditario romano*, 2nd edn, 2 vols. (Milan, 1963–7); and Watson, *Law of Succession in the later Roman Republic*.

[Stuttgart Vulgate] *1. accesserunt autem filiae Salphaad filii Epher filii Galaad filii Machir filii Manasse qui fuit filius Ioseph quarum sunt nomina Maala et Noa et Egla et Melcha et Thersa 2. steteruntque coram Mosen et Eleazaro sacerdote et cunctis principibus populi ad ostium tabernaculi foederis atque dixerunt 3. pater noster mortuus est in deserto nec fuit in seditione quae concitata est contra Dominum sub Core sed in peccato suo mortuus est hic non habuit mares filios cur tollitur nomen illius de familia sua quia non habet filium date nobis possessionem inter cognatos patris nostri 4. rettulitque Moses causam earum ad iudicium Domini 5. qui dixit ad eum 6. iustam rem postulant filiae Salphaad da eis possessionem inter cognatos patris sui et ei in hereditate succedant 7. ad filios autem Israhel loqueris haec 8. homo cum mortuus fuerit absque filio ad filiam eius transibit hereditas 9. si filiam non habuerit habebit successores fratres suos 10. quod si et fratres non fuerint dabitis hereditatem fratribus patris eius 11. sin autem nec patruos habuerit dabitur hereditas his qui ei proximi sunt eritque hoc filiis Israhel sanctum lege perpetua sicut praecepit Dominus Mosi.*

The Collator's biblical passage has many differences from the Vulgate but is again closer to the Lyons Codex of the Old Latin Bible, with some probable editing on the Collator's part. In general, on this biblical passage see John Sturdy, *Numbers* (Cambridge, 1976), 193–5, and Levine, *Numbers*, 341–8. For comparison with other Near Eastern laws, see *LH* 165–72. Hyamson, 133, argued that verses 8–10 fell out of the textual tradition of the *Collatio*. While the argument that these verses were lost due to scribal error is possible, we have seen that the Collator often edited the biblical passages to make the comparison with Roman law stronger. It seems more likely that he is doing the same thing here. Additionally, the Collator somewhat compresses the text of the other parts of the passage. For instance, he cuts out the ancestry of Zelophehad (or Salfad), the names of the daughters, and the detail that he was not in the company of Korah and those who opposed Moses' leadership during the Exodus (all of which stand in the Vulgate, Septuagint, and Hebrew texts). These instances are all in keeping with the Collator's editorial practice. It should be noted that this is the only title of the *Collatio* not to include the phrase *Moyses dicit* ('Moses says') at the beginning, but rather *Scriptura divina sic dicit* ('the Divine Scripture says thus'). However, this introductory fomula could still be the Collator's voice, because we see at Coll. 6. 7. 1 the phrase *lex divina sic dicit* ('the Divine Law says thus'). Such phraseology rules out the possibility that the Collator might have been a pagan.

16. 2

This passage comes from Gaius, *Liber Institutionum*, 3. 1–17. While we have a large amount of this famous jurist's work in a palimpsest that was discovered in 1816 by B. G. Niebuhr, the first part of Book 3 (i.e. 1–5) is missing and is restored from the *Collatio* (and the sixth-century *Institutes* of Justinian, 3. 1). For an apograph of the palimpsest, which suffered further from applications of chemical solutions by zealous nineteenth-century scholars, see W. Studemond (ed.), *Gaii Institutiones* (Leipzig, 1873), especially 17–18. The text of Gaius, *Inst.*, 3. 5–17 shows some variants from the passage in the *Collatio*. See further, the *apparatus criticus* of E. Seckel and B. Kübler, *Gai Institutiones* (Stuttgart, 1935; reprinted 1969). On the interrelationship of the texts, see Wieacker, *Textstufen*, 195–6, and, more recently, Nelson, *Überlieferung, Aufbau und Stil von Gai Institutiones*, 116–23. In general, on this part of Gaius' work, see Nelson and Manthe, *Gai Institutiones III. 1–87*.

Throughout Title 16, I follow Gordon and Robinson, *Institutes of Gaius*, 544, who translate forms of *suus heres* as 'immediate heirs.' Hyamson's more awkward 'self-successors' is unclear to the modern reader as is also the literal 'one's own heirs', while F. de Zulueta (tr.), *The Institutes of Gaius, Part I* (Oxford, 1946) left the phrase in Latin. Traditionally, *sui heredes* are Roman citizens who were in *patria potestas* when the *paterfamilias* was alive and normally would inherit his wealth after his death.

The *causae probatio* at Coll. 16. 2. 5 was a legal process through which a child born to a Roman citizen and a non-citizen woman could gain inheritance rights (see further, Berger, *Encyclopedic Dictionary*, 383). The *Lex Aelia Sentia* mentioned at 16. 2. 5, was a law from the early empire (4 CE) that restricted manumission. See further, Berger, 'Lex Aelia Sentia', *Encyclopedic Dictionary*, 547; J. Gardner, *Being a Roman Citizen* (London, 1993), 41–4; and Sherwin-White, *Roman Citizenship*, 280–94. On the process of manumission and its role in Roman inheritance law, see Gardner, *Family and Familia*, 6–20. On women's role in inheritance in Roman law, see J. Gardner, *Women in Roman Law and Society* (London, 1986), 163–204.

There is a problem with the text at Coll. 16. 2. 8 as the phrase *altera dimidia* stands in the nominative singular and means 'the other half'. At some point in the manuscript tradition a clause from the *Institutes* must have dropped out from this passage. It is insightful that the manuscripts all render the *dimidia* as *dimidiam*, and W even changed *altera* to *alteram*, showing that the copyists were attempting to fix an existing problem in the text. This implies that the reading had already existed in the manuscript at the stage of α. The phrase *de agnatis* ('concerning agnates') that appears in the *Collatio* at Coll. 16. 2. 9 seems to be a gloss that crept into the manuscript tradition (in which case it must have happened early as it is in B and W, and so must have stood at least in α). On the *patrueles* and *consobrinos* at Coll. 16. 2. 10, see A. C. Bush, '*Consobrinus* and Cousin', *The Classical Journal* 68 (1972–3), 161–5.

Forms of *ius* at 16. 2. 5, 12, 14, 15, 16, and 17 have been variously translated as 'law' (in the collective sense), 'right', 'legal right', and 'legal principle' depending on the context (see above at Coll. 1. 6). In general, on the relationship between Gaius' description and the traditional inheritance law of the Twelve Tables, see Lucrezi, *La successione intestata*, 28–35. On this part of the Twelve Tables, Tabula V. 4–5, see further, Crawford, *Roman Statutes*, II, 640–2.

16. 3

Ps. Paulus, *Sententiae*, Book 4 (Krüger, 4. 8. 1–20; Liebs, 4. 7. 1–20). This passage in the *Collatio* is crucial for the reconstruction of this passage from the *Sententiae* (see further, Krüger). Parts of this passage (Coll. 16. 3. 14–20) also survive in *LRV* 4. 8. 1–3. Liebs, 'pseudopaulinischen Sentenzen', 197, hypothesizes that the anonymous compiler of the *Sententiae* might have obtained some of this information from Modestinus, due to the close similarity of Coll. 16. 3. 14 with a quotation from Modestinus' *Pandects* in the *Digest* (38. 7. 5 pr.).

This passage contains many revealing aspects of the Roman law of testaments. Cutting the string of a testament was a practical way of making a will invalid. In classical Roman law, the only way for a testator to make a will invalid was to write a new testament. On the *exceptio doli* mentioned at Coll. 16. 3. 1, see Berger, 'Exceptio doli', *Encyclopedic Dictionary*, 459 and, more recently, A. Wacke, 'La "exceptio doli" lo rende possibile: fedecommesso in favore di terza e fedecomissaria liberazione dell' obbligo di restituzione della dote', *Iura* 46 (1995), 21–45.

At 16. 3. 4, on the *Lex Iulia de maritandis ordinibus*, of 18 BCE, and the *Lex Papia Poppaea*, 9 CE in the consulship of M. Papius Mutilus and Q. Poppaeus Secundus, see Berger, 'Lex Iulia de maritandis ordinibus', *Encyclopedic Dictionary*, 553; Crawford, *Roman Statutes*, II, 801–9; Treggiari, *Roman Marriage*, 60–80; Evans Grubbs, *Law and Family in Late Antiquity*, 103–39 (on Constantine's repeal of some provisions); and McGinn, *Prostitution, Sexuality, and the Law*, 70–139. Later Roman jurists treated these laws in a unified sense and at times denoted them collectively in the singular tense as is the case in our passage.

At Coll. 16. 3. 7 (and 16. 3. 16), there is an allusion in Ps. Paulus to the Roman legal concept of *erroris causae probatio*. This was a Roman legal Roman formula dating at least to the *Lex Aelia Sentia* (4 CE) denoting marriages between parties of different status. This statute provided a process by which male children of mixed marriages (i.e. citizen and non-citizen) could gain citizenship and succession rights from the praetor or provincial governor (see above on the *causae probatio* at Coll. 16. 2. 5). Presumably, this would ensure a large supply of potential soldiers or, more likely, win continued loyalty for Octavian and his successors. See Gaius, *Inst.* 1. 28–32b, 1. 66–7. See further, M. Kaser, *Römische Privatrecht*, 2nd edn (Munich, 1971), I, 279–80 (more recent editions of this book have eliminated this entry, perhaps because it was so rare). More fully, see C. Terreni, 'Gaio e L'"Erroris Causae Probatio"', *Labeo* 45 (1999), 333–67. Forms of *ius* at 16. 3. 2, 5, and 16 have been variously translated as 'legal principle' and 'law' (in the collective sense), depending on the context (see above at Coll. 1. 6).

For emancipation at 16. 3. 15, see Gardner, *Family and Familia*, 6–113. At 16. 3. 20 on the *Lex Voconia* of 169 BCE, see Berger, 'Lex Voconia', *Encyclopedic Dictionary*, 56; A. J. B. Sirks, '*Sacra*, succession and the *lex Voconia*', *Latomus* 53 (1994), 273–96; Treggiari, *Roman Marriage*, 365–6; T. van der Meer, 'The Voconian Law: Nova or phoenix?', *TR* 67 (1999), 115–23; and A. Weishaupt, *Die lex Voconia* (Vienna, 1999).

16. 4

Ps. Ulpian, *Liber singularis regularum*, 26. 1 and 1a. For other sections of this passage, see P. Krüger, *Ulpiani Liber Singularis Regularum* in *Collectio Librorum Iuris Anteiustiniani* (Berlin, 1878), II; Lenel,

Paling., II, col. 1016; and, more recently, Avenarius, *Der Pseudo Ulpianische*, 489–91, and his *Die Pseudo-Ulpianische*, 60–2. For the Twelve Tables citation, see Crawford, *Roman Statutes*, II, 640–2. At 16. 4. 2, *iura* is translated as legal rights denoting powers that emanated from earlier laws (see above at Coll. 1. 6).

16. 5

Although the last book entitled *Institutes* quoted by the Collator was that of Gaius at Coll. 16. 2, the text here dos not come from Gaius but instead stems from the *Institutes* of the last author quoted, i.e. Ulpian. The text here presumably came from the Title *De Successionibus ab Intestato* from Ulpian's *Institutes*. See Lenel, *Paling.*, II, cols. 929–30. On the text here and its connection to Ulpian, and probable lack of glosses, see Wieacker, *Textstufen*, 212–13.

16. 6

Ulpian, *Institutes*. See Lenel, *Paling.*, II, cols. 929–30. On the text, see Wieacker, *Textstufen*, 212–13. For the *erroris causae probatio* at Coll. 16. 6. 1, see above at Coll. 16. 2. 5 and 16. 3. 7.

16. 7

Ulpian, *Institutes*. See Lenel, *Paling.*, II, cols. 929–30. On the text, see Wieacker, *Textstufen*, 212–13. On emancipation, see Gardner, *Family and Familia*, 6–113.

16. 8

Although Coll. 16. 8. 1 implies this passage comes from the Title *De Suis Heredibus*, the content suggests it might also be from the same section of Ulpian's *Institutes* used in Coll. 16. 5–7. See further, Lenel, *Paling.*, II, cols. 929–30. On the text, see Wieacker, *Textstufen*, 212–13. For the Twelve Tables citation at Coll. 16. 8. 2, see Crawford, *Roman Statutes*, II, 646–8, on Tabula V. 8.

16. 9

Ulpian, *Institutes.* See Lenel, *Paling.*, II, col. 930. On the text here and its connection to Ulpian, see Wieacker, *Textstufen*, 212–13. For the process of emancipation at 16. 9. 2, see Gardner, *Family and Familia*, 6–113. For the Twelve Tables citation at Coll. 16. 9. 2, see Crawford, *Roman Statutes*, II, 646–8 on Tabula V. 8. The *occasione iuris* at 16. 9. 2 refers to a legal technicality that is to someone's advantage. On *occasio*, see Berger, *Encyclopedic Dictionary*, 606. For the *decima* at Coll. 16. 9. 3 (later repealed by *CJ* 9. 57. 2 of 410), see Berger, *Encyclopedic Dictionary*, 426.

Table 1: The Collator's Alleged Sources

Abbreviations given here will be used in Table 3

1. Paulus

    (a) *Liber responsorum* [LR]

    Book 5
    Under Title *Ex locato et conducto*: Coll. 10. 9

    (b) Ps. Paulus, *Liber singularis de iniuriis* [LSI]

    Under Title *De Iniuriis*: Coll. 2. 5
    Under Title *Quemadmodum iniuriarum agatur*: Coll. 2. 6

    (c) Ps. Paulus, *Liber singularis de poenis paganorum* [LSPP]

    Under Title *De abigeis*: Coll. 11. 6

    (d) Ps. Paulus, *Liber singularis de poenis omnium legum* [LSDOL]

    Under Title *Ad legem Iuliam de adulteris*: Coll. 8. 2

    (e) Ps. Paulus, *Liber singularis de adulteriis* [LSA]

    Under Title (name not given): Coll. 4. 2; 4. 3; 4. 4; 4. 6

    (f) Ps. Paulus, *Sententiae* [Sent.]

    Book 1
    Under Title *Finium regendorum*: Coll. 13. 2

    Book 2
    Under Title *Ad legem Corneliam de adulteriis*: Coll. 4. 12; 5. 2
    Under Title *De nuptiis*: Coll. 6. 3
    Under Title *De furibus*: Coll. 7. 5
    Under Title *De deposito*: Coll. 10. 7

    Book 4
    Under Title *De intestatorum successionibus*: Coll. 16. 3

    Book 5
    Under Title *Ad legem Corneliam de sicariis et veneficis*: Coll. 1. 2; 1. 3; 1. 4; 1. 7; 1. 13; 2. 7; 3. 2; 7. 2; 8. 4

Under Title *De testibus et de quaestionibus*: Coll. 8. 3; 9. 3
Under Title *De legem Corneliam testamentariam*: Coll. 8. 5; 8. 6
Under Title *De abactoribus*: Coll. 11. 2; 11. 3; 11. 4; 11.5
Under Title *De incendariis*: Coll. 12. 2; 12. 3; 12. 4; 12. 6
Under Title *Ad legem Fabiam*: Coll. 14. 2

2. Ulpian

(a) *Liber de officio proconsulis* [LOP]

Book 7
Under Title *De sicariis et veneficis*: Coll. 1. 3; 1. 6; 1. 11
Under Title *De mathematicis et vaticinatoribus*: Coll. 15. 2

Book 8
Under Title *De dominorum saevitia*: Coll. 3. 3
Under Title *De furibus*: Coll. 7. 4
Under Title *De poena legis Corneliae testamentariae*: Coll. 8. 7
Under Title *Ad legem Iuliam de vi publica et privata*: Coll. 9. 2
Under Title *De abigeis*: Coll. 11. 7, Coll. 11. 8
Under Title *De naufragis et incendiariis*: Coll. 12. 5
Under Title *De termino mota*: Coll. 13. 3

Book 9
Under the Title *Ad legem Fabiam*: Coll. 14. 3

(b) *Institutionum Libri* [Inst.]

Under Title *De legitimis hereditatibus*: Coll. 16. 5; 16. 6; 16. 7
Under Title *De suis heredibus*: Coll. 16. 8; 16. 9

(c) *Liber ad edictum* [LAE]

Book 18
Under Title *Si fatebitur iniuria occisum esse*: Coll. 2. 4; 12. 7
Under Title *Si quadrupes pauperiem dederit*: Coll. 7. 3

(d) Ps. Ulpian, *Liber singularis regularum* [LSR]

Under Title *De iniuriis*: Coll. 2. 2
Under Title *De nuptiis*: Coll. 6. 2
Under Title *De legitimis hereditatibus*: Coll. 16. 4

3. Papinian

(a) *Liber definitionum* [LD]

Book 2
Under Title *De iudicatis*: Coll. 2. 3

(b) *Liber responsorum* [LR]

Book 15
Under the Title *Ad legem Iuliam de adulteriis*: Coll. 4. 5

(c) Ps. Papinian, *Liber singularis de adulteriis* [LSA]

No title given: Coll. 4. 7; 4. 8; 4. 9; 4. 10; 4. 11; 6. 6

4. Modestinus

Liber differentiarum [LD]

Book 2
Under Title *De deposito vel commodato*: Coll. 10. 2

Book 6
Under Title *De scientibus et ignorantibus*: Coll. 1. 12

5. Gaius

Institutiones [Inst.]

Book 3
No Title given: Coll. 16. 2

6. *Codex Gregorianus* [CG]

Book 4
Under Title *Ad legem Corneliam de sicariis et veneficis*: Coll. 1. 8; 1 9; 1.10
Under Title *De deposito*: Coll. 10. 8

Book 5
Under Title *De nuptiis*: Coll. 6. 4

Book 7
Under Title *De maleficis et Manichaeis*: Coll. 15. 3

Book 14
Under Title *De accusationibus*: Coll. 3. 4

7. *Codex Hermogenianus* [CH]

    Under Title *De nuptiis*: Coll. 6. 5
    Under Title *De deposito*: Coll. 10. 3; 10. 4; 10. 5; 10. 6

8. Contemporary Laws [CL]

    Valentinianus, Theodosius, et Arcadius Auggg. *ad Orientium vicarium urbis Romae* (= *CTh* 9. 7. 6): Coll. 5. 3

Table 2: Biblical Quotations in the Collatio[1]

Collatio	Biblical Citation
1. 1	Numbers 35: 16, 17, 20, 21
1. 5	Numbers 35: 22–5
2. 1	Exodus 21: 18–19
3. 1	Exodus 21: 20–1
4. 1	Lev. 20: 10; Exodus 22: 16–17
5. 1	Lev. 20: 13
6. 1	Lev. 20: 11–12
6. 7	Deut. 27: 20–3; Lev. 28: 12–18
7. 1	Exodus 22: 2–3
8. 1	Deut. 29: 16–20
9. 1	Exodus 20: 16
10. 1	Exodus 22: 7–11
11. 1	Exodus 22: 1, 3
12. 1	Exodus 22: 6
13. 1	Deut. 19: 14
14. 1	Exodus 21: 16; Deut. 24: 7
15. 1	Deut. 18: 10–14
16. 1	Numbers 27: 1–11

[1] For earlier attempts at lists of the Collator's Biblical quotations, see Mommsen, *Collatio*, 131–4; Hyamson, 277; Smits, *Collatio*, 44–71; Schulz, 'biblischen Texte', 20–43; and Frakes, '*Lex Dei* and Latin Bible', 425–41.

Table 3: Simultaneous List of Citations of Sources

Coll.	Bible	Paulus	Ulpian	Modestinus	Papinian	Gaius	CG	CH	CL
1									
1	Num. 35: 16–17, 20–21								
2		Sent. 5							
3			LOP 7						
4		Sent. 5							
5	Num. 35: 22–5								
6			LOP 7						
7		Sent. 5							
8							4		
9							4		
10							4		
11			LOP 7						
12				LD 6					
13		Sent 5							
2									
1	Ex. 21: 18–19								
2			LSR						
3					LD2				
4			LAE 18						
5		LSI							
6		LSI							
7		Sent. 5							
3									
1	Ex. 21: 20–1								
2		Sent. 5							
3			LOP 8						
4							14		
4									
1	Lev. 20: 10; Ex. 22:16–17								
2		LSA							
3		LSA							
4		LSA							
5					LR 15				
6		LSA							

Coll.	Bible	Paulus	Ulpian	Modestinus	Papinian	Gaius	CG	CH	CL
7					LSA				
8					LSA				
9					LSA				
10					LSA				
11					LSA				
12		Sent. 2							
5									
1	Lev. 20: 13								
2		Sent. 2							
3									CTh 9.7.6
6									
1	Lev. 20: 11–12								
2			LSR						
3		Sent. 2							
4							5		
5								De Nupt.	
6					LSA				
7	Deut. 27: 20–3; Lev. 28: 12–18								
7									
1	Ex. 22: 2–3								
2		Sent. 5							
3			LAE 18						
4			LOP 8						
5		Sent. 2							
8									
1	Deut. 29: 16–20								
2		LSPOL							
3		Sent. 5							
4		Sent. 5							
5		Sent. 5							
6		Sent. 5							
7			LOP 8						
9									
1	Ex. 20: 16								
2			LOP 8						
3		Sent. 5							
10									
1	Ex. 22: 7–11								
2				LD 2					

Table 3—*continued*

Coll.	Bible	Paulus	Ulpian	Modestinus	Papinian	Gaius	CG	CH	CL
3								De Depos.	
4								De Depos.	
5								De Depos.	
6								De Depos.	
7		Sent. 2							
8							4		
9		LR 5							
11									
1	Ex. 22: 1. 3								
2		Sent. 5							
3		Sent. 5							
4		Sent. 5							
5		Sent. 5							
6		LSPP							
7			LOP 8						
8			LOP 8						
12									
1	Ex. 22: 6								
2		Sent. 5							
3		Sent. 5							
4		Sent. 5							
5			LOP 8						
6		Sent. 5							
7			LAE 18						
13									
1	Deut. 19: 14								
2		Sent. 1							
3			LOP 8						
14									
1	Ex. 21: 16; Deut. 24: 7								
2		Sent. 5							
3			LOP 9						
15									
1	Deut. 18: 10–14								
2			LOP 7						
3							7		

Coll.	Bible	Paulus	Ulpian	Modestinus	Papinian	Gaius	CG	CH	CL
16									
1	Num. 27: 1–11								
2						Inst. 3			
3		Sent. 4							
4			LSR						
5			Inst.						
6			Inst.						
7			Inst.						
8			Inst.						
9			Inst.						

Table 4: Variant Surviving Texts of Collator's Sources in the Corpus Iuris Civilis

A. *DIGEST*

Coll.	*Digest*
1. 6	48. 8. 1. 3
1. 7	48. 8. 17
1. 11	48. 8. 4. 1
1. 13	48. 6. 11
2. 4	9. 2. 27. 17
3. 3	1. 6. 2
4. 3	48. 5. 39. 8
7. 3	9. 2. 3 and 5
7. 4	47. 17. 1
8. 3	22. 5. 16
8. 7	48. 10. 9. 3
9. 2	22. 5. 3. 5
9. 3	22. 5. 24
10. 2	16. 3. 23
10. 7	16. 3. 29
11. 7	47. 14. 1. Pr.
11. 8	47. 14. 1. 2–3
12. 5	47. 9. 12
12. 7	9. 2. 27. 7–12
13. 3	47. 21. 2
16. 3. 14	38. 7. 5. Pr.

B. *CODE OF JUSTINIAN*

Coll.	*CJ*
1. 8	9. 16. 1
1. 9	9. 16. 1
1. 10	9. 16. 4
6. 4	5. 4. 17
10. 6	4. 34. 10
10. 8	4. 34. 1
10. 9	4. 65. 1

C. *INSTITUTES OF JUSTINIAN*

Coll.	*Institutes*
2. 5. 1	4. 4. Pr.
3. 3	1. 8. 2
16. 2	3. 1. 1–2b

Works Cited

1. EDITIONS AND TRANSLATIONS OF THE *COLLATIO LEGUM MOSAICARUM ET ROMANARUM*

Baviera, J. (ed.), 'Mosaicarum et Romanarum Legum Collatio' in S. Riccobono *et al.* (eds.), *Fontes Iuris Romani Antejustiniani, Pars Altera: Auctores* (Florence, 1940, reprinted 1968), II.

Bluhme, F. (ed.), *Lex Dei sive Mosaicarum et Romanarum legum collatio* (Bonn, 1833) (subsequently included in E. Böcking, A. von Bethmann-Hollweg, and E. Pugge (eds.), *Corpus Iuris Anteiustiniani* (Bonn, 1841), I).

Girard, P. (ed.), 'Mosaicarum et Romanarum Legum Collatio' in P. Girard and F. Senn (eds.), *Textes de Droit Romain*, 7th edn (Paris, 1967), I.

Huschke, P. (ed.), 'Lex Dei sive Mosaicarum et Romanarum Legum Collatio' in P. Huschke (ed.), *Iurisprudentia Anteiustiniana* (Leipzig, 1860), II (reissued in a 6th edition with revisions by E. Seckel and B. Kuebler, 1927).

Hyamson, M. (ed. and tr.), *Mosaicarum et Romanarum Legum Collatio* (Oxford, 1913).

Mommsen, T. (ed.), *Mosaicarum et Romanarum Legum Collatio* in Paul Krüger, T. Mommsen, and Wilhelm Studemund (eds.), *Collectio Librorum Iuris Anteiustiniani* (Berlin, 1890), III.

Montemayor Aceves, M. (ed. and tr.), *Mosaicarum et Romanarum Collatio (Comparación de Leyes Mosaicas y Romanas)* (Mexico City, 1994).

Pithou, P. (ed.), *Fragmenta Quaedam Papiniani, Pauli, Ulpiani, Gaii, Modestini, aliorumque veterum Iuris auctorum ex integris ipsorum libris ante Iustiniani Imp. tempora collecta, et cum Moysis legibus collata* (Paris, 1573).

Smits, N., *Mosaicarum et Romanarum legum Collatio* (Haarlem, 1934).

Spruit, J. E. and Bongenaar, K. E. M. (eds.), 'Mosaicarum et Romanarum Legum Collatio' in J. E. Spruit and K. E. M. Bongenaar (eds.), *Fragmenta Vaticana, Collatio, Consultatio, Scholia Sinaitica, Probus* (Zutphen, 1987).

2. EDITIONS AND TRANSLATIONS OF OTHER PRIMARY SOURCES CITED IN FOOTNOTES

Allenbach, J. (ed.), *Biblia Patristica* (Paris: CNRS, 1986).

Amidon, P. (tr.), *The Church History of Rufinus of Aquileia, Books 10 and 11* (Oxford, 1997).

Avenarius, M. (ed. and tr.), *Die Pseudo-Ulpianische Einzelschrift der Rechtsregeln (liber singularis regularum)* (Göttingen, 2005).

Babbitt, F. (tr.), *Plutarch's Moralia* (Cambridge, MA, 1936: Loeb Classical Library), V.

Barrow, R. H. (ed. and tr.), *Prefect and Emperor: The Relationes of Symmachus* AD *384* (Oxford, 1973).

Beyerle, K. (ed.), *Lex Baiuvariorum* (Munich, 1926).

Blume, F. C. (tr.), *Annotated Justinian Code*, George William Hopper Law Library, University of Wyoming, ed. Timothy Kearly, 2nd edn (Laramie, 2009) (available on line at <http://uwacadweb.uwyo.edu/blume&justinian/>).

Böhringer, L. (ed.), *De Divortio Lotharii Regis et Theutbergae Reginae* (Hannover, 1992).

Bram, J. R. (tr.), *Ancient Astrology—Theory and Practice: Mathesis Libri VII by Firmicus Maternus* (Park Ridge, NJ, 1975).

Burgmann, L. and Troianos, S. (eds.), *Nomos Mosaikos* in D. Simon (ed.), *Fontes Minores* (Frankfurt, 1979), III.

Cameron, Averil and Hall, S. (tr.), *Eusebius: Life of Constantine* (Oxford, 1999).

Connolly, R. (tr.), *Didascalia Apostolorum* (Oxford, 1929).

Crawford, M. (ed.), *Roman Statutes*, 2 vols. (London, 1996).

Creed, J. L. (ed.), *Lactantius: De Mortibus Persecutorum* (Oxford, 1984).

Diez-Macho, A. (ed.), *Neophyti 1. Targum Palestinense Ms de la Biblioteca Vaticana* (Madrid, 1968–79).

Drijvers, H. J. W. (ed. and tr.), *The Book of the Laws of Countries: Dialogue on Fate of Bardaisan of Edessa* (Assen, 1965).

Eckhardt, K A. (ed. and tr.), *Germanenrechte, Texte und Übersetzungen II/2: Alamannen und Bayern* (Weimar, 1934).

Ehrman, B. (tr.), *The Apostolic Fathers* (Cambridge, MA: Loeb Classical Library, 2003).

Elliger, K. and Rudoph, W. (eds.), *Biblia Hebraica Stuttgartensia* (New York, 1987: American Bible Society).

Field, F. (ed.), *Origenis Hexaplorum quae supersunt* (Hildesheim, 1964).

Fremantle, W. H., Lewis, G., and Martley, W. (tr.), *Jerome: Letters and selected works*, NPNF, 2nd series (New York, 1893), VI.

Funk, F. X. von (ed.), *Didascalia et Constitutiones Apostolorum* (Paderborn, 1905).

Glover, T. R. (ed.), *Tertullian, Apology, De Spectaculis* (Cambridge, 1966).

Godefroy, J. (ed.), *Codex Theodosianus* (Leipzig, 1738; revision of earlier edition of Lyons, 1665).

Gordon, W. M. and Robinson, O. F. (tr.), *The Institutes of Gaius* (London, 1988).

Green, R. P. H. (ed.), *Augustine: De Doctrina Christiana* (Oxford, 1995).

Greer, R. and Mitchell, M. (tr.), *The 'Belly-Myther' of Endor: Interpretations of 1 Kingdoms 28 in the Early Church* (Atlanta, 2007).

Haenel, G. (ed.), *Codex Theodosianus* (Bonn, 1842).

—— *Lex Romana Visigothorum* (Berlin, 1849).

—— *Iuliani epitome latina Novellarum Iustiniani* (Leipzig, 1873).

Harmon, A. M. (tr.), *The Works of Lucian*, 4 vols. (Cambridge, MA: Loeb Classical Library, 1925).

Hartranft, C. D. (tr.), *The Ecclesiastical History of Sozomen*, NPNF (New York, 1890).

Heimbach, G. (ed.), *Basilicorum libri* LX, 3 vols. (Leipzig, 1833–43).

Holy Bible: New Revised Standard Version Bible with Apocrypha (Oxford, 1991).

Krüger, P. (ed.), *Codex Iustinianus* (Berlin, 1877).

—— *Pauli Libri Quinque Sententiarum* in *Collectio Librorum Iuris Anteiustiniani, Tomus Alter* (Berlin, 1878).

—— *Codices Gregorianus et Hermogenianus* in P. Krüger, T. Mommsen, and W. Studemond (eds.), *Collectio Librorum Iuris Anteiustiniani* (Berlin, 1890), III.

Lenel, O., *Palingenesia Iuris Civilis*, 2 vols. (Graz, 1960 reprint).

Levine, B., *Numbers 21–36: A new translation with introduction and commentary*, The Anchor Bible Commentary 4.A (New York, 2000).

Metzger, M. (ed.), *Les Constitutions Apostoliques* (Paris, 1985), I.

Milgrom, J., *Leviticus 17–22: A new translation with introduction and commentary* (New York, 2000).

Mommsen, T. (ed.), *Fragmenta Vaticana* in T. Mommsen, P. Krüger, and W. Studemond (eds.), *Collectio Librorum Iuris Anteiustiniani* (Berlin, 1890), III.

Mommsen, T. and Krüger, P. (eds.), *Digesta Iustiniani Augusti* (Berlin, 1870); reprinted as *Corpus Iuris Civilis I: Institutiones et Digesta*, 21st edn (Zurich, 1970).

Mommsen, T. and Meyer, P. M. (eds.), *Theodosiani libri XVI cum Constitutionibus Sirmondianis*, 2 vols. (Berlin, 1905, publ. 1904).

Monro, C. H. (tr.), *Digest IX. 2: Lex Aquilia* (Cambridge, 1898).

Mynors, R. (ed.), *XII Panegyrici Latini* (Oxford, 1964).

Nelson, H. L. W. and Manthe, U. (eds.), *Gai Institutiones III. 1–87: Intestaterbfolge und sonstige Arten von Gesamtnachfolge* (Berlin, 1992).

Nelson, H. L. W. and Manthe, U. (eds.) *Gai Institutiones III. 88–181: Die Kontraktsobligationen* (Berlin, 1999).

—— *Gai Institutiones III. 182–225: Die Deliktsobligationen* (Berlin, 2007).

Nestle, E. and Aland, K. (eds.), *Novum Testamentum Graece*, 27th edn (Stuttgart, 1993).

Nixon, C. E. V. and Rodgers, B. S. (tr.), *In Praise of Later Roman Emperors: The Panegyrici Latini* (Berkeley, 1994).

Pharr, C. (tr.), *The Theodosian Code* (Philadelphia, 1952).

Pietersma, A. (tr.), *A New English Translation of the Septuagint* (Oxford, 2000).

Propp, W. H. C., *Exodus 19–40: A new translation with introduction and commentary*, The Anchor Bible Commentary V.2A (New York, 2006).

Quentin, H. (ed.), *Biblia Sacra Iuxta Latinam Vulgatam Versionem ad Codicum Fidem. Libros Exodi et Levitici ex Interpretatione Sancti Hieronymi* (Rome, 1929).

—— *Biblia Sacra Iuxta Latinam Vulgatam Versionem ad Codicum Fidem. Libros Numerorum et Deuteronomii ex Interpretatione Sancti Hieronymi* (Rome, 1936).

Reeve, M. (ed.), *Vegetius: Epitoma Rei Militaris* (Oxford, 2004).

Rivers, T. (tr.), *Laws of the Alamans and Bavarians* (Philadelphia, 1977).

Robert, U. (ed.), *Pentateuchi Versio Latina Antiquissima e Codice Lugdunensi* (Paris, 1881).

—— *Heptateuchi parties posterioris versio Latina antiquissima e codice Lugdunensi* (Lyons, 1900).

Sabatier, P. (ed.), *Bibliorum sacrorum Latinae versiones antiquae seu Vetus Italica* (Reims, 1743).

Scheltema, H. (ed.), *Basilicorum libri LX*, 17 vols. (Groningen 1953–88).

Schulz, F. (ed.), *Die Epitome Ulpiani der Cod. Vat. Reginae 1128* (Bonn, 1926).

Schwind, E. von (ed.), *Lex Baiwariorum*, MGH *Leges nationum Germanicarum* (Hannover, 1926; reprinted in 1997), V(2).

Scott, S. P. (tr.), *The Civil Law*, 12 vols. (Cincinnati, 1932).

Seckel, E. and Kübler, B. (eds.), *Gai Institutiones* (Stuttgart, 1935; reprinted 1969).

Selb, W. and Kaufhold, H. (ed. and tr.), *Das Syrisch-Römische Rechtsbuch*, 3 vols. (Vienna, 2002).

Studemond, W. (ed.), *Gaii Institutiones* (Leipzig, 1873).

Tanakh: A new translation of the Holy Scriptures (Philadelphia: Jewish Publication Society of America, 1985).

Thompson, E. A. (ed.), *A Roman Reformer and Inventor: Being a new text of the treatise 'De rebus bellicis'* (Oxford, 1952).

Thomson, R. W. (tr.), *The Lawcode (Datastangirk') of Mxit'ar Gos* (Amsterdam, 2000).

Tischendorf, C. von (ed.), *Novum Testamentum Graece*, 7th edn (Leipzig, 1869).

Vööbus, A. (ed.), *The Didascalia Apostolorum in Syriac*, 2 vols. (Leuven, 1979).

Watson, A. (ed. and tr.), *The Digest of Justinian*, 4 vols. (Philadelphia, 1985).

Weber, R. *et al.* (eds.), *Biblia Sacra Iuxta Vulgatam Versionem*, 5th rev. edn (Stuttgart, 2007).

Westcott, B. F. and Hort, F. J. A. (eds.), *The New Testament in the Original Greek* (New York, 1882), II.

Wevers, J. W. *et al.* (eds.), *Septuaginta Vetus Testamentum Graecum* (Göttingen, 1974–99).

Williams, F. (tr.), *The Panarion of Epiphanius of Salamis*, 2 vols. (Leiden, 1987–90)

Ziwsa, C. (ed.), *Gesta apud Zenophilum* in C. Ziwsa (ed.), *S. Optati Milevitani libri VII*, CSEL 26 (Vienna, 1893).

Zulueta, F. de (tr.), *The Institutes of Gaius, Part I* (Oxford 1946).

3. SECONDARY SOURCES CITED IN FOOTNOTES AND COMMENTARY

Ackroyd, P. R. and Evans, C. F. (eds.), *The Cambridge History of the Bible*, I: *From the Beginnings to Jerome* (Cambridge, 1970).

Airlie, S., 'Private bodies and the body politic in the divorce case of Lothar II', *Past and Present* 161 (1998), 3–38.

Albertario, E., *Animus furandi, contributo alla dottrina del furto nel diritto romano e nel diritto bizantino* (Milan, 1923).

Ankum, H., 'Papinian, ein dunkler Jurist?', *Orbis Iuris Romani* 1 (1996), 5–32.

Anonymous, *Letters of Papinian* (New York, 1779).

Arangio-Ruiz, V., 'Sul liber singularis Regularum', *BIDR* 30 (1921), 178–219.

Arjava, A., 'The survival of Roman family law after the Barbarian settlements' in Mathisen, *Law, Society, and Authority in Late Antiquity*, 33–51.

Arnold, D. and Bright, P. (eds.), *De Doctrina Christiana: A classic of Western culture* (Notre Dame, 1995).

Athanassiadi-Fowden, P., *Julian and Hellenism* (Oxford, 1981).

Athanassiadi, P. and Frede, M. (eds.), *Pagan Monotheism in Late Antiquity* (Oxford, 1997).

Avenarius, M., *Der Pseudo-Ulpianische liber singularis regularum: Entstehung, Eigenart und Überlieferung einer hochklassischen Juristenschrift* (Göttingen, 2005).

Bagnall, R., Cameron, Alan, Schwartz, S., and Worp, K., *Consuls of the Later Roman Empire* (Atlanta, 1987).

Bagnall, R., *Egypt in Late Antiquity* (Princeton, 1993).

Barnes, T. D., *Tertullian* (Oxford, 1971).

—— 'The date of Vegetius', *Phoenix* 33 (1979), 254–7.

—— *Constantine and Eusebius* (Cambridge, MA, 1981).

—— *The New Empire of Diocletian and Constantine* (Cambridge, MA, 1981).

—— 'Constantine's prohibition of pagan sacrifice', *AJP* 105 (1984), 69–72.

—— *Athanasius and Constantius* (Cambridge, MA, 1993).

—— *From Eusebius to Augustine* (Aldershot, 1994).

—— *Ammianus Marcellinus and the Representation of Historical Reality* (Ithaca, 1998).

—— 'Monotheists all?', *Phoenix* 55 (2001), 142–62.

—— 'Damascus or Demessus?', *Zeitschrift für Papyrologie und Epigraphik* 151 (2005), 266–8.

Barnwell, P., 'Emperors, jurists and kings: Law and custom in the late-Roman and early-medieval West', *Past and Present* 168 (2000), 6–29.

Barone-Adesi, G., *L'eta della 'Lex Dei'* (Naples, 1992).

Barrett, C. K., 'The interpretation of the Old Testament in the New' in Ackroyd and Evans (eds.), *The Cambridge History of the Bible*, I, 377–411.

Bartlet, J. V., 'Fragments of the *Didascalia Apostolorum*', *JTS* 18 (1916–17), 301–9.

Barton, T., *Ancient Astrology* (London, 1994).

Bauckham, R., 'James and the Gentiles (Acts 15. 13–21)' in Ben Witherington (ed.), *History, Literature, and Society in the Book of Acts* (Cambridge, 1996), 154–84.

—— *James: Wisdom of James, Disciple of Jesus the Sage* (London, 1999).

Bauman, R., *Lawyers in Roman Republican Politics: A study of the Roman jurists in their political setting, 316 BC 82 BC* (Munich, 1983).

—— *Lawyers in Roman Transitional Politics: A study of the Roman jurists in their political setting in the late Republic and Triumvirate* (Munich, 1985).

—— *Lawyers and Politics in the Early Roman Empire: A study of the relations between the Roman jurists and the emperors from Augustus to Hadrian* (Munich, 1989).

—— 'The death of Ulpian: The irrestible force and the immovable object', *ZRG (R.A.)* 112 (1995), 385–99.

—— *Crime and Punishment in Ancient Rome* (London, 1996).

Baumstark, A., 'Die Evangelienzitate Novatians', *Oriens Christianus*, 3rd series, 5 (1930), 1–14.

Becker, E., 'Konstantin der Grosse, der "neue Moses": Die Schlacht am Pons Milvius und die Katastrophe am Schilfmeer', *Zeitschrift der Kirchengeschichte* 31 (1910), 161–71.

Behrends, O., 'Papinians Verweigerung oder die Moral eines Juristen', *Literatur und Rechts* 1 (1996), 243–91.
Behrens, D., *Die vis maior und das klassische Haftungssystem* (Giessen, 1936).
Berger, A., 'Lex Fabia', *RE* supp. 7 (Stuttgart, 1940), cols. 386–94.
—— 'Some remarks on cattle-stealing in Roman law', *Seminar* 2 (1944), 23–40.
—— *Encyclopedic Dictionary of Roman Law* (Philadelphia, 1953).
Bertrand-Dagenbach, C., *Alexandre Sévère et l' Histoire Auguste* (Brussels, 1990).
Beseler, G., *Beiträge zur Kritik der römischen Rechtsquellen* (Tübingen, 1910–20).
—— 'Confestim-Continuo', *ZRG (R.A.)* 51 (1931), 188–202.
Bianchini, M., Review of Barone-Adesi, *Iura* 43 (1992), 144–8.
Bingham, S., 'Life on an island: A brief study of places of exile in the first century AD', *Studies in Latin Literature and Roman History* 12 (2003), 376–400.
Birdsall, J. N., 'The New Testament text', in Ackroyd and Evans (eds.), *The Cambridge History of the Bible*, I, 308–77.
Birks, P., Review of Honoré's *Ulpian*, *The Irish Jurist* 18 (1983), 151–81.
Birley, A., *Septimius Severus: The African emperor* (London, 1999).
Bischoff, B., *Latin Palaeography: Antiquity and the Middle Ages*, tr. D. Ó. Crónín and D. Ganz (Cambridge, 1990).
Blockley, R. C., *East Roman Foreign Policy* (Leeds, 1992).
Blu[h]me, F., 'Über Pithou's Handschrift der Lex Dei, oder Legum Mosaicarum et Romanarum Collatio', *Zeitschrift für geschichtliche Rechtswissenschaft* 10 (1842), 298–308.
Blumenthal, U.-R., *The Investiture Controversy: Church and monarchy from the ninth to the twelfth century* (Philadelphia, 1988).
Bonifacio, F., 'Richerche sul de Deposito Irregolare in Diritto Romano', *BIDR*, n. s. 8 (1947), 80–152.
Bonner, G., 'Augustine as biblical scholar', in Ackroyd and Evans (eds.), *The Cambridge History of the Bible*, I, 541–63.
Bonte, P. (ed.), *Épouser au plus proche, inceste, prohibitions et stratégies matrimoniales autour de la Méditerranée* (Paris, 1994).
The Book of Common Prayer (Oxford, 1928).
Boswell, J., *Christianity, Social Tolerance, and Homosexuality: Gay people in Western Europe from the beginning of the Christian era to the fourteenth century* (Chicago, 1980).
Bouffartigue, J., *L' Empereur Julien et la culture de son temps* (Paris, 1992).
Bowersock, G., *Julian the Apostate* (Cambridge, MA, 1978).
Boyarin, D., *Border Lines: The partition of Judaeo-Christianity* (Philadelphia, 2004).
Bradbury, S., 'Constantine and the problem of anti-pagan legislation in the fourth century', *CP* 89 (1994), 120–39.

Bradley, K., *Slaves and Masters in the Roman Empire: A study on social control* (Brussels, 1984).
Brandt, H., 'Lancizolle (de Leuze de L.), Karl Wilhelm v.' in *Neue Deutsche Biographie* (Berlin, 1892), XIII, 474–5.
Brassloff, S., 'Herennius Modestinus', *RE* 8, 1 (Stuttgart, 1912), cols. 668–75.
Braun, R. and Richer, J. (eds.), *L'Empereur Julien: De l'histoire à la légende* (Paris, 1978).
Brennan, T. C., *The Praetorship in the Roman Republic*, 2 vols. (Oxford, 2000).
Brown, P., *Augustine of Hippo* (Berkeley, 1967).
—— 'The diffusion of Manichaeism in the Roman Empire', *JRS* 59 (1969), 92–103.
—— *The World of Late Antiquity* (London, 1971).
—— *The Making of Late Antiquity* (Cambridge, MA, 1978).
Brown, R., *An Introduction to the New Testament* (NY, 1997).
Brown, W., Review of von Schwind (ed.), *Lex Baiwariorum, The Medieval Review* [online], 00.05.02.
Browning, R., *The Emperor Julian* (Berkeley, 1976).
Bruce-Mitford, R. L. S., 'The art of the Codex Amiatinus', *Journal of the British Archaeological Association*, 3rd series, 32 (1969), 1–25.
Brunnenmeister, E., *Das Tödtungsverbrechen im altrömischen Recht* (Leipzig, 1887).
Buckland, W. W., *The Roman Law of Slavery* (Cambridge, 1908).
Buhlmann, J. and Gilman, D. (eds.), *Louis Le Caron, Dialogues* (Droz, 1986).
Bürge, A., *Retentio im römischen Sachen und Obligationenrecht* (Zurich, 1979).
Burke, P., *The French Historical Revolution: The Annales School, 1929–89* (Stanford, 1990).
Burkitt, F. C., *The Old Latin and the Itala* (Cambridge, 1896).
—— 'Saint Augustine's Bible and the Itala', *JTS* 11 (1910), 258–68 and 447–58.
Burns, J. Patout, *Cyprian the Bishop* (London and New York, 2002).
Bush, A., '*Consobrinus* and Cousin', *The Classical Journal* 68 (1972–3), 161–5.
Cameron, Alan, 'The date and identity of Macrobius', *JRS* 55 (1965), 25–38.
—— 'Gratian's repudiation of the pontifical robe', *JRS* 58 (1968), 96–102.
—— *Claudian: Poetry and propaganda at the court of Honorius* (Oxford, 1970).
Cameron, Alan and Long, J., *Barbarians and Politics at the Court of Arcadius* (Berkeley, 1993).
Cameron, Averil, 'Constantinus Christianus' (Review of Barnes, *Constantine and Eusebius* and *New Empire of Diocletian and Constantine*), *JRS* 73 (1983), 184–90.
—— *Later Roman Empire, AD 284–430* (Cambridge, 1993).

Cameron, Averil and P. Garnsey (eds.), *The Cambridge Ancient History*, XIII: *The Late Empire, AD 337–425* (Cambridge, 1998)

Cannato, C., *Richerche sulla risponsabilità contrattuale nel diritto romano* (Milan, 1996).

Cantarella, E., *Studi sull'omicidio in diritto greco e romano* (Milan, 1976).

Carcaterra, A., *Le definizioni dei giuristi romani: Metodo mezzi e fini* (Naples, 1966).

Carella, B., 'The source of the Prologue to the laws of Alfred', *Peritia* 19 (2005), 91–118.

Carey, F. M., 'The Scriptorium of Reims during the archbishopric of Hincmar (845–882 A. D.)' in L. Webber Jones (ed.), *Classical and Mediaeval Studies in Honor of Edward Kennard Rand* (New York, 1938).

Carmichael, C., *The Origin of Biblical Law: The Decalogues and the Book of the Covenant* (Ithaca, 1992).

—— *Law, Legend, and Incest in the Bible: Leviticus 18–20* (Ithaca, 1997).

Ceci, L., *Le etimologie dei giureconsulti romani* (Rome, 1966).

Cenderellli, A., *Ricerche sul 'Codex Hermogenianus'* (Milan, 1965).

Cervenca, G., 'Ancora sul Problema della datazione della "Collatio Legum Mosaicarum et Romanarum"', *SDHI* 29 (1963), 253–60.

Chandler, D. 'Who was Papinian?: The meaning(s) of the lyrical ballad's epigraph', *English Language Notes* 39 (2002), 31–41.

Chapman, J., 'St. Cyprian of Carthage', *The Catholic Encyclopedia* (New York, 1908), IV, 583.

Clark, E. A., *The Origenist Controversy* (Princeton, 1992).

Cloud, J. D., 'The primary purpose of the lex Cornelia de Sicariis', *ZRG (R.A.)* 86 (1969), 258–86.

—— 'Lex Iulia de vi: Part I', *Athenaeum* 76, n. s. 66 (1988), 578–95.

—— 'Lex Iulia de vi: Part II', *Athenaeum* 77, n. s. 67 (1989), 427–65.

—— 'A "philologist" looks at the "Lex Scantinia"' in *Iuris Vincula: Studi in Onore di Mario Talamanca* (Naples, 2001), II, 201–25.

—— 'Leges de Sicariis: The first chapter of Sulla's *lex de sicariis*', *ZRG (R.A.)* 126 (2009), 114–55.

Cohen, B., *Jewish and Roman Law* (New York, 1966).

Coleridge, S. T. and Wordsworth, W. *Lyrical Ballads*, 2nd edn (London, 1800).

Conrat (Cohn), M., *Geschichte der Quellen und Literatur des Römischen Rechts im früheren Mittelalter* (Leipzig, 1891), I.

—— 'Hieronymus und die Collatio', *Hermes* 35 (1899), 344–7.

Corbett, P. E., *The Roman Law of Marriage* (Oxford, 1930).

Corcoran, S., *The Empire of the Tetrarchs: Imperial pronouncements and government AD 284–324*, 2nd edn (Oxford, 2000).

—— 'The sins of the fathers: A neglected Constitution of Diocletian on incest', *Legal History* 21 (2000), 1–34.

Corcoran, S., 'The publication of law in the era of the Tetrarchs' in Demandt, Goltz, and Schlange-Schöningen (eds.), *Diokletian und die Terarchie* (2004), 56–73.

—— 'Before Constantine' in Lenski (ed.), *The Cambridge Companion to the Age of Constantine* (2006), 35–58.

—— 'The Tetrarchy: Policy and image as reflected in imperial pronouncements' in D. Boschung and W. Eck (eds.), *Die Tetrarchie: eine neues Regierungssystem und seine mediale Präsentation* (Wiesbaden, 2006), 31–61.

—— 'The heading of Diocletian's prices edict at Stratonicea', *Zeitschrift für Papyrologie und Epigraphik* 166 (2008), 295–302.

Costa, E. *Papiniano, Studi di Storia interna del diritto romano* (Bologna, 1899), IV.

Cramer, F. H., *Astrology in Roman Law and Politics* (Philadelphia, 1954).

Cramp, R., *Wearmouth and Jarrow Monastic Sites* (Swindon, 2005).

Crane, E., *The World History of Beekeeping and Honey Hunting* (New York, 1999).

Cribiore, R., *The School of Libanius in Late Antique Antioch* (Princeton, 2007).

Crifò, G., *Ricerche sull' 'exilium' nel periodo repubblicano* (Milan, 1961).

—— 'Ulpiano. Esperienze e responsabilità del giurista' in H. Temporini (ed.), *ANRW* (Berlin, 1976), II(15), 708–89.

Croke, B., 'Arbogast and the death of Valentinian II', *Historia* 25 (1976), 235–44.

—— 'AD 476: The manufacture of a turning point', *Chiron* 13 (1983), 81–119.

Croke, B. and Harries, J. (eds.), *Religious Conflict in Fourth-Century Rome* (Sydney, 1982).

Crone, P., *Pre-Industrial Societies* (Oxford, 1989).

Crook, J. A., 'Lex Cornelia de falsis', *Athenaeum* 65 (1987), 163–71.

Cullmann, O., *Early Christian Worship*, tr. A. Todd and J. Torrance (London, 1962).

Curran, J., 'From Jovian to Theodosius' in Averil Cameron and P. Garnsey (eds.), *The Cambridge Ancient History*, XIII: *The Late Empire, AD 337–425* (Cambridge, 1998), 78–110.

Cursi, M. F., *Iniuria cum damno: antigiuridicità e colpevolezza nella storia del danno Aquiliano* (Milan, 2002).

Dagron, G., *Naissance d'une capitale* (Paris, 1974).

D'Ales, A., *Novatien: Étude sur la théologie romaine au milieu du iiie siècle* (Paris, 1924).

Dalla, D., *Ubi Venus mutatur: Omosessualità e Diretto nel mondo Romano* (Milan, 1987).

Dam, R. van, *Leadership and Community in Late Antique Gaul* (Berkeley, 1985).

Daniels, A. von, *De Saxononici speculi origine ex juris communis* (Berlin, 1852).

—— *Alter und Ursprung des Sachsenspiegels* (Berlin, 1853).

—— *Handbuch der deutsche Reichs-und Staatenrechtsgeschichte* (Tübingen, 1859), I, 219–21.

Darnton, R., *The Great Cat Massacre and Other Episodes in French Cultural History* (New York, 1984).

Daube, D., 'Nocere and Noxa', *Cambridge Law Journal* 7 (1939), 23–54.

—— '*Collatio* 2. 6. 5' in I. Epstein, E. Levine, and C. Roth (eds.), *Essays in Honor of the Very Reverend Dr. J. H. Hertz* (London, 1943), 111–29 (republished in David Daube, *Collected Studies in Roman Law* (Frankfurt, 1991), I, 107–22).

—— 'Utiliter agere', *Iura* 11 (1960), 69–148.

—— 'The Old Testament prohibitions of homosexuality', *ZRG (R.A.)* 103 (1985), 447–8.

Davis, N. Z., *The Return of Martin Guerre* (Cambridge, MA, 1983).

Degrassi, A., *I Fasti Consolari dell'Impero Romano* (Rome, 1952).

Demandt, A., Goltz, A., and Schlange-Schöningen, H. (eds.), *Diokletian und die Tetrarchie. Aspekte einer Zeitenwende* (Berlin, 2004).

Demelius, G., *Die Exhibitionspflicht in ihrer Bedeutung für das classische und heutige Recht: juristische Untersuchung* (Graz, 1872).

Dessau, H., 'Über Zeit und Persönlichkeit der Scriptores Historiae Augustae', *Hermes* 24 (1889), 337–92.

Digeser, E. D., *The Making of a Christian Empire: Lactantius and Rome* (Ithaca, 2000).

—— 'Religion, law and the Roman polity: The era of the Great Persecution' in C. Ando and J. Rüpke (eds.), *Religion and Law in Classical and Christian Rome* (Stuttgart, 2006), 68–84.

—— 'Christian or Hellene? The Great Persecution and the problem of identity' in Frakes and Digeser, *Religious Identity in Late Antiquity* (2007), 36–57.

Diosdi, G., 'Gaius, der Rechtsgelehrte (mit einer Bibliographie von R. Wittmann)' in H. Temporini (ed.), *ANRW* (Berlin, 1976), II(15), 605–31.

Dirksen, H. E., 'Über die Collatio Legum Mosaicarum et Romanarum' in F. D. Sanio (ed.), *H. E. Dirksen's Hinterlassene Schrift zur Kritik und Auslegung der Quellen römischer Rechtsgeschichte und Alterthumskunde* (Leipzig, 1871), II, 100–29.

—— 'Hincmar, Erzbischof von Rheims, als Kenner der Quellen des römischen Rechts' in F. D. Sanio (ed.), *H. E. Dirksen's Hinterlassene Schrift zur Kritik und Auslegung der Quellen römischer Rechtsgeschichte und Alterthumskunde* (Leipzig, 1871), II, 130–41.

Dodds, E. R., *Pagan and Christian in an Age of Anxiety: Some aspects of religious experience from Marcus Aurelius to Constantine* (Cambridge, 1965).

Dohrmann, H., *Anerkennung und Bekämpfung von Menschenopfern im römischen Strafrecht der Kaiserzeit* (Frankfurt, 1995).

Dolezalek, G., *Verzeichnis der Handschriften zum römischen Recht bis 1600* (Frankfurt, 1972), II.

Dominicis, M. A. de, 'Ancora sulla Collatio Legum Mosaicarum et Romanarum', *BIDR* 8 (1966), 337–42.

D'Ors, A., 'Contribuciones a la historia del crimen falsi' in *Studi in onore di Edoardo Volterra* (Milan, 1977), II, 527–58.

Drake, H. A., Review of Barnes, *Constantine and Eusebius*, *AJP* 103 (1982), 462–6.

—— 'Firmicus Maternus and the politics of conversion' in G. Schmeling and J. Mikalson (eds.), *Qui Miscuit Utile Dulci: Festschrift essays for Paul Lachlan MacKendrick* (Wauconda, 1998), 133–49.

—— *Constantine and the Bishops* (Baltimore, 2000).

—— 'Socrates' question' in Frakes and Digeser, *Religious Identity in Late Antiquity* (2007), 228–41.

Draper, J., 'Torah and troublesome Apostles in the *Didache* community' in J. Draper (ed.), *The Didache in Modern Research* (Leiden, 1996), 340–63.

Drijvers, H. J. W., *Bardaisan of Edessa* (Assen, 1966).

Driver, S. R., *The Book of Exodus* (Cambridge, 1911).

Droge, A., *Homer or Moses? Early Christian interpretations of the history of culture* (Tübingen, 1989).

Du Plessis, P., 'Subletting and the Roman law of letting and hiring: Interpreting C. 4.65.6', *Revue Internationale des droits de l'Antiquité* 52 (2005), 131–44.

—— 'Between theory and practice: New perspectives on the Roman law of letting and hiring', *Cambridge Law Journal* 65 (2006), 423–37.

—— 'The Roman concept of *lex contractus*', *Roman Legal Tradition* 3 (2006), 79–94.

Edmondson, J. C., 'Mining in the later Roman Empire and beyond: Continuity or disruption', *JRS* 79 (1989), 84–102.

Edwards, M., 'Pagan and Christian in the age of monotheism' in S. Swain and M. Edwards (eds.), *Approaching Late Antiquity: The transformation from early to late empire* (Oxford, 2004), 211–34.

—— 'The beginnings of Christianity' in Lenski (ed.), *The Cambridge Companion to the Age of Constantine* (2006), 137–58.

Ehrman, B., *The New Testament: A historical introduction to the early Christian writings*, 4th edn (NY and Oxford, 2008).

Ensslin, W., *Die Religionspolitik des Kaisers Theodosius d. Gr.* (Munich, 1953).

Errington, R. Malcolm, 'Constantine and the pagans', *GRBS* 29 (1988), 309–18.

—— 'The praetorian prefectures of Virius Nicomachus Flavianus', *Historia* 41 (1992), 439–61.

—— 'Christian accounts of the religious legislation of Theodosius I', *Klio* 79 (1997), 398–443.

—— *Roman Imperial Policy from Julian to Theodosius* (Chapel Hill, 2006).

Evans-Jones, R., 'The action of the Twelve Tables "ex causa depositii"', *Labeo* 34 (1988), 188–208.

Fahey, M., *Cyprian and the Bible* (Tübingen, 1971).

Faro, S., 'Sull'anno della morte di Ulpiano', *Index: Quaderni camerti di studi romanistici* 30 (2002), 251–87.

Ferrary, J.-L., 'Lex Cornelia de sicariis et veneficis', *Athenaeum* 79, n. s. 69 (1991), 417–34.

Ferrill, A., *The Fall of Rome: The military explanation* (London, 1986).

Fiensy, D. A., *Prayers Alleged to be Jewish: An examination of the Constitutiones Apostolorum* (Chico, 1983).

Finegan, J., *The Archeology of the New Testament* (Princeton, 1992).

Finley, M. I., *Ancient Slavery and Modern Ideology* (London, 1980).

—— *The Ancient Economy*, 2nd edn (Berkeley, 1985).

Flume, W., 'Fritz Schulz+', *ZRG (R.A.)* 75 (1958), 499–506.

Fonrobert, C., 'The *Didascalia Apostolorum*: A Mishna for the Disciples of Jesus', *JECS* 9 (2001), 485–509.

Fournier, P., 'Le Liber ex lege Moysi et les tendances biblique du droit canonique irlandais', *Revue Celtique* 30 (1909), 221–34.

Fowden, G., *Empire to Commonwealth: Consequences of monotheism in late antiquity* (Princeton, 1993).

Fox, R. Lane, *Pagans and Christians in the Mediterranean World from the Second Century AD to the Conversion of Constantine* (New York, 1988).

Frakes, R. M., 'Cross-references to the lost books of Ammianus Marcellinus', *Phoenix* 49 (1995), 232–46.

—— '*Graecus* and *Res Gestae*: Ammianus Marcellinus and his intended audience', *Studies in Latin Literature and Roman History* 10 (2000), 392–442.

—— 'Some thoughts on the lost books of Ammianus Marcellinus', *Ancient World* 31 (2000), 48–53 (reprinted in R. M. Frakes and D. L. Toye, *The Dance of Hippocleides: A Festschrift for Frank J. Frost* (Golden, CO, 2002), 48–53).

—— '*Item Theodosianus*? (Observations on Coll. V. 3. 1)', *QUCC* n. s. 71(2) (2002), 163–8.

—— 'The *Collatio* and the *Codex Gregorianus* (Observations on Coll. I. 10, VI. 4, VI. 6, XV. 3)', *Index: Quaderni camerti di studi romanistici* 33 (2005), 293–300.

—— 'The dynasty of Constantine Down to 363' in Lenski (ed.), *The Cambridge Companion to the Age of Constantine* (2006), 91–107.

—— 'A note on *Collatio* 12. 6. 1 and Paulus', *Roman Legal Tradition* 3(2) (2006), 1–5.

—— 'The *Lex Dei* and the Latin Bible', *HTR* 100: 4 (2007), 425–41.

Frakes, R. M., 'The manuscript tradition of the *Lex Dei*', *ZRG (R.A.)* 124 (2007), 290–304.

Frakes, R. M. and Digeser, E. D. (eds.), *Religious Identity in Late Antiquity* (Toronto, 2007).

Francisci, P. de, 'Ancora intorno alla "Collatio Legum Mosaicarum et Romanarum"', *BIDR* 5 (1963), 97–101.

Frede, M. 'Monotheism and pagan philosophy in later antiquity' in Athanassiadi and Frede (eds.), *Pagan Monotheism in Late Antiquity*, 41–67.

Fredricksen, P., *Augustine and the Jews: A Christian defense of Jews and Judaism* (NY, 2008).

Freher, M., 'Parergon', reprinted in E. Otto (ed.), *Thesaurus Iuris Romani*, 2nd edn (Utrecht, 1733), I, cols. 852–948.

Frier, B., 'Bees and lawyers', *Classical Journal* 78 (1982), 105–14.

—— 'Law on the installment plan', Review of Honoré's *Ulpian*, *Michigan Law Review* 82 (1984), 856–68.

—— *The Rise of the Roman Jurists: Studies in Cicero's Pro Caecina* (Princeton, 1985).

—— 'Why did the Jurists change Roman law? Bees and lawyers revisited', *Index: Quaderni camerti di studi romanistici* 22 (1994), 135–49.

Fuller, R. and Westberg, D., *Preaching the Lectionary: The Word of God for the church today*, 3rd edn (Collegeville, MN, 2006).

Funk, F. X. von, *Die apostolischen Konstitutionen, eine literarhistorische Untersuchung* (Rottenburg am Neckar, 1891).

Futrell, A., *Blood in the Arena: The spectacle of Roman power* (Austin, 1997).

Galtier, P., 'La Date de la Didascalia des Apotres', *RHE* 13 (1947), 315–51.

Gandolfi, G., *Il Deposito nella problematica della giurisprudenza romana* (Milan, 1976).

Gardner, I. M. F. and Lieu, S. N. C., 'From Narmouthis (Medinat Madi) to Kellis (Ismart El-Kharab): Manichaean documents from Roman Egypt', *JRS* 86 (1996), 146–69.

Gardner, J., *Women in Roman Law and Society* (London, 1986).

—— *Being a Roman Citizen* (London, 1993).

—— *Family and Familia in Roman Law and Life* (Oxford, 1998).

Garnsey, P., *Social Status and Legal Privilege in the Roman Empire* (Oxford, 1970).

—— *Ideas of Slavery from Aristotle to Augustine* (Cambridge, 1996).

Garnsey, P. and Humfress, C., *The Evolution of the Late Antique World* (Cambridge, 2001).

Gaudemet, J., *La Formation du droit seculier et du droit de l'eglise aux IV et V siecles* (Paris, 1957).

—— 'A propos du "furtum" a l'epoque classique' in A. Gaurino and M. Bretone, *Mnemeion Siro Solazzi* (Naples, 1964), 141–53.

Gerkens, J.-F., '*Vis maior* and *vis cui resisti non potest*' in R. van den Bergh and G. van Niekerk (eds.), *Ex iusta causa traditum: Essays in honour of Eric H. Pool* (Pretoria, 2005), 109–20.

Gibbon, E., *Decline and Fall of the Roman Empire*, Modern Library edition (New York, n.d.).

Ginzburg, C., *The Cheese and the Worms: The cosmos of a sixteenth-century miller* (Baltimore, 1980).

Giovanni, L. de, 'Effecti della Constitutio Antoniniana: un' ulteriore prospettiva d'indagine' in *Fraterna Munera: Studi in onore di L. Amirante* (Salerno, 1998), 145–59.

Giuffrè, V., 'Papiniano: fra tradizione ed innovazione' in H. Temporini (ed.), *ANRW* (Berlin, 1976), II(15), 632–66.

Goodenough, E. R., 'The political philosophy of Hellenistic kingship', *Yale Classical Studies* 1 (1928), 55–102.

Gradenwitz, O., *Interpolationen in den Pandekten: kritische Studien* (Berlin, 1887).

Grafton, A., *Joseph Scaliger: A study in the history of classical scholarship*, I: *Textual Criticism and Exegesis* (Oxford, 1983).

Grafton, A. and Williams, M., *Christianity and the Transformation of the Book: Origen, Eusebius, and the Library of Caesarea* (Cambridge, MA, 2006).

Grant, R. M., 'Theophilus of Antioch to Autolycus', *Harvard Theological Revew* 40 (1947), 227–56.

—— 'Marcion and the critical method' in P. Richardson and J. Hurd (eds.), *From Jesus to Paul: Studies in honour of Francis Wright Beare* (Waterloo, ON, 1984), 207–15.

—— *Irenaeus of Lyons* (London, 1997).

Grasmück, E., *Exilium: Untersuchungen zur Verbannung in der Antike* (Paderborn, 1978).

Gravina, G. V., *Il Papiniano*, included in the *Tragedie Cinque* (Naples, 1712).

Greenslade, S. L., *Church and State from Constantine to Theodosius* (London, 1954).

Greenspoon, L., 'Mission to Alexandria: Truth and legend about the creation of the Septuagint, the first Bible translation', *Bible Review* 5 (1989), 34–41.

Gröschler, P., *Actiones in factum: eine Untersuchung zur Klage-Neuschöpfung im nichtvertraglichen Bereich* (Berlin, 2002).

Grubbs, J. Evans, *Law and Family in Late Antiquity: The Emperor Constantine's marriage legislation* (Oxford, 1995).

Gruen, E., 'Fact and fiction: Jewish legends in a Hellenistic context' in P. Cartledge, P. Garnsey, and E. Gruen (eds.), *Hellenistic Constructs* (Berkeley, 1997), 72–88.

Gryphius, A., *Grossmütiger Rechtsgelehrter oder Sterbender Aemilius Paulus Papinianus, Trauerspil* (Breslau, 1659).

Guarino, A., 'Studi sull' "incestum"', *ZRG (R.A.)* 63 (1943), 175–267.

Gustafson, M., 'Condemnation to the mines in the later Roman Empire', *HTR* 87 (1984), 421–33.

Gwynn, D., *The Eusebians: The polemic of Athanasius of Alexandria and the construction of the 'Arian Controversy'* (Oxford, 2007).

Haas, C., 'Imperial religious policy and Valerian's persecution of the Church', *Church History* 52 (1983), 133–44.

Haehling, R. von, *Die Religionszugehörigkeit der hohen Amtsträger des römischen Reiches seit Constantins I. Alleinherrschaft bis zum Ende der Theodosianischen Dynastie (324–450 bzw. 455 n. Chr.)* (Bonn, 1978).

Hall, L. Jones, 'Cicero's *instinctu divino* and Constantine's *instinctu divinitatis*: The evidence of the Arch of Constantine for the senatorial view of the 'Vision' of Constantine', *JECS* 6 (1998), 647–71.

—— *Roman Berytus: Beirut in late antiquity* (London, 2004).

Hanson, R. P. C., 'Biblical exegesis in the early Church' in Ackroyd and Evans (eds.), *The Cambridge History of the Bible*, I, 423–4.

Harnack, A. von, *Marcion: das Evangelium vom fremden Gott*, 2nd edn (Leipzig, 1924).

Harries, J., 'The Roman Imperial Quaestor from Constantine to Theodosius II', *JRS* 78 (1988), 148–72.

—— 'The background to the Code' in Harries and Wood, *The Theodosian Code* (1993), 1–16.

—— 'How to make a law code' in M. Austin, J. Harries, and C. Smith (eds.), *Modus Operandi: Essays in honor of Geoffrey Rickman* (London, 1998), 63–78.

—— *Law and Empire in Late Antiquity* (Cambridge, 1999).

—— *Cicero and the Jurists: From citizens' law to the lawful state* (London, 2006).

—— 'Violence, victims, and legal tradition in late antiquity' in H. A. Drake (ed.), *Violence in Late Antiquity: Perceptions and practices* (Aldershot, 2006), 85–102.

—— *Law and Crime in the Roman World* (Cambridge, 2007).

Harries, J. and Wood, I. (eds.), *The Theodosian Code: Studies in the imperial law of late antiquity* (London, 1993).

Harris, W. V., 'The Roman father's power of life and death' in R. S. Bagnall and W. V. Harris (eds.), *Studies in Roman Law in Memory of A. Arthur Schiller* (Leiden, 1986), 81–95.

Hartmann, L., 'Abigeatus', *RE* (Stuttgart, 1893), I, col. 97.

Healy, J., *Mining and Metallurgy in the Greek and Roman World* (London, 1978).

Heather, P., *The Fall of the Roman Empire: A new history of Rome and the Barbarians* (Oxford, 2006).

Hedrick, C. W., *History and Silence: The purge and rehabilitation of memory in late antiquity* (Austin, 2000).

Heimbach, G. E., Review of Haenel's *Codex Theodosianus, Neue Jenaische Allgemeine Literatur-Zeitung* 2(175–7) (Leipzig, 1843), 709–20.

Hengel, M., *The Septuagint as Christian Scripture: Its prehistory and the problem of its canon* (Edinburgh, 2002).

Herzog, R. and Schmidt, P. L. (eds.), *Handbuch der Lateinischen Literatur der Antike* (Munich, 1997), VIII(4).

—— *Handbuch der Lateinischen Literatur der Antike* (Munich, 1989), VIII(5).

Hitzig, H. F., *Iniuria. Beiträge zur Geschichte der Injuria im griechischen und römischen Recht* (Munich, 1899).

Hohenlohe, C., *Ursprung und Zweck der Collatio Legum Mosaicarum et Romanarum* (Vienna, 1935).

—— 'Noch einmal Ursprung und Zweck der Collatio Mosaicarum et Romanarum Legum', *Archiv für Katholisches Kirchenrecht* 119 (1939), 352–64.

—— 'Um die Geheimnisse der "Collatio legum mosaicarum et romanarum"', *SDHI* 5 (1939), 486–90.

Honoré, T., *Gaius* (Oxford, 1962).

—— 'Proculus', *TR* 30 (1962), 472–509.

—— *Tribonian* (London, 1978).

—— 'The making of the Theodosian Code', *ZRG (R.A.)* 103 (1986), 133–222.

—— 'Scriptor Historiae Augustae', *JRS* 77 (1987), 156–76.

—— *Emperors and Lawyers*, 2nd edn (Oxford, 1994).

—— *Law in the Crisis of Empire, 379–455 AD* (Oxford, 1998).

—— *Ulpian: Pioneer of Human Rights*, 2nd edn (Oxford, 2002).

—— 'How Tribonian organized the compilation of Justinian's Digest', *ZRG (R.A.)* 121 (2004), 1–43.

Honoré, T. (ed.), *Virius Nicomachus Flavianus* (Konstanz, 1989).

Hopkins, K., *Death and Renewal* (Cambridge, 1983).

Humfress, C., 'Law and legal practice in the age of Justinian' in M. Maas (ed.), *Cambridge Companion to the Age of Justinian* (Cambridge, 2005), 161–84.

—— 'Civil law and social life' in Lenski (ed.), *The Cambridge Companion to the Age of Constantine* (2006), 205–25.

—— *Orthodoxy and the Courts* (Oxford, 2007).

Huschke, P., 'Über Alter und Verfasser der Legum Mosaicarum et Romanarum Collatio', *Zeitschrift für geschichtliche Rechtswissenschaft* 13 (1846), 1–49.

Jacobs, A., '"Papinian commands one thing, our Paul another": Roman Christians and Jewish law in the *Collatio Legum Mosaicarum et Romanarum*' in C. Ando and J. Rüpke (eds.), *Religion and Law in Classical and Christian Rome* (Stuttgart, 2006), 85–99.

Johnstone, S., 'On the uses of arson in classical Rome', *Studies in Latin Literature and Roman History* 6 (1992), 41–69.

Jolowicz, H. F. and Nicholas, B., *Historical Introduction to the Study of Roman Law*, 3rd edn (Cambridge, 1972),

Jones, A. H. M., *The Later Roman Empire, 284–602: A social, economic, and administrative survey* (London, 1964; reprint Baltimore, 1986).

Jones, A. H. M. and Skeat, T. C., 'Notes on the genuineness of the Constantinian documents in Eusebius' Life of Constantine', *JEH* 5 (1954), 196–200.

Jones, A. H. M., Martindale, J. R., and Morris, J. (eds.), *Prosopography of the Later Roman Empire* (Cambridge, 1971), I.

Jörs, P., 'Aemilius Papinianus', *RE* 1, 1 (Stuttgart, 1893), cols. 572–5.

—— 'Codex Gregorianus', *RE* (Stuttgart, 1900), IV(1), cols. 161–4.

—— 'Codex Hermogenianus', *RE* (Stuttgart, 1900), IV(1), cols. 164–67.

—— 'Collatio legum Mosaicarum et Romanarum', *RE* (Stuttgart, 1900), IV, cols. 367–70.

—— 'Domitius Ulpianus', *RE* (Stuttgart, 1905), V(1), cols. 1435–509.

Jülicher, A., *Itala: Das Neue Testament in altlateinischer Überlieferung* (Berlin, 1938).

Kaiser, W., *Die Epitome Iuliani* (Frankfurt, 2004).

Kalb, W., *Die Jagd nach Interpolationen in den Digesten: sprachliche Beiträge zur Digestenkritik* (Nuremberg, 1897).

Kaser, M., 'Testimonium', *RE* (Stuttgart, 1934), supp. 5a, cols. 1021–61.

—— *Römische Privatrecht*, 2nd edn (Munich, 1971), I.

Kaser, M. and Knütel, R., *Römische Privatrecht*, 18th edn (Munich, 2005).

Kaster, R., *Guardians of Language: The grammarian and society in late antiquity* (Berkeley, 1988).

Kaufhold, H., Review of G. Galbiati and Sergio Noja, *Precetti e Canoni giuridico-morali per arabi christiani, Vol. I, Oriens Christianus* 53 (1969), 266–70.

Kelly, C., *Ruling the Later Roman Empire* (Cambridge, MA, 2004)

——'Bureaucracy and government' in Lenski (ed.), *The Cambridge Companion to the Age of Constantine* (2006), 183–204.

Kelly, D., 'Jean du Tillet, archivist and antiquary', *Journal of Modern History* 38 (1966), 337–54.

—— 'Gaius Noster: Substructures of Western social thought', *American Historical Review* 84 (1979), 619–48.

Kelly, Gavin, *Ammianus Marcellinus: The allusive historian* (Cambridge, 2008).

Kelly, Gordon, *A History of Exile in the Roman Republic* (Cambridge, 2006).

Kelly, J. M., *Roman Litigation* (Oxford, 1966).

Kennedy, H. A. A., 'Latin Versions, The Old' in J. Hastings (ed.), *A Dictionary of the Bible*, 3 (Edinburgh, 1900), 47–62.

Kenrick, J., 'The Versio Itala, its age, name and origin', *Theological Review* 11 (1874), 318–30.

Keresztes, P., 'The Imperial Roman government and the Christian Church II: From Gallienus to the Great Persecution' in W. Haase (ed.), *ANRW* (Berlin, 1979), II (23.1), 375–86.

Kim, Y., 'Epiphanius of Cyprus and the geography of heresy' in Drake, *Violence in Late Antiquity*, 235–51.

King, N. Q., *The Emperor Theodosius and the Establishment of Christianity* (Philadelphia, 1960).

Klami, H. T., *'Mutua magis videtur quam deposita' Über die Geldverwahrung im Denken der Römischen Juristen* (Helsinki, 1969).

Klek, J. and Armbruster, L., *Die Bienenkunde des Altertums*, 3 vols. (Leipzig, 1919–21).

Kolb, F., 'Der Bussakt von Mailand: Zum Verhaltnis von Staat und Kirche in der Spätantike' in H. Boockman, K. Jürgensen, and G. Stottenberg (eds.), *Geschichte und Gegenwart: Festschrift für K. D. Erdmann* (Neumünster, 1980), 41–74.

—— *Diocletian und die erste Tetrarchie: Improvisation oder Experiment in der Organisation monarchischer Herrschaft?* (Berlin, 1987).

Kovac, M., 'Bora or summer storm: Meterological aspect of the Battle of Frigidus' in R. Bratoz, *Westillyricum und Nordostitalien in der Spätrömischen Zeit* (Ljubljana, 1996), 109–19.

Kübler, B., 'Griechische Tatbestände in dem Werken der Kasuistischen Literatur', *ZRG (R.A.)* 29 (1908), 183–226.

—— 'Gaius', *RE* (Stuttgart, 1910), VII(1), cols. 489–508.

—— Review of Hohenlohe, *Ursprung*, *ZRG (R.A.)* 56 (1936), 361–2.

Kunkel, W., *Die Römischen Juristen: Herkunft und soziale Stellung*, 2nd edn (Cologne, 1967).

Lachmann, K., 'Verbesserungen des Textes der Collatio', *Zeitschrift für geschichtliches Rechtswissenschaft* 10 (1842), 309–14.

La Rosa, F., 'Il valore originario di' "iniuria" nella "lex Aquilia"', *Labeo* 44 (1998), 366–76.

Ladurie, E. Le Roy, *Montaillou: The promised land of error*, tr. G. Braziller (New York, 1978).

Lamb, J. A., 'The place of the Bible in the liturgy' in Ackroyd and Evans (eds.), *The Cambridge History of the Bible*, I, 563–86

Lambertini, R., *Plagium* (Milan, 1980).

Lampe, P., *From Paul to Valentinus: Christians at Rome in the first two centuries*, English tr. of *Die Christen in den ersten beiden Jahrhunderten* (London, 2003).

Larsen, C. W. R., 'Theodosius and the Thessalonian Massacre revisted—yet again', *Studia Patristica* 10 (1970), 297–301.

Lawson, F., *Negligence in the Civil Law* (Oxford, 1950).

Lee, A. D. , 'Traditional religions' in Lenski (ed.), *The Cambridge Companion to the Age of Constantine*, 159–79.

Lendon, J., *Empire of Honour: The art of government in the Roman world* (Oxford, 1997).

Lenel, O., 'Kritisches und Exegetisches', *ZRG (R.A.)* 8 (1887), 195–206.

Lenski, N., 'Evidence for the *Audientia Episcopalis* in the new letters of Augustine' in Mathisen (ed.), *Law, Society, and Authority in Late Antiquity* (2001), 83–97.

—— *Failure of Empire: Valens and the Roman state in the fourth century* AD (Berkeley, 2002).

Lenski, N. (ed.), *Cambridge Companion to the Age of Constantine* (Cambridge, 2006).

Levy, E., 'Paulus und der Sentenzenverfasser', *ZRG (R.A.)* 50 (1930), 272–94.

—— Review of Volterra, *Collatio, ZRG (R.A.)* 50 (1930), 698–705.

Liebs, D., *Hermogenians Iuris Epitomae* (Göttingen, 1964).

—— 'Rechtsschulen und Rechtsunterricht im Prinzipat' in H. Temporini (ed.), *ANRW* (Berlin, 1976), II(15), 197–286.

—— 'Römische Provinzialjurisprudenz' in H. Temporini (ed.), *ANRW* (Berlin, 1976), II(15), 288–362.

—— Review of Honoré's *Ulpian, Gnomon* 56 (1984), 441–50.

—— *Die Jurisprudenz im spätantiken Italien (260–640 n. Chr.)* (Berlin, 1987).

—— 'Hermogenians Prätorianerpräfektur inschriftlich bezeugt', *ZRG (R.A.)* 107 (1990), 385–6.

—— 'Die pseudopaulinischen Sentenzen I', *ZRG (R.A.)* 112 (1995), 151–71.

—— 'Die pseudopaulinischen Sentenzen II', *ZRG (R.A.)* 113 (1996), 132–242.

—— *Römische Jurisprudenz in Gallien* (Berlin, 2002).

—— 'Zur Überlieferung und Entstehung des Breviarium Alaricianum', *Atti dell' Accademia Romanistica Constantiniana* 14 (2003), 653–71.

—— *Römische Jurisprudenz in Africa*, 2nd edn (Berlin, 2005).

Lieu, S., *Manichaeism in the Later Roman Empire and Medieval China*, 2nd edn (Tübingen, 1992).

—— *Manichaeism in Mesopotamia and the Roman East*, 2nd edn (Leiden, 1999).

—— *Manichaean Texts from the Roman Empire* (Cambridge, 2004).

Lilja, S., *Homosexuality in Republican and Augustan Rome* (Helsinki, 1983).

Litewski, W., 'Die Personen des römischen Verwahrungsverhältnisses', *RIDA* 3, série 47 (2000), 235–349.

Lizzi Testa, R., 'Christian emperor, Vestal Virgins and priestly colleges: Reconsidering the end of Roman paganism', *Ant. Tard.* 15 (2007), 251–62.

Löhr, W. A., 'Some observations on Karl-Heinz Schwarte's "Diokletian's Christengesetz"', *Vigiliae Christianae* 56 (2002), 75–95.

Longo, C., 'Appunti sul Deposito Irregolare', *BIDR* 18 (1905), 121–56.

Longo, G., 'Crimen plagii', *Annali della facoltà giuridica dell' università di Genova* 13 (1974), 381–482.

Loschiavo, L., 'La legge che dio trasmise a Mosè. Fortuna medioevale di un' operetta volgare', *Rechtsgeschichte* 2 (2003), 72–86.

Lotz, A., *Der Magiekonflikt in der Spätantike* (Bonn, 2005).

Lübtow, U. von, 'Die Aufgaben des römischen Praetors auf dem Gebiet der Zivilrechtspflege' in *Studi in onore di A. Biscardi* (Milan, 1983), IV.

Luck, G., *Arcana Mundi: Magic and the occult in the Greek and Roman worlds*, 2nd edn (Baltimore, 2006).

Lucrezi, F., 'Constantino e gli aurispici', *Atti dell' academia di scienze morali e politiche* 97 (1987), 171–98.

—— 'L'uccisione del proprio Schiavo nella Collatio' in *Iuris Vincula: Studi in Onore di Mario Talamanca* (Naples, 2001), 21–92.

——*L'uccisione dello schiavo in diritto ebraico e romana* (Turin, 2001).

—— 'Sulla data di redazione della Collatio alla luce di due costituzioni costantiniane', *Atti dell' Accademia Romanistica Costaniniana* 14 (2003), 599–613.

—— *La Successione intestata in diritto ebraico e romano. Studi sulla Collatio* (Turin, 2005), III.

—— 'Lex Dei e comparazione Giruidico', *AARC* 15 (2005), 57–82.

Luomanen, P., 'Where did another rich man come from? The Jewish-Christian profile of the story about a rich man in the "Gospel of the Hebrews" (Origen, Comm. In Matth. 15.14)', *Vigiliae Christianae* 57 (2003), 243–75.

MacCormack, G., 'Criminal liability for fire in early and classical Roman law', *Index: Quaderni camerti di studi romanistici* 3 (1972), 382–96.

—— 'Terminus motus', *RIDA* 26 (1979), 239–60.

—— 'Juristic interpretation of the *Lex Aquilia*' in *Studi in onore di Cesare Sanfilippo* (Milan, 1982), I, 253–83.

—— 'Sources' in E. Metzger (ed.), *A Companion to Justinian's Institutes* (Ithaca, 1999), 1–17.

MacDonell, J. and Manson, E. (eds.), *Great Jurists of the World* (Boston, 1914), II.

Manthe, U., 'Ethische Argumente im Werk Papinians', *Orbis Iuris Romani* 10 (2005), 143–66.

Margolis, M., 'Additions to field from the Lyons Codex of the Old Latin', *Journal of the American Oriental Society* 33 (1913), 254–58.

Marlowe, E., 'Framing the sun: The Arch of Constantine and the Roman cityscape', *The Art Bulletin* 88 (2006), 223–42

Martini, R., *Le definizioni dei giuristi romani* (Milan, 1966).

Masi, A., 'Contributi ad una Datazione della "Collatio Legum Mosaicarum et Romanarum"', *BIDR* 3 (1961), 285–321.

Mathisen, R., '*Adnotatio* and *Petitio*: The emperor's favor and special exceptions in the early Byzantine Empire' in D. Feissel and J. Gascou (eds.), *La pétition à Byzance* (Paris, 2004), 23–32.

Mathisen, R. (ed.), *Law, Society, and Authority in Late Antiquity* (Oxford, 2001).
Mattei, P., 'L'anthropologie de Novatien: Affinités, perspectives, et limites', *REAug* 38 (1992), 232–59.
Matthews, J., *The Roman Empire of Ammianus* (London, 1989).
—— *Western Aristocracies and Imperial Court*, AD *364–425*, 2nd edn (Oxford, 1990).
—— 'Ammianus on Roman law and lawyers' in J. den Boeft *et al.*, *Cognitio Gestorum: The historiographic art of Ammianus Marcellinus* (Amsterdam, 1992), 47–57.
—— 'The making of the text' in Harries and Wood, *The Theodosian Code* (1993), 19–44.
—— *Laying Down the Law: A study of the Theodosian Code* (New Haven, 2000).
—— 'Roman law and Barbarian identity in the late Roman West' in S. Mitchell (ed.), *Ethnicity and Culture in Late Antiquity* (London, 2000), 31–44.
—— 'The Roman Empire and the proliferation of elites', *Arethusa* 33 (2000), 429–46.
—— 'Interpreting the *Interpretationes* of the *Breviarium*' in Mathisen (ed.), *Law, Society, and Authority in Late Antiquity* (2001), 11–32.
Mattingly, H., 'The religious background of the "Historia Augusta"', *HTR* 39 (1946), 213–15.
McGinn, T. A. J., '"Ne Serva Prostituatur": Restrictive covenants in the sale of slaves', *ZRG (R.A.)* 107 (1990), 315–53.
—— *Prostitution, Sexuality, and the Law in Ancient Rome* (Oxford, 1998).
McGurk, P., 'The oldest manuscripts of the Latin Bible' in Richard Gameson (ed.), *The Early Medieval Bible: Its production, decoration and use* (Cambridge, 1994), 1–23.
McIntosh, J., *A Study of Augustine's Versions of Genesis* (Chicago, 1912).
McLean, N., 'The Lyons Old Latin Heptateuch', *JTS*, o. s. 2 (1901), 305–8.
McLynn, N., *Ambrose of Milan* (Berkeley and Los Angeles, 1994).
Meer, T. van der, 'The Voconian Law: Nova or phoenix?', *TR* 67 (1999), 115–23.
Merkel, J., *Die Lehre von der successio graduum unter Intestaterben* (Tübingen, 1876).
Metzger, B., *The Early Versions of the New Testament: Their origin, transmission, and limitations* (Oxford, 1977).
—— *The Text of the New Testament: Its transmission, corruption, and restoration*, 3rd edn (Oxford, 1992).
—— *The Canon of the New Testament: Its origins, development, and significance* (Oxford, 1997).
Metzger, E., *A Companion to Justinian's Institutes* (Ithaca, 1999).

Meyer, E. A., *Legitimacy and Law in the Roman World: Tabulae in Roman belief and practice* (Cambridge, 2004).
Meyvaert, P., 'Bede, Cassiodorus, and the Codex Amiatinus', *Speculum* 71 (1996), 827–83.
Mikat, P., *Die Inzestverbote des Dritten Konzils von Orléans (538), Ein Beitrag zur Geschichte des Fränkischen Eherects* (Opladen, 1993), 38–40.
—— *Die Inzestgesetzgebung der merowingisch-fränkischen Konzilien (511–626/27)* (Padeborn, 1994).
Millar, F., *The Emperor in the Roman World* (London, 1977).
—— 'Condemnation to hard labour in the Roman Empire from the Julio-Claudians to Constantine', *PBSR* 52 (1984), 124–47.
—— 'A new Approach to the Roman jurists', *JRS* 76 (1986), 272–80.
—— *A Greek Roman Empire: Power and belief under Theodosius II (408–450)* (Berkeley, 2006).
Milne, H. J. M. and Skeat, T. C., *Scribes and Correctors of the Codex Sinaiticus* (London, 1938).
Molnár, I., 'Das adulterium als ein das Ansehen der römischen Familie verletzendes Verbrechen' in Hans-Georg Knothe (ed.), *Status Familiae: Festschrift für Andreas Wacke* (Munich, 2001), 345–64.
Momigliano, A., 'Pagan and Christian historiography in the fourth century' in A. Momigliano (ed.), *The Conflict between Paganism and Christianity in the Fourth Century* (Oxford, 1963), 79–99.
Moreau, P, *Incestus et prohibitae nuptiae* (Paris, 2002).
Morris, C., *The Papal Monarchy: The Western Church from 1050 to 1250* (Oxford, 1989).
Mueller, F., *Vegetius: Abriss des Militärwesens* (Stuttgart, 1997).
Murison, A. F., Review of Hyamson, *CR* 27 (1913), 274–77.
Murphy, F. X., *Rufinus of Aquleia, (345–411): His life and works* (Washington, DC, 1945).
Navarra, M., 'Note in tema di "utilitas": Modestino e Coll. 10. 2', *Labeo* 50 (2004), 84–134.
Nelson, H. L. W., *Überlieferung, Aufbau und Stil von Gai Institutiones* (Leiden, 1981).
Nelson, J. and Drotning, E. (eds.), *Luther's Small Catechism*, tr. T. Wengert (Minneapolis, 2001).
Nicholson, E., *The Pentateuch in the Twentieth Century: The legacy of Julius Wellhausen* (Oxford, 1998).
Nicolson, A., *God's Secretaries: The making of the King James Bible* (New York, 2003).
Nock, A. D., 'The emperor's divine *comes*', *JRS* 37 (1947), 102–16.
Noethlichs, K. L., *Die Juden im christlichen Imperium Romanum [4.-6. Jahrhundert]* (Berlin, 2001).
Nogrady, A., *Römisches Strafrecht nach Ulpian: Buch 7 bis 9 De officio proconsulis* (Berlin, 2006).

Nörr, D., 'Papinian and Gryphius. Zum Nachleben Papinians', *ZRG (R.A.)* 83 (1966), 308–33.

—— 'Drei Miszellen zur Lebensgeschichte des Juristen Salvius Julianus' in A. Watson (ed.), *Daube Noster* (Edinburgh, 1974), 233–52.

—— *Rechtskritik in der römischen Antike* (Munich, 1974).

—— *Causa Mortis* (Munich, 1986).

—— 'Zur Taxatio bei der Actio Iniuriarum', *Collatio Iuris Romani: Études Dédiées À Hans Ankum* (Amsterdam, 1995), II, 389–401.

Novick, P., *That Noble Dream: The 'objectivity question' and the American historical profession* (Cambridge, 1988).

O'Corrain, D., 'Irish vernacular law and the Old Testament' in P. Ni Chathain and M. Richter (eds.), *Ireland and Christendom: The Bible and the missions* (Stuttgart, 1987), 284–310.

O'Donnell, J., *Cassiodorus* (Berkeley, 1979).

—— *Augustine Confessions II: Commentary on Books 1–7* (Oxford, 1992).

Oliviero, G., 'A proposito di succcessio ordinum nell'eredità in testata della Dodici Tavole', *SDHI* 68 (2002), 625–31.

O'Meara, D. J., *Platonopolis: Platonic political philosophy in late antiquity* (Oxford, 2003).

Ostersetzer, I., 'La "Collatio legum Mosaicarum et Romanarum," Ses origins—son but', *Revue des Études Juives* 97 (1934), 65–96.

Ott, J. N., Review of C. Paucker, *Spicilegium addendorum lexicis latinis composuit adnotavit*, *Zeitschrift für die österreichischen Gymnasien* 26 (1875), 517–18.

Pagels, E., *Beyond Belief: The secret Gospel of Thomas* (New York, 2003).

Papandrea, J., *The Trinitarian Theology of Novatian of Rome: A study in third-century orthodoxy* (Lewiston, NY, 2008).

Parkes, M. B., *The Scriptorium of Wearmouth-Jarrow* (Jarrow, 1982).

Paschoud, F., 'Raisonnements providentialistes dans l'Histoire Auguste', *BHAC* 1977/78 (*Antiquitas* IV 14), 163–78.

—— 'La Storia Augusta come testimonianza e riflesso della crisi d'identità degli ultimi intellettuali pagani in Occidente' in G. Bonamente and A. Nestori (eds.), *I Cristiani e l'Impero nel IV secolo* (Macopata, 1988), 155–6.

—— 'Chronique d'historiographie tardive', *Ant. Tard.* 15 (2007), 349–64.

Pastori, F., *Il commodato in diritto romano* (Bologna, 1995).

Paulus, C., 'Testimonium', *Der Neue Pauly* (Stuttgart, 2002), XII, cols. 189–91.

Pepe, L., *Richerche sul furto nelle XII tavole e nel diritto attico* (Milan, 2004).

Pharr, C., 'The interdiction of magic in Roman law', *TAPA* 63 (1932), 269–95.

Phillips, A., *Deuteronomy: Commentary* (Cambridge, 1973).

Piazza, M., *La disciplina del falso nel diritto romano* (Padua, 1991).

Pieler, P., 'Lex Christiana' in D. Simon, D. (ed.), *Akten des 26. Deutschen Rechtshistorikertages* (Frankfurt, 1987), 485–503.

Pika, W., *Ex causa furtiva condicere im klassichen römischen Recht* (Berlin, 1988).

Platschek, J., Review of Nogrady's *Ulpian*, *TR* 76 (2008), 396–99.

Polay, E., *Iniuria Types in Roman Law* (Budapest, 1986).

Potter, D., *Prophecy and History in the Crisis of the Roman Empire* (Oxford, 1990).

Pottier, B., 'L' Histoire Auguste, le consul Aurélien et la réception de la Notitia Dignatatum en occident', *Ant. Tard.* 14 (2006), 225–34

Pretto-Sakmann, A., '"You never can tell with bees": Good advice from Pooh for students of the *Lex Aquilia*' in A. Burrows and A. Rodger (eds.), *Mapping the Law: Essays in honour of Peter Birks* (Oxford, 2006), 475–96.

Price, J., Review of Rutgers, *Journal of the American Oriental Society* 117 (1997), 720–1.

Prieto, M. F., *La difamación en el derecho romano* (Valencia, 2002).

Pringsheim, F., *Zum Plan einer neuen Ausgabe der Basiliken: Begründung ihrer Notwendigkeit und Gesichtspunkte für ihre Herstellung* (Berlin, 1956).

Pugliese, G., 'Noxia', *Law Quarterly Review* 88 (1972), 543–8.

—— 'A suggestion on the Collatio', *Israel Law Review* 29 (1995), 161–75.

Pugsley, D., 'On Tribonian and his Latin style' in R. Ruedin (ed.), *Melanges en l'honneur de Carlo Augusto Cannata* (Basel, 1999), 171–7.

Puliatti, S., *Incesti Crimina: Regime Giuridico da Augusto a Giustiniano* (Milan, 2001).

Rabello, A. M., 'Alcune note sulla "Collatio Legum Mosaicarum et Romanarum" e sul suo luogo d'origine' in *Scritti sull'Ebraismo in memoria di Guido Bedarida* (Florence, 1966), 177–86.

—— 'Sull'ebraicita' dell'autore della "Collatio Legum Mosaicarum et Romanarum"', *La Rassegna mensile di Israel* 33 (1967), 339–49.

—— 'Sul Decalogo "Cristianizzato" e l'autore della "Collatio Legum Mosaicarum et Romanarum"', *La Rassegna mensile di Israel* 55 (1989), 133–5.

—— 'La Datazione della Collatio Legum Mosaicarum et Romanarum e il Problema di una sua seconda redazione o del suo uso nel corso del quarto secolo' in J.-M. Carrié and L. Lizzi Testa (eds.), *Humana Sapit: Etudes d'Antiquité tardive offerts à Lellia Cracco Ruggini* (Brepols, 2002), 411–22.

Rad, G. von, *Deuteronomy: A commentary*, tr. Dorotea Barton (Philadelphia, 1966).

Radin, M., 'The privilege of confidential communication between lawyer and client', *California Law Review* 16 (1928), 487–97.

Ranke, L. von, 'Vorrede zur ersten Ausgabe', *Geschichten der romanischen und germanischen Völker von 1494 bis 1514*, 3rd edn (Leipzig, 1885).

Rapp, C., 'Comparison, paradigm, and the case of Moses in panegyric and hagiography' in M. Whitby (ed.), *The Propaganda of Power: The role of panegyric in late antiquity* (Leiden, 1998), 277–98.

Ratti, S. 'Nicomaque Flavien Senior Auteur de L'Histoire Auguste' in *Historiae Augustae Colloquium Bambergense* (Mai, 2005), ed. G. Bonamente and H. Brandt (Bari, 2007), 305–17.

—— 'Nicomaque Flavien Senior et l'Histoire Auguste: la découverte de nouveaux liens', *REL* 85 (2007), 204–19.

Reed, J. S. B., Review of Hyamson, *JRS* 3 (1913), 150–1

Reynolds, L. D. and Wilson, N. G., *Scribes and Scholars*, 3rd edn (Oxford, 1991).

Rilinger, R., *Humiliores-Honestiores: zu einer sozialen Dichotomie in Strafrecht der römischen Kaiserzeit* (Munich, 1988).

Rives, J., 'The Decree of Decius and the religion of empire', *JRS* 89 (1999), 135–54.

—— 'Magic in Roman law: The reconstruction of a crime', *Classical Antiquity* 22 (2003), 313–39.

—— 'Magic, religion, and law: The case of the *Lex Cornela de sicariis et veneficiis*' in C. Ando and J. Rüpke (eds.), *Religion and Law in Classical and Christian Rome* (Stuttgart, 2006), 47–67.

Rizzelli, G., '"Stuprum" e "adulterium" nella cultura augustea e la "Lex Iulia de adulteriis,"' *BIDR* 90 (1987), 355–88.

Robertis, F. de, *La Legittimazione attiva nell'actio furti* (Bari, 1950).

—— *Risponsibilita contrattuale nel diritto romano* (Bari, 1994).

—— *Damnum Iniuria Datum*, 2 vols. (Bari, 2000–2).

Roberts, C. H. and Skeat, T. C., *The Birth of the Codex* (London, 1983).

Robinson, I., *The Papacy, 1073–1198: Continuity and innovation* (Cambridge, 1990).

Robinson, O. F., 'An aspect of *Falsum*', *TR* 60 (1992), 29–38.

—— *The Criminal Law of Ancient Rome* (London, 1995).

—— *Penal Practice and Penal Policy in Ancient Rome* (London, 2007).

Rodger, A., 'Behind the scenes in Roman law', Review of Honoré's *Tribonian, Emperors and Lawyers*, and *Ulpian*, *Oxford Journal of Legal Studies* 3 (1983), 383–404.

Rodriguez, S. Bello, 'Un rescripto de Adriano sobre el crimen de abigeatus: civiliter vel criminaliter agere?' in A. Murillo Villar (ed.), *La responsibilidad civil de Roma al derecho moderno* (Burgos, 2001), 93–104.

Rodriguez-Martin, J.-D., 'A handbook for Alaric's codification', *RIDA* 3, série 46 (1999), 451–63.

Romanelli, P., '*Constitutio Antoniniana*', *Romanitas* 4 (1962), 29–41.

Rönsch, H., *Itala und Vulgata*, 2nd edn (Marburg, 1875).

—— *Semasiologische Beiträge zum lateinischen Wörterbuch* (Leipzig, 1887).

Rotondi, G., 'Studi sulle fonti del codice giustinianeo' in *Scritti Giuridici* (Pavia, 1922), 110–283.

Rubin, Z., 'Further to the dating of the *Constitutio Antoniniana*', *Latomus* 34 (1975), 430–6.

Rudorff, A., *Über den Ursprung und die Bestimmung der Lex Dei oder Mosaicarum et Romanarum legum Collatio* (Berlin, 1868).

Ruggini, L. Cracco, 'Ebrei e Romani a Confronti nell' Italia Tardoantica', *Italia Judica* (Rome, 1983), 38–65.

Rutgers, L. V., *The Jews in Late Ancient Rome: Evidence of cultural interaction in the Roman diaspora* (Leiden, 2000).

Ryan, F. X., 'The *Lex Scantinia* and the prosecution of censors and aediles', *CP* 89 (1994), 159–62.

Sachsse, C. R., Review of von Daniels, *De Saxononici speculi origine ex juris communis*, *Kritische Zeitschrift für die gesammte Rechtswissenschaft* 1 (1853), 173–216.

Saller, R., *Patriarchy, Property, and Death in the Roman Family* (Cambridge, 1994).

—— 'Family and household' in A. K. Bowman, P. Garnsey, and D. Rathbone (eds.), *Cambridge Ancient History, XI: The High Empire,* AD *70–192*, 2nd edn (Cambridge, 2000), 855–74.

Salzman, M. R., *On Roman Time: The Codex calendar of 354 and the rhythms of urban life in late antiquity* (Berkeley, 1990).

—— *The Making of a Christian Aristocracy* (Cambridge, MA, 2002).

Samter, R., 'War Gajus der männliche pseudonym einer Frau?', *Deutsche Juristenzeitung* 13 (1908), 1386–91.

Sanguinetti, A., *Dalla querela alla portio legitima: aspetti della successione necessaria nell' epoca tardo imperiale e giustinianea* (Milan, 1996).

Sarna, N. M. and Shanks, H., 'Israel in Egypt: The Egyptian sojourn and the Exodus' in H. Shanks (ed.), *Ancient Israel: From Abraham to the Roman destruction of the Temple*, 2nd edn (Washington, DC, 1999), 33–54.

Sasse, C., *Die Constitutio Antoniniana* (Wiesbaden, 1958).

Savigny, F. C. von, *Geschichte des Römischen Rechts im Mittelalter* (Heidelberg, 1850).

Scherillo, G., Review of Volterra, *Collatio*, *Archivo giuridico* 104 (1930), 255–65.

—— 'Teodosiano, Gregoriano, Ermogeniano' in *Studi in memoria di U. Ratti* (Milan, 1934), 247–323.

Schildenberger, J., 'Die Itala des hl. Augustinus' in B. Fischer and V. Fiala (eds.), *Colligere fragmenta: Festschrift Alban Dold* (Beuron, 1950), 84–102.

Schiller, A., 'Provincial cases in Papinian', *Acta Juridica* 1 (1958), 221–42.

Schmitz, H., *Die Bussbücher und Bussdisciplin der Kirche nach handschriftlichen Quellen dargestellt* (Mainz, 1883).

Schrage, E., 'La date de la "Collatio Legum Mosaicarum et Romanarum", étudiée d'après les citations bibliques' in J. A. Ankum et al. (eds.), *Mélanges Felix Wubbe* (Fribourg, 1993), 401–17.

Schultz, F., 'Das Ediktsystem in den Paulus-Sentenzen', *ZRG (R.A.)* 47 (1927), 39–52.

—— 'Die biblischen Texte in der Collatio Legum Mosaicarum et Romanarum', *SDHI* 2 (1936), 20–43.

—— *History of Roman Legal Science* (Oxford, 1946).

—— 'The manuscripts of the "Collatio Legum Mosaicarum et Romanarum"' in M. David, B. A. van Gröningen, and E. M. Meijers (eds.), *Symbolae van Oven* (Leiden, 1946), 313–32 (reprinted in *Bullettino dell'Istituto di Diritto Romano* 55 (1951), 50–69).

—— *Classical Roman Law* (Oxford, 1951).

Schumacher, L., *Sklaverei in der Antike* (Munich, 2000).

Schwartz, E., 'Artapanos', *RE* (Stuttgart, 1895), II(1), col. 1306.

Seeck, O., 'Das sogenannte Edikt von Mailand', *Zeitschrift für Kirchengeschichte* 12 (1891), 381–6.

—— 'Die Zeitfolge der Gesetze Constantins', *ZRG (R.A.)* 10 (1899), 1–44, 177–255.

—— 'Gratianus (3)', in *RE* (Stuttgart, 1912), VII(2), cols. 1831–40.

—— *Regesten für Kaiser und Päpste* (Stuttgart, 1919).

Seeck, O. and Veith, G., 'Die Schlacht am Frigidus', *Klio* 13 (1913), 451–67.

Segre, G., 'Sul Deposito Irregolare in Diritto Romano', *BIDR* 19 (1907), 197–234.

Shanks, H. and Witherington, B., *The Brother of Jesus* (New York, 2003).

Shaw, B., 'Raising and killing children: Two Roman myths', *Mnemosyne* 54 (2001), 31–77.

Shaw, B. and Saller, R., 'Close-kin marriage in Roman society?', *Man: Journal of the Royal Anthropological Institute*, n. s. 19 (1984), 432–44.

Sherman, C. P., 'The study of law in Roman law schools', *Yale Law Journal* 17 (1907–8), 499–512.

Sherwin-White, A. N., *The Roman Citizenship*, 2nd edn (Oxford, 1973).

Siems, H., 'Lex Baiuvariorum' in *Handwörterbuch zur deutschen Rechtsgeschichte* (Berlin, 1978), II, 1887–901.

—— 'Lex Baiuvariorum', *Reallexikon der Germanischen Altertumskunde* (Berlin and New York, 2001), XVIII, 304–15.

Sirks, A. J. B., 'The sources of the Code', in Harries and Wood, *The Theodosian Code* (1993), 45–67.

—— '*Sacra*, succession and the *lex Voconia*', *Latomus* 53 (1994), 273–96.

—— *The Theodosian Code: A study* (Friedrichsdorf, 2007).

Sitzia, F., 'D. 19.2.15.2: "vis maior" e "vitia ex ipsa re"' in C. Cascione (ed.), *Fides humanitas ius: studi in onore di Luigi Labruna* (Naples, 2007), VII, 5211–27.

Skeat, T. C., 'The Codex Vaticanus in the fifteenth century', *JTS*, n. s. 35 (1984), 454–65.

Small, J. P., *Wax Tablets of the Mind: Cognitive studies of memory and literacy in classical antiquity* (London, 1997).

Smelik, K. A. D., 'The Witch of Endor: I Samuel 28 in rabbinic and Christian exegesis till 800 AD', *Vigiliae Christianae* 33 (1979), 160–79.

Smith, R., *Julian's Gods* (London, 1995).

Sogno, C., *Symmachus: A political biography* (Ann Arbor, 2006).

Solazzi, S., 'Per la Data della "Collatio Mosaicarum et Romanarum Legum"' in his *Scritti di Diritto Romano*, 3 (Naples, 1960), 481–502.

Solin, H., *Die Stadtrömischen Sklavennamen: Ein Namenbuch* (Stuttgart, 1996).

Sotty, R., *Recherche sur les utiles actiones: la notion d'action utile en droit romain classique* (Grenoble, 1977).

Spagnuolo, V., '*Actio iniuriarum noxalis*', *Labeo* 15 (1969), 33–76.

Sparks, H. D. F., 'The Latin Bible' in H. Wheeler Robinson (ed.), *The Bible in its Ancient and English Versions* (Oxford, 1940), 100–27.

—— 'Jerome as biblical scholar' in Ackroyd and Evans (eds.), *The Cambridge History of the Bible* (1970), I, 510–41.

Sperandio, M., *Codex Gregorianus: origini e vicende* (Naples, 2005).

Springer, M., 'Die Schlacht am Frigidus als quellenkundliches und literaturgeschichtliches Problem' in R. Bratoz (ed.), *Westillyricum und Nordostitalien in der Spätrömischen Zeit* (Ljubljana, 1996), 45–93.

Stanojevic, O., *Gaius Noster, Plaidoyer pour Gaius* (Amsterdam, 1989).

Stark, R., *The Rise of Christianity* (Princeton, 1996).

Stertz, S. A., 'Christianity in the Historia Augusta', *Latomus* 36 (1977), 694–715.

Stolmar, R., *Actio Utiles: Grundlagen, Wesen, Voraussetzungen, Andwendungen, Wirkungen* (Sindelfingen, 1984).

Straub, J., *Studien zur Historia Augusta* (Bern, 1952).

—— *Heidnische Geschichtsapologetik in der christlichen Spätantike: Untersuchungen über Zeit und Tendenz der Historia Augusta* (Bonn, 1963).

—— 'Eugenius', *RAC* 6 (1966), cols. 860–77.

Streeter, B. H., *The Four Gospels: A study of origins, treating of the manuscript tradition, sources, authorship, and date* (New York, 1924).

Sturdy, J., *Numbers* (Cambridge, 1976).

Syme, R., *Ammianus and the Historia Augusta* (Oxford, 1968).

—— *Emperors and Biography: Studies in the Historia Augusta* (Oxford, 1971).

Szidat, J., 'Die Usurpation des Eugenius', *Historia* 28 (1979), 487–508.

Szirmai, J. A., *The Archaeology of Medieval Bookbinding* (Aldershot, 1999; reprint 2007).

Talmon, S., 'The Old Testament text' in Ackroyd and Evans (eds.), *The Cambridge History of the Bible*, I, 159–99.

Taubenschlag, R., 'Testimonium Falsum', *RE* (Stuttgart, 1934), supp. 5a, col. 1061.

—— 'Terminus Motus', *RE* (Stuttgart, 1934), supp. 5a, cols. 784–5.

Taylor, V., *The Gospels: A short introduction*, 9th edn (London, 1960)

Terreni, C., 'Gaio e L' "Erroris Causae Probatio"', *Labeo* 45 (1999), 333–67.

Thulin, K., 'Haruspices', *RE* (Stuttgart, 1912), VII(2), cols. 2341–468.

Tiede, D., 'Religious propaganda and Gospel literature' in W. Haase (ed.), *ANRW* (Berlin, 1984), XXV(2), 1705–29.

Tischendorf, C. von (tr.), *When Were Our Gospels Written?* Religious Tract Society in London (New York, 1866).

Tougher, S., *Julian the Apostate* (Edinburgh, 2007).

Tove, E., *Textual Criticism of the Hebrew Bible*, 2nd edn (Minneapolis, 2001).

Treggiari, S., *Roman Marriage: Iusti Coniuges from the time of Cicero to the time of Ulpian* (Oxford, 1991).

Triebs, F., *Studien zur Lex Dei* (Freiburg, 1905), I.

—— *Studien zur Lex Dei*, II: *Das Römische Recht der Lex Dei über das Sechste Gebot des Dekalogs* (Freiburg, 1907).

—— *Die Lex Iulia de adulteriis coercendis auf Grundlage der sog. Lex Dei (Collatio Legum Mosaicarum et Romanarum)* (Breslau, 1910).

Trigger, B. G., *Understanding Early Civilizations* (Cambridge, 2003).

Turner, C. H., 'Jean du Tillet: A neglected scholar of the sixteenth century', appendix V in J. K. Fotheringham (ed.), *The Bodleian Manuscript of Jerome's Version of the Chronicle of Eusebius, reproduced in Collotype* (Oxford, 1905), 48–63.

Turpin, W., 'The purpose of the Roman law codes', *ZRG (R.A.)* 104 (1987), 620–30

—— '*Formula*, *Cognitio*, and proceedings *extra ordinem*', *RIDA* 46 (1999), 499–574.

Valditara, G., *Damnum iniuria datum*, 2nd edn (Turin, 2005).

Valiño, E., *Actiones utiles* (Pamplona, 1974).

Vanderspoel, J., *Themistius and the Imperial Court* (Ann Arbor, 1995).

Vessey, M., 'The origins of the Collectio Sirmondiana' in Harries and Wood, *The Theodosian Code*, 178–99.

Voci, P., *Diritto ereditario romano*, 2nd edn, 2 vols. (Milan, 1963–7).

Völkl, A., *Die Verfolgung der Körperverletzung im frühen Römischen Recht* (Vienna, 1984).

Volterra, E., *Collatio Legum Mosaicarum et Romanarum* (Rome, 1930).

Vööbus, A., *Early Versions of the New Testament* (Stockholm, 1954).

Wacke, A., 'La "exceptio doli" lo rende possibile: fedecommesso in favore di terza e fedecomissaria liberazione dell' obbligo di restituzione della dote', *Iura* 46 (1995), 21–45.

Walters, D., 'From Benedict to Gratian: The Code in medieval ecclesiastical authors' in Harries and Wood, *The Theodosian Code*, 200–16.

Warmington, B., 'The sources of some Constantinian documents in Eusebius' Ecclesiastical History and the Life of Constantine', *Studia Patristica* 18 (1986), 93–8.

Wasserstein, A. and Wasserstein, D., *The Legend of the Septuagint: From classical antiquity to today* (Cambridge, 2007).

Watson, A., 'Two studies in textual history', *TR* 209 (1962), 209–42
—— *The Law of Succession in the Later Roman Republic* (Oxford, 1971).
—— *Law Making in the Later Roman Republic* (Oxford, 1974).
—— 'Roman slave law and Romanist ideology', *Phoenix* 37 (1983), 53–65.
—— Review, *Times Literary Supplement* (16 February, 1985), 164.
—— *Roman Slave Law* (Baltimore, 1987).
Weishaupt, A., *Die lex Voconia* (Vienna, 1999).
Wellhausen, J., *Geschichte Israels*, 2 vols. (Berlin, 1878).
Wenger, L., *Die Quellen des römischen Rechts* (Vienna, 1953).
West, M. L., *Textual Criticism and Editorial Technique* (Stuttgart, 1973).
—— 'Towards monotheism' in Athanassiadi and Frede (eds.), *Pagan Monotheism in Late Antiquity* (1997), 21–40.
White, H. J., 'The Codex Amiatinus and its birthplace', *Studia Biblica et Ecclesiastica: Essays chiefly in biblical and patristic criticism* (Oxford, 1890), II, 273–309.
Wieacker, F., *Textstufen Klassischer Juristen* (Göttingen, 1960).
—— *Römische Rechtsgeschichte* (Munich, 1988), I.
Wiedemann, T., *Emperors and Gladiators* (New York, 1992).
Wilamowitz-Möllendorff, U. von, *Geschichte der Philologie* (Stuttgart, 1921; reprinted 1998).
Wilken, R., *Judaism and the Early Christian Mind: A study of Cyril of Alexandria's exegesis and theology* (New Haven, 1971).
—— *John Chrysostom and the Jews* (Berkeley, 1983).
Williams, M., *The Monk and the Book: Jerome and the making of Christian scholarship* (Chicago, 2006).
Williams, S., *Diocletian and the Roman Recovery* (London, 1985).
Williams, S. and Friell, G., *Theodosius: The empire at bay* (New Haven, 1994).
Witherington, B., *Jesus the Sage* (Minneapolis, 1994).
Wittchow, F., *Exemplarisches Erzählen bei Ammianus Marcellinus* (Munich, 2001).
Wittig, J., *Der Ambrosiaster "Hilarius". Ein Beitrag zur Geschichte des Papstes Damasus* (Breslau, 1906), I.
Wittmann, R., *Die Körperveletzung an Freien im klassischen römischen Recht* (Munich, 1972).
Wlassak, M., 'A. Agerius', *RE* (Stuttgart, 1895), I, col. 794.
Wolff, H.-J., 'Vorgregorianische Reskriptensammlungen', *ZRG (R.A.)* 69 (1952), 128–53.
Wood, I., 'The Code in Merovingian Gaul', in Harries and Wood, *The Theodosian Code*, 161–71.
Woods, D., 'The Constantinian origin of Justina (Themistius, *Or.*3.43b)', *CQ* 54 (2004), 325–7
Wormald, P., *The Making of English law: King Alfred to the twelfth century* (Oxford, 1999).

Würthwein, E., *Der Texte des Alten Testament* (Stuttgart, 1988), tr. E. F. Rhodes, *The Text of the Old Testament* (Grand Rapids, 1995).

Wytzes, J., *Der Streit um den Altar der Viktoria* (Leiden, 1936).

Ziegler, L., *Die lateinischen Bibelübersetzungen vor Hieronymus und die Itala des Augustinus* (Munich, 1879).

Zimmerman, R., *The Law of Obligation: Roman foundations of the civilian tradition* (Cape Town, 1990).

Select Index of Names and Topics

This intentionally selective index includes names of ancient and medieval authors and historical figures as well as titles of laws, titles of works, institutional offices, concepts, and major developments developed in the historical study and Commentary. In general, items only in footnotes are omitted. To avoid redundancy with the tables and Commentary, it does not include such topics from the Latin text or English translation.

Aaron (brother of Moses) 244
Abraham 148, 272
Actio ad exhibendum 286
Actio in factum 293–4
Actio utiles 260
Actiones in simplum 286
Adnotatio 249–50
Adronicus, Flavius Aurelius Altenicus 284
Adultery 4, 62–3, 136, 257–63
Agatho 249
Agerius, Aulus 254
Agnates 306
Agrippina 268
Agrippinus, Julius 286–7
Alaric (Visigothic chief) 32
Alaric II (Visigothic king) 32–3
Alcuin 40, 42
Alexander of Abonoteichus 109
Alfred (the Great) 50 n. 58, 274
Altar of Victory 21, 25, 30, 149
Alypius 127, 142
Ambrose (bishop of Milan) 27–30, 125–6, 128, 139, 150
Ambrosiaster 125 n. 6
Ammianus Marcellinus 22–3, 128–9, 143, 148–9
Annales School 5, 150 n. 111
Antonine Constitution 16, 72, 78, 285
Antoninus Pius (emperor) 289, 301
Apograph of Scaliger 5, 49–50, 247
Apollonius (of Tyana) 148
Apologetics 151
Aquilian Law (see *lex Aquilia*)
Arbogast 30–1, 149
Arcadius (emperor) 26, 29, 31–2, 59, 133, 257
Archives 32, 42, 58, 61, 81, 129
Ardashir II (Persian emperor) 26
Arson 4, 104, 114, 119, 290–5
Artapanus 137
Astrology 4, 107–9, 299–302
Asylum 246
Audience (of Collator, possible) 140–51
Augustine (of Hippo) 85–7, 110, 127–9
Aurelius 284–5

Bardaisan 242 n. 1
Basilika (Byzantine lawbook) 34
Bees 294
Berytus (law school at) 79, 127
Bestiality 114 n. 43, 272–3
Bible (history of) 83–4
Bible (Collator's version) 90–97
Bible (Old Latin) 84–95
Biscop, Benedict 96
Bishops 133–4, 141, 145, 150
Blood avenger (in Hebrew law) 116–7, 243–4
'Book of the Covenant' 251–2
Boundary stones (markers) 4, 104–5, 116–7, 295–6
Breviarium or *Breviary* (Visigothic lawbook) 32–3, 54, 56
Butheric 266–7

Callistratus (jurist) 281, 296
Caracalla (emperor) 72, 75, 77, 248, 259, 286, 298
Carolingian Renaissance 40–2
Cassius, Avidius 301
Causae probatio 305, 307–8
Cautio 293
Celsus (jurist) 294
Ceolfrith 96
Chaldeans 300, 302
Charisius, Arcadius (jurist) 78
Charlemagne 33, 40

Charles Martel (Frankish *major domo*) 33, 39
Christianity 3–4, 13, 17–19, 24, 27, 29, 84, 138, 140–151
Church councils (Merovingian) 37–8, 57, 110
Cicero 141, 273–4
Class background (of Collator, possible) 126–9
Claudius (accidentally killed) 250
Claudius (emperor) 121 n. 58, 268, 271
Clement of Alexandria 137
Code of Justinian 2–3, 33, 45, 58, 80, 107–8
Codex (book form) 121
Codex Bellovacensis 47–8
Codex Grandior 96
Codex Gregorianus 53, 57–8, 61, 63, 79–80, 107–110, 248, 249, 257, 269, 270, 302
Codex Hermogenianus 53, 57–8, 80–1, 269–70, 283, 284
Codex Iustinianus (see *Code of Justinian*)
Codex Sinaiticus 96
Codex Theodosianus (see *Theodosian Code*)
Codex Vallicelliano 46–7
Codex Vaticanus 96
Codex Vesontinus 262–3
Cognitio extra ordinem 276
Collatio Legum Mosaicarum et Romanarum (see Title)
Commentaries (juristic) 12, 14, 74
Commodus (emperor) 259
Conceptum (receiving stolen goods) 276
Constans (emperor) 20–22, 266, 270
Constantine (emperor) 17–22, 71, 142, 145–6, 301, 307
Constantine II (emperor) 20
Constantius I (emperor) 269, 284
Constantius II (emperor) 20–23, 29–30, 120, 266, 300–1
Constitutio (see Roman law)
Consultatio (5th century lawbook) 70
Contumelia 275
Cornelian law (see *lex Cornelia*)
Corpus Iuris Civilis 12, 33
Cotta, Marcus Aurelius 279
Coveting 104–6
Crispus 18
Croesus 108
Cyprian 85
Damasus (bishop of Rome) 88
Dating (of *Collatio*, possible) 57–65
De Adulteriis (of Paulus) 70
De doctrina Christiana (of Augustine) 85–7
Decalogue (see Ten Commandments)
Decima 309
Decreta (see Roman law)
Defensor civitatis 142
Deportatio 244
Deposit 4, 104–5, 117, 120, 136, 282–7
Deuteronomy (book of) 83, 272–3, 277
Didache 135, 137
Didascalia Apostolorum 137–8
Digest 5–6, 12, 33, 71–4, 118–20, 247, 253, 256
Dio, Cassius 270
Diocletian 12–17, 110, 284, 302
Diosimus 285
Diu positum 286
Divination 19–20, 22–3, 110, 142, 300–1
Dolo malo 245, 298
Doves 294

Edict (of the Urban Praetor) 14–5, 45, 74
'Edict of Milan' 17–8, 146
Edicta (see Roman law)
Editions (of *Collatio*) 1–2, 49–50
Effractores (burglars) 276
Elagabalus (emperor) 68
Emancipation 307, 309
Epaphroditus 247
Ephiphanius (4th century author) 25
Episcopalis audientia (or bishop's court) 18, 141, 145
Eshnunna, Laws of 242
Eudoxia (empress) 32
Eugenius (usurper) 30–1, 149–50
Eunuchs 118
Eusebius (of Caesarea) 137–8, 146
Eustathius 284
Eutropius (imperial advisor) 32
Evaristus, Marius 250
Exceptio doli 306
Exilium 244, 248, 262
Exodus (Book of) 83, 88

Fabian law (see *lex Fabia*)
False testimony (or perjury) 4, 101–2, 277–279

Father, Law of the 261
Firmicus Maternus 141–2
Flavianus, Flavius 270
Flavianus, Virius Nicomachus 28, 31, 265
Fragmenta Vaticana 64, 70
Frankfurt School 5
Frigidus River (battle of) 31, 149
Furtum (theft) 4, 100–1, 103, 119, 273–6

Gaius (jurist) 33, 67, 75, 78–9, 97, 305–6
Galerius (emperor) 17, 269, 284
Geminus, Gaius Fufius 279
Geminus, Lucius Rubellius 279
Genesis (Book of) 83, 89
Gentianus, Terentius 296
Gladiators 289–90
Gnostics 27
Gospels 84, 88, 144 n. 87
Governor (provincial) 73, 276
Gratian (emperor) 24–6, 31

Hadrian (emperor) 74, 247, 250, 256, 289, 296
Hammurabi (*Code* or *Laws of*) 242
Haruspex (and *Haruspices*) 19–20, 22, 24
Herodotus 108
Hincmar (Medieval bishop) 35, 40–6, 53, 65, 110
Historia Augusta 60–61, 73, 142–3, 147–8, 265
Homicide 4, 100–1, 114 n. 43, 243–250
Homosexuality 4, 41, 53–4, 57, 59, 81, 98 n. 173, 100, 117, 263–7
Honestiores 16, 278
Humiliores 16, 278
Huns 26

Identity (of Collator) 1–2, 124–130, 149–151
Incest 4, 44, 57, 100–1, 115, 120, 267–273
Infamia 276
Inheritance 4, 97, 100, 105 n. 19, 110, 111, 303–309
Iniuria (injury) 4, 100, 251–55, 275, 292–4
Institutes (of Gaius) 79, 305–6
Institutes (of Justinian) 33, 69, 79, 254, 256, 265, 305–6
Institutionum libri (of Ulpian) 73–4, 97
Investiture Contest (or Controversy) 29
Irenaeus (bishop of Lyons) 24
Itala (alleged version of Latin Bible) 82 n. 109, 85–7, 90 n. 146, 131
Ius (as label) 247, 250, 255 n. 4, 259, 261, 266, 269, 284, 286, 306

James ('the Just') 135
Jerome (Latin translator of Bible) 41–2, 88–9, 125, 139
Jesus 84, 130, 139, 144, 147
John (Chrysostom) 139
Jovian (emperor) 24
Julian (emperor) 21–5, 30, 138–9, 147, 149–51
Julian (author of *Epitome*) 38–40
Julian (proconsul) 302
Julian law (see *lex Iulia de*)
Iulianus, Salvius 14–15, 74
Iulius (Alfius) 256
Justa (or Justus) 248
Justinian 3, 5, 12, 33, 38, 45, 285

Kidnapping (*plagium*) 4, 60, 81–2, 100, 104–6, 297–9
Korah 303–4

Labeo, Marcus Antistius (jurist) 16 n. 16, 254, 294
Lactantius 17–8
Law of Citations 51–3, 67, 75–6, 78
Lawyers (Roman) 12, 15, 17, 72, 126–8, 129, 141–4
Legitimacy (of emperors) 13–14
Lex (see Roman law)
Lex Aelia Sentia 305, 307
Lex Aquilia 14, 74, 105, 119, 126, 254, 293–4
Lex Baiuvariorum 39, 103 n. 14, 111
Lex Cornelia de falsis (or *Lex Cornelia Testamentaria)* 278
Lex Cornelia de sicariis et veneficis 244, 292
Lex Dei (see Title)
Lex duodecim tabularum (see Twelve Tables)
Lex Fabia 60, 298
Lex Iulia de adulteriis coercendis 259, 265, 268
Lex Iulia de maritandis ordinibus 259, 307
Lex Papia Poppaea 307

Lex Romana Visigothorum (see *Breviarium*)
Lex Scantin(i)a 265
Lex Voconia 307
Leviticus (book of) 83, 88, 89, 95, 264, 266, 268, 272–3
Libanius 21 n. 38, 127
Liber de officio proconsulis (of Ulpian) 73, 97, 112
Liber definitionum (of Papinian) 77, 252
Liber differentiarum (of Modestinus) 78, 250, 283
Liber ex legi Moysi 50 n. 58, 105, 139 n. 68
Liber responsorum (of Papinian) 68–9, 260
Liber responsorum (of Paulus) 77, 286
Liber singularis de adulteriis (of Ps. Papinian) 67, 76, 113, 115, 261–2, 271
Liber singularis de adulteriis (of Ps. Paulus) 53, 67, 70, 113, 258, 259, 260
Liber singularis de iniuriis (of Ps. Paulus) 53, 69, 254
Liber singularis de poenis omnium legum (of Ps. Paulus) 70, 278
Liber singularis de poenis paganarum (of Ps. Paulus) 69, 289, 292
Liber singularis regularum (of Ps. Ulpian) 67, 74–5, 252, 307–8
Library (of Collator) 97–98, 114
Libri ad edictum (of Ulpian) 74, 97
Libo, Lucius Scribonius 279
Licinius 17–18
Licinus 279
Livy 61, 108
Locatio conductio 287, 293
Location (of Collator) 59, 129, 143, 147, 150
Lot 272
Lothar II (Frankish king) 35, 40
Lucian 109
Lyons manuscript (of Latin Bible) 89–91, 94

Magic 4, 14, 19–21, 24, 104, 108–9, 299–302
Magister libellorum 72, 75, 78, 80
Magnentius (Flavius Magnus) 22–23
Magnus Maximus (usurper) 26–7, 59
Mandata 290
Manichaeism 4, 14, 61, 100, 103–4, 106–110, 299, 301–302
Manus 259
Manuscripts (of *Collatio*) 1–2, 35–7, 40–49
Manuscript Tradition (of *Collatio*) 36–51
Mar Adda (a Manichee) 61
Marcellus (jurist) 258
Marcian (jurist) 247
Marcianus (proconsul) 256
Marcion (of Sinope) 136
Marcus Aurelius (emperor) 259, 301
Marriage 267–272
Martyrs (Scillitan) 84
Masoretic text (of Hebrew Bible) 83 n. 112, 134
Masters (cruelty of) 62, 101, 255–7
Matthew (Gospel of) 124, 143–4
Maxentius (emperor) 21, 145
Maximian (emperor) 249, 269, 284, 285, 302
Messalla, Marcus Valerius 279
Mestrius (soldier) 286
Method (of Collator) 111–123
Milvian Bridge (battle of) 17
Mines 289–90
Mitzvot 83, 140
Modestinus 67, 71, 77–78, 111, 112, 126, 250, 283, 306
Monotheism 3–4, 145–9
Moses 1, 83, 100, 135–140, 244, 266, 304
Munatius, Flavius 284

Ne prostituatur 256
Negidius, Numerius 254
Neratius (jurist) 294–5
New Revised Standard Version (NRSV) 242, 288
Novels 33, 38
Noxa 252–3, 292
Novatian 85
Numbers (Book of) 83, 88, 89, 95, 113, 116, 246

Occasio 309
Occasione iuris 309
Octavian or Augustus (emperor) 12, 259
Odilo (Duke of Bavaria) 39
Odoacer 32

Origen 88, 122 n. 64, 136
Orpheus 148

Pacatus (governor) 301
Pagan and Paganism (labels) 3–4, 20–5, 29–31, 143–49
Pandect 95–7
Papinian (Aemilius Papinianus) 67, 71, 75–7, 111, 126, 252–3, 259, 260, 269–70
Papinianists 76
Patria potestas (power of the father) 305
Patricius 127
Paul (apostle) 264
Paulus, Iulius (jurist) 53, 67–72, 111, 126, 254, 259, 260, 286–7
Peisistratus 108
Pentateuch 83, 88, 96–7, 114, 136
Pepin III (Frankish king) 40
Persecution (of Christians) 13–14, 17, 87, 302
Pliny (the younger) 136
Polytheist and polytheism (see Pagan)
Pomponius Flaccus, Lucius (consul) 301
Pomponius, Sextus (jurist) 16 n. 16, 275
Pontifex Maximus 22, 25
Praetorian Prefect 28, 68, 72, 75, 80
Principate 12–13, 279
Proculus (jurist) 293, 295
Prostitution 54, 57, 256, 265–6, 276, 281
Purpose (of Collator, possible) 1–2, 124, 133, 143–151

Quadratilla, Septimia 285
Quaestio de sicariis 245
Quaestiones perpetuae 245
Quintilian 274

Rei vindicatio 286
Relegatio 248
Renaissance (Carolingian) 40, 42
Renaissance (Italian) 49, 56
Rescripta 15, 58, 72, 75, 269
Religion (of Collator) 129–140
Roman Jurists (classical) 14–6, 33, 67–8
Roman Law (definition) 14–5
Roman Law making (process of) 2, 14–6, 63
Romanists 105
Romulus (King of Rome) 60–1, 261
Romulus Augustulus (emperor) 32
Rufinus (imperial advisor) 32
Rufinus (of Aquilia) 125
Rufinus, Licinius (jurist) 125
Rufus (consul) 301
Rustling (of livestock) 287–90

Sabinus (jurist) 295
Sabinus, Julius 256
Sack of Rome 32
Sacratus, Aurelius 257
Sacrifice (pagan) 19–30
Salfad (or Zelophehad) 304
Samuel (Hebrew prophet) 300
Sarah 272
Saul (Hebrew king) 300
Scaevola, Quintus Cervidius 68
Second legislation (of Judaism) 138
Sententiae (of Ps. Paulus) 53, 70–72, 244, 247–8, 285, 302, 306
Septuagint 82, 84–5, 94, 130, 135
Severus Alexander (emperor) 68–9, 72, 147, 249, 286
Severus, Septimius 72, 77, 260, 295
Shapur III (Persian emperor) 26
Shechem Dodecalogue 116, 272, 295
Sirmondian Constitutions 56, 268
Slaves 4, 62–3, 100, 255–7, 262, 292, 298
Sodomy 35, 41, 264, 266
Sorcery (see Magic)
Sozomen (Church historian) 28, 266
Stemma (of *Collatio* manuscripts) 2, 37, 50, 51
Stilicho 32
Structure (of *Collatio*) 4, 99–111
Stuprum 4, 35, 41, 43, 53, 100, 263–7
Succession (see inheritance)
Sulla (Lucius Cornelius) 14, 244, 278, 292
Suus heres 305
Symmachus 22, 28, 30, 147
Syncretism 3–4, 145–8

Tablets (*tabulae*) 121
Taurus, Sisenna Statilius 279
Temple (in Jerusalem) 23, 122 n. 60
Ten Commandments 99–109, 111, 135–140, 144, 264
Tertullian 84–5, 136–7, 143, 265
Testimony (of family members) 4, 100, 101–2, 280–1
Tetragrammaton 116
Tetrarchs and Tetrarchy 13–14, 31

Theodosian Code 2–3, 12, 33, 45, 57, 58, 63, 80, 107
Theft (see *furtum*)
Theodorus, Marchus Ofellius 248
Theodosius (emperor) 26–31, 54, 59, 62, 63, 142, 149, 151, 265
Theodosius II (emperor) 33, 51
Theophilus (of Antioch) 136
Theutberga (Frankish queen) 35, 40, 41, 53
Tiberianus, C. Iunius 270
Tiberius (emperor) 301
Title (of *Collatio Legum Mosaicarum et Romanarum* vs. *Lex Dei*) 1, 42
Toleration (religious) 17–29
Trajan (emperor) 136
Trent, Council of 88
Tribonian 5, 67, 118, 120, 249
Twelve Tables 11, 14, 45, 261, 273–4, 275, 286, 291, 296, 306, 308, 309

Ulpian (Domitius Ulpianus) 60, 67, 72–75, 97, 107, 111, 126, 244, 245, 247, 250, 253, 256, 275, 276, 279, 281, 289, 290, 291–2, 292–4, 296, 298, 301, 308, 309
Umbricia (or Umbra) 256
Urseius (jurist) 295

Valens (emperor) 24–6, 150
Valentinian (emperor) 24–5, 150
Valentinian II (emperor) 25–30, 57, 59, 62, 265–7
Valentinian III (emperor) 32, 51–52
Vestal Virgins 22, 29 n. 89, 68
Vetus Latina (see Bible, Old Latin)
Virgin 258
Vis maior 287
Visigoths 26, 32–3, 80
Vivianus (jurist) 293–4
Voice (of Collator) 60, 81–2, 244, 245, 253, 266, 268, 270, 271–2, 273–4, 298–9, 304
Vulgate 41, 47, 82, 88–9

Wearmouth-Jarrow (monastery of) 96
Witch (of Endor) 300
Writing (ancient methods) 121–3

Zelophehad (or Salfad) 304
Zenobia (usurper) 61

Index of Modern Scholars

This index includes names of scholars mentioned in the text of the chapters of the historical study and the Commentary, but does not include all names from footnotes or brief passing references.

Armbruster, L. 294
Avenarius, M. 252, 268, 308

Barnes, T. D. 3 nn. 8 and 10, 19 n. 31, 269, 302
Barone-Adesi, G. 53 n. 64, 64 n. 104, 132 n. 38
Bauman, R. 68 n. 6, 278, 289, 298
Behrens, J.-F. 287
Berger, A. 69, 71, 242, 244, 245, 247, 248, 253, 286, 288, 293, 294, 305, 306, 307, 309
Beseler, G. 70, 71, 283
Bingham, S. 248
Bluhme, F. 46, 50, 247
Brown, P. 11, 302
Bürge, A. 283
Bush, A. C. 306

Cameron, Av. 146 n. 94, 147 n. 101
Cannata, C. 283
Carella, B. 274
Carmichael, C. M. 252, 268
Cervenca, G. 256, 263, 275, 298, 299
Charondas (see Le Caron)
Cloud, J. D. 244, 265, 281
Corcoran, S., 249, 268, 269, 270, 283, 284, 298, 302
Cracco-Ruggini, L. 132 n. 3
Crane, E. 294
Crawford, M. 244, 254, 259, 261, 273, 275, 281, 286, 291, 296, 298, 306, 307, 308, 309
Crifo, G. 72 n. 31, 262
Cujas, Jacques (Jacobus Cujacius) 49, 263

Dalla, D. 265, 266
Daube, D. 1, 2, 4, 253, 255, 264, 283
De Dominicis, M. 263, 275, 298, 299
De Francisci, P. 256, 263, 275, 298, 299
Degrassi, A. 279
De Robertis, F. 283, 293
Demelius, G. 286
De Zulueta, F. 305
Dirksen, H. E. 298
Dohrmann, H. 301
Drake, H. A. 18 nn. 25 and 27, 19 n. 31
Drijvers, H. J. W. 242 n. 1
Driver, S. R. 252, 291, 298
Du Plessis, P. 287, 293
Du Tillet, Jean (Joannes Tilius) 48

Edmondson, J. 289
Ensslin, W. 266
Evans-Jones, R. 286

Feissel, D. 250
Ferrary, J.-L. 244
Frakes, R. M. 246, 249, 265, 268, 270, 292
Frier, B. 294
Futrell, A. 290

Gardner, J. 261, 263, 305, 307, 308, 309
Garnsey, P. 244, 248, 262, 278, 288
Gascou, J. 250
Gerkens, J.-F. 287
Gibbon, E. 11
Godefroy, J. 54
Gordon, W., 305
Grasmück, E. 244, 248, 262
Gröschler, P. 293
Grubbs, J. Evans 269, 307
Gustafson, M. 289

Haenel, G. 55–7, 244, 248, 263
Harries, Jill 104, 106, 109, 111, 133, 244, 259, 272, 274, 276, 296
Harris, W. V. 26
Healy, J. 289
Hitzig, H. F. 254

Hohenlohe, C. 266
Honoré, A. M (Tony) 72 n. 31, 75, 77, 248, 249, 250, 257, 265, 269, 270, 286, 287, 293, 296
Hopkins, K. 290
Huschke, P. 50, 54, 55, 57, 125, 248, 258
Hyamson, M. 2, 54, 55, 67, 141, 242, 244, 272, 281, 282, 288, 293, 295, 296, 297, 304, 305

Jacobs, A. 125 n. 6, 132 n. 37
Jörs, P. 55, 141

Kaiser, W. 37 n. 4
Kaser, M. 307
Kaufhold, H. 83 n. 110, 266, 274
Kelly, Gordon 248, 262
Klek, J. 294
Krüger, P. 244, 245, 247, 248, 249, 250, 255, 256, 257, 262, 264, 265, 268, 269, 275, 276, 278, 279, 281, 285, 288, 289, 291, 292, 296, 298, 302, 306, 307
Kübler, B. 305

Lancizolle, K. W. 46
Lawson, F. 294
Le Caron, Loys (or Louis) Charondas 49
Lenel, O. 245, 247, 250, 252, 253, 254, 256, 258, 259, 260, 261, 262, 268, 271, 275, 276, 278, 279, 280–1, 283, 289, 290, 291, 292, 296, 298, 301, 307, 308, 309
Levine, B. 244, 246, 304
Levy, E. 71, 131
Liebs, D. 71, 81, 244, 245, 247, 250, 252, 254, 255, 256, 262, 264, 265, 266, 268, 275, 276, 278, 279, 281, 285, 288, 289, 291, 292, 294, 296, 298, 302, 306
Lilja, S. 265
Longo, C. 285
Loschiavo, L. 104, 138
Lucrezi, F. 256, 306

MacCormack, G. 293
Manthe, U. 305
Masi, A. 253, 256, 262, 263, 275, 298, 299
Mathisen, R. 249
McGinn, T. 256, 259, 265, 276, 281, 307
Milgrom, J. 258, 264, 268
Millar, F. 289, 290
Mommsen, T. 1–2, 5, 43–44, 46, 47, 50, 55, 102–3, 105, 242, 247, 254, 258, 274, 278, 282, 292, 296, 297, 300,
Montemayor Aceves, M. 104, 286
Murison, A. 252

Navarra, M. 283
Nelson, H. L. W. 305
Niebuhr, B. G. 79, 305
Nörr, D. 254, 255, 289, 294
Nogrady, A. 245, 247, 250, 256, 276, 279, 281, 289, 290, 292, 296, 298, 301

Ostersetzer, I. 131–2
Ott, J. N. 264

Paschoud, F. 265
Pastori, F. 283
Pharr, C. 109–110, 302
Phillips, A. 277, 297, 300
Pithou, P. 48–50, 248, 258
Platschek, J. 247
Pretto-Sakmann, A. 294
Prieto, M. 275
Propp, W. 251, 256, 258, 280, 283, 288
Pugliese, G. 253

Rabello, A. M. 53 n. 64, 132 n. 36
Rad, G. von 272, 295, 300
Ranke, Leopold von 5
Ratti, S. 265
Rives, J. 14 n. 10, 20 n. 35, 108 n. 27
Robinson, O. 305
Rönsch, H. 264
Rotondi, G. 257, 270
Rutgers, L. V. 132–3, 141
Ryan, F. X. 265

Sabatier, P. 89 n. 141, 263, 267
Saller, R. 261
Scaliger, J. 5, 49–50, 247, 260
Scherillo, G. 131
Schulz, F. 2, 37, 40, 45, 50, 64–5, 131–2, 141, 242, 250, 258, 263, 273, 283, 294, 297, 300
Seckel, E. 305
Selb, W. 266, 274
Shaw, B. 261
Sherwin-White, A. 259, 305

Sirks, A. J. B. 307
Sitzia, F. 287
Smelik, K. 300
Smits, N. 103, 131–2, 143, 242, 263
Solazzi, S. 4 n. 14, 133, 253
Solin, H. 247
Sotty, R. 260
Spagnuolo, V. 253
Stolmar, R. 260
Studemond, W. 305
Sturdy, J. 304

Terreni, C. 307
Thomson, R. 291
Treggiari, S. 307
Triebs, F. 102 n. 7, 246, 253, 254, 259, 260, 261, 262, 268, 275

Valditara, G. 293
Valiño, E. 260
Van der Meer, T. 307
Volterra, E. 2, 57–8, 82 n. 109, 130–2

Wacke, A. 306
Watson, A. 262, 293, 294
Weishaupt, A. 307
Wellhausen, J. 83 n. 111, 300
Wieacker, F. 66–7, 70, 247, 250, 252, 253, 254, 256, 258, 259, 260, 261, 262, 271, 275, 276, 279, 283, 289, 290, 292, 294, 296, 298, 301, 305, 308, 309
Wittmann, R. 253, 254
Wlassak, M. 254
Wormald, P. 274

Index Locorum

This index includes passages that are directly discussed or closely developed in the text of the historical study and in the Commentary. I have not included sources that are briefly cited in footnotes or in the tables. To avoid redundancy, I have avoided listing *Collatio* passages when they appear in their respective sections of the Commentary

Legal Sources

Code of Justinian

1. 4. 7 133
1. 11. 1 21
1. 55. 8 142
4. 5. 6 256
4. 34. 1 286
4. 34. 10 285
4. 65. 1 286
5. 4. 17 269
5. 5. 4 271
5. 5. 6 269
9. 9. 1 260
9. 9. 2 260
9. 14. 1 62, 256
9. 16. 1 248, 249
9. 16. 4 249
9. 18 (Title) 107, 302
9. 18. 3 19 n. 32, 20 n. 34
9. 18. 4 20 n. 35
9. 18. 5 22
9. 20. 7 60, 82, 298
9. 57. 2 309

Collatio

1. 1 43, 90, 91, 113, 246
1. 1. 3–4 91
1. 2–4 113
1. 5 113
1. 5. 1–4 91, 117
1. 7 46, 112
1. 11 118
1. 12 111, 126
1. 13 112, 118
2. 1. 1 94, 114, 119
2. 3 111, 292
2. 4 118, 126, 292
2. 5 69, 112
2. 6 112
2. 7 112
3. 1 114
3. 2 61–2, 112, 253
4. 4 71
4. 5 77 n. 73, 111
4. 7 76, 111, 112, 113
4. 8 76, 111, 112
4. 9 76, 111, 112
4. 10 76, 111, 112
4. 11 62, 76, 111, 112
4. 12 62, 76, 112, 263, 264
5. 1 53
5. 2. 1 53
5. 3. 1 57–8, 61, 64–5, 81, 99, 117, 129, 130–2, 273
6. 1 113, 117 n. 53, 129 n. 23
6. 2 115
6. 3 115
6. 4 115
6. 5 115, 284
6. 6 76, 111, 115
6. 7 58 n. 89, 115, 304
7. 1. 1 11, 119, 141
7. 2 63, 112
7. 3 119, 245
7. 5 112
8. 3 112
8. 4 112, 244
8. 5 112
8. 6 112
8. 7 112
9. 1 113, 277
9. 2 112
10. 1 113, 120
10. 2 78 n. 83, 111
10. 7 119
10. 7. 1–4 120
10. 7. 9 119
11. 1 113

12. 1 113
12. 7 119, 253
13. 1 146 n. 99, 297
14. 2. 2 82
14. 3 107
14. 3. 6 60–1, 66, 81
15 (Title Heading) 106–9
15. 1 110
15. 2 107, 110
15. 3 107–10
15. 3. 3 61
16. 2 111
16. 5–9 113

Digest
1. 1 244
1. 6. 2 256
1. 10 256
2. 4. 1 256
9. 2. 3 275
9. 2. 5 119, 275
9. 2. 27 118–9, 253
9. 2. 27. 1–35 253
9. 2. 27. 7–12 292
9. 2. 27. 10 293
9. 2. 27. 17 253
11. 3 256
16. 3. 23 283
16. 3. 29 pr. 119
16. 3. 29 285
22. 5. 3 281
22. 5. 16 278
22. 5. 24 281
23. 2. 57 268
47. 9. 12 pr. 119
47. 9. 12 119, 292
47. 14. 1 pr. 289
47. 14. 1. 2–3 290
47. 17. 1 276
47. 21. 2 296
48. 5. 38. 7 269
48. 5. 39. 4 268
48. 5. 39. 8 259
48. 6. 11 118, 250
48. 8. 1. 3 247
48. 8. 4 pr 118
48. 8. 4. 1 118, 250
48. 8. 4. 2 118
48. 8. 17 247
48. 10. 9. 3 279
48. 12. 6 260
48. 15. 1 298
48. 15. 2 260, 298
48. 15. 6 298
48. 15. 7 298
48. 16. 16 70
48. 19. 5. 2 250
50. 4. 18. 26 78
50. 16. 223 pr. 285
68. 18 262

Gaius, *Inst.*
1. 13–15 259
1. 28–32b 307
1. 53 62
1. 61 268
1. 66–67 307
3. 1–17 305
3. 5–17 305
3. 183–6 276
3. 191 276
4. 75–7 292

Institutes of Justinian
1. 8. 2 256
3. 1 305
4. 4 pr. 254
4. 4 69
4. 18. 4 265

Laws of Hammurabi
1–4 277
8 274, 288
14 297
21 274
22 274
112 283
120–126 283
129 258, 263
130 258
129–136 258
154–157 278
165–172 304
196–223 252
206 252
207 252

Laws of Eshnunna
36–37 283

Lex Romana Visigothorum (Breviarium)
1. 16. 1 296
2. 12. 1–2 286
2. 27. 1 262
2. 32. 1–9 276
4. 8. 1–3 306
5. 17. 1–3 281

5. 17. 5 278
5. 20. 1 288
5. 20. 2 288
5. 25. 1 244, 278
5. 25. 2 247
5. 27. 2 278

Syro-Roman Lawbook
#76a 274
#76b 266

Theodosian Code
1. 4. 2 71
1. 4. 3 52, 67, 75–6
2. 1. 10 133
3. 12. 1 269, 270
3. 12. 2 120, 270
3. 12. 4 57
9. 7. 4 62, 262, 263
9. 7. 6 42, 54, 57, 81, 265–66
9. 12. 1 62, 256
9. 12. 2 62
9. 14. 2 63
9. 16 (Title) 107
9. 16. 1 (=*CJ* 9. 18. 3) 248, 249
9. 16. 2 (=*CJ* 9. 18. 3) 19 n. 32
9. 16. 3 (=*CJ* 9. 18. 4) 20 n. 35
9. 16. 4 (=*CJ* 9. 18. 9) 22, 249
9. 16. 6 22
9. 16. 7–8 25
9. 18. 1 60, 298–9
9. 19. 1 82
9. 19. 1–4 278
9. 40. 1 19 n. 32
16. 1. 2 27
16. 8. 1 18 n. 26
16. 8. 2–4 18 n. 26
16. 8. 5 18 n. 26
16. 10. 3 20
16. 10. 4 (=*CJ* 1. 11. 1) 21
16. 10. 5 21
16. 10. 6 21
16. 10. 10 29 n. 87
16. 10. 11 30
16. 10. 12 30
16. 10. 21 142

Literary Sources

Ammianus Marcellinus
17. 4 23 n. 50
19. 10. 1–4 22 n. 49
30. 4. 2–22 143
31. 9. 5 266

Aurelius Victor
Caes., 41. 24 266

Cicero
Pro Mil. 3. 9 273–4

De Rebus Bellicis
Pr. 1 147
Pr. 5 147
21 147

Dionysius of Halicarnassus
Roman Antiquities, 2. 26 261

Eutropius
Brev. 10. 9 266

Herodotus
1. 25–59 108

Historia Augusta
Life of Tacitus, 1 60–1
Life of Carus, 6. 1 265

Isidore of Seville
Etymologies
5. 1 139 n. 68
5. 25 286

Julian
Contra Galileos, 152 B-E 139

Libanius
Or. 1. 98–9 21 n. 38

Livy
1. 16 61
1. 56. 9–13 108 n. 30

Lucian
Alexander the False Prophet, 5 109 n. 33

Panegyrici Latini
12. 2. 4 146
12. 2. 5 146
12. 10. 4 146
12. 16. 2 146
12. 26. 1 146

Pliny
NH 8. 220 294
NH 11. 12 294

Plutarch
De Pyth. Or. 408c 108–9

Quintilian
Inst. Or. 5. 14. 18 274

Symmachus
Rel. 3. 5 147 n. 102

Rel. 3. 7 22 n. 47
Rel. 3. 8 147 n. 102

Themistius
Or. 5. 70b 24 n. 57

Varro
Rerum rusticarum, 3. 7–8 294

Vegetius
2. 18. 4 147
2. 21. 1 147

Zonaras
13. 5. 15 266
13. 6. 7–9 266

Zosimus, *Historia Nova*
2. 40 20 n. 35
2. 42 266

Bible

Genesis 8: 15–9: 1 272
Genesis 9: 9–17 272
Genesis 19: 33–36 272
Genesis 20: 12 272
Exodus 20: 2–17 99
Exodus 20: 16 277, 280
Exodus 21: 2 117
Exodus 21: 16 297
Exodus 21: 18–19 93–4, 251–2
Exodus 21: 20–21 255–6
Exodus 22: 1 and 3 287–8
Exodus 22: 2–3 63, 274, 288
Exodus 22: 5 291
Exodus 22: 6 114, 290–1
Exodus 22: 7–11 282
Exodus 22: 16–17 257–8
Exodus 22: 7, 8, 11 47, 117, 282–3
Leviticus 18: 12, 13, 18, 16 271–3
Leviticus 18: 22 117
Leviticus 20: 10 113, 257–258
Leviticus 20: 11–12 113, 115, 267
Leviticus 20: 13 41, 53, 65, 113, 117, 263
Numbers 27: 1–11 303–4
Numbers 35: 16–17 113, 115, 243
Numbers 35: 18–19
Numbers 35: 20–1 115, 243
Numbers 35: 22–5 91–93
Deuteronomy 5: 6–21 99
Deuteronomy 18: 10–14 107, 299–300
Deuteronomy 19: 14 116–7, 295
Deuteronomy 19: 16–20 277–8, 280
Deuteronomy 19: 19 277
Deuteronomy 24: 7 297–8
Deuteronomy 25: 5–10 120–1
Deuteronomy 27: 17 116, 295
Deuteronomy 27: 20–23 271–3
1 Samuel: 28. 7–25 300
Matthew 5: 17–19 144
Matthew 19: 16–19 124, 144
Romans 1: 26–7 264
1 Corinthians 6: 1–11 145
1 Corinthians 6: 9 264
James 2: 8–13 135
Acts 15: 4–29 135

Ecclesiastical Sources

Ambrose
Ep. 74 28 n. 79

Augustine
Conf., 5. 3–11 302
De doctrina Christiana, 2. 36 87
De doctrina Christiana, 2. 52–3 85–6
De civitate dei, 6. 8 266
Quaest. in Hept., 2. 71 95 n. 164
Quaest. in Hept., 2. 84 95 n. 164
Quaest. in Hept., 4. 10 95 n. 164
Quaest. in Hept., 5. 59 95 n. 164, 272
De bono coniugali, 1. 17–20 272

Didache
2. 1–3 135 n. 51

Didascalia Apostolorum
6. 16. 1–2 137–8
6. 19. 5 138

Eusebius of Caesarea
HE, 10. 5. 2–14 17 n. 13
VC, 2. 24–42 146

Hincmar
De Divortio Lotharii Regis et Theutbergae Reginae, Responsio 12 35, 41–6

Lactantius
DMP, 33–5 17 n. 23
DMP, 48. 2 17–8

Lucifer of Cagliari
De Athan. 1. 3 280
De Athan. 1. 7 277

Methodius of Olympus
Symposium, Logos 1. 2 272

Paulinus
V. Ambr., 31 31 n. 97

Sozomen
HE, 7. 25. 1–9 28 n. 82, 29 n. 82, 266–7

Speculum (Ps. Augustine)
c. 42 280
c. 45 258
c. 55 300
c. 58 255
c. 74 288

Tertullian
De Pudic. 6. 3. 4 136 n. 55
Apologia 45.4 136–7, 143 n. 85
De Monogamia 12. 3 265

Inscriptions
CIL VI, 1139=*ILS* 694 143 n. 93
CIL VI, 2145=*ILS* 1261 29 n. 89